in Eighteenth~Century Style

31 Squash
Zucchini
32 Late Seeding Bed (Corn)
Sweet Corn **30**
28 Artichoke
29 Late Seeding Bed (Various)
27 Purslane and Spring Onions & planting bed for Artichokes
25 & 26 Asparagus

23 & 24 Snow Peas
Broccoli

Flat Leaved Parsley **21 & 22**
Oregano
Peas

20 Espalier Tree Walk: Apples and Pears (young)

Roquette **17a & b** with Radish border

19 Carrots and Turnips

18 Rhubarb

Dill with Marigold border **16b**

16a Fennel with Marigold border

Bay Tree with Privet border

Onions **12b** with Privet border

13 with Parsley border
Sorrel

14 Beets

15a Turnips **15b**

15a Lettuce

ROBERT CARRIER

GREAT DISHES
OF
THE
WORLD

ROBERT CARRIER

GREAT DISHES
OF
THE
WORLD

MARSHALL CAVENDISH

Editor: Frances Jones
Designer: Pedro Prà-Lopez

Published by Marshall Cavendish Books Limited
58 Old Compton Street
LONDON W1V 5PA

Originally published in 1963 by
Thomas Nelson and Sons Ltd

This edition first published 1982

ISBN 0 85685 945 1

Typeset in Bembo by ABM Typographics Ltd., Hull
Colour reproduction by Lithospeed Ltd., London
Printed and bound in Italy by L.E.G.O., Vicenza, Italy

FOREWORD

THE HISTORY OF every nation lies visible on its table. Its wars and victories, its occupation in defeat, the marriages of its kings, its religion, its overseas empires – all have left behind them a dish or two destined to be adopted into the national life.

The Medicis, by marrying the Louis, transformed the French table, which then claimed the credit and conquered the world with its cuisine. The Auld Alliance, forged by endless interlocking marriages between the two kingdoms, still leaves many mementos in the Frenchified names of Scotland's food. A revolution gave us restaurants, when the chefs of the aristocracy were reduced to serving the very people who had so rudely cut off the heads they used to feed.

Civilisation itself, in fact, is founded upon food, for it began with the domestication of animals and the cultivation of crops. As soon as people could stay still – were released at last from the travail of following the game on which they fed – they ceased to live from hand to mouth, began to build up stocks and to store their wealth. With this wealth they bought leisure, and leisure brought them culture.

Then the wanderlust returned, forced on mankind again by the demands of food. The drives out from the Near East in search of pasture spread civilisation to Europe.

Greece and Rome flourished and fell, but Europe in the Dark Ages still needed spices. The quest for these, hidden behind the oratory of Saint Bernard and Peter the Hermit, led to the wonder of the East being rediscovered in the Crusades. For it was food, and not religion, that drove our forefathers to set out for years on the Crusades, to open up again the spice routes to the East closed down by the explosion of Mohammedanism in the Arabian desert.

It was food, once more, that made men brave uncharted seas – filled, as they thought, with monsters and evil spirits – to find the spice islands in the West. For spices were the measure by which wealth was counted in the Middles Ages, so coveted were they. So coveted, indeed, that Columbus died disgraced for having found only gold in America, and not the spices that he had promised.

This book assembles some of the most famous dishes of the world, dishes evolved from civilisations long past, dishes that have been favoured by every people that has tried them. Some still have to achieve international popularity. Each one of them is part of the story of mankind. So let us approach them reverently. They have all history behind them. The first taste of some may surprise you, but adventure your palate as your ancestors did. And remember, the history of the world is written in this food. Culture stems from the stomach as well as the brain.

CONTENTS

SUCCESS WITH RECIPES

'I dislike feeling at home when I'm abroad,' said Bernard Shaw, his eyes fixed disapprovingly on those English tourists who spend their holidays searching for a good cup of tea and some plain, decent cooking. But what the master of paradox failed to mention was the delight of feeling abroad when we are at home.

The easiest way to carry yourself back to some favourite haunt is to recreate at home the dishes you enjoyed there. Or you can transport yourself to countries you have never even visited by sampling their cuisine. There is a tremendous variation in the food styles of the different nations of the world. Add to this the diverse regional cuisines of France, Italy, the United States and China, to name just a few, and you will have some idea of the delights that await you in this book.

Over the past thirty years I have been collecting recipes on my travels abroad, experimenting with them in my own kitchens in America, Italy, Germany, France and England.

This book is the outcome of those years of pleasure, for an undoubted pleasure it has been, resulting in a collection of some of the world's most exciting recipes – GREAT DISHES OF THE WORLD – each guaranteed to bring you the delights of travel without any of its inconveniences. No visas, no endless waits at airports, no inoculations and no luggage are necessary for the enjoyment of these dishes. Only the excitement of preparing something new, of tasting a quite original flavour, of sampling the exotic.

Do not be alarmed by the foreign names of some of these dishes, or by the seeming multiplicity of the ingredients used. You will find that you already have most of them in your kitchen, and in the next few chapters I hope to show that most cooking – even of elaborate dishes – is merely the result of combining a number of very simple operations; but like everything else – walking, talking, driving a car, painting a picture – you learn best by actually *doing*.

In our grandparents' time, there were elaborate bicycling schools where people spent months learning how to stay balanced on two wheels. It seems that in the beginning we have to learn everything the hard way; later, it becomes almost second nature.

The great thing in cooking, according to the experts, is to master the principles and then to allow the application of the rules to special cases to follow as a matter of course. Thus, when you have learned how to cook a steak to pink-centred, charcoaled perfection, you will not need special lessons for grilling a lamb chop; when you have learnt to make half a dozen sauces, you will be able to make half a hundred without extra effort.

Whenever you try a new method of cooking, do not be disappointed if you are unsuccessful at the first or even the second attempt, but try to find out the cause of failure and remedy it the next time. For recipes are not like doctors' prescriptions; they cannot be repeated too often. In every case you must use your own judgement with regard to the time required for each cooking process.

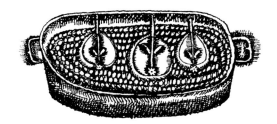

HOW TO USE THIS BOOK

Read the recipe all the way through before you start to cook. Check that you have all the necessary ingredients and equipment. If any of the general directions are not completely clear to you, read the introductory material in the next few chapters.

SECTION 1, 'THE GOOD INGREDIENTS', tells you what basic ingredients are necessary; gives you French chefs' tricks with butter, olive oil and diced green bacon to add flavour and substance to stews, *ragoûts* and casseroles; and shows how finely chopped onion, shallot and garlic can lend excitement to the simplest sauces.

SECTION 2, 'A SHORT GUIDE TO COOKING TERMS', defines the meaning of any cooking term used in this book that might be unfamiliar to you.

SECTION 3, 'BASIC EQUIPMENT', describes the equipment I find most useful in my kitchen.

THE GOOD INGREDIENTS

M ANY COOKS TODAY make the mistake of trying to economise on the basic necessities of good cooking: the best quality butter; olive oil from Provence; fat bacon; quality wines and rich stocks for cooking; coarse sea salt (the famous *gros sel* of French cuisine) and freshly ground black pepper; onion, garlic and shallots; the best wine vinegar and a selection of fresh herbs and spices. This is a false economy, for with these materials at hand you can make any number of excellent casserole dishes using the same basic cooking techniques.

Of course, you will have to acquire a *tour de main;* you will have to know how to make stocks and soups, sauces and soufflés, and learn the techniques of roasting and baking. You must become accustomed to your oven, to your mixer, to your omelette pan . . . and to the foods you are likely to cook.

Nothing replaces quality and freshness. All food should be eaten fresh. I find that a salad picked from the garden ten minutes before Sunday luncheon is worth five of the same from the corner grocer's; and a fish caught fresh from the coastal waters of St. Tropez makes a better *bouillabaisse* than those kept on ice in the best Paris restaurants.

So avoid buying foods too far in advance. I find that meats, fish, butter, milk, fruits and vegetables all tend to lose freshness and flavour when stored too long. If you are going to refrigerate foods, fresh or cooked, keep them in covered containers to preserve moisture.

And remember that it is not necessary to serve highly complicated dishes when you entertain. Greatness in cooking is apparent primarily in the plain dishes – those sound traditional country casseroles of the French regional cuisine, for instance – properly prepared with butter of farmhouse freshness and simmered for hours in the slowest of ovens.

There are countless recipes for the pot roasts and *ragoûts* of lamb, veal and beef, and the great country stews of poultry, meat and game, which have many points in common in their preparation. (1) Whether or not the meat has been larded, it is usually dredged with flour and sautéed until golden in hot fat – butter, oil, salt pork, or a combination of the three. (2) It is then usually flamed in cognac, Calvados or some other alcohol, before being moistened with rich stock, wine or cream, and slowly simmered to perfection. (3) Finally, the extracts given out by the meat in the cooking process, however delicious they may be, are almost always enriched by the addition of onions, shallots, garlic and a selection of fresh herbs or spices.

These country recipes, whether *bœuf à la gardiane,* tender chunks of beef braised in red wine as cooked in the Camargue region of France, or *matelote à la bourguignonne,* a *ragoût* of freshwater fish, eel, pike and carp, flamed in cognac and served in a rich wine sauce, or any of the other delicious casserole dishes of meat, fish, poultry or vegetables which you will find described in the pages of this book, all follow the same basic cooking techniques.

COOKING FATS

To my mind there is nothing that quite replaces butter in cooking. If you want the best results, all butter and all cooking oils should be of the best quality. And although margarine has become very popular in recent years, I see no great advantage in using it; if a vegetable fat is called for, by far the most practical and pleasant to use are the vegetable oils – olive, corn and peanut.

For slow frying, I like to mix olive oil and butter in equal quantities, putting the oil in the pan first to keep the butter from browning; or I use a combination of olive oil and corn oil for the lighter *ragoûts* of chicken, rabbit or vegetables.

For the earthier casseroles, I combine olive oil and butter and add diced cubes of fat salt pork or green bacon to create a rich emulsion with plenty of flavour. Lard, dripping and what the French often call the *graisses nobles* – goose, duck and chicken fats – are also indicated for certain dishes, and a supply of good olive oil is essential for salads and as a sauce for spaghetti and bean dishes cooked in the Italian manner.

THE AROMATICS

Onions: The onion is perhaps the oldest known vegetable in the world. Onions are said to have been one of the foodstuffs eaten by the Egyptian workmen who built the Pyramids.

The onion is a sublime flavourer for casserole dishes and stews. Try the French trick of gently frying finely chopped onions, shallots and garlic in olive oil and butter before adding meat and vegetables for a meat casserole. This aromatic trio will add greatly to the end result of your dish. But a word of warning — do not let them turn colour before adding the meat. They should be just transparent.

A little onion chopped finely — a tablespoon or two, no more — browned in butter with a little finely chopped parsley and a hint of garlic adds greatly to the savour of grilled steak or lamb chops. Add a whole onion, stuck with a pungent clove or two, to chicken or beef stock; serve a dish of creamed onions with roast lamb. If onions are small enough, present them in a baked pastry case for added effect.

I like onions with a Provençal stuffing of ground veal, diced fat salt pork, finely chopped onion and garlic, minced fresh tarragon and parsley, beaten egg, boiled rice, freshly grated Parmesan cheese and salt and freshly ground black pepper to taste.

Try small white onions, glazed, as a garnish for party dishes. To make glazed onions: peel small white onions and cook them very slowly, uncovered, in enough butter and water to half-cover them. Sprinkle the onions with sugar and salt and baste them frequently. The onions should be translucent and melting.

Shallots: The delicate, violet-tinted shallot, another member of the onion family, is usually finely chopped and sautéed in a little butter as a flavourful addition to casseroles, stews, sauces and grilled or sautéed meat, fish and poultry. Shallots are easy to grow if you have a patch of soil in the sun. Once you start them, they are virtually perpetual, as they reproduce by dividing. A grilled fillet steak, served with hot melted butter and sprinkled with finely chopped parsley and shallots, is delicious. Chopped shallots in small game birds — quail, partridge, grouse — add greatly to the flavour; chopped shallots can also be used effectively in wine sauces and in stuffings for meat roasts. Fish dishes improve greatly with the addition of a little finely chopped shallot to the sauce.

Leeks: The leek, probably brought to Britain by the early Romans, was commonly cultivated in Egypt in the time of the Pharaohs. Closely allied to the onion — but with the bulbous part cylindrical and the leaves broad and flat — the leek was celebrated in Italy in the time of Pliny. It was held in great esteem by the Emperor Nero, who used to eat leeks for several days each month to clear his voice.

The leek is grown in this country as a vegetable, with properties very similar to the onion but of a milder character. I like to combine leeks with onions and garlic as an aromatic threesome for the great French soups, *pot-au-feu* and *poule-au-pot*. They are, of course, an integral part of cock-a-leekie and Scotch broth, and, puréed with chicken stock, cream and potatoes, make one of the most famous soups in the world — vichyssoise. Try leeks on their own, puréed with chicken stock and cream, for a delicious cream of leek soup. Serve this versatile vegetable in a variety of ways: leeks *à la grecque* (leeks boiled in dry white wine and olive oil with finely chopped onions and carrots), leeks *à la vinaigrette* (leeks poached in water and served with a vinaigrette sauce), leeks *au gratin* (leeks baked in a cream sauce) and leeks *Mornay* (poached leeks served with a well-flavoured cheese sauce).

Chives: The most 'polite' of the onion family, with its delicate flavour, the chive is one of the most popular culinary seasonings. Use finely chopped chives with finely chopped chervil, parsley and tarragon to make the delicate combination for an *omelette aux fines herbes*. Carry this subtlety one step further for a *soufflé aux fines herbes*. Vichyssoise would not be vichyssoise without its sprinkling of chives. Use this plant finely chopped to add a delicious hint of onion to salad dressings and as a garnish for vegetables. Try it also with cream of asparagus and bean soup.

Garlic: When garlic first appeared in history, it was considered to have magic properties like the mandrake root. It was a wonder drug, perhaps the oldest drug in the world — a primeval 'cure-all' for the ancients. In describing its most potent powers, the Roman historian, Pliny, claimed that garlic was so good 'the very smell of it drove away serpents and scorpions'.

Today, French and Italian cooks cannot possibly get along without this most beloved and most hated of seasoners. And in this country, garlic is slowly creeping back into favour, working its way up the social ladder in thousands of kitchens in the years since the war.

Without this pungent bulb, many dishes would almost lack their reason for being. Who would give a second thought to *bouillabaisse* — that golden-coloured, highly-flavoured *bouillon* of fish from the Mediterranean — without the aromatic flavours of garlic and saffron? And could we call a salad— tender green lettuce leaves, bathed in olive oil and home-made wine vinegar seasoned with salt and freshly ground black pepper to taste — a real salad if it did not contain at least a hint of garlic? I like to add a clove or two of garlic to hearty French or Italian casseroles of meat or vegetables and to pasta sauces. And I always insert a sliver or two into roast lamb, pork or beef before cooking.

In some cases, it is the strong, garlicky flavour that gives the dish its character; in others, the appeal comes from the special bouquet that garlic imparts to the food rather than from its own flavour.

In using garlic, I think it best to consider three basic facts. First, the heavy flavour that offends many people evaporates if you crush the garlic before using it. This seems to eliminate the strong odour and flavour and leaves a pleasing pungency. Second, this same heavy flavour of the garlic – like that of the onion – disappears if you simmer it in a liquid. And third, garlic acquires a bitter taste if allowed to cook in butter or oil long enough to take on colour. In making garlic-flavoured butter sauces for sautéed foods, add the crushed garlic to butter already heated, or lightly browned and just heated through, before you pour the sauce over the food.

One of my favourite garlic recipes in this vein is the famous Italian spaghetti dish, *spaghetti al' aglio e olio,* which simply means spaghetti served with an oil and garlic sauce.

Professional chefs' recipes usually specify 'crushed' garlic. You can crush a small amount of garlic by bringing the flat side of a big heavy knife down sharply on the chopped pieces. I like to crush each clove of garlic flat with the palm of my hand – delicate fibrous casing and all – and put four or five of these crushed cloves with an equal number of sage leaves in the centre of a boned roast of pork. Roll up the meat, tie it securely and roast it in the usual way, and you will have *rôti de porc à la Provençale.*

French cooks always call a small amount of crushed garlic *'une pointe d'ail'* – as much as you pick up on the point of a small sharp knife. When they want to crush larger amounts of garlic, they use a small mortar and pestle. Cooks in this country can purchase garlic presses which are quite efficient. But whichever method you use, do not forget to clean thoroughly any boards, knives or other utensils used with garlic, because a lingering garlic flavour on kitchen equipment is far from desirable.

HERBS

The British are not adventurous with herbs: mint, parsley, sage, and possibly thyme and chives, are virtually the only ones they use. All the herbs mentioned here can be used fresh, dried or frozen. Drying them is a simple task. Harvest herbs when plant first begins to show flowers; dry in a well-ventilated room and store in air-tight containers in a cool, dry place. To quick-freeze herbs: blanch in boiling water; plunge immediately in iced water; drain off excess moisture; seal in aluminium foil and place in the freezer. Frozen herbs should be thawed at room temperature before using.

All seasoning should, of course, be to taste, and herbs – like perfume – should be used subtly. Experiment, with a light hand at first, to discover the distinction herbs can contribute to your cooking. Then, as you become more expert, use fresh herbs liberally to make your favourite dishes more personally yours.

In general, I like to add most herbs towards

the end of cooking. In this way they cannot cook too long, thus losing savour, or imparting a bitter taste to food.

Thyme: Pungent and aromatic, thyme is used to flavour stews, soups and sauces; it goes particularly well with dishes in which wine is used. There are many varieties of this herb, wild and cultivated. Lemon thyme adds zest and flavour to scrambled eggs, egg sandwich spreads and creamed eggs. Mix thyme to taste with salt and freshly ground black pepper and rub over beef, lamb or veal before roasting. Casseroles of meat or poultry are greatly enhanced in flavour if a little thyme is added shortly before cooking time is up. Try this herb warmed in butter with grilled lobster, shrimps and prawns. Add it to butter to dress carrots, mushrooms, onions and potatoes.

Parsley: This is the best known and the most generally used of all herbs – invariably thought of in this country as a garnish for meat, fish and vegetables. Modern dieticians have discovered a wealth of vitamins in parsley. Use it chopped finely to enhance the flavour of sauces, soups and stews, fish and meat salads, stuffings, and as an intrinsic part of the traditional faggot of mixed herbs (the French call it a *'bouquet'*), which adds such a wonderful something to French country cooking. Parsley sauce is an excellent accompaniment to boiled or steamed fish, or boiled chicken.

Marjoram: One of the most popular of herbs – and one of the most versatile. It is very pungent: a little marjoram goes a long way. Stews, soups, braised meats, sausages, pork roasts and chops, all call for interesting uses of marjoram. This herb is also very good with fish. Try a little finely chopped with buttered carrots, spinach or turnips for a subtle, new flavour. Its aromatic, slightly bitter taste is excellent in poultry stuffings.

Saffron: Saffron – now one of the world's most costly flavouring agents – comes from the stigma of a certain type of crocus. Once greatly esteemed in this country as a flavourer of breads, cakes, soups and stews, saffron is now more or less forgotten. Not so in Italy, where it lends its special flavour and colour to *risotto alla Milanese* (saffron rice), in France, where it is an integral part of *bouillabaisse* and Provençal fish soups, and in Spain, where it is one of the essential ingredients of *paella*, Spain's national dish of chicken, sausage, seafood and saffron-flavoured rice. Use saffron to add colour and zest to rice dishes and fish soups of all kinds. Try it in baking, for example in saffron buns and saffron bread.

Tarragon: Known to most as a flavouring for wine vinegar, this fresh, green herb is delicious when chopped finely and combined with melted butter and a little lemon juice as a sauce for fish. The delicate, pungent taste of this difficult-to-grow herb, and its delightful perfume, make it a must in any herbal list. Add chopped fresh tarragon to a salad; use it to add special interest to fricasséed or roast chicken. Use it in aspics with chicken, eggs or shellfish. Tarragon is the indispensable ingredient of *sauce Béarnaise* and adds its inimitable savour to green mayonnaise. Its faintly *anise* flavour is good in marinades for meat and fish.

Mint: The very smell of this popular herb is supposed to stimulate appetite. In England it is king: there are about fourteen varieties of mint grown in this country. Spearmint, the most popular, is used for flavouring peas and potatoes, and in the preparation of mint sauce to accompany roast lamb. Try it, too, in salads and salad dressings. Fresh pea soup, whether served hot or cold, is the better for the clean, clear flavour of fresh mint, as are pot cheeses, ices, wine cups and, of course, mint julep.

Try other mint varieties – grow them in

The herb garden at Hintlesham
Hall is laid out in eighteenth-
century style (see above and
endpapers). Each bed has a crop
and border specially chosen
for the most exciting colours
and shapes—cool green curly
lettuces edged with rows of
blue-green chives (see left)
and cascading wigwams of green
beans teamed with bright orange
nasturtiums (far left).

15

your garden or on the window sill – for further flavour flourishes: pineapple and *eau-de-Cologne* mint snipped into salads, or crystallised for cakes, or tied in bunches to flavour wine cups and *tisanes;* apple mint for poultry stuffings, fruit cups and for jellies made from crab-apples and gooseberries.

Fennel: Fennel is used extensively by the Italians and the Mediterranean French. This feathery herb, which looks something like dill, is excellent in fish sauces and salad dressings. Fennel seeds – famous for their use in liqueurs of the *anisette* variety – add a subtle flavour and texture to pastries.

Dried fennel stalks are used by the French for flaming *loup de mer* and as an aromatic in *bouillabaisse* and *soupe de poissons.*

The bulbs of fresh fennel (*finocchio* in Italian, *fenouil* in French) are also eaten as a salad. In this case the thickened stalk or bulb is sliced thinly and dressed with olive oil and lemon juice, and seasoned with salt and freshly ground black pepper to taste. Eaten this way, it has a delightful *anise* or liquorice flavour.

Rosemary: A sprinkling of fresh rosemary leaves complements the flavour of lamb and kid. Add chopped fresh rosemary, blended with chopped parsley and butter, to any baked chicken dish for a delightful change. The fresh, sweet, pinewoods flavour of this herb, which has been used since antiquity, adds an indescribable taste to sauces, stews and cream soups. Try it with steak or veal chops, using finely chopped rosemary leaves as you would pepper for a steak *au poivre*. No other seasoning is necessary. Rosemary is much better used fresh than dried.

Coriander: Fresh coriander is used in practically all cooking in Mexico and South America, where it is called *cilantro.* It is also used extensively by the Chinese and Japanese,

who call it Chinese parsley. Its exotic flavour is the highlight of *ceviche* (raw fish salad), *guacamole* (mashed avocado salad) and other Mexican dishes. In this country we use coriander leaves or seeds in chutneys, with lemon sauce for venison, and with braised celery or cream of celery soup. Its flavour seems to bring out the celery taste.

Chervil: This delicate, feathery herb is a member of the parsley family. A little chervil is excellent in a delicate butter sauce such as *sauce Hollandaise.* Finely chopped chervil, parsley, chives and tarragon go to make the subtle combination of fresh herbs necessary for an *omelette aux fines herbes.* Chervil alone makes a cheese omelette very special. It is very good with most stews and soups and an excellent garnish for salads. Try sprinkling finely chopped fresh chervil on grilled fish just before you remove it from under the grill.

Basil: One of the choicest and most aromatic of herbs, basil is difficult to grow in this climate. It is very popular with the Spaniards, the Italians, the French and the Portuguese, who use the spicy and aromatic basil in many of their dishes. It has a delightful odour, and some claim it is clove-like in flavour. Basil is especially fine with lamb chops to which its leaves and tender stems give a sweet, mildly pungent flavour. Combine chopped snippets of basil with oregano, chives and melted butter and serve with spaghetti; sprinkle a teaspoon of finely chopped basil leaves and parsley on sliced, chilled tomatoes to make a salad that literally breathes 'South of France'. Use it to flavour salads, soups, stews and sauces.

Bouquet garni: It is a bunch of herbs, either tied together or bound into a tiny cheesecloth sack, and cooked with the food. The herbs are usually bound so that they may be lifted out at the end of cooking and discarded, but my French cook, Naomi, used to chop up her *bouquet* herbs as finely as possible and incorporate them into the sauce. A simple *bouquet* consists of merely a few sprigs of parsley, chives and a bay leaf. A *bouquet garni* is made up of two sprigs parsley, two sprigs thyme, one branch celery, one sprig marjoram, one bay leaf and one sprig rosemary.

Oregano: Closely related to marjoram and sometimes called wild marjoram, oregano seems to go specially well with tomatoes and tomato sauces and is a natural for pasta sauces. A touch of this herb makes grilled tomatoes delicious. Try oregano when baking onions or roasting pork or lamb. This herb is much used in Italy to flavour the many varieties of pizza. Use oregano in stuffing for meat or fowl, in basting sauces and marinades.

Sage: Sage is used a good deal in Italian and Provençal dishes. In *saltimbocca* thin slices of veal are rolled with *prosciutto* (Parma ham) and a sage leaf, and fried gently in butter. In Provence, *daurade au sauge* (sea-bream cooked with sage) and *carré de porc au sauge* (roast pork with sage) are well-known specialities. Because of its strong, bold flavour, it must be used with great care – especially in stuffings for chicken, duck and goose, where it is apt to swamp other, more delicate flavours. It is fragrant, though a little bitter, and is good with pork, goose and sausage.

Dill: A lacy, delicately flavoured herb, dill is used in many German, Russian and Swedish recipes. Far too little is used in England today, where it is best known as a flavouring for vinegar and pickles. Fresh sprigs of this herb mix well with many vegetables and with salads and fish. Try cucumbers with sour cream and fresh dill; new potatoes with lemon butter and fresh dill; potato salad with crumbled bacon and fresh dill in the dressing; fish salads with dill.

SPICES

The fortunes of some of Europe's greatest families were founded on the peppercorn. Medieval spice merchants became very rich men, for a pound of ginger would buy a sheep, a pound of cloves would buy a cow and a sack of pepper would buy a man. In fact, at one time pepper was so expensive that it was sold by the individual peppercorn.

We owe a lot to spices today. Not only the more exotic flavour of our foods – special dishes such as steak *au poivre,* Madras chicken curry and saffron rice – but the discovery of a whole new world. The Arabs, leading spice merchants to the world, had kept the secret of their source of supply so closely guarded that the West did not discover where these riches could be obtained until Marco Polo visited the Orient in the thirteenth century. His written account of his three voyages astonished the world. As a result of his tales, Columbus set out on the voyage of exploration that was to end in the discovery of the islands of the Caribbean, and of America; Vasco da Gama rounded the continent of Africa to reach India for the first time by sea; and Magellan, after two years of hardship and adventure, discovered the Spice Islands of New Guinea where cloves, nutmeg, cinnamon, pepper and other spices grew in abundance.

HOW TO USE SPICES: Be selective. Unless you are following a tested recipe do not combine too many at one time. And remember that the correct spice combination for any food is the one that tastes right to you. There are no rules. The use of spices is an art, not a science.

TEST YOUR SPICES OCCASIONALLY: If spices are kept too long they lose their wonderful distinctive aroma. Be ruthless about throwing out any spices that have gone stale and replace them with a fresh supply.

Allspice: Allspice is the dried, hard, unripe berry of the pimento or allspice tree, a member of the bay family. It was thought by Columbus to be the much sought after 'pepper', and was brought back in great triumph to Europe. Often called the Jamaican pepper, it closely resembles the true pepper in shape, but has a delicately fragrant flavour – pungent and aromatic – that tastes like a blend of cinnamon, nutmeg and mace, strongly spiced with cloves. The French call this spice *'quatre épices'.*

Allspice is excellent for game, poultry stuffings and sausage mixtures. Use it ground or whole in stews, *ragoûts,* sauces and gravies, whole for pickles and marinades; add two or three berries to a fresh pea soup; to flavour chutneys, ketchup and spiced fruits. Use it with a light hand to flavour delicate sauces for fish and eggs; let its fragrance accent hot puddings, fruit pies and some cakes.

Aniseed: Strongly flavoured and highly scented if used too lavishly, aniseed has a light, wonderfully pleasant liquorice flavour when used with a gentle touch in cooking. Sometimes called 'sweet cumin', to which it has a slight similarity in flavour, it is used widely in confectionery, and in cake and pastry making. French cooks pound aniseed with lump sugar to flavour sponge cakes, custards or creams.

Aniseed is distilled to make Pernod and *anisette,* two French liqueurs of distinction. Use Pernod to flavour fish chowders; you will find that a few drops lend a certain excitement to oysters Rockefeller. A 'stew' of lobsters is enhanced with the volatile essence of this Mediterranean liqueur.

Sprinkle aniseed on cakes and biscuits. Use it in the Oriental manner to add flavour and excitement to fish and game.

Cardamom: Cardamom – which belongs to the ginger family – once had a reputation as an aphrodisiac and was consequently used by certain chefs of the French court for its reputedly 'warming' qualities.

Cardamom has much of the same fire as ginger, allspice and black pepper, and is used in India as one of the prime ingredients of hot curry powders and sauces. I like to use cardamom seeds whole for pickling and for curries; finely ground in pastries, sweet sauces and cakes.

Cardamom goes particularly well with orange. Try a little, too, sprinkled on melon, or just a hint of this fragrant spice to give a touch of the East to after-dinner coffee.

Chile powder: A blend – like curry powder – of several ingredients, chile powder (also called chili powder and not to be confused with powdered chilli) is a delicious combination of the finely ground pods of several kinds of hot peppers, paprika, cumin seed, dried garlic and oregano.

Rich in colour and in flavour, chile powder is much used in Mexican and South-Western American cooking, as well as in tropical countries to flavour native dishes – stews, meats, sauces and soups.

Cinnamon: A spice highly prized by the ancients, cinnamon is made from the dried spicy inner bark of the cinnamon tree, first cousin to the cassia and the bay. Its fragrant odour and sweet spicy flavour are the perfect foil, when used in moderation, for fish and fish sauces.

Combine cinnamon with pepper, ginger, cloves and mace. Use this mixture as a 'dry marinade' to rub on pork chops and game be-

Spices, once so rare they were literally worth their weight in gold, are now a familiar sight in the kitchen. Use these riches from Africa and the East to give a magic touch to your cooking.

fore cooking. Add a hint of cinnamon and cloves to Dijon mustard to flavour baked ham.

Spice mulled wines with cinnamon. Let this spice add interest to sweets, cakes and puddings. Sprinkle it over coffee, sliced fresh fruits and puddings. Cinnamon toast – spread the bread with blended butter, sugar and cinnamon before cooking – is delicious.

Its highly fragrant odour and sweet, aromatic flavour are a 'must' for apple pies, dumplings, sauces and puddings.

Cloves: Cloves – like pepper – were one of the first Oriental spices to excite the cupidity of Western spice traders. First used by the Chinese, the clove has a hot spicy flavour and a highly aromatic scent.

Use whole cloves for pickling, for pork, ham and gammon, and fruit dishes. Take advantage of the clove's natural affinity for onion, pork and ham. Use ground cloves in spice cakes, gingerbreads, puddings and sweets.

No apple pie is considered complete without a faint hint of clove, but be careful not to overdo it.

Coriander: Sweet yet tart in flavour, coriander is a favourite ingredient of hot curries and sauces and has been used for centuries in Middle Eastern cooking.

Coriander is delicious when rubbed on pork before roasting; or on pork chops before cooking. Use dried coriander to flavour Moroccan dishes; with dried bean soups, or in poultry stuffings.

Try this spice with meats, cheeses, pickles; use it sparingly in puddings and pastries.

Cumin seed: An important ingredient of all chili and curry powders, cumin is much used in Far Eastern and Oriental foods. Its strong, aromatic scent and pungent flavour (similar to caraway seed, but much stronger) are used extensively in Mexican cookery, Indian curries, and as a delicious flavourer for meat loaf, lamb and chicken dishes and anything made with dried beans.

I like to use the seeds whole as an attractive 'wrapping' for cubes of cream cheese.

Curry powder: Commonly known as a spice, curry powder is in reality a blend of many herbs and spices. Commercial varieties may contain eight to thirty-eight different sorts. Connoisseurs of curry have special formulae of freshly ground herbs and spices for various dishes. The following list – which reads like a complete herb and spice index – will give you some idea of the principal ingredients it is possible to include in a well-blended curry powder: allspice, aniseed, bay leaves, cardamom, cinnamon, cloves, coriander, cumin, dill, fennel, garlic, ginger, mace, mustard, nutmeg, black pepper, red pepper, paprika, poppy seeds, saffron, turmeric, etc. The relative strength of the blend depends, of course, on how much hot pepper is used.

Mustard: Mustard was well known to the ancient Romans, who imported it into Gaul where it quickly found favour. The French moisten powdered white and black mustards with *verjuice* (to make Dijon mustard), with wine (to make Bordeaux mustard), and add herbs for various special mustard blends such as *moutarde verte*.

ENGLISH MUSTARD – produced in this country since 1720, when it was first ground and sifted commercially – is a blend or powdered white and black mustards, with a little turmeric added to make the mustard powder a rich golden yellow. It is very hot in flavour.

I like to use mustard to flavour sauces and gravies for meats and game; in pickles, chutneys and relishes, and, of course, in salad dressings.

Ginger: One of the earliest Oriental spices to be known in Europe, ginger originally came from Southern China where the ripe roots were carefully selected, boiled in several waters to remove some of their fire, and then preserved in thick syrup. Ginger was known to the ancient Greeks and Romans. It was used in India in early times. In England, ginger was well known before the Conquest.

This extremely pungent spice should be creamy white in colour when ground. It is smooth-skinned and light buff in colour when whole.

Ground ginger adds much to apple sauces, chutneys and stewed fruits. Try blending ground ginger with black pepper and crushed salt, and rubbing it over steaks and lamb chops before grilling.

Sprinkle ground ginger lightly on fish before grilling. Add lightly to fruit and wine sauces.

Mace: Mace is the dried outer sheath of the kernel of the fruit of the nutmeg tree, and similar, if stronger, in flavour. It is an expensive spice – only a quarter of an ounce is obtained per pound of nutmeg harvested.

Use ground mace for pickling, marinades, brines and game sauces. Use it with a lighter hand for cakes, sweets and puddings. Add mace with impunity to any sweet in which chocolate plays a leading part.

Oyster stew – a great favourite in New England – would not be the same without a dash of mace. Try mace with fish, shellfish, eggs and vegetables in a rich cream sauce. Cauliflower and carrots, particularly, take kindly to a hint of mace, and puréed potatoes, enriched with cream and butter, are all the better for a dash of this versatile spice.

Nutmeg: Delicate and at the same time very aromatic, nutmeg is the dried seed of the fruit of the nutmeg tree. Usually used as a substitute for, or as an adjunct to, mace, this spice is very stimulating to the palate.

The whole nut keeps its flavour almost indefinitely. Ground nutmeg, however, soon loses its flavour, so it is much better to keep it in nut form and grate it as you need it.

Use nutmeg as you would mace.

Paprika: One of the spices the Turks brought with them to Western Europe was paprika, or Turkish pepper, as it was called in the sixteenth century – the same 'sweet' pepper or *aji* discovered by Columbus in the New World. Warmly aromatic and a rich red in colour, paprika is used a great deal in French, Spanish, Moroccan and Hungarian cookery.

Use this mild sweet cousin of the red pepper to add colour and flavour to eggs, seafood and vegetables. Fish dishes, cream soups and cooked cheese dishes all benefit from a sprinkling of paprika. And, of course, it is a prime ingredient of chicken or veal paprika, and of the Hungarian national dish, *gulyas*.

Pepper: One of the prime motivating factors for Columbus's voyage to find the Spice Islands, pepper is our most widely used spice. Columbus found two kinds of pepper: the black seeds whose aroma was much like that of cloves, cinnamon and nutmeg – our famous allspice, for centuries called Jamaican pepper – and the spicy vegetable which the Mayan natives called *aji* (the red pepper family).

BLACK PEPPER – one of the first spices to be introduced to Europe – is the dried, unripe fruit of the *piper nigrum* found in the East Indies. This spice lends flavour and excitement to most foods. It quickly loses flavour and aroma when ground. I prefer to grind it with a pepper mill as I need it.

WHITE PEPPER – less pungent and less aromatic than black pepper – is the same seed freed from

21

its outer skin. It is perfect for lighter sauces and in any dish where specks of black pepper would be unsightly.

RED PEPPER – the most pungent of all spices – is very hot, pungent and biting. Use it sparingly to lend excitement to fish, shellfish, *canapé* spreads and salad dressings. It is perfect for curry and barbecue sauces, and for the hot stews and *ragoûts* of Africa and the Caribbean.

Turmeric: Made from the dried and ground stem or root of a plant of the ginger family, turmeric is similar in flavour to ginger, but more discreet.

Famous mainly for the rich yellow tinge it gives to foods, turmeric is often used to colour and flavour mixed pickles, and curry and mustard powders.

THE THICKENERS

Most of the country-styled dishes – the peasant casseroles of France, Italy and Spain which are becoming so popular in this country – need no elaborate sauces to enhance their flavour. It is the slow, careful reduction of oil, butter and wine with shallots, garlic and the juices of meat, chicken or fish, cooked slowly *en cocotte* which gives to each of these dishes its own delicious flavour and texture. They contain their own sauce, in fact, and the addition of flour, thickening or a made-up sauce to such a dish is not usually necessary.

There are times, however, when you will want to make sauces and gravies a little more full-bodied or substantial. Then it is best to resort to the French chef's *beurre manié* (kneaded bits of butter and flour added to the casserole at the last minute). For dishes with a white stock or cream base like *blanquette de veau* or *matelote à la Normande,* combine egg yolks, cream and a dash of lemon juice.

Beurre manié
When the sauce should be very slightly thickened at the last moment, a *beurre manié* is indicated. Take a piece of butter (about one good tablespoon) and knead it to a smooth paste with the same amount of flour; this is stirred into the sauce bit by bit a few minutes before serving, and given just sufficient time to simmer for the flour to be cooked.

Egg yolks
Egg yolks are useful to bind, enrich and give substance to a sauce. If your sauce should turn out to be too thin, you can thicken it by adding the yolk of an egg or two, thoroughly beaten up. Add a little of the hot liquid to the beaten yolks, beat again and pour the combined mixture into the main body of your sauce, whisking all the time. Heat through without boiling, or the yolks will cook and disintegrate.

THE MOISTENERS

Wine
The use of wine in Continental cooking dates back to Roman days. In a certain number of French and Italian dishes – *ragoûts,* soups, *daubes* – it is indispensable. When wine is cooked, the alcohol evaporates, leaving a wonderful flavour which permeates the dish. Never throw away the dregs of wine left in bottles . . . this is the best cook's trump card. Use wine to flavour gravies; drop a spoonful into your salad dressing; add a touch at the last minute to veal chops sizzled in butter. To attempt wine cookery with poor wine is more than just a mistake, it is pure heresy.

Stock
Most country casseroles, sauces and a great many delicious soups are based on good chicken or beef stock of the rich home-made variety. A pint or two of stock can be kept on

hand for one week in a covered jar in the re-frigerator, or stored indefinitely in the freezer. I make stock in regular weekly bouts; the butcher sends the appropriate boiling fowl, veal and beef bones, and meat, as a regular weekly order. In this way, I am free, through-out the week, to make any number of *consom-més,* risottos, soups and sauces. Liquids from the stockpots enrich casseroles of meat and poultry; vegetables are cooked in stock for extra tastiness. Stock on hand is a must for good cooking.

Cream

Cream is a luxurious complement to the do-main of sumptuous cookery. It is used by the Norman French mainly in the form of *sauce Normande,* which begins with a roux made of butter and flour. To this is added a condensed liquid obtained by boiling vegetables and herbs until the *bouillon* has become an essence of their flavours, enriched either by white wine or egg yolks, depending on the dish for which the sauce is destined. The cream is added last, along with more butter and a dash of lemon juice. *Sauce Normande* is particularly good with various egg dishes, and a wonderful accom-paniment to fish and chicken dishes.

COOKING WITH WINE

Wine is much more than just a flavouring agent: used with discretion, it gives an umis-takable fillip to the simplest dishes. In *ragoûts* and marinades it is a wonderfully effective 'ten-deriser' for the drier or tougher cuts of meat.

Wine in this country is sufficiently low in cost to allow it to be used generously in cook-ing. Try wine for stewing and basting; use it adventurously as a delicious substitute for other liquids or as an agent to blend flavours in a *ragoût* or a casserole. Add red wine to a marinade for beef, lamb, pork or game. Use

wine – both red and white – to lend excitement to soups and sauces.

Think of wine in cooking as just another of the necessary good ingredients like butter, olive oil, parsley, onions and herbs. Allow it to round out and add savour to the general flavour of your cooking. And a note for teetotallers: wine loses its alcohol content in cooking and its taste actually changes.

There are no set rules for cooking with wine. White wines go well with the white meats of veal, poultry and fish, but they also add body and flavour to a Provençal *daube* of beef. And one of the most delicious fish recipes I know is turbot cooked in red wine.

Wine can be used to add savour to many, many good things. *Bœuf à la bourguignonne* was my first introduction to the delights of wine cookery, tender chunks of beef sautéed until golden in butter and olive oil with a few *lardons* of fat salt pork and then simmered to tender perfection in red wine with tiny white onions and button mushrooms. Steak *à la Bordelaise* features rump steak or fillet, grilled for a few minutes on each side, and served with a deli-cious red wine sauce.

Try *salmis* of grouse this season. This age-old recipe roasts birds until partially cooked, cuts them into serving pieces and serves them with golden *croûtons* in a rich wine sauce. Chic-ken, too, is delicious when prepared in this way, as are pheasant and partridge.

Coq-au-vin, a tender chicken browned in butter, flamed in cognac and then simmered in a stock made rich with wine and herbs, is also a favourite of mine. Ham goes especially well when cooked with dry white wine. We all know gammon served with a Madeira sauce; but have you tried simple pork sausages sim-mered in red wine which has been thickened with a tablespoon or two of fresh bread-crumbs?

Dry sherry, Marsala or Madeira add im-mediate savour to a clear soup, but be careful only to use a very small amount. Baste fish and seafood with a mixture of equal parts of melted butter and dry sherry, vermouth or dry white wine.

Transform a potato salad by dressing it with olive oil, wine vinegar and dry white wine and season with salt and freshly ground black pepper, to taste.

Marinate duck or game overnight in red wine with sliced carrots and onions, fresh herbs and a dash of cognac for added tenderness and flavour. Brown meat first in butter and then simmer in marinade juices until done.

Fruit, too, gains in flavour when cooked in wine. Poach hard-fleshed fruits such as pears, peaches, cherries, nectarines and apricots – with or without skins – in red or white wine, water and sugar until tender. After poaching, remove fruit from its liquid and chill. Serve fruit in its own liquid which has been separately chilled.

And remember, the better the wine you use, the better the final dish.

THE EMERGENCY SHELF

No household should be without its emergency shelf, stocked with canned and packaged 'convenience' foods, ready for unexpected guests or an impromptu dinner party.

I like to entertain and I always make sure that I have the ingredients for one or two surprise menus ready for use in case I invite guests back after a cocktail party or after the theatre. Impromptu meals – whipped up in a minute without the fuss and bother that often go into a full-scale dinner party – can be enormous fun. And success is practically assured with a little forethought and planning.

In the country, particularly, where friends are more apt to drop in for drinks and stay for supper, I rely on my emergency shelf for simple casseroles or knife-and-fork soups that come almost entirely from package or can. Spaghetti, for instance, with an Italian tomato sauce simmered for an hour before the meal, allows just enough time for a drink or two in front of the fire with guests before lunch or dinner is served. Precede with an Italian *antipasto* platter — canned or bottled artichoke hearts, green and black olives, a slice or two of foil-wrapped *salame,* canned anchovies, sardines and fresh tomatoes — follow with a green salad and brandied fruits — pears, peaches, apricots and cherries — and your reputation is made.

Or, instead of spaghetti, serve a quick *paella* made with saffron rice liberally spiked with prawns, minced clams, quartered mushrooms, peas and strips of pimento. Easy to prepare, if you make sure that you have the following ingredients in store: rice for risotto, saffron, chicken stock cubes for *bouillon,* a Spanish onion and one can each of prawns, minced clams, mushrooms, peas and pimento. Tiny cocktail sausages and a small roast chicken or cooked lobster, cut into serving pieces, make this dish almost regal. Follow with a green salad, a chocolate mousse or fruit fool and coffee. More than enough to keep any party going.

The egg, of course, reigns supreme as a stand-by for emergency meals. An omelette, filled with creamed tuna or curried ham and shrimp, makes an excellent light luncheon dish or a hot first course before a cold meat. Try a cheese soufflé with garlic *croûtons,* or one made with canned salmon flavoured with freshly grated Parmesan cheese, lemon juice and cayenne pepper. Make a chocolate or lemon-flavoured soufflé for a festive finish to a family meal.

Paper-thin pancakes filled with emergency shelf ingredients — curried seafood, diced canned ham and mushrooms in a cheese sauce, mashed sardines, minced clams — can turn a simple country lunch into party fare. Try a ham and chicken salad in a fruit dressing made of sliced oranges, bananas, whipped cream and mayonnaise flavoured with a dash of brandy. Perfect after a hot seafood chowder.

Keep these stand-by supplies on your emergency shelf.
When shopping for emergency shelf items, remember that most can be kept for an almost unlimited time. So buy in quantity when you find them reduced in a sale; you will save both time and money. Best for quick meals are canned ham, chicken, fish, seafood and luncheon meats.

I always have eggs, milk, cream, Parmesan cheese and a small supply of Spanish onions, garlic, carrots, tomatoes and lettuce on hand. In addition to these 'perishables', I like to keep the following staples for emergency entertaining:

Soups and stock cubes
Cream of mushroom
Tomato
Turtle
Green pea
Clam broth
Chicken stock cubes
Beef stock cubes

Canned Vegetables
Mushrooms
Small white onions
Italian peeled tomatoes
Tomato purée
Tomato juice
Artichoke hearts
Peas

Canned or bottled meats
Ham
Chicken
Liver pâté

Canned Fruits
Pears
Pineapple
Peaches
Apricots
Cherries

Canned Fish
Salmon
Tuna
Crabmeat
Sardines
Anchovies
Minced clams
Cod's roe

Pasta and rice
Spaghetti
Noodles
Green noodles
Risotto rice

Miscellaneous
Olive oil
Wine vinegar
Canned milk
Mayonnaise
Olives
Pickles
Relishes
Truffles

A GUIDE TO COOKING TERMS

Acidify:
To add lemon juice or vinegar to a sauce or cooked dish.

Acidulated water:
(1) Water mixed with an acidifying agent – lemon juice or vinegar – used to blanch sweetbreads, veal or chicken. (2) Lemon juice and water in equal quantities added to sliced apples, pears or bananas to stop them turning brown.

Aspic:
The culinary name for calf's foot jelly, or jelly made with bones of meat, fish or poultry. Any meat, fish, poultry, game or vegetable may be served 'in aspic'.

Bain-marie:
A French kitchen utensil designed to keep liquids at simmering point without coming to the boil. It consists of a saucepan standing in a larger pan which is filled with boiling water. A *bain-marie* is a great help in keeping sauces, stews and soups hot without overcooking. In domestic kitchens, a double saucepan can do double duty as a *bain-marie*.

Bake:
To cook in dry heat in the oven. This term is usually used only for breads, cakes, cookies, biscuits, pies, tarts and pastries. When meats are cooked in the oven, the term used is 'to roast'.

Baking blind:
A pastry shell that is baked without any filling is liable to collapse at the sides if it is not supported. Also, the base may bubble up (less likely if it has been pricked properly). To prevent this happening, the shell is baked 'blind'.

First line the pastry shell with greaseproof paper or aluminium foil. Fill it with dried beans. Push the beans up against the sides of the shell to ensure that they are supported.

Then place the tin on a baking sheet and bake in a preheated oven (200°C/400°F/gas 6) for 10 minutes. Remove from the oven and carefully lift out paper (or foil) and beans. Reduce oven temperature to 180°C/350°F/gas 4 and bake for 8 to 10 minutes for a half-baked case, 10 to 15 minutes for a fully-baked one.

Barbecue:
To cook meat, poultry, game or fish in the

A well-equipped kitchen and an expert chef are essential for any good restaurant.

open on a grill or spit over charcoal. Originally this term meant cooking a whole animal over an open fire, or in a pit. Barbecued foods are usually basted with a highly-seasoned sauce during cooking.

Bard:
To cover meat, poultry, game and sometimes fish with thin strips of pork fat or green bacon before roasting or braising.

Baste:
To pour or spoon liquid over food as it cooks to moisten and flavour it.

Batter:
Something that is beaten. Usually means the mixture from which pancakes, puddings and cakes are made. The batter used for pancakes and for coating purposes is made of eggs, flour, milk and/or water, and is fairly liquid.

Beat:
To mix with a spoon, spatula, whisk, electric blender or food processor; to make a mixture smooth and light by enclosing air.

Beurre manié:
Equal quantities of butter and flour kneaded together and added bit by bit to a stew, casserole or sauce to thicken it.

Blanch:
To preheat in boiling water or steam. This can be done for several reasons: (1) to loosen outer skins of fruits, nuts or vegetables; (2) to whiten sweetbreads, veal or chicken; (3) to remove excess salt or bitter flavour from bacon, gammon, ham, Brussels sprouts, turnips, endive, etc.; (4) to prepare fruits and vegetables for canning, freezing or preserving.

Boil:
To cook in any liquid – usually water, wine or stock, or a combination of the three – brought to boiling point and kept there.

Boiling point:
The temperature at which bubbles rise continually and break over the entire surface of a liquid.

Bouillon:
A clear soup, broth or stock made with beef, veal or poultry, and vegetables. *Bouillon* must be strained before using.

Bouquet garni:
A bunch or 'faggot' of culinary herbs used to flavour stews, casseroles and sauces. A *bouquet garni* can be small, medium or large, according to the flavour required for the dish and, of course, according to what the cook has at hand.

Bread:
To roll in, or coat with, breadcrumbs before cooking.

Broil:
See 'grill'.

Brunoise:
Finely diced vegetables – carrots, celery, onions, leeks (and sometimes turnips) – simmered in butter and stock until soft. Used to flavour soups, stuffiings, sauces and certain dishes of fish and shellfish.

Caramelise:
To melt sugar in a thick-bottomed saucepan, stirring continuously, until it is a golden brown syrup.

Chaud-froid:
A jellied white sauce made of butter, flour, chicken stock, egg yolks, cream and gelatine. Used to glaze chicken, ham, etc.

Chill:
To place in refrigerator or other cold place until cold.

Clarify:
To clear a stock or broth by adding slightly beaten egg whites and crushed egg shells and bringing liquid to the boil. The stock is then cooled and strained before using.

Cool:
To allow to stand at room temperature until no longer warm to the touch. *(Not* to put in the refrigerator.)

Court-bouillon:
The liquid in which fish, poultry or meat is cooked to give added flavour. A simple *court-bouillon* consists of water to which you have added 1 bay leaf, 2 celery stalks, 1 Spanish onion, 2 carrots and salt and freshly ground black pepper, to taste. Other additives are wine vinegar, stock, olive oil, garlic, shallots, cloves, etc.

Cream:
To work one or more foods with a heavy spoon or a firm spatula until the mixture is soft and creamy. To cream butter and sugar: beat softened butter with electric mixer (or rub against sides of bowl with a wooden spoon) until smooth and fluffy. Gradually beat or rub in sugar until thoroughly blended and mixture is light and fluffy.

Croûtons:
Bread trimmed of crusts, cut to shape (triangles, hearts, dice), rubbed with cut garlic clove (optional) and sautéed in oil or butter.

Cut in:
When making pastry to combine fat and dry ingredients with two knives, scissor-fashion, or with a pastry blender.

Deep-fry:
To cook in deep hot fat until crisp and golden. Also known as French-fry.

Devil:
(1) To grill food with a mixture of butter, mustard, Worcestershire sauce and fresh breadcrumbs. (2) To cook or serve with a hot 'devil' sauce.

Disjoint:
To cut poultry, game or small animals into serving pieces by dividing at the joint.

Dissolve:
To mix a dry ingredient with liquid until it is absorbed.

Dredge:
To coat food with a fine-particled substance by dusting, sprinkling, or rolling the food in flour, cornflour, cornmeal, sugar, etc.

Dust:
To sift or sprinkle lightly with a fine-particled substance such as flour, sugar or seasonings.

Duxelles:
Finely chopped mushrooms and onion (or shallots), sautéed in butter until soft. Mixture should be quite dry. Used to flavour poached fish and shellfish; dress a fillet of beef or leg of baby lamb before it is wrapped in pastry; or to garnish a *papillote.*

Fillet:
(1) Special cut of beef, lamb, pork or veal; boned breast of poultry and game; fish cut off the bone lengthwise. (2) To cut any of the above to use in cooking.

Fish fumet:
A highly concentrated fish stock, made by reducing well-flavoured fish stock. Used to

poach fish, fish fillets or fish steaks and flavour sauces. Corresponds to essence for meats.

Flame:
To pour alcohol over a dish and ignite it.

Flute:
To flute pastry, make short slanting kinks with a floured knife along the pastry edge.

Fold-in:
When a mixture has been beaten until light and fluffy, other ingredients must be 'folded in' very gently with a spatula so that the air will not be lost. Blend in new ingredients little by little, turning mixture very gently. Continue only until the ingredients are evenly blended.

Fricassée:
To cook chicken or veal in fat until golden, and then in a sauce. Fricassée is, in fact, a form of braising.

Garniture:
The garnish or trimming added to a cooked dish, or served at the same time on a separate dish; vegetables, rice, pasta, *croûtons,* etc.

Glaze:
A thin coating of syrup or aspic – sometimes coloured with caramel – which is brushed over sweets, puddings, fruits (syrup), or cooked ham, tongue, chicken, beef, pork, veal, etc. (aspic). Food must be cold and quite dry before aspic will set.

Grate:
To reduce to particles with a grater.

Gratin:
To cook *'au gratin'* is to brown food in the oven – usually covered in a sauce and dotted with breadcrumbs, cheese and butter – until crisp, golden coating forms.

Grill:
To cook by direct heat such as an open fire, or, more usually, by charcoal, gas or electricity.

Julienne:
Cut into fine strips the length of a matchstick: used for leeks, carrots etc.

Knead:
To work dough with hands until it is of the desired elasticity or consistency.

Lard:
(1) Common cooking fat obtained by melting down of pork fat. (2) Culinary process by which *lardons* of pork fat or green bacon are threaded through meat, poultry, game and sometimes fish to lend flavour and moisture to food.

Lardons:
(1) Strips of pork fat or green bacon used as above. (2) Diced pork fat or green bacon, blanched and sautéed to add flavour and texture to certain stews, *daubes, ragoûts* and casseroles.

Liaison:
To thicken a sauce, gravy or stew: (1) by addition of flour, cornflour, arrowroot, rice flour, potato flour, or a *beurre manié* (flour and butter); (2) by stirring in egg yolk, double cream, or in the case of certain dishes of poultry or game, blood.

Macédoine:
(1) A mixture of raw or cooked fruit for a fruit salad. (2) a mixture of cooked diced vegetables dressed with a cream sauce or mayonnaise, or aspic, usually served as an *hors d'oeuvre* salad, or as a garnish.

Marinade:
A highly-flavoured liquid – usually red or white wine or olive oil or a combination of the

two – seasoned with carrots, onion, bay leaf, herbs and spices. Marinades can be cooked or uncooked. The purpose of a marinade it to impart flavour to the food and to soften fibres of tougher foods.

Marinate:
To let food stand, or steep, in a marinade.

Mask:
To cover cooked food with sauce.

Mince:
To reduce to very small particles with a mincer, chopper or knife.

Mirepoix:
Finely diced carrots, onion, celery (and sometimes ham), simmered in butter until soft. Used to add flavour to dishes of meat, poultry, fish and shellfish.

Oven-fry:
To cook meat, fish or poultry in fat in the oven, uncovered, basting food with fat from time to time.

Parboil:
To precook or boil until partially cooked.

Pare or peel:
(1) To cut off outside skin or covering of a fruit or vegetable with a knife or parer. (2) To peel fruits such as oranges or bananas.

Papillote:
To cook *'en papillote'* is the culinary term for cooking food enclosed in an oiled paper or foil case *(papillote).*

Poach:
To cook gently in simmering (not boiling) liquid so that the surface of the liquid barely trembles.

Pit:
To remove pit, stone or seed, as from cherries.

Pound:
To reduce to very small particles, or a paste, with a mortar and pestle.

Purée:
To press through a fine sieve or food mill to produce a smooth soft food.

Quenelle:
The finely pounded flesh of fish, shellfish, veal, poultry or game, mixed with egg whites and cream and pounded over ice to a velvety smooth paste. These featherlight dumplings are then poached in stock or water.

Ragoût:
A stew made from even-sized pieces of meat, poultry or fish. There are two types: 'brown' ragoût in which the main ingredient is sautéed in fat until brown and then simmered with stock, meat juices or water, or a combination of these, until tender; *Navarin de mouton* is an example of a 'brown' *ragoût.* In a 'white' ragoût (Irish stew is a typical one) the meat or fish is not browned before stewing.

Reduce:
To cook a sauce over a high heat, uncovered, until it is reduced by evaporation to the desired consistency. This culinary process improves both flavour and appearance.

Render:
To free fat from tissue by melting at low heat.

Roast:
To cook meat by direct heat on a spit or in the oven. 'Baking' would be a better term for meat which is cooked in the oven, for in a closed area vapour accumulates and changes the texture and flavour of true roast.

Roux:
The gentle amalgamation of butter and flour over a low heat; capable of absorbing at least six times its own weight when cooked. (1) To make a white roux: melt 2 tablespoons butter in the top of a double saucepan; add 2 tablespoons of sieved flour and stir with a wire whisk for 2 to 3 minutes over water until the mixture amalgamates but does not change colour. (2) A pale roux: cook as above, stirring continuously, just a little longer (4 to 5 minutes) or until the colour of roux: cook as above until mixture acquires a fine light brown colour.

Salmis:
To cook jointed poultry or game in a rich wine sauce after it has been roasted until almost done. Often done in a chafing dish at the table.

Salpicon:
Finely diced meat, poultry, game, fish, shellfish, or vegetables, bound with a savoury sauce and used to fill *canapés* and individual *hors d'oeuvre* pastry cases. Also used to make rissoles, croquettes and stuffings for eggs, vegetables and small cuts of poultry or meat.

Sauté:
To fry lightly in a small amount of hot fat or oil, shaking the pan or turning food frequently during cooking.

Scald:
To heat to temperature just below boiling point. I use a double saucepan to scald cream or milk. This prevents scorching.

Score:
To make evenly-spaced, shallow slits or cuts with a knife.

Sear:
To brown and seal the surface of meat quickly over high heat. This prevents juices from escaping.

Sift:
To put through a sifter or a fine sieve.

Simmer:
To cook in liquid just below boiling point, with small bubbles of steam rising occasionally to the surface.

Skewer:
(1) To keep in shape with skewers. (2) The actual skewer, made of metal or wood, which is used to keep meats, poultry, game, etc., in shape while cooking. (3) The skewer, a piece of metal or wood sometimes called 'brochette', used to hold pieces of chicken, fish, poultry, etc., to be grilled over charcoal, or under gas or electricity.

Sliver:
To cut or shred into long, thin pieces.

Steam:
To cook food in vapour over boiling water or stock. This process is often used in Oriental cooking.

Steep:
To let food stand in hot liquid to extract flavour or colour.

Whisk:
To beat rapidly with a whisk, rotary beater or electric mixer in order to incorporate air and increase volume.

Zest:
The finely grated rind of lemon or orange.

The busy, colourful fruit and vegetable market in the rue Mouffetard, Paris.

BASIC EQUIPMENT

W HEN CATHERINE DE MEDICI brought Italian cooks to France, she also brought the key to the whole future of eating in one kitchen gadget – the fork. The knife, I grant you, is pretty important, and so is the spoon. A knife alone, however, meant that you still had to use your hands for a good part of the meal and that restricted you to roasts and boiled meats and all the rigmarole of medieval food. But with the introduction of the fork, sauces and every subtlety became possible and the art of present-day cookery was born.

There are gadgets and gadgets. Some are indispensable, some so complicated that it is almost easier to beat by hand for 20 minutes than to assemble and dismantle the monsters. You may have your own idiosyncrasies – I have my automatic slicing machine, bought in a weak moment, which I have used six times during the past two years. But, for the most part, the equipment I use in my kitchen is as simple as Catherine de Medici's fork.

INDISPENSABLE ITEMS

Chopping bowl
One of the most used utensils in my kitchen is a small wooden chopping bowl with a knife which has a curved blade specially designed to fit it. In this I cut all parsley, *fines herbes,* garlic, shallots and onions. It is always in view, ready for use, in my kitchen, as is a thick chopping board. I hate to have to search for such necessary and constantly used items.

Chopping board
Make sure your chopping board is thick enough to withstand many washings without

warping, and large enough to hold food that falls away from the knife whatever the size of the item being chopped.

Mortar and pestle
A rather more esoteric bit of basic equipment in my kitchen is the stone mortar and pestle which are also always in readiness for pounding dried breadcrumbs, herbs to make a sauce, or meats for a *pâté.* I like a large-sized mortar, so that I can use it to pound anchovies for a Provençal *anchoiade* or poached salt cod for a *brandade de morue.*

Electric food processor

But perhaps my favourite cooking tool of all is the new Magimix food preparation machine which goes further faster than any blender, or mincer, or mixer, that I know. The Magimix is not an inexpensive gadget; indeed its high purchase price might make any novice cook stop short to catch her breath. But it is one of the most used tools in my kitchen. It makes hamburger and minced meats for meat loaves, or *pâtés,* literally in a second; it blends raw meat, fish, or poultry to a super fine mousse for *quenelles* and mousses in a matter of minutes; it grinds breadcrumbs perfectly at the push of its safety lid; makes the quickest grated Gruyère or Parmesan cheese that I've ever seen; and blends cooked vegetables and cooked fish with cream and stock to make a quick and easy purée for smooth soups and *bisques* in seconds.

One of the things I like best about it is that if you are going to process onions, parsley, breadcrumbs, pork, pork fat, veal and chicken livers to make a *terrine,* or *pâté,* you don't have to wash the blade, or the bowl, as you process each ingredient. A great time and effort saver. And when it comes to washing the machine, all you have to do is wash the sharp blade, the bowl and the cover: three separate pieces that are easy to dismantle and put together again.

CUTLERY FOR THE KITCHEN

Most food preparation calls for some kind of cutting, slicing or chopping. You will find that a good selection of kitchen knives is one of the first requisites of a well-equipped kitchen. I have had a special chopping table made for my kitchen at Hintlesham complete with a sink and waste disposal unit dropped into the thick chopping block top and special slots cut into the block to hold my regularly used knives.

Basic knife wardrobe

In any department store or ironmonger's, you will find an extensive array of kitchen knives with different shapes, lengths and edges. Many of the imported modern German knives have scalloped or serrated edges which offer special advantages in cutting and hold their cutting edge indefinitely. These are the knives from my own Robert Carrier Cook Knife Range that I find the most useful.

Ham slicer

The long 22-24cm/9-9½in ham knife is perfect for cutting thin parallel slices of ham or gammon and is also good for poultry.

Carving knife

Use for all roasts and steaks. The blade should be 18-22cm/7-9in long. I find a long knife with serrated edge is good, too, for cold meats, cheeses and sausages, as well as for most bread and pastry cutting.

French cook's knife

You will need one large and one small. Use to dice, chop or slice raw vegetables and fruits.

Small paring knife

Good for paring potatoes, cucumbers, carrots and onions. A paring knife with a pointed tip and a 7.5cm/3in blade is most satisfactory.

Boning knife

Its slightly curved blade is excellent for boning meats, poultry and game. I find it is a knife I pick up for almost everything.

Cleaver

Useful for sectioning heavy pieces of meat, cutting joints, and for game and lobster. I also use mine, flat-sided, as a meat tenderiser.

KITCHEN IMPLEMENTS

Of all the everyday tools that are in constant use in every kitchen, these are among the most versatile.

Cooking fork
Select one with a long handle and stainless steel prongs.

Wooden and metal spoons
Both long and short are necessary to fit a variety of saucepan sizes.

Slotted metal cooking spoon
Useful for making sauces and gravies smooth and for skimming stocks and sauces.

Spatula
A flexible spatula of stainless steel for icing cakes, loosening food and turning omelettes.

Ladle
Available in a variety of sizes; for ladling soups, sauces and gravies.

Wire whisks
Either round or flat, for whisking sauces and egg whites.

Measuring equipment
Accurate measurements are essential to any kind of cooking. If they are kept within easy reach of cooking and preparation areas, measuring becomes automatic. A set of individual MEASURING SPOONS in plastic or metal – 15ml/1 tablespoon, 5ml/1 teaspoon, 2.5ml/½ teaspoon and 1.5ml/¼ teaspoon – is ideal for measuring small quantities of ingredients. A MEASURING CUP marked off in centilitres and fluid ounces is also useful, as is a pair of KITCHEN SCALES.

Kitchen grater
Round- or square-shaped with different-sized cutting sides for grating cheese, lemon and orange rinds, nutmeg, etc. New stainless steel graters are on the market which make maintenance much easier.

Pepper and salt mills
These kitchen aids offer the extra advantage of freshly ground seasonings.

Sieves
A conical sieve used for the straining of sauces is one of the most useful kitchen utensils. A 15cm/6in conical sieve is a good size for all purposes. I also find the ordinary round bottomed sieves useful for the sieving and draining of vegetables.

Mixing bowls
Every kitchen should have a series of mixing bowls large enough for all ingredients to be used. I like a series of 3 bowls in assorted sizes, as well as a mammoth bowl with a lip which I find most useful.

COOKWARE

Saucepans
When buying new equipment, make sure you choose good sturdy saucepans of heavy metal. Though more expensive at first, they are well worth the initial outlay, for heavy saucepans will hold the meat better, will not dent or warp so easily and will not allow foods to scorch. I prefer stainless steel, stainless steel combined with aluminium, or copper saucepans, in the largest sizes available. I find that if I cook for

more than 3 persons, it is always the largest saucepan that I reach for. I prefer saucepans with straight sides.

Double saucepan
Used for making most sauces and for keeping sauces hot without danger of curdling or separating. It is absolutely necessary for delicate emulsion sauces such as Béarnaise or Hollandaise.

Frying pan
A large black-iron frying pan with a thick bottom is one of the best cook's aids ever invented. I have 2, a pan for omelettes and a large all-purpose pan. To keep frying pans in good condition, never put them away dirty and never clean with a metal knife or metal sponge. A frying pan should be cleaned by heat, with salt applied when the pan is very hot, and a paper towel.

Before using your iron frying pan for the first time, prepare it by heating it over a hot flame until all protective varnish or grease has disappeared. Then wipe it clean with a paper towel. Cover the bottom generously with oil or lard and heat this fat in the oven or over heat. Pour off the excess grease and leave the residue in the pan. If food still sticks when you use the pan, repeat the process.

CASSEROLES

You will soon find you want a casserole 'wardrobe' – several sizes of every type of casserole made – but if your kitchen is on the small side, I suggest you start with the following: 2 large casseroles for buffet suppers and large gatherings; 2 medium-sized casseroles for dinners of 4 to 8; and several small casseroles for vegetables and for intimate dinners for 2.

The choice is large: heatproof, classic copper and ovenproof earthenware from France; modern Swedish metal designs in all shapes, colours and sizes; and the very latest, stainless steel combined with aluminium, made by Cuisinox for ICTC.

Iron casseroles
I am particularly happy to see the arrival in this country of iron *cocottes* and casseroles such as I have been used to in America. There, our 'Dutch oven', a large round casserole in heavy black iron with a close-fitting lid, was the stand-by for every kind of cooking. Wonderful for pot roasts and for casseroles of chicken, meat and game, it worked very well as an emergency frying pan . . . and I have even baked an upside-down peach pudding in one. These iron casseroles come in 3 or 4 practical sizes. They are prepared and maintained in the same way as iron frying pans. Be sure to keep them well oiled as they a have a tendency to rust in this climate if left dry.

But perhaps my favourite casseroles are the traditional orange-coloured enamelled iron casseroles from France produced by Le Creuset. Wonderfully decorative in my kitchen, they are solid, hard-wearing and wonderful to use. Their traditional shapes are perfect for every sort of cooking.

Asbestos mat
If your casserole is not heatproof, you will need an asbestos mat to put under it for top-of-the-stove cookery.

CHAPTER 1

APPETISERS

HORS D'OEUVRE VARIES

MOST OF THE glamorous restaurants of the world serve a galaxy of titbits, both hot and cold, which fly under the banner of *hors-d'œuvre variés*. These appetite stimulants are usually wheeled up to your table on a two- or three-tiered trolley, each tier of which can hold up to twenty small dishes or *raviers* containing a colourful assortment of vegetables, marinated in olive oil and lemon juice and served *à la vinaigrette,* or prepared *à la grecque* with wine, olive oil, finely chopped onion, carrot and herbs. These trolleys come to us via France from Russia where the *hors-d'œuvre* idea originated in the Russian *zakouski* table, set up in a room adjoining the reception room and wheeled in to satisfy far-travelling guests before dinner. Thus it is not surprising to find Russian salad, hard-boiled eggs with a mayonnaise or sour cream dressing, and pickled and preserved fish of all kinds included in the usual *hors-d'œuvre* assortment. The formula for *hors-d'œuvre* and *entrées chaudes* varies according to the whim of the *maître de la maison.* At the old Restaurant de la Boule d'Or in Paris, for example, the *hors-d'œuvre* were limited to cucumbers in cream, sliced *saucisson,* tomato salad, asparagus *vinaigrette,* a duck pâté and a delicious dish of artichoke hearts, button onions and mushrooms *à la grecque.* The three hot *entrées* of the house were *quiche Lorraine,* a savoury tart of eggs, cheese and bacon; *pissaladière,* a Provençal tomato and onion tart; and a dish of delicately browned ham patties.

La Petite Auberge, a famous restaurant located in Noves, in the South of France, offers an *hors-d'œuvre* dish that is really a meal in itself. Their famous vegetable appetiser consists of the following cooked and raw vegetables: button onions cooked

---

Right: A tempting selection of hors d'oeuvre variés, including Bean Salad Vinaigrette (top right), Turbot Salad 'White Tower' (centre), *Onions 'Monégasque' (centre right), Lentils and Sausages 'Forum of the Twelve Caesars' (lower left), and Oriental Rice (lower right).*

in white wine and lemon juice, flavoured with nutmeg, pepper and herbs; leeks with a herb-flavoured French dressing; coarsely grated raw carrots dressed with mustard-flavoured mayonnaise; finely sliced green peppers with an onion dressing; raw mushroom salad; poached celery with a Provençal dressing in which pounded anchovies, olive oil and wine vinegar play their part; highly-spiced saffron rice studded with raisins; tomato slices with a tarragon cream sauce; marinated artichoke hearts; and asparagus tips, topped with puréed tomatoes, lightly flavoured with mustard and mayonnaise. Any one of these would be delicious by itself as an *hors-d'œuvre;* or try a combination of two or more to provide colour, flavour and texture contrasts.

The real purpose of the *hors-d'œuvre* course is to stimulate the appetite, not to drown it. A correctly chosen complement of dishes should not contain too much mayonnaise or other dressings but it should contain both cooked and raw foods so that tastes and textures vary as much as possible. Serve *hors-d'œuvre* to best advantage in individual dishes or bowls.

The famous vegetable appetiser from La Petite Auberge restaurant in Noves, in the South of France.

LENTILS AND SAUSAGES 'FORUM OF THE TWELVE CAESARS'

SERVES 4-6

225g/½lb lentils
2 Spanish onions, peeled and halved
2 cloves
2 bay leaves
ham bone, or 100g/¼lb bacon
16 cocktail sausages, or 8 small chipolata sausages
90ml/6 tbls red wine vinegar
5ml/1 tsp Dijon mustard
150ml/¼pt olive oil
salt and freshly ground black pepper
30ml/2 tbls finely chopped onion
30ml/2 tbls finely chopped parsley
4-8 lettuce leaves
2 small tomatoes, quartered

1. Soak lentils overnight in water to cover. Drain.
2. Preheat oven to hot (230°C/450°F/gas 8).
3. Place lentils in a large saucepan with halved onions, cloves, bay leaves and ham bone or bacon. Add 1.4L/2½pt water and simmer lentils until tender, about 2 hours. Remove onions, cloves and ham bone or bacon. Drain and allow to cool.
4. Bake sausages in oven until cooked through and cool.
5. Make a French dressing by combining wine vinegar, Dijon mustard and olive oil and season with salt and freshly ground black pepper to taste.
6. Pour dressing over lentils; add finely chopped onion and parsley, and toss well. Arrange on a bed of lettuce leaves on a serving platter with lentil salad on top; place sausages down the centre of the dish and serve with tomatoes.

BEAN SALAD VINAIGRETTE

SERVES 4-6

700g/1½lb young green beans
salt
2.5ml/½ tsp Dijon mustard
30-45ml/2-3 tbls red wine vinegar
90-120ml/6-8 tbls olive oil
salt and freshly ground black pepper
finely chopped parsley
finely chopped garlic

1. Top and tail young green beans and cook them in plenty of boiling salted water until they are barely tender.
2. Meanwhile, make a French dressing by combining Dijon mustard, red wine vinegar and olive oil, and season with salt and freshly ground black pepper, finely chopped parsley and garlic to taste.
3. Drain beans and toss immediately while still warm in the dressing. Chill before serving.

MEDITERRANEAN FISH SALAD

SERVES 4-6

350g/¾lb turbot, cleaned and gutted
350g/¾lb halibut, cleaned and gutted
salt
150ml/¼pt milk
150ml/¼pt olive oil
juice of 1-2 lemons
salt and freshly ground black pepper
100g/¼lb Norwegian shrimps
30-60ml/2-4 tbls finely chopped parsley
30-60ml/2-4 tbls finely chopped shallots
1 garlic clove, finely chopped

1. Cut turbot and halibut into cubes about 10mm/½in thick and poach in boiling salted water to which you have added milk to make the fish white. Reduce heat so that water barely bubbles. When fish can be flaked with a fork, drain. Remove skin and bones while the fish is still warm.

2. Meanwhile make a salad dressing by combining olive oil and lemon juice, and season with salt and freshly ground black pepper to taste.

3. Combine cooked fish with shrimps and toss immediately in the salad dressing.

4. Just before serving, add finely chopped parsley, shallots and garlic to salad and toss gently. Transfer to a serving platter and serve immediately.

ONIONS 'MONEGASQUE'

SERVES 6-8

2 medium-sized carrots, coarsely chopped
olive oil
1kg/2lb button onions, peeled
150ml/¼pt dry white wine
60ml/4 tbls lemon juice
50g/2oz sultanas
30ml/2 tbls tomato purée
2 bay leaves
2.5ml/½ tsp dried thyme
salt and freshly ground black pepper
cayenne pepper
15ml/1 tbls finely chopped parsley

1. Sauté coarsely chopped carrots in 60ml/4 tbls olive oil until soft and golden. Combine in a saucepan with peeled onions, 450ml/¾pt water, dry white wine, lemon juice, sultanas, tomato purée, bay leaves, dried thyme, and salt and freshly ground black pepper and cayenne pepper to taste. Simmer for about 1 hour, or until onions are cooked through and sauce has reduced a little. Chill.

2. Just before serving, correct seasoning; pour over a little olive oil and sprinkle with finely chopped parsley.

NOTE: I sometimes add a little ground saffron and a little more tomato purée to this recipe for extra emphasis.

ORIENTAL RICE

SERVES 4-6

2.5ml/½ tsp ground saffron
1.5ml/¼ tsp ground cumin
90ml/6 tbls dry white wine
*600ml/1pt hot **Basic chicken stock**
  (see page 66)*
350g/¾lb risotto rice
½ green pepper, seeded and diced
½ red pepper, seeded and diced
½ Spanish onion, coarsely chopped
salt and freshly ground black pepper

DRESSING
90-120ml/6-8 tbls olive oil
30-45ml/2-3 tbls red wine vinegar
30ml/2 tbls finely chopped parsley
salt and freshly ground black pepper

1. Dissolve ground saffron and cumin in dry white wine and CHICKEN STOCK and combine in a large saucepan with rice, diced peppers, and chopped onion. Season with salt and freshly ground black pepper to taste. Cover pan and simmer until all the liquid is absorbed and the rice is tender. Add some more liquid if necessary.

2. Meanwhile, make a dressing by combining olive oil, red wine vinegar and finely chopped parsley, and season with salt and freshly ground black pepper to taste. Add more olive oil or wine vinegar if necessary.

3. Drain rice well and toss in dressing. Transfer to a serving platter and serve immediately.

HARICOTS BLANCS EN SALADE

SERVES 4-6

350g/³/₄lb dry white beans
1 Spanish onion, finely chopped
90ml/6 tbls olive oil
1 garlic clove, finely chopped
1 bay leaf
5ml/1 tsp salt
1 medium-sized green pepper, seeded and diced
60ml/4 tbls red wine vinegar
salt and freshly ground black pepper

DRESSING

¹/₂ Spanish onion, finely chopped
60ml/4 tbls finely chopped parsley
1 garlic clove, finely chopped
5ml/1 tsp prepared mustard
salt and freshly ground black pepper
olive oil
juice of ¹/₂ lemon

GARNISH

finely chopped parsley
anchovy fillets
black olives

1. Soak dry white beans overnight in water to cover. Drain.
2. In a flameproof casserole, sauté finely chopped onion in 30ml/2 tbls olive oil until onion just begins to turn colour. Add finely chopped garlic, bay leaf, salt and 1.4L/2¹/₂pt water and simmer beans in this stock until beans are tender, about 2 hours. Drain.
3. Add the diced green pepper to beans along with 60ml/4 tbls olive oil and wine vinegar. Season with salt and freshly ground black pepper to taste.
4. Make a dressing by combining finely chopped onion, parsley and garlic with mustard in a bowl. Season with salt and freshly ground black pepper to taste. Mix well and then pour in olive oil, drop by drop, as if you were making a mayonnaise, beating the mixture all the time until thick. Flavour with lemon juice.
5. Arrange salad in a salad bowl; pour over salad dressing and toss until well mixed. Garnish with finely chopped parsley, anchovy fillets and black olives, and serve.

JEWISH CHOPPED CHICKEN LIVERS

SERVES 4

350g/³/₄lb chicken livers
120ml/8 tbls chicken fat
1 Spanish onion, finely chopped
2 hard-boiled eggs
1 celery stalk, finely chopped
¹/₄-¹/₂ small green pepper, seeded and finely chopped
salt and freshly ground black pepper
hot toast, to serve

1. Sauté chicken livers in 90ml/6 tbls melted chicken fat until they are firm, but not cooked through. Remove livers from pan.
2. Sauté finely chopped onion in remaining chicken fat until transparent and cooked through.
3. Chop hard-boiled eggs coarsely and put through the finest blade of your mincer with chicken livers.
4. Combine chicken liver and egg mixture in a large bowl with sautéed onion, finely chopped celery, and green pepper, and enough additional chicken fat to make mixture smooth. Season to taste with salt and freshly ground black pepper. Serve with hot toast.

MARINATED HERRING FILLETS IN SOUR CREAM

SERVES 6-12

12 fresh herring fillets
600ml/1pt soured cream
30ml/2 tbls red wine vinegar
30ml/2 tbls olive oil
3 medium-sized onions, very finely sliced
12 green peppercorns
3-6 small bay leaves
salt
1 large sour apple
½ lemon, very thinly sliced

1. Wash herring fillets; pat dry and arrange in a serving bowl.
2. Combine soured cream, red wine vinegar and olive oil. Add very finely sliced onions, green peppercorns, bay leaves, and salt. Pour over herrings. Cover and place in a refrigerator. Marinate for 24 hours.
3. Just before serving, peel, core and slice the apple very thinly. Add the apple and lemon slices to the herring mixture and toss well.

TURBOT SALAD 'WHITE TOWER'

SERVES 4-6

1kg/2lb turbot fillets
salt
150ml/¼pt milk
150ml/10 tbls olive oil
juice of 2 lemons
freshly ground black pepper
60ml/4 tbls finely chopped parsley
60ml/4 tbls coarsely chopped onion

1. Cut turbot into slices about 10mm/½in thick and poach in 1L/2pt boiling salted water to which you have added milk to make fish white. Reduce heat so that water barely bubbles. It is important that the turbot cooks very

gently so that it does not lose its juices in the stock. When fish can be flaked with a fork, drain.
2. Meanwhile, make a dressing by combining olive oil and lemon juice, and season with salt and freshly ground black pepper to taste.
3. Remove skin and bones from turbot while still warm and then toss immediately in dressing. Add finely chopped parsley and coarsely chopped onion, and allow to cool. Do not refrigerate.
4. Just before serving, correct seasoning, adding more olive oil and lemon juice, if necessary. This dish is best served soon after it has been prepared, as it tends to lose flavour if kept too long.

CEVICHE *(Mexican Seafood Cocktail)*

SERVES 4

450g/1lb halibut, or any firm white non-fatty fish
juice of 2 fresh limes or lemons
225g/½lb tomatoes, peeled and seeded
1 small green pepper, seeded and diced
60ml/4 tbls olive oil
60ml/4 tbls finely chopped parsley
60ml/4 tbls finely chopped coriander leaves
15-30ml/1-2 tbls red wine vinegar
dash of Tabasco
2.5ml/½ tsp dried oregano
salt and freshly ground black pepper
1 avocado pear, peeled and diced
6 stuffed olives, sliced

1. Fillet, skin and dice raw fish. Place in a porcelain or earthenware bowl (not metal); pour over lime or lemon juice and marinate for 3 hours, turning fish pieces with a wooden spoon from time to time, so that juice turns the fish snowy-white and non-transparent. It will look and flake like cooked fish.
2. Dice peeled tomatoes and add to fish.
3. Add diced green pepper to fish mixture to-

gether with olive oil, finely chopped parsley and coriander leaves, red wine vinegar, Tabasco and dried oregano. Season with salt and freshly ground black pepper, to taste.

4. Serve Ceviche chilled, garnished with diced avocado pear and sliced stuffed olives.

TARAMASALATA

SERVES 4-6

1 jar smoked cod's roe, about 100g/¼lb
6 slices of white bread
¼ Spanish onion, grated
1-2 garlic cloves, mashed
120-160ml/8-12 tbls olive oil
juice of 1 lemon
15ml/1 tbls finely chopped parsley
green olives
hot toast, to serve

1. Place cod's roe in a mortar. Trim crusts from bread; soak bread in water; squeeze almost dry and add to cod's roe. Pound mixture to a smooth paste.

2. Stir grated onion and mashed garlic into paste. Then add olive oil and lemon juice alternately in small amounts, stirring well, until mixture acquires a smooth, uniform consistency. Strain through a fine sieve. The above can be done in an electric blender, in which case the mixture does not need to be sieved.

3. Transfer Taramasalata to a serving bowl; sprinkle with finely chopped parsley and garnish with green olives. Serve with hot toast. I also like to stuff 5cm/2in lengths of crisp celery with this mixture as a light appetiser.

COLD SALMON PATE

1kg/2lb raw fresh salmon
60ml/4 tbls dry sherry
30ml/2 tbls cognac

2 bay leaves
salt and freshly ground black pepper
175g/6oz raw whiting
175g/6oz raw cod
2 slices of stale bread
milk
2 egg yolks, lightly beaten
50g/2oz butter
100g/¼lb smoked salmon, cut into fingers
60ml/4 tbls finely chopped chives
60ml/4 tbls finely chopped parsley
lemon juice
***Sauce verte** (see page 86)*

1. Skin and bone salmon; cut the best parts of it into short fingers about 6mm/¼in thick and marinate these for about 2 hours in dry sherry and cognac, with bay leaves and salt and freshly ground black pepper to taste. Turn salmon fingers occasionally so that all sides are impregnated with the sherry/cognac mixture.

2. Preheat oven to moderate (180°C/350°F/gas 4).

3. Skin and bone whiting and cod and place in electric blender with the remainder of the salmon. Add bread which you have dipped in milk, lightly-beaten egg yolks and 50g/2oz butter. Season with salt and freshly ground black pepper to taste. Moisten mixture with sherry/cognac marinade and blend well. Pass mixture through a fine sieve.

4. Roll marinated salmon 'fingers' in chopped chives and parsley. Dip smoked salmon 'fingers' into a little lemon juice and then roll in chopped chives and parsley mixture.

5. Butter a terrine or ovenproof pâté dish and cover the bottom with a layer of fish mixture; place prepared 'fingers' of marinated salmon and smoked salmon on this; cover with a layer of fish mixture, and so on until terrine is full, finishing with a layer of fish mixture. Cover and cook in preheated oven for 45 to 60 minutes.

6. Serve pâté cold with SAUCE VERTE.

GUACAMOLE (*Avocado Appetiser*)

SERVES 6

2 ripe avocado pears
juice of 1 lemon
1 garlic clove, mashed to a paste with a little salt
4 tomatoes, peeled, seeded and coarsely chopped
½ Spanish onion, finely chopped
2 stalks celery, finely chopped
½ medium-sized green pepper, finely chopped
15ml/1 tbls finely chopped coriander leaves or
* parsley*
30-60ml/2-4 tbls olive oil
salt and freshly ground black pepper

1. Peel and mash avocados lightly with a
wooden spoon. Keep the stones. Add lemon
juice, mashed garlic, coarsely chopped tomatoes, and finely chopped onion and celery
or green pepper to mashed avocados.
2. Stir finely chopped coriander leaves or
parsley and olive oil into mashed avocado mixture and season with salt and freshly ground
black pepper to taste. Leave the avocado stones
in the sauce until ready to serve to keep sauce
from changing colour. Mexicans serve
guacamole with *tostaditos* (deep-fried wedges of
tortilla).

TOMATOES GUACAMOLE

SERVES 4

8 large tomatoes
salt
2 ripe avocado pears
juice of 1 lemon
1 garlic clove, mashed
15-30ml/1-2 tbls onion juice
freshly ground black pepper
chilli powder
2 stalks celery, finely chopped
½ medium-sized green pepper, finely chopped
15-30ml/1-2 tbls finely chopped coriander leaves
* or parsley*

1. To prepare tomato cases, plunge tomatoes
into boiling water for a minute, one by one,
and remove their skins with a sharp knife. Slice
cap off each and carefully scoop out all pulp
and seeds. Season inside of each tomato cup
with salt and turn upside down on a tray to
drain. Cover tomato cups loosely with
aluminium foil and chill in refrigerator until
ready to use.
2. To make *guacamole* filling; peel and mash
avocados lightly with a wooden spoon. Add
lemon juice and mashed garlic and season with
onion juice, salt and freshly ground black pepper and chilli powder to taste. Fold in finely
chopped celery or green pepper, and chill.
3. Just before serving, fill each tomato cup
with *guacamole* mixture and sprinkle with
finely chopped coriander leaves or parsley.

TERRINE DE CANARD A L'ORANGE

Every French restaurant boasts its *pâté maison;* every great chef cherishes his own special terrine recipe incorporating chicken, duck or game. My favourite – and one of the world's great dishes – is *terrine de canard à l'orange,* a terrine made with the fillets of breast of duck marinated in orange juice, cognac, Noilly Prat and Madeira, and encased in a savoury *farce* made up of the finely ground meats of the duck, together with pork, pork fat and veal, flavoured with the marinade juices, herbs and spices.

Far from being difficult to prepare, a terrine such as this one fits particularly well into the scheme of the busy host or hostess. It can be prepared in advance – several days in fact – and chilled, thus eliminating much last-minute cooking; it is also easy to serve.

Terrines are usually baked in heavy earthenware baking dishes, round or oval in shape with straight sides and with a small hole in the cover to allow the steam to escape. Always line the bottom and sides of the dish with thin slices of fat salt pork or bacon. I usually cut mine paper-thin on a rotary cutter. Failing this, a useful trick is to cut the slices at least 6mm/¼in thick; place them between two pieces of greaseproof paper; and then pound them with a wooden mallet to about 3mm/⅛in in thickness. You will find that they cover the sides of your pâté dish better this way.

Aspic plays a major part in most terrine recipes. When I make a terrine, I always place a weighted board or plate on top of it to weigh it down as it cools. The terrine shrinks in cooling and this weight (use an iron, canned foods or a brick) compresses it just enough to eliminate the tiny air holes that make it difficult to slice when chilled. The terrine should be firm and moist, and must not fall apart as you cut it. The aspic serves to hold it together, as well as adding to the general flavour and appearance.

Any well-flavoured *consommé* will serve as a base for your aspic. For terrines of game and poultry, the bones of the animal or bird should be used in making the stock. It is usually wise to make sure that the aspic will set by chilling it thoroughly and remelting it just prior to use. If the aspic fails to set during this preliminary chilling, strengthen it by adding a little unflavoured gelatine to the mixture.

Previous pages: One of the world's great dishes – Terrine de Canard à l'Orange.

49

TERRINE DE CANARD A L'ORANGE

1 duck
6 duck or chicken livers
100g/4oz raw veal
100g/4oz cooked ham
100g/4oz fresh pork fat
2 eggs, well beaten
225g/¹/₂lb pork fat, thinly sliced
3 very thin slices of orange
***Madeira aspic** (see page 67)*

MARINADE
60ml/4 tbls cognac
60ml/4 tbls Noilly Prat
60ml/4 tbls Madeira
60ml/4 tbls orange juice
¹/₂ Spanish onion, finely chopped
2.5ml/¹/₂ tsp dried thyme
2.5ml/¹/₂ tsp dried savory
1.5ml/¹/₄ tsp grated nutmeg
5ml/1 tsp grated orange rind
5ml/1 tsp finely chopped parsley
2 bay leaves, crumbled
salt and freshly ground black pepper

1. Skin and bone duck; remove breast fillets and cut into long, thin strips about 6mm/¹/₄in in diameter. Reserve remaining meat and carcass.

2. Make marinade by combining cognac, Noilly Prat, Madeira and orange juice with finely chopped onion, dried thyme, savory and grated nutmeg, grated orange rind, finely chopped parsley, and crumbled bay leaves. Season with salt and freshly ground black pepper to taste. Marinate duck strips in this mixture overnight, covered. Drain. Reserve marinade.

3. Preheat oven to moderate (190°C/375°F/gas 5).

4. Chop remaining duck meat finely with duck or chicken livers, veal, ham and fresh pork fat. Reserve duck carcass. Stir in reserved marinade and well beaten eggs.

5. To test the pâté mixture for flavour, bake a spoonful of the mixture in the preheated oven until cooked through. Taste and correct seasoning, adding a little more alcohol, spices or salt and freshly ground black pepper to mixture, if desired. The mixture should be very well flavoured.

6. Line the bottom and sides of an ovenproof terrine dish with thin slices of pork fat. Press in a thick layer of the finely chopped meat mixture; arrange strips of duck over pâté mixture with a few slices of pork fat 6mm/¹/₄in in diameter, if available. Cover with another layer of mixture. Top with thin slices of pork fat. Cover terrine; place in a pan of hot water and bake in preheated oven for about 1 to 1¹/₄ hours.

7. Remove cover and place a weighted board or plate on the terrine to compress it gently as it cools. Take terrine from its container, remove outside fat and replace in a clean dish. Decorate with thin slices of orange and cover with MADEIRA ASPIC. Allow pâté to 'mature' in the refrigerator for 2 or 3 days before serving.

PATE MAISON

225g/¹/₂lb bacon, thinly sliced
cognac, warmed
1kg/2lb calf's liver, minced
225g/¹/₂lb pork liver, minced
2 eggs
90ml/6 tbls double cream
30ml/2 tbls lemon juice
2 garlic cloves, crushed
1.5ml/¹/₄ tsp grated nutmeg
salt and freshly ground black pepper
1 truffle, coarsely chopped (optional)
100g/4oz chicken livers, coarsely chopped and
  sautéed in a little butter until just pink

1. Preheat oven to slow (170°C/325°F/gas 3).
2. Cut rinds from bacon slices and line a pâté

mould with bacon: sprinkle with cognac.

3. Mix minced livers with eggs, double cream, lemon juice, crushed garlic and ground nutmeg. Season with salt and freshly ground black pepper to taste. Pour over warmed cognac and ignite it. Mix well with fork and half-fill pâté mould with mixture. Place coarsely chopped truffle, if desired, and sautéed chicken livers in a row down centre. Cover with rest of pâté; then cover top with bacon. Cover mould; stand in pan of hot water and bake in preheated oven for about 2 hours.

4. Remove pâté from oven and allow to cool. Put weight on top to press down firmly, and chill overnight in the refrigerator. Turn pâté out of mould just before serving.

TRUFFLED DUCK PATE

1 medium-sized duck, with liver
4 shallots, finely chopped
pinch of dried thyme
4 bay leaves
150ml/¼pt dry white wine
salt and freshly ground black pepper
450g/1lb calf's liver, diced
90ml/6 tbls butter
4 Cox's orange pippin apples
5ml/1 tsp sugar
juice of ½ lemon
2 eggs, beaten
60ml/4 tbls cognac
1.5ml/¼ tsp grated nutmeg
225g/½lb fat salt pork, thinly sliced
2 truffles
Madeira aspic *(see page 67)*

1. Skin and bone duck. Cut the breast meat into long, thin strips.
2. Combine finely chopped shallots, dried thyme and 2 bay leaves, crumbled, with dry white wine and season with salt and freshly ground black pepper to taste. Marinate duck

strips in this mixture for at least 2 hours. Drain.
3. Preheat oven to moderate (180°C/350°F/gas 4).
4. Sauté diced calf's liver and duck liver in 60ml/4 tbls butter until medium rare.
5. Peel, core and slice apples; add sugar and cook in lemon juice and remaining butter until soft.
6. Pass livers and apples through a sieve; add beaten eggs and cognac, season with ground nutmeg and salt and freshly ground black pepper to taste. Blend mixture until smooth.
7. Line a pâté dish or earthenware casserole with thin slices of fat salt pork. Add half the liver and apple mixture and place layers of marinated duck fillets on it. Stud with truffles rolled in thin slices of fat salt pork, reserving enough truffle for decoration. Cover with remaining liver and apple mixture and top with remaining fat salt pork. Place the 2 remaining bay leaves on top of pâté and cover; place in a pan of hot water and bake in preheated oven for about 1½ hours.
8. Remove cover and place a weighted plate on the pâté to compress it gently as it cools. Take pâté from its container; remove outside fat and replace in a clean pâté dish or casserole. Decorate with slices of truffle and cover with MADEIRA ASPIC. Allow pâté to 'mature' in the refrigerator for 2 or 3 days before serving.

MOUSSE DE FOIE GRAS EN BRIOCHE

120ml/8 tbls double cream
225g/½lb canned pâté de foie gras
60ml/4 tbls cognac
30ml/2 tbls finely chopped parsley
50g/2oz mushrooms, finely chopped
100g/4oz butter
salt and freshly ground black pepper
Brioche dough *(see page 345)*
1 egg yolk, diluted with a little milk

1. Whip cream in an electric blender, or food processor. until fairly stiff.

2. Combine *pâté de foie gras,* cognac and finely chopped parsley and blend thoroughly with whipped cream.

3. Sauté finely chopped mushrooms in 100g/4oz butter over a low heat for 5 minutes, or until golden. Season with salt and freshly ground black pepper to taste.

4. Stir hot mushroom and butter mixture into pâté mixture and let stand at room temperature for at least 1 hour.

5. Line a large well buttered brioche mould with a sheet of BRIOCHE DOUGH 4cm/1½in thick and about 2.5cm/1in wider in circumfer-

ence than is required to line the mould.

6. Set the pâté in a ball in the brioche-lined mould and cover gently with the overhanging dough. Form a piece of the dough the size of a cup into a ball and set the ball on top of the brioche. Let the mould stand for 20 minutes in a warm place to allow the dough to rise.

7. Preheat oven to hot (230°C/450°F/gas 8) at least 10 minutes before end of the dough rising time.

8. Brush the top of brioche with diluted egg yolk and bake in preheated oven until the brioche is browned and cooked through. Cool the brioche before lifting out onto a serving dish. Serve warm or cold.

QUICHE LORRAINE

This hot cheese pie makes frequent and delicious appearances on tables throughout France and increasingly often in this country. Slender wedges are served as an appetiser before dinner; larger portions make a perfect light luncheon dish when accompanied by a tossed green salad; and individual quiches provide a delectable first course for a more substantial meal.

Essentially a custard, well flavoured with cheese and baked in a pie shell, the quiche varies from country to country. Germany and Switzerland have their own versions of this popular dish, but the most famous of all is the French *quiche Lorraine.* In Alsace-Lorraine, the home of the quiche, each village has its own special recipe and each jealously proclaims that its quiche is the authentic one. In some recipes, only cheese and custard are used; in others, finely chopped onions sautéed in butter add their subtle flavour; and in still others, *lardons* of fat salt pork or green bacon are added. I find the quiche an easily and quickly-made, light-hearted *entrée.* But be careful, for your quiche should be satin-smooth on the inside with a crisp, golden crust, so do not let it wait for guests. Serve it immediately, for it is at its best when piping hot.

Traditionally, *quiche Lorraine* is made with *lardons* of fat salt pork or green bacon, but try these variations on the basic theme, substituting for the bacon one of the following:

Quiche aux crabes: Remove tendons and bits of shell from cooked crab; flake and add to quiche mixture. Shrimps, prawns and diced lobster may also be added for a *quiche aux fruits de mer.*

Quiche aux champignons: Clean and slice mushrooms thinly; sauté in butter and lemon juice; drain well and add to quiche mixture.

Quiche au poisson: Poach halibut or turbot fillets in a well-flavoured *court-bouillon* of water and dry white wine, flavoured with onion, carrot, bay leaf, salt, and freshly ground black pepper; drain well; remove skin and bones and flake fish into quiche mixture.

Quiche aux fines herbes: At Hintlesham Hall in Suffolk we often serve a *quiche aux fines herbes* – a delicate green quiche mixture of blended eggs and cream flavoured with finely chopped fresh herbs from the garden and freshly grated Gruyère cheese.

QUICHE LORRAINE

SERVES 4-6

Fingertip pastry for 20cm/8in pastry case (see page 347)
1 egg white, beaten
4 egg yolks
300ml/1/2pt single cream
salt and freshly ground black pepper
freshly grated nutmeg
100g/4oz green bacon (cut in one piece), or fat salt pork
30ml/2 tbls butter
100g/4oz Gruyère cheese, diced

1. Line pastry tin with FINGERTIP PASTRY. Prick bottom with a fork and place in the refrigerator to set for 30 minutes.
2. Preheat oven to moderately hot (200°C/400°F/gas 6).
3. Bake pastry case blind in preheated oven for 10 minutes. (For directions on how to bake blind see page 26.) Remove pastry case from oven and cool. Then brush bottom of the pastry case with a little beaten egg white. Lower oven temperature to moderate (190°C/375°F/gas 5).
4. Whisk egg yolks; add single cream and whisk until thick and lemon-coloured. Flavour with salt and freshly ground black pepper to taste, and a touch of freshly grated nutmeg.
5. Cut green bacon or fat salt pork into thin strips; remove rind and blanch bacon in boiling water for 3 minutes; sauté strips in butter until golden. Drain.
6. Arrange diced cheese and green bacon strips in pastry case. Pour over the cream and egg mixture and bake in the preheated oven for 25 to 30 minutes. Serve hot.

QUICHE AUX FINES HERBES

SERVES 6-8

Fingertip pastry for 25cm/10in pastry case
  (see page 347)
1 egg white, beaten
4 eggs
150ml/¼pt double cream
150ml/¼pt milk
60ml/4 tbls freshly grated Parmesan cheese
salt and freshly ground black pepper
freshly grated nutmeg
60ml/4 tbls finely chopped onion
30ml/2 tbls butter
1 lettuce, shredded
15ml/1 tbls finely chopped chives
15ml/1 tbls finely chopped tarragon
15ml/1 tbls finely chopped parsley
2.5ml/½ tsp dried rosemary

1. Line pastry tin with FINGERTIP PASTRY. Prick bottom with a fork and place in the refrigerator to set for 30 minutes.
2. Preheat oven to moderately hot (200°C/400°F/gas 6).
3. Bake pastry case blind for 10 minutes (see page 26). Remove pastry case from oven and cool. Then brush bottom of the pastry case with beaten egg white. Lower oven temperature to moderate (190°C/375°F/gas 5).
4. Beat eggs together with double cream and milk. Stir in freshly grated Parmesan and when well mixed, season with salt, freshly ground black pepper and grated nutmeg, to taste.
5. Sauté finely chopped onion in butter until just coloured; add shredded lettuce and toss quickly, about ½ minute, just to heat lettuce through. Force through a fine sieve.
6. Combine onion and lettuce with finely chopped herbs and add to eggs and cream.
7. To assemble quiche: fill pastry shell with herb mixture and bake in preheated oven for 25 to 30 minutes. Serve hot, lukewarm, or cold, cut in wedges.

AMERICAN CLAM TART

SERVES 4-6

Fingertip pastry for 20cm/8in pastry case (see
  page 347)
1 egg white, beaten
400g/14oz can chopped clams
3 slices of bacon
15ml/1 tbls butter
60ml/4 tbls finely chopped onion
60ml/4 tbls finely chopped parsley
3 eggs
150ml/¼pt double cream
salt and freshly ground black pepper

1. Line pastry tin with pastry, fluting the edges. (For fluting pastry see page 30). Prick bottom with a fork and place in the refrigerator to set for 30 minutes.
2. Preheat oven to moderately hot (200°C/400°F/gas 6).
3. Bake blind (see page 26) in preheated oven for about 10 minutes, just long enough to set the crust without browning it. Remove pastry case from oven and allow to cool. Then brush the bottom of the pastry case with a little beaten egg white. Lower oven temperature to moderate (180°C/350°F/gas 4).
4. Drain clams, reserving juice.
5. Sauté bacon in butter until crisp. Remove and drain. Sauté finely chopped onion in fats until transparent. Remove and drain.
6. Crumble bacon and combine with chopped clams, sautéed onion and finely chopped parsley. Spoon mixture into pastry case.
7. Lightly beat eggs; add double cream and reserved clam juice and season with salt and freshly ground black pepper to taste. Pour custard mixture into pastry case and bake in the preheated oven for 25 to 30 minutes, or until the crust is brown and the custard has set.

Quiche aux Fines Herbes.

ITALIAN SPINACH PIE

SERVES 4-6

Fingertip pastry for 20cm/8in pastry case (see page 347)
1 egg white, beaten
350g/³⁄₄lb frozen spinach, thawed
60ml/4 tbls butter
salt and freshly ground black pepper
225g/¹⁄₂lb cottage cheese
3 eggs, lightly beaten
25-50g/1-2oz Parmesan cheese, freshly grated
90ml/6 tbls double cream
freshly grated nutmeg

1. Line pastry tin with pastry, fluting the edges (see page 30). Prick bottom with a fork and place in the refrigerator to set for 30 minutes.
2. Preheat oven to moderately hot (200°C/400°F/gas 6).
3. Bake blind (see page 26) in preheated oven for about 10 minutes, just long enough to set the crust without browning it. Remove pastry case from oven and allow to cool. Brush bottom of pastry case with a little beaten egg white. Lower oven temperature to moderate (180°C/350°F/gas 4).
4. Cook spinach in butter until wilted and season with salt and freshly ground black pepper to taste. Drain thoroughly and then add cottage cheese with beaten eggs, Parmesan cheese, cream and nutmeg, to taste. Spread mixture in pastry case and bake in preheated oven for 25 to 30 minutes, or until the crust is brown and the cheese custard mixture has set.

PISSALADIERE

SERVES 4-6

Fingertip pastry for 20cm/8in pastry case (see page 347)
1 egg white, beaten

60ml/4 tbls olive oil
6 large ripe tomatoes, peeled, seeded and chopped
45ml/3 tbls tomato purée
3 Spanish onions
30ml/2 tbls butter
freshly chopped rosemary or tarragon
60ml/4 tbls grated Parmesan cheese
50g/2oz can anchovy fillets, drained
black olives
extra oil for anchovies and olives

1. Line pastry tin with FINGERTIP PASTRY, fluting the edges (see page 30). Prick bottom with a fork and place in the refrigerator to set for 30 minutes.
2. Preheat oven to moderately hot (200°C/400°F/gas 6).
3. Bake blind (see page 26) in preheated oven for about 10 minutes, just long enough to set the crust without browning it. Remove pastry case from oven and allow to cool. Then brush the bottom of the pastry case with a little beaten egg white.
4. Lower oven temperature to moderate (180°C/350°F/gas 4).
5. Heat olive oil; add ripe tomatoes and tomato purée. Cook over a low heat to get rid of excess moisture, mashing occasionally with a wooden spoon to form a purée.
6. Slice Spanish onions and simmer in butter with a little freshly chopped rosemary or tarragon, until soft and golden but not brown.
7. Sprinkle bottom of pastry case with Parmesan cheese; add cooked onions and then cover with the tomato purée. Arrange anchovies in a lattice-work on top and place a black olive in the centre of each square. Brush olives and anchovies lightly with oil and bake in preheated oven for 25 to 30 minutes.
NOTE: I sometimes mix cooked tomato purée and simmered onions together and flavour the mixture with additional freshly grated Parmesan cheese for a softer-flavoured variation of this famous dish.

MINIATURE FISH CRESCENTS

SERVES 4

100g/4oz butter, softened
100g/4oz cream cheese, creamed
100g/4oz flour
2 cans sardines in oil, drained
lemon juice
curry powder
salt and freshly ground black pepper
2 hard-boiled eggs, finely chopped
30ml/2 tbls finely chopped parsley

1. Combine butter and cream cheese, and stir until mixture is well blended. Add flour and mix with a fork. Knead dough and form it into a ball. Refrigerate for 1 hour.

2. To prepare filling: mash sardines; add a little lemon juice and curry powder and season with salt and freshly ground black pepper to taste. Add finely chopped eggs and parsley, and mix well.

3. Roll dough out on a floured surface to about 10mm/½in thick. Cut into 10cm/4in squares. Cut squares in half to form triangles. Chill until dough is a little firm. Preheat oven to hot (230°C/450°F/gas 8).

4. Place 5ml/1 tsp of sardine filling in centre of each triangle. Roll from wide edge towards point, twisting ends to seal. Turn ends to form a small crescent.

5. Place on baking sheet. Bake in preheated oven for about 10 minutes, or until golden brown.

CHAPTER 2

SOUPS

— SOUPE A L'OIGNON —

F RENCH ONION SOUP always spelled Paris in its most romantic mood: an aromatic vision of Les Halles at four in the morning, with its busy crowded streets filled with the clamorous cries of an awakening city, where home-returning revellers mingled with hard-working marketmen for their one communal meal of the day.

Les Halles does not exist in Paris any more – it has moved to Rungis. But my mind often goes back to the busy old market and to a tiny, crowded, smoky little workmen's café which stayed open all night. There, porters and fruiterers, lorry drivers and butchers, complete with blood-stained aprons, used to eat and drink around the crowded *zinc* in the early hours of the morning, and consume countless portions of the house speciality: an appetising *soupe à l'oignon,* served with a piping-hot crust of bubbling cheese.

Today, the café still exists – enlarged and bedizened with a smart upstairs restaurant for chic Parisians and foreign visitors. But downstairs it is still the same noisy, crowded, smoky room where a few remaining marketmen gather to swap early morning drinks and stories. And the onion soup is as good and as famous as ever.

French onion soup is nothing if not adaptable. Take a few onions, a little water or a little stock, a slice or two of toasted bread and a sprinkling of grated cheese, and you have a deliciously warming and inexpensive soup. Add a little dry white wine, a glass of champagne, or a dash or two of brandy and you have a soup fit for the gods.

Pile an ovenproof earthenware bowl high with slices of oven-toasted French bread; cover each layer with freshly grated Gruyère cheese; fill the bowl with your favourite French onion soup, place it in the oven until the bowl is smoking hot, golden with melted cheese and toasted bread, and you have *soupe à l'oignon gratinée* as it is served in Les Halles.

Soupe à l'Oignon, the traditional warming pick-me-up for late-night revellers.

SOUPE A L'OIGNON

SERVES 4-6

24 small white onions
60ml/4 tbls butter
sugar
1.4L/2¹/2pt **Basic beef stock** *(see page 65)*
60-90ml/4-6 tbls cognac
salt and freshly ground black pepper
4-6 slices of French bread, toasted and buttered
100g/4oz Gruyère cheese, freshly grated

1. Peel and slice onions thinly.
2. Heat butter in a large saucepan with a little sugar; add the onions and cook them very, very gently over a low flame, stirring constantly with a wooden spoon until they are an even golden brown. Add BASIC BEEF STOCK gradually, stirring constantly until the soup begins to boil. Then lower the heat: cover and simmer gently for about 1 hour.
3. Just before serving, add cognac to soup and season with salt and freshly ground black pepper to taste. Serve in a heated soup tureen, or individual serving bowls, each one containing a toasted and buttered slice of French bread heaped with freshly grated Gruyère cheese.

SOUPE A L'OIGNON GRATINEE

SERVES 4-6

1.4L/2¹/2pt well-flavoured **Soupe à l'oignon**
   (see above)
slices of oven-toasted French bread
100g/4oz Gruyère cheese, freshly grated

1. Preheat oven to hot (230°C/450°F/gas 8).
2. Place a layer of oven-toasted sliced French bread in the bottom of an ovenproof casserole and sprinkle generously with freshly grated Gruyère cheese. Cover with another layer of French bread and sprinkle with plenty of freshly grated Gruyère as above.

3. Bring the onion soup to the boil; pour over bread and cheese and bake in the preheated oven until cheese is bubbling and golden brown.

ONION SOUFFLE SOUP

SERVES 4-6

1.4L/2¹/2pt well-flavoured **Soupe à l'oignon**
   (see previous column)
450ml/³/4pt hot **Béchamel sauce** *(see page 80)*
90ml/6 tbls freshly grated Gruyère cheese
2 egg whites, stiffly beaten
salt and freshly ground black pepper
freshly grated nutmeg
4-6 slices of French bread, toasted and buttered

1. Preheat oven to hot (230°C/450°F/gas 8).
2. To make the soufflé: stir freshly grated Gruyère cheese into the hot BÉCHAMEL SAUCE. Allow to cool.
3. Fold in stiffly beaten egg whites and season with salt, freshly ground black pepper and freshly grated nutmeg to taste.
4. Bring the SOUPE A L'OIGNON to the boil. Pour into individual ovenproof dishes or an ovenproof casserole; top with toasted and buttered slices of French bread and spoon cheese soufflé mixture over this. Bake in preheated oven for 8 to 10 minutes, or until the soufflé has risen and is golden. Serve immediately.

COLD BORSCH

SERVES 6-8

700g/1¹/2lb lean beef
beef bones (optional)
salt
4 sprigs of parsley
2 leeks, coarsely chopped
2 large carrots, coarsely chopped
1 bay leaf

1 garlic clove
6 black peppercorns
450g/1lb cooked beetroot, peeled and diced
2 potatoes, peeled and diced
½ medium-sized red cabbage, coarsely chopped
2 Spanish onions, coarsely chopped
225g/½lb mushrooms, sliced
300ml/½pt soured cream

1. Dice the lean beef and put into a large saucepan (together with beef bones if desired) and 2L/4pt salted water. Bring the water slowly to the boil; skim carefully, and add parsley, coarsely chopped leeks and carrots, bay leaf, garlic clove and black peppercorns. Simmer, covered, for 1½ hours, skimming from time to time.
2. Remove meat from the soup. Strain soup through a fine sieve into a clean saucepan. Add diced beetroot and potatoes, coarsely chopped red cabbage, onions and sliced mushrooms. Bring to the boil. Skim, and simmer, uncovered, for 1 hour.
3. Strain soup into a tureen and chill.
4. Just before serving, stir in soured cream.

ITALIAN LEEK AND PUMPKIN SOUP

SERVES 4-6

450g/1lb pumpkin flesh
225g/½lb potatoes
1 Spanish onion
50g/2oz butter
100g/4oz fresh haricot or broad beans
600ml/1pt milk
salt
cayenne pepper
50g/2oz leeks
*600ml/1pt hot **Basic chicken stock***
  (see page 66)
150ml/¼pt double cream
*100g/4oz **Boiled rice** (see page 179)*
30-45ml/2-3 tbls chopped chervil or parsley

1. Dice peeled pumpkin, and peel and dice potatoes. Chop the onion.
2. Melt half the butter in a large saucepan and simmer chopped onion until golden.
3. Add diced pumpkin, potatoes, beans and milk to pan and bring to the boil. Reduce heat and simmer for 45 minutes, stirring from time to time to prevent scorching, adding a little more milk if the mixture becomes too dry.
4. Strain soup through a fine sieve into a clean saucepan and season with salt and cayenne pepper to taste.
5. Cut leeks into fine strips and cook in the remaining butter. Add to the soup, along with CHICKEN STOCK, and bring slowly to the boil.
6. Just before serving, stir in double cream, BOILED RICE and chopped chervil or parsley. Transfer to a heated soup tureen, or individual serving bowls and serve immediately.

'FONDA DEL SOL' ARGENTINIAN PUMPKIN SOUP

SERVES 6

1¼kg/2½lb pumpkin flesh
*1L/2pt **Basic chicken stock** (see page 66)*
1 Spanish onion, chopped
6 spring onions
4 tomatoes
300ml/½pt single cream
salt and freshly ground black pepper
150ml/¼pt salted whipped cream

1. Dice peeled pumpkin and put into a saucepan; add CHICKEN STOCK, chopped onion, spring onions and tomatoes, and simmer until tender. Allow to cool.
2. Purée soup in an electric blender, or food processor; add single cream and season with salt and freshly ground black pepper to taste. Pour into prechilled cups.
3. Just before serving, place a dollop of salted whipped cream on each portion.

CORN AND TUNA BISQUE

SERVES 4

15ml/1 tbls butter
15ml/1tbls flour
450ml/³/4pt milk
1 chicken stock cube, crumbled
salt and freshly ground black pepper
400g/14oz can sweetcorn, drained
200g/7oz can tuna, drained and shredded
curry powder, or dry sherry (optional)

1. Melt butter in the top of a double saucepan; add flour and cook for a few minutes, stirring constantly until well blended. Add milk and crumbled chicken stock cube and season with salt and freshly ground black pepper to taste. Simmer, stirring from time to time, until the soup has slightly thickened.
2. Stir in sweetcorn and bring to the boil; add shredded tuna and heat through. Correct seasoning. Transfer to a heated soup tureen, or individual serving bowls, and serve immediately. (Add a little curry powder or sherry, if desired.)

SCANDINAVIAN FRUIT SOUP

SERVES 6

1.4kg/3lb assorted fruits (peaches, plums, pears,
*   cherries, apricots, berries, etc.)*
45ml/3 tbls lemon juice
sugar
ground cinnamon
15ml/1 tbls cornflour
150ml/¹/4pt soured cream
45ml/3 tbls dry white wine (optional)

1. Stone and slice fruits, but do not peel.
2. Combine fruits in a saucepan with 850ml/1¹/2pt water and lemon juice. Add sugar and ground cinnamon to taste. Cover and simmer until fruits are soft. Purée in an electric blender, or food processor, then pass mixture through a sieve. Return to a clean pan.
3. Dissolve cornflour in a little cold water. Add to puréed fruits and bring to the boil, then simmer gently until soup thickens. Add wine before removing from heat, if desired. Transfer to a soup tureen and chill.
4. Serve soup cold with soured cream.

POT-AU-FEU

Pot-au-feu – the great knife-and-fork soup often called the national soup of France – is one of the most rewarding dishes in the world to make. Although it looks complicated at first glance, you will find that this soup of many parts is well worth the effort involved. It is, in fact, two dishes – a beef broth or *bouillon,* and a main dish of boiled beef or, as the French term it, *'le bouilli',* the ancestor via Scotland of British 'bully beef'.

Serve the broth first and follow with the *bouilli* accompanied by vegetables from the *bouillon:* carrots, leeks, onions and sometimes – cooked separately rather than in the *bouillon* – cabbage and potatoes.

To make a pot-au-feu, you will need:
2kg/4lb lean beef
1kg/2lb shin of beef (meat and bone)
100g/¼lb ox liver
2 chicken livers
4L/8pt water, or water and stock
coarse salt
4 carrots
2 turnips
4 leeks
2 celery stalks
1 fat garlic clove
1 Spanish onion, stuck with 2 cloves
1 bouquet garni (bay leaf, few sprigs of parsley
  and thyme)

The secret of making a good *pot-au-feu* is to begin by covering the ingredients with cold water, bringing it slowly to the boil, a mere ripple on the surface, and then allowing it to simmer gently for hours without interruption at a low, regular heat.

Ask your butcher to bone the meat – chosen from the silverside, shoulder, top rib, or top round, (although the last-mentioned is inclined to be a little tough in comparison to the others,) or a combination of two of these, plus some shin of beef (meat and bone) so useful in making a *bouillon* because of its gelatinous qualities. If I have it at hand, I sometimes add a knuckle of veal or a good-sized marrow bone to these basics for extra flavour.

Your butcher will also cut the meat into large pieces, tie it up securely and break the bones for you. All you have to do when you are ready to make your *pot-au-feu* is to lay the bones in the bottom of a large stockpot; place the meat, ox liver and chicken livers on top and add water, or water and stock, and put the stockpot on the lowest possible heat so that the water comes to the boil very slowly. As it does so, the gradual heating of the water will enlarge the fibre of the meat and dissolve the gelatinous substances which it contains.

When the liquid barely begins to simmer in the pot, add a little coarse salt to help the scum rise to the surface of the *bouillon*.

The scum which forms is thick and brownish-grey in colour. Let it become sufficiently compact and then skim it off with a slotted spoon, being careful to scrape away any remaining at the sides of the pot. When the water just begins to tremble, add half a glass of cold water to stop the boiling and to bring a new rise of scum to the surface. Skim and repeat this process several times for 10 to 15 minutes, until the scum is just a white froth which will of its own accord be consumed in the cooking.

Add the carrots, leeks, turnips, celery stalks and garlic, the onion stuck with cloves, and the *bouquet garni*. If the vegetables bring a little more scum to the surface, skim carefully and cover the stockpot with a lid, tilting it so that the steam can escape. If you want your meats to remain tender, keep heat as low as possible so that the stock just trembles gently at one point only. The cooking time for your *pot-au-feu* varies a little according to the size of the pieces of meat. But as none should weigh more than 1kg/2lb, 3 hours from the time you add the vegetables will be about right.

THE VEGETABLES
The flavour and appearance of the vegetables in your *pot-au-feu* will be better if they are not overcooked. For the best results, carrots and turnips, cut in quarters, can be added to the *bouillon* immediately after it has been skimmed. Leeks, split if they are big and with most of the green cut off, should be tied together with the celery stalks and added an hour after the other vegetables along with an onion, stuck with cloves, garlic and a *bouquet garni*. In the North of France they add a small *bouquet* of fresh chervil to the stock when the *pot-au-feu* is three-quarters cooked, and some cooks like to improve the colour of the *bouillon* by adding a few pea pods dried in the oven. Cabbage, not

usually a part of the classic *pot-au-feu,* can be cooked separately, in water at first and then in a little of the *bouillon,* and served with the meat and vegetables. Potatoes, too, are sometimes served with a *pot-au-feu.*

THE BOUILLON

Bring 2L/3½pt of the *bouillon* to a fast boil; dip soup ladle into the *bouillon* at the point where the boiling is most active. The fat will be forced to the side of the pot and your resulting *bouillon* will be less greasy. Pass the *bouillon,* one ladleful at a time, through a fine muslin laid in a sieve. Allow it to cool for a few minutes; skim any remaining fat from the surface; pour *bouillon* into a clean saucepan and re-heat.

THE MEAT AND VEGETABLES

Remove the beef and vegetables carefully from the stockpot and drain. Cut the strings from the meat and remove any small bones separated in cooking. Cut the meat to facilitate serving and place it in the centre of a heated serving dish. Surround with cooked vegetables, grouping them by colour. If you have added cabbage, place it in a sort of *bouquet* at one side of the dish. Potatoes can be served with the other vegetables or apart.

You can serve the *bœuf bouilli* alone 'au gros sel', or you can accompany it by one or two kinds of mustard and small bowls of pickled gherkins, cocktail onions and small carrots, pimentoes and green tomatoes in vinegar. I personally like to serve it with a sauce of whipped cream and freshly grated horseradish or, as in Italy, with *salsa verde,* a piquant green sauce.

OTHER USES FOR REMAINING BOUILLI

Put beef through the mincer; mash equal quantities of boiled potatoes. Mix all together and work them well to blend, then bind with an egg and add salt and freshly ground black pepper to taste. Butter a mould; fill with meat mixture; cover with a buttered paper and cook in a moderate oven (190°C/375°F/gas 5) for 30 minutes. This is delicious when served with a tomato or sour cream sauce.

Quite good meat balls or croquettes can be made in the same manner: mince the beef; combine with mashed potatoes and grated Gruyère cheese or Parmesan cheese; season with a little nutmeg, salt and freshly ground black pepper, shape into balls and sauté in butter until golden.

POULE-AU-POT

SERVES 6-8

2.7kg/6lb boiling fowl
450g/1lb lean pickled pork
1 small cabbage
1 large turnip
1 Spanish onion, stuck with 4 cloves
freshly ground black pepper
dried thyme
hot water, or water and **Basic chicken stock**
  (see page 66)
bay leaf
butter

VEGETABLE GARNISH
12 small white onions
12 small carrots
12 small potatoes
450g/1lb green beans, tied in bundles

1. Clean, singe and truss the boiling fowl.
2. Wash the pickled pork thoroughly and halve it. Place in a small casserole or saucepan just large enough to hold it. Cover with cold water and bring it rapidly to the boil. Drain.
3. Clean and quarter cabbage and turnip, and place the vegetables in the bottom of a large stockpot, together with the onion. Place the

fowl and the blanched pickled pork on the vegetables and sprinkle with freshly ground black pepper and a little dried thyme. Add enough hot water, or water and CHICKEN STOCK, barely to cover; place a bay leaf on top of the fowl and cover with a piece of buttered paper. Place lid tightly on the stockpot; bring slowly to the boil; skim; reduce heat, and simmer gently for 1½ to 2 hours, skimming surface of barely bubbling liquid of impurities from time to time.

4. Add small onions, carrots, potatoes and

green beans to the stockpot and continue to cook for about 45 minutes longer, or until the fowl is tender and the vegetables are cooked.

5. To serve, place the fowl in the centre of a heated platter and place a piece of pork on each side. Surround the meat with the vegetables, grouped according to colour, and pour over a little of the broth.

NOTE: If pickled pork is unobtainable, use 350g/¾lb raw gammon and treat it as pickled pork in step 2.

BASIC STOCKS

It has been said that a cook's reputation rises or falls by the quality of his or her soups. A soup must be substantial enough to satisfy and at the same time light enough not to slacken enthusiasm for what follows. What an easy way to gain a reputation, for with the best home-made stocks you can provide a whole series of delicious soups from the world-famous *soupe à l'oignon* of the French to the pride of the Greek cuisine, *avgolemono* (a handful of cooked rice, eggs whisked with the juice of a lemon and some fine rich chicken stock), a gold-tinted soup that is delicately creamy and fresh.

BASIC BEEF STOCK *(Classic Method)*

MAKES ABOUT 1.7L/3pt

1kg/2lb shin of beef (meat and bone)
1kg/2lb shin of veal (meat and bone)
60ml/4 tbls beef, veal or pork dripping
6 small carrots, chopped and browned in butter
1 Spanish onion, chopped and browned in butter
2 celery stalks, roughly chopped
1 bouquet garni (1 sprig parsley and thyme and
*   1 bay leaf)*
1 fat garlic clove
4-6 black peppercorns
100g/4oz lean raw ham

1. Bone meat, cut into large pieces and tie together. Set aside.
2. Break up the bones as finely as possible; sprinkle with 45ml/3 tbls of the dripping and brown them in a hot oven for 40-45 minutes. When they are slightly browned, add chopped and browned carrots and onion, celery, *bouquet garni*, garlic and black peppercorns, but no salt. Stir well and continue to cook for 15 minutes, stirring from time to time.
3. Transfer vegetables and bones to a large stockpot or saucepan, add 3L/5½pt cold water and bring slowly to the boil. Skim carefully, wipe the edge of the saucepan, put the lid half

65

on and allow the stock to cook gently for 4 hours. Then strain the liquid through a fine sieve into a large bowl and allow to cool. Skim off fat and reserve stock for use in next step.

4. Put the meat and ham in a saucepan just large enough to hold it. Brown in remaining drippings then pour off excess fat. Add 300ml/ ½pt of the prepared stock; cover and simmer very gently over a low heat until the stock is almost completely reduced, turning the meat from time to time so that it is bathed on all sides in the stock. Pour the remainder of the stock into the saucepan; bring to the boil and then simmer very gently and evenly with the lid off.

5. As soon as the meat is tender and the stock is rich and well flavoured, strain through a fine sieve into a large bowl. Cool and skim off fat, then store in the refrigerator. Use within 4 days. The meat may be served in a great variety of ways.

BASIC BEEF STOCK *(Quick Method)*

MAKES ABOUT 1.7L/3pt

450g/1lb veal knuckle
450g/1lb beef knuckle
60ml/4 tbls beef, veal or pork dripping
1kg/2lb lean beef
2 chicken feet (optional)
2 leeks (white parts only)
1 Spanish onion stuck with 2 cloves
2 celery stalks, roughly chopped
2 large carrots, roughly chopped
4 sprigs of parsley
1 fat garlic clove
salt and freshly ground black pepper

1. Have veal and beef knuckles coarsely chopped by your butcher. Sprinkle them with meat dripping and brown in a hot oven for 40-45 minutes.
2. Transfer bones to a large stockpot with lean

beef, chicken feet, if you have any, and leeks, onion stuck with cloves, celery stalks, chopped carrots, parsley sprigs and garlic clove. Cover with 3L/5½pt cold water and bring slowly to the boil, removing the scum as it accumulates on the surface. Simmer gently for 1 hour; add salt and freshly ground black pepper to taste, and continue to simmer for another hour, or until the meat is tender. Correct seasoning and strain the stock through a fine sieve into a large bowl. Skim off fat and store stock in the refrigerator. Use within 4 days.

BASIC CHICKEN STOCK *(Classic Method)*

MAKES ABOUT 1.7L/3pt

2.7kg/6lb boiling fowl
450g/1lb veal knuckle
2 chicken feet (optional)
salt
6 black peppercorns
2 leeks, white parts only, cut into 7.5cm/3in
  segments
6 small carrots
1 Spanish onion stuck with 2 cloves
2 celery stalks, cut into 7.5cm/3in segments
1 bouquet garni (parsley, 1 sprig of thyme and 1
  bay leaf)
1 garlic clove

1. Place boiling fowl in a large stockpot with veal knuckle and chicken feet (for their extra gelatine content) and cover with 3L/5½pt cold water. Add salt and black peppercorns and bring slowly to the boil. Skim; reduce heat and simmer, with the water barely bubbling, for at least 1 hour, skimming the scum from the surface if necessary.
2. Add leek segments, carrots, onion stuck with the cloves, celery segments, *bouquet garni* and garlic clove to stockpot and continue to simmer for 1½ to 2 hours, or until the chicken is tender.

3. Transfer chicken and vegetables to a serving dish and reserve for later use. Skim fat from the surface of the stock; correct seasoning and strain through a fine sieve into a large bowl. Cool; skim off fat and store stock in the refrigerator for later use. Use within 4 days.

BASIC CHICKEN STOCK (*Quick Method*)

MAKES ABOUT 1.7L/3pt

2kg/4lb boiling fowl
450g/1lb veal knuckle
2 leeks, white parts only, cut into 7.5cm/3in
  segments
2 large carrots, cut into 5cm/2in segments
2 celery stalks, tops included, cut into 7.5cm/3in
  segments
1 Spanish onion, stuck with cloves
1 fat garlic clove
4 sprigs of parsley
salt and freshly ground black pepper

1. Place fowl and veal knuckle in a large stockpot with 3L/5½pt cold water and bring slowly to the boil, skimming until the scum no longer rises to the surface. Simmer for 1 hour, skimming again if necessary.
2. Add leeks, carrots and celery segments, onion stuck with cloves, garlic clove and parsley sprigs. Season with salt and freshly ground black pepper to taste, and continue to simmer gently for 1 hour.
3. Remove the fowl, veal knuckle and vegetables from the stock. correct seasoning and strain stock through a fine sieve into a large bowl. Cool: skim fat and store in the refrigerator for later use. Use within 4 days.

BASIC ASPIC (*Classic Method*)

MAKES ABOUT 1.7L/3pt

450kg/1lb shin of beef (meat and bone)
duck or chicken carcass
1 calf's foot, or 4 chicken feet
1 Spanish onion, sliced
1 leek, sliced
1 carrot, sliced
1 celery stalk, chopped
salt and freshly ground black pepper
1 bouquet garni (1 sprig of parsley and thyme and 1
  bay leaf)
1 egg white
100g/4oz raw lean beef, chopped

1. Ask your butcher to chop shin of beef into pieces.
2. Combine first 9 ingredients in a large stockpot; cover with cold water and bring slowly to the boil. Simmer gently for about 4 hours, skimming from time to time. Strain and cool before skimming off the fat.
3. To clarify the stock, beat egg white lightly, combine with chopped raw lean beef and add to the stock; bring very slowly to the boil, stirring constantly. After the stock has boiled up a few times, it will be clarified. Lower the flame and simmer the stock very gently for about 25 minutes. Strain while hot through a fine cloth.
4. Allow to cool until very syrupy and on the point of setting. It is then ready to use or will keep in the refrigerator for several days.

SHERRY ASPIC: Stir in 60ml/4 tbls dry sherry.

MADEIRA ASPIC: Stir in 60ml/4 tbls Madeira.

TARRAGON ASPIC: When clarifying aspic jelly, add several tarragon sprigs.

This recipe will make 2L/4pt of jelly and will keep for several days in the refrigerator.

BEEF CONSOMME

MAKES ABOUT 1.7L/3pt

*2L/4pt **Basic beef stock** (see page 65)*
450g/1lb minced lean beef
2 leeks, chopped
2 celery stalks, chopped
2 carrots, chopped
½ Spanish onion, chopped
freshly ground black pepper
whites and shells of 2 eggs

1. Strain BASIC BEEF STOCK and combine in a large saucepan with minced beef, chopped leeks, celery, carrots and onion. Season with freshly ground black pepper to taste.
2. Beat egg whites; crumble shells. Add to BEEF STOCK and bring slowly to the boil. Simmer for 1 hour; strain through a fine cloth and cool.
3. Skim off fat from the surface of the cooled stock and pour carefully into storage jars, being careful not to disturb any sediment which lies at bottom of stock. Consommé will keep for at least a week in the refrigerator, but must be reboiled before use.

CHICKEN CONSOMME

MAKES ABOUT 1.7L/3pt

*2L/4pt **Basic chicken stock** (see page 66)*
whites and shells of 2 eggs

1. Strain CHICKEN STOCK into a large saucepan.
2. Beat egg whites and lightly crumble shells; add to CHICKEN STOCK and bring slowly to the boil. Simmer for 1 hour; strain through a fine sieve and cool. Skim and keep as for BEEF CONSOMME.

STRACCIATELLA ALLA ROMANA

SERVES 4-6

3 eggs
45ml/3 tbls chopped parsley
45ml/3 tbls freshly grated Romano or Parmesan cheese
*1.2L/2½pt well-seasoned **Basic chicken stock** (see page 66)*

1. Beat eggs. Stir chopped parsley and freshly grated cheese into egg mixture.
2. Bring CHICKEN STOCK to a fast boil and gradually add egg mixture, stirring constantly. Lower the heat and stir while soup simmers for 5 minutes more. Transfer to a heated soup tureen, or individual bowls.

TORTELLINI IN BRODO

SERVES 4-6

225g/½lb flour
3 eggs
5ml/1 tsp olive oil
salt
50g/2oz prosciutto, minced
100g/4oz cooked chicken, minced
50g/2oz cooked pork, minced
30ml/2 tbls chopped basil, tarragon or chervil
30ml/2 tbls grated Parmesan cheese
freshly ground black pepper
freshly grated nutmeg
*1.4L/2½pt **Basic chicken stock** (see page 66)*

1. Make a well in the flour on a large pastry board; break 2 eggs into the well; add olive oil and a good pinch of salt, and slowly mix flour and eggs together. Work the dough with your hands for 15 minutes, adding more flour if necessary. Sprinkle board with more flour and roll out dough as thinly as possible with a rolling pin.
2. Sprinkle a clean tea towel lightly with flour

and lay the sheet of pasta dough on it to dry for 10 minutes before cutting.
3. Cut rolled dough into circles with a 4cm/ 1½in round cookie or biscuit cutter.
4. To make stuffing, combine minced meats, 1 egg, chopped basil, tarragon or chervil and grated Parmesan cheese, and season with salt, freshly ground black pepper and freshly grated nutmeg to taste. Place 2.5ml/½ tsp of this mixture in the centre of each circle of dough.

5. Moisten the edges, then fold dough over almost to the other side, enclosing the stuffing. Seal the moistened edges together, then wrap the half-moons around the top of your index finger, connecting the two ends to make a little bell shape.
6. Bring CHICKEN STOCK to the boil; add the *tortellini* and cook for about 20 minutes, or until tender. Transfer to a heated soup tureen and serve immediately.

BLENDER SOUPS

It is the destiny of some new instruments of modern times to change at one fell swoop the whole structure and habit of today's living. Such an instrument was the fork; such were the rotary whisk, the refrigerator, the deep-freeze – and such, I am sure, is the electric blender, or food processor.

Here, with one relatively inexpensive attachment, all the hitherto hard-to-create dishes of French *haute cuisine* are yours for the making: delicious pâtés and terrines of meat, game and poultry; featherlight *quenelles,* those delicate morsels of forcemeat of pike, salmon and lobster; creamy purées of peas, artichoke hearts, leeks and potatoes; and the whole delightful gamut of cooling summer soups.

The blender, or food processor, is a wonderful tool and, if used correctly, will perform any number of difficult culinary operations in a wink of the proverbial eye. It can whisk soups at a speed that is spectacular, smoothing almost any miscellaneous collection of ingredients into a rich flavoursome purée. The following recipes for special refreshing soups can all be made with the blender, or processor, in shorter time than it takes me to tell you about them; and without this magic tool, they can be quickly and easily made in minutes, if not in seconds, with the aid of a *mouli légume* (food mill), available from the kitchen departments of better stores throughout the country. Without either of these two machines, you will have to resort to a large fine-meshed sieve and a wooden spoon to achieve your smooth purée.

Most vegetable soups are more rich and mellow when prepared in a well-flavoured stock rather than milk or water. If the soup is of celery, cauliflower or Jerusalem artichokes, or other vegetables that cannot be satisfactorily simmered in butter, the vegetables should be parboiled for 8 to 10 minutes, well drained, chopped and added to the simmering chicken or beef stock. When I use leeks, spinach, onions, carrots, mushrooms or cucumber, they are first chopped, then sautéed gently in butter without being allowed to colour, and then added to the stock.

From this point on, the preparation of most vegetable cream soups is the same. The vegetables are cooked in the gently simmering stock until quite soft; vegetables and stock are whisked in the blender, or processor, or pressed through a fine sieve; seasoning is added; cream and egg yolks are stirred in and the soup is allowed to thicken in the top of a double saucepan until it is of the right consistency.

COLD BEETROOT SOUP

SERVES 4

1/2 Spanish onion, sliced
30ml/2 tbls butter
225g/1/2lb cooked beetroot, peeled and sliced
1 boiled potato, peeled
juice of 1 large lemon
salt and freshly ground black pepper
300ml/1/2pt double cream
300-450ml/1/2-3/4pt chilled **Basic chicken stock**
   (see page 66)

1. Sauté sliced onion in butter until soft, but not coloured.
2. Put peeled and sliced beetroot, sautéed onion and boiled peeled potato through electric blender or food processor until smooth (or press through a fine sieve); add lemon juice and season with salt and freshly ground black pepper to taste. Chill.
3. Just before serving, combine double cream and chilled CHICKEN STOCK. Add to beetroot mixture and blend for almost 1 minute, or until well-mixed. Transfer to a soup tureen, or individual soup bowls, and serve.

CURRIED APPLE SOUP

SERVES 4

30ml/2 tbls butter
1 Spanish onion, coarsely chopped
   600ml/1pt **Basic chicken stock** *(see page 66)*
15ml/1 tbls curry powder
15ml/1 tbls cornflour
2 egg yolks, well beaten
150ml/1/4pt hot double cream
2 tart green eating apples
salt and freshly ground black pepper
juice of 1/2 lemon
watercress leaves

1. Melt butter; add coarsely chopped onion and cook until soft, but not coloured. Stir in BASIC CHICKEN STOCK and curry powder; add cornflour mixed with a little cold water. Bring to the boil, then simmer for 8 minutes.
2. Add well beaten egg yolks to hot double cream and mix well. Stir a little of the hot soup into the egg and cream mixture. Then gradually add the egg and cream mixture to the hot soup, stirring well.
3. Remove from the heat immediately and transfer mixture to an electric blender, or food processor, with 1 apple, peeled, cored and sliced. Blend until smooth. Season with salt

and freshly ground black pepper to taste. Transfer to a soup tureen and chill.

4. Peel, core and dice remaining apple and marinate in lemon juice to keep colour.

5. Just before serving, stir diced apple into soup; garnish with watercress leaves and serve.

GAZPACHO *(Spanish Iced Soup)*

SERVES 4

2 small garlic cloves
6 large tomatoes, peeled
1 Spanish onion, coarsely chopped
1 large green pepper, coarsely chopped
1 cucumber, peeled and cut into cubes
105ml/7 tbls olive oil
60ml/4 tbls lemon juice
300ml/½pt tomato juice, chilled
150ml/¼pt well-flavoured **Basic chicken stock,**
  chilled (see page 66)
salt
cayenne pepper
30ml/2 tbls butter
2 slices of bread, diced

1. Blend 4 tomatoes and 1 garlic clove in an electric blender or food processor; add half the coarsely chopped onion, quarter of the coarsely chopped green pepper, and half the cucumber cubes; blend again. Strain mixture into a soup tureen and chill in the refrigerator.

2. Just before serving, blend together 90ml/ 6 tbls olive oil, the lemon juice, chilled tomato juice and CHICKEN STOCK. Season with salt and cayenne pepper to taste. Stir into the above mixture and add several ice cubes.

3. Gazpacho is traditionally served accompanied by small bowls of raw vegetables and garlic *croûtons*. Guests help themselves to a little of each. To prepare, chop the remaining vegetables – tomatoes, onion, green pepper and cucumber – and put each vegetable into a separate bowl. Heat butter with 15ml/1 tbls of olive oil and remaining clove of garlic. Remove garlic clove and sauté diced bread in GARLIC BUTTER (see page 87) until crisp and golden. Drain on absorbent paper; transfer to a small serving bowl and serve soup with these accompaniments.

'FOUR SEASONS' WATERCRESS VICHYSSOISE

SERVES 6

5 potatoes, peeled and sliced
2 large leeks, sliced
1½ bunches of watercress, chopped
1 ham bone (optional)
1.1L/2pt **Basic chicken stock** *(see page 66)*
salt and freshly ground black pepper
600ml/1pt double cream, chilled
sprigs of watercress

1. Cook vegetables and watercress with ham bone (if desired) in CHICKEN STOCK until tender.

2. Purée soup in blender or food processor, or pass through a fine sieve. Season with salt and pepper to taste and chill.

3. Just before serving, add chilled double cream. Garnish with watercress.

VICHYSSOISE VERTE

SERVES 4-6

225g/½lb raw potatoes, peeled and diced
50g/2oz raw leeks, chopped
225g/½lb raw green peas
900ml/1½pt **Basic chicken stock** *(see page 66)*
salt and freshly ground black pepper
celery salt
450ml/¾pt double cream
15ml/1 tbls finely chopped chives

1. Simmer diced potatoes, chopped leeks and green peas in CHICKEN STOCK until barely tender.

2. Purée vegetables and stock in an electric blender or food processor, or press through a fine sieve. Season with salt and freshly ground black pepper and celery salt to taste. Cool mixture slightly and stir in double cream. Transfer to a soup tureen and chill thoroughly. Sprinkle with finely chopped chives before serving.

LEEK AND POTATO SOUP

SERVES 4-6

6 large leeks
60ml/4 tbls butter
4 medium-sized potatoes
850ml/1 ¹/₂pt **Basic chicken stock** *(see page 66)*
salt and freshly ground black pepper
freshly grated nutmeg
300ml/¹/₂pt double cream
15ml/1 tbls finely chopped chives

1. Cut the green tops from the leeks and cut the white parts into 2.5cm/1in segments. Melt butter in a large saucepan and sauté the white parts gently until soft. Do not allow to brown.

2. Peel and slice potatoes and add to leeks together with CHICKEN STOCK. Season with salt, freshly ground black pepper and freshly grated nutmeg, to taste. Simmer until vegetables are tender.

3. Purée vegetables and stock in an electric blender or food processor. Stir in double cream. Return soup to saucepan and simmer, stirring, for about 3 minutes, taking care that soup does not boil or it will curdle. Transfer to heated soup tureen and serve sprinkled with chives.

CREAM OF CAULIFLOWER SOUP

SERVES 4

1 cauliflower, about 1kg/2lb
salt
60ml/4 tbls butter
60ml/4 tbs flour
850ml/1 ¹/₂pt **Basic chicken stock** *(see page 66)*
1 Spanish onion, coarsely chopped
1 celery stalk, coarsely chopped
2 sprigs of parsely, coarsely chopped
2 egg yolks
150ml/¹/₄pt double cream
freshly ground black pepper
freshly grated nutmeg

1. Poach cauliflower in boiling salted water for 5 minutes. Drain.

2. Melt butter in a large saucepan; add flour and cook, stirring continuously, until a smooth paste is formed. Add CHICKEN STOCK, coarsely chopped onion, celery and parsely, and simmer for 20 minutes.

3. Strain stock into a clean saucepan, add cauliflower and cook until cauliflower is softened.

4. Purée soup in an electric blender or food processor, or pass through a fine sieve. Stir in egg yolks and double cream. Simmer, stirring, for about 3 minutes, taking care that the soup does not boil, or it will curdle. Season with salt, freshly ground black pepper and a little freshly grated nutmeg. Serve in a heated soup tureen or individual soup bowls.

— ITALIAN MINESTRONE —

If, as has been claimed, one of the best things ever to come out of Italy is spaghetti in all its myriad variations, one of the finest uses for pasta is in the many wonderful soups and *brodi* of the Italian provinces. Delicate broths of chicken or beef – *cappelletti in brodo* (chicken stock studded with subtly flavoured 'little monks' caps' of meat and herbs) and *farfallini in brodo* (beef stock with small pasta bows) vie with the thick fish soups of the coastal regions – *zuppa di pesce alla romana* (fish soup Roman style), and *cacciucco* (squid, lobster, scallops and sliced fish, simmered in stock with olive oil and dry white wine) – for first place in our affections. But the most famous of them all, and certainly one of the 'great dishes of the world', is Italian minestrone.

Minestrone is, by its very nature, a peasant soup; basically a mixture of beans and fresh vegetables simmered in bean broth and rich beef stock or water with meats, herbs, olive oil, pasta and freshly grated cheese. But like most great peasant dishes, it is fit for the most sophisticated palate.

Italian restaurants serve it as a first course, but in some Italian homes it often provides the whole meal. I like minestrone so thick, so full-bodied, so rich with meat and vegetables, that you can practically cut it with a knife.

The variations on the minestrone theme are legion. I sometimes add spinach or sliced courgettes to the vegetables; diced Italian sausage, ham or ham bone do no real harm; and when in season, a handful of finely chopped fresh basil elevates this country soup into the *gourmet* class.

Serve minestrone with additional cheese – freshly grated Parmesan cheese or, if available, Roman *pecorino* – and a slice or two of Italian bread, even though the Italians themselves frown on eating bread with a soup that contains pasta.

Overleaf: Italian Minestrone—basically a mixture of beans and fresh vegetables, simmered in bean broth and rich beef stock or water, with meats, herbs, olive oil, pasta and freshly grated Parmesan cheese.

73

MINESTRONE

SERVES 6-8

225g/½lb dried kidney or haricot beans
2-3 fresh sage leaves
450g/1lb fat salt pork, diced
2 garlic cloves, finely chopped
1 Spanish onion, cut into quarters or eighths
*2L/4pt **Basic beef stock***
(see page 65)
4 carrots, finely sliced
4 celery stalks, finely sliced
½ small head cabbage, roughly sliced
4 curly endive sprigs, roughly sliced
4-6 tomatoes, sliced
225g/½lb green beans, sliced
100g/4oz frozen peas
100-150g/4-6oz macaroni, broken into 5cm/2in
lengths, or use 'elbow' macaroni
salt and freshly ground black pepper
30ml/2 tbls finely chopped parsley
30ml/2 tbls olive oil
60-90ml/4-6 tbls freshly grated Parmesan cheese

1. Soak dried kidney or haricot beans overnight in cold water. Drain.
2. Place beans in 1L/2pt water with sage leaves and bring to the boil. Skim, reduce heat, then cover and simmer for 2 hours. Skim from time to time, as necessary. The beans must be cooked slowly to stay whole. Drain.
3. Dice fat salt pork, and sauté in a thick-bottomed casserole until golden brown.
4. Sauté finely chopped garlic and onion segments with fat salt pork until golden. Then add BEEF STOCK, finely sliced carrots and celery and simmer gently for 30 minutes.
5. Add cabbage, endive, tomatoes and green beans to soup with cooked beans and bring to the boil. Skim and reduce heat until soup barely simmers; cover and simmer for 1 hour.
6. Twenty minutes before serving, add frozen peas and macaroni lengths, or 'elbow' maca-

roni; bring to the boil and then simmer until macaroni is tender. If soup is too thick, add a little water. Season with salt and freshly ground black pepper to taste. Just before serving, stir in finely chopped parsley and the olive oil. Serve in a heated soup tureen and sprinkle with freshly grated Parmesan cheese.

PASTA E FAGIOLI

SERVES 6-8

225g/½lb dried kidney or haricot beans
1 beef marrow bone, about 10cm/4in long
60ml/4 tbls tomato purée
1 Spanish onion, finely chopped
1 garlic clove, finely chopped
45ml/3 tbls olive oil
45ml/3 tbls finely chopped parsley
5ml/1 tsp salt
10ml/2 tsp dried oregano
freshly ground black pepper
cayenne pepper
225g/½lb macaroni, broken into pieces, or use
'elbow' macaroni
30ml/2 tbls freshly grated Parmesan cheese

1. Soak dried kidney or haricot beans overnight in cold water. Drain.
2. Combine beans, marrow bone, tomato purée and 2L/4pt cold water in a large saucepan. Bring to the boil. Skim. Reduce heat: cover and simmer for 2 hours, skimming from time to time, as necessary.
3. Sauté onion and garlic in olive oil until transparent. Add to soup together with finely chopped parsley, salt and dried oregano. Season with freshly ground black pepper and cayenne pepper to taste, and simmer, covered, for about 20 minutes. Then add macaroni pieces or 'elbow' macaroni and continue to cook until tender. Serve in a heated soup tureen sprinkled with Parmesan cheese.

SOUPE AU PISTOU

SERVES 6-8

450g/1lb dried haricot beans
450g/1lb French beans, cut into 5mm/¹/₄in slices
4 small courgettes, sliced
4 medium-sized carrots, sliced
2 leeks, sliced
2 potatoes, peeled and diced
50g/2oz Parmesan cheese, freshly grated
salt and freshly ground black pepper

PISTOU SAUCE
8 large garlic cloves
8 sprigs of fresh basil
175ml/6fl oz olive oil
120ml/8 tbls freshly grated Parmesan cheese

1. Soak dried haricot beans overnight in cold water. Drain.
2. Put drained haricot beans into a saucepan with 2L/4pt cold water. Bring to the boil and skim. Add sliced French beans, sliced courgettes, carrots, leeks and diced potatoes. Season with salt and freshly ground black pepper to taste, and cook briskly.
3. When vegetables are tender, add pistou sauce (see below) and cook gently for 5 minutes more. Serve this hearty soup with freshly grated Parmesan cheese.
4. To make pistou sauce: mash garlic cloves in a mortar; add fresh basil sprigs and continue mashing. Add olive oil to this sauce very gradually and blend thoroughly. Then add Parmesan cheese and pound until smooth.

ZUPPA DI FAGIOLI

SERVES 4-6

225g/¹/₂lb dried white beans
salt and freshly ground black pepper
60ml/4 tbls olive oil

2 garlic cloves, chopped
30ml/2 tbls finely chopped parsley

1. Soak white beans overnight in cold water. Drain.
2. Put beans into a stockpot with 1.4L/2¹/₂pt cold water. Bring to the boil; skim and simmer as slowly as possible for 2 to 3 hours, or until beans are tender.
3. Remove half the beans; blend them to a smooth purée in an electric blender or food processor, or press them through a fine sieve. Add this purée to the soup and season with salt and black pepper to taste.
4. Heat olive oil in a small pan and cook chopped garlic in oil until just golden. Add chopped parsley to this mixture and pour into the soup. Stir well. Transfer to a heated soup tureen or individual soup bowls.

GREEN PEA SOUP

SERVES 6

2 Spanish onions, thinly sliced
350g/³/₄lb dried green peas
6-8 black peppercorns
15ml/1 tbls salt
4 cloves
5ml/1 tsp dried mustard
2 celery stalks, thinly sliced
100g/4oz bacon, cut into thin strips
1.5ml/¹/₄ tsp dried oregano
fried croûtons

1. Combine first 8 ingredients in a large saucepan, add 1.7L/3pt cold water and bring to the boil. Skim and then cook very slowly, covered, for 2 to 3 hours, adding more water if soup becomes too thick.
2. Add dried oregano after soup has cooked for 2 hours. Serve in a heated soup tureen, or individual soup bowls, accompanied by fried *croûtons*.

LENTIL SOUP

SERVES 4-6

175g/6oz dried green lentils
*1.4L/2½pt **Basic beef stock** (see page 65)*
ham knuckle, or 100g/4oz fat salt pork
2 potatoes, peeled and diced
15ml/1 tbls butter
15ml/1 tbls flour
freshly ground black pepper

1. Wash lentils and drain. Cover with cold water and leave to soak for 2 hours. Drain.

2. Cover with cold water again and bring to the boil. Boil for 10 minutes, and drain again. Add BEEF STOCK and ham knuckle, or fat salt pork, to lentils and bring to the boil. Reduce heat; cover and simmer gently for 2½ to 3 hours, or until lentils are tender.
3. Twenty minutes before lentils are done, add diced potatoes.
4. Just before serving, make a *beurre manié* by creaming together the butter and flour. Whisk this into the soup, bit by bit, and continue to cook for a few minutes longer. Season with black pepper to taste, and serve.

CHAPTER 3

SAUCES

GREAT SAUCES

According to the *Dictionary of Jovial Gastronomy*, 'a sauce-maker must be adroit and sensitive to the most delicate nuance as sauce-making includes chemistry, harmony, flavour voluptuousness, vigilance and other virtues . . . all crossed by the lightning stroke of genius.' No wonder so many cooks hesitate to look into this awesome subject and discover for themselves that, given a few practical rules and a little experience, the whole magic realm of sauce-making is theirs for the asking. But don't get me wrong, I don't claim that your version of *quenelles de brochet* will ever equal the ethereal *pain de poisson* served with an unctuous *sauce Cardinale* created daily by Alexandre Dumaine in his restaurant at Saulieu.

Yet sauces, like soups and stocks, have their place in everyday good cooking as well as in the kitchens of international hotels. A home-made sauce can lend a certain magic to the simplest of ingredients and make a memorable meal out of humble beginnings.

The French have a way with sauces. Ever since the days of the famous Carême, sauce-making has been the key to French *haute cuisine* and ranks foremost among the many skills that any aspiring cook must learn, practise and finally master.

A selection of equipment and basic ingredients used to produce the classic white sauce.

WHITE SAUCES

Béchamel – named after the *maître d'hôtel* of Louis XIV – is the mother sauce of all white sauces and is exceedingly simple to prepare. A simple Béchamel sauce can be made with just flour, butter, milk and a little minced onion, but I think you will find that the following classic recipe, which includes chopped veal, adds greatly to the savour of this delicious sauce. The secret of making a good white sauce – like most other sauces – is to cook it slowly.

BECHAMEL SAUCE (*Classic Method*)

MAKES ABOUT 600ml/1pt

75ml/5 tbls butter
½ onion, finely chopped
30ml/2 tbls flour
900ml/1½pt hot milk
1 chicken leg or thigh, bone and all, coarsely
*   chopped*
50g/2oz lean veal or ham, chopped
1 celery stalk, chopped
1 small sprig of thyme
½ bay leaf
6 white peppercorns
freshly grated nutmeg

1. Melt 45ml/3 tbls butter in a thick-bottomed saucepan, or in the top of a double saucepan and cook chopped onion over a low heat until it is soft and transparent, but not coloured.
2. Stir in flour and cook, stirring constantly, for 2 to 3 minutes, until flour is cooked through. Add a quarter of the hot milk and cook, stirring vigorously. As the sauce begins to thicken, add the remaining hot milk, stirring constantly until sauce begins to bubble.
3. In another saucepan, simmer chopped chicken leg or thigh, chopped lean veal or ham and celery in 30ml/2 tbls butter over a very low heat. Season with thyme, bay leaf, peppercorns and nutmeg to taste. Cook for 5 minutes, stirring to keep meat from browning.
4. Add meat and celery to sauce; reduce heat and simmer for 45 minutes to 1 hour, stirring occasionally.
5. When sauce is reduced to the proper consistency (two-thirds of original quantity), strain through a fine sieve and into a bowl, pressing meats and vegetables well to extract all the flavour. Dot surface of sauce with tiny pieces of butter to keep a skin from forming.

CREAM SAUCE . . . for fish, poultry, eggs and vegetables.
Add 60ml/4 tbls double cream to 600ml/1pt hot BECHAMEL SAUCE (see above) and bring to boiling point. Add drops of lemon juice.

AURORE SAUCE . . . excellent with eggs, chicken or shellfish.
Add 30-45ml/2-3 tbls tomato purée to 600ml/1pt hot BECHAMEL SAUCE (see above).

ONION SAUCE . . . for fish, lamb or veal.
Peel and chop 1 Spanish onion, cover with hot water and parboil for 3 to 5 minutes. Drain and

cook onion in a saucepan with a little butter until soft. Add 600ml/1pt hot BECHAMEL SAUCE (see page 80) and cook for approximately 15 minutes. Strain sauce through a fine sieve, pressing the vegetables well to extract all juice; return to heat and gradually beat in 60ml/4 tbls double cream. Correct seasoning with salt and white pepper to taste.

CHICKEN VELOUTE SAUCE

MAKES ABOUT 600ml/1pt

30ml/2 tbls butter
30ml/2 tbls flour
900ml/1¹/2pt well-flavoured boiling **Basic chicken stock** *(see page 66)*
salt
white peppercorns
4 button mushrooms, chopped

1. Melt butter in thick-bottomed saucepan or in the top of a double saucepan; add flour and cook for 2 to 3 minutes, stirring constantly, until flour is cooked through.
2. Add boiling CHICKEN STOCK and salt and white peppercorns to taste and cook, stirring vigorously. Add chopped mushrooms, reduce heat and simmer, stirring occasionally, and skimming from time to time, until the sauce is reduced to two-thirds of the original quantity and is very thick but light and creamy.
3. Strain sauce through a fine sieve, pressing mushrooms against sieve to extract all their flavour. Dot surface of sauce with tiny pieces of butter to keep skin from forming. Serve with poached chicken or hard-boiled eggs.

RICH CHEESE SAUCE

MAKES ABOUT 300ml/¹/2pt

45ml/3 tbls butter
45ml/3 tbls flour

450ml/³/4pt hot **Basic chicken stock** *(see page 66)*
300ml/¹/2pt double cream
45ml/3 tbls freshly grated Gruyère cheese
45ml/3 tbls freshly grated Parmesan cheese
salt and freshly ground black pepper
freshly grated nutmeg

1. Melt butter in thick-bottomed saucepan or in the top of a double saucepan; stir in flour and cook for 2 to 3 minutes stirring constantly, until smooth. Blend in hot CHICKEN STOCK and then double cream, stirring vigorously.
2. Stir in grated Gruyère cheese and Parmesan cheese and season with salt and freshly ground black pepper to taste, and a little freshly grated nutmeg. Reduce heat and simmer for about 20 minutes, stirring from time to time to keep skin from forming. When sauce is reduced to two-thirds of original quantity, strain through a fine sieve. Good for poultry, fish, vegetables and eggs.

RICH PRAWN SAUCE

MAKES ABOUT 300ml/¹/2pt

75ml/5 tbls butter
45ml/3 tbls flour
450ml/³/4pt **Fish fumet** *(see page 111), strained*
300ml/¹/2pt double cream
350g/³/4lb frozen prawns, defrosted and coarsely chopped
salt and freshly ground black pepper
cayenne pepper
30ml/2 tbls cognac, warmed

1. Melt 45ml/3 tbls butter in a thick-bottomed saucepan, or in the top of a double saucepan; stir in flour and cook for 2 to 3 minutes, stirring constantly, until smooth. Add strained FISH FUMET slowly, stirring vigorously, until sauce is rich and creamy. Reduce heat and simmer for 20 minutes; then add double cream and continue cooking, uncovered, stirring from time to time to keep skin from forming, until the sauce is reduced to two-thirds of the original quantity.

2. Sauté coarsely chopped prawns in 30ml/ 2 tbls butter until heated through; season with salt, freshly ground black pepper and cayenne pepper to taste. Flame with cognac and add to sauce. Good for poached fish and fish and shellfish soufflés.

BROWN SAUCES

There is only one basic brown sauce, *sauce espagnole* which is used as the base for many famous French sauces. As this sauce keeps very well, make it by the litre and store it in the refrigerator in a covered jar for future use. *Sauce espagnole,* or basic brown sauce, will keep indefinitely in the refrigerator if it is boiled up again once a week, and returned to the refrigerator in a clean jar.

Use *sauce espagnole* as a base for many exciting sauces, and as it is, to lend interest to braised onions, carrots and celery, or to add to the butter that steaks and chops have been cooked in.

SAUCE ESPAGNOLE

MAKES ABOUT 600ml/1pt

1 Spanish onion
sugar
45ml/3 tbls beef dripping
75g/3oz fat salt pork, or green bacon, diced
3 carrots, coarsely chopped
2 celery stalks, coarsely chopped
45ml/3 tbls flour
1.7L/3pt home-made boiling **Basic beef stock** *(see page 65)*
1 bouquet garni (3 sprigs of parsley, 1 sprig of thyme and 1 bay leaf)
1 garlic clove, peeled
150ml/¼pt rich **Tomato sauce** *(see page 83)*
salt and freshly bround black pepper

1. Slice onion crossways into 4 fat slices. Sprinkle cut sides of onion with a little sugar and caramelise them on each side in a thick-bottomed iron frying pan.

2. Melt beef dripping in a large heavy saucepan; add diced fat salt pork or green bacon, coarsely chopped carrots and celery, and cook until golden. Add caramelised onion slices to other vegetables.

3. Sprinkle with flour and cook gently over a very low heat, stirring frequently, until all the vegetables are well browned. Add a third of the boiling BEEF STOCK together with a *bouquet garni* and garlic clove, and cook, stirring frequently, until sauce thickens.

4. Add half remaining stock and cook very slowly over a very low heat, uncovered, stirring occasionally, for about 1½ to 2 hours until reduced to half the original quantity. Skim off scum and fat occasionally.

5. Add TOMATO SAUCE and cook for a few minutes longer. Then strain through a fine sieve into a bowl, pressing the vegetables against the sieve to extract all their juice.

6. Return mixture to a clean saucepan; add remaining stock and continue to cook slowly until the sauce is reduced to about 600ml/1pt, skimming the surface from to time. Strain again. Correct seasoning and cool, stirring occasionally. Store sauce espagnole in a covered jar in the refrigerator until ready for use.

RICH SAUCE ESPAGNOLE

A richer Sauce Espagnole is used by most professional chefs and even though it is a little more trouble, the results are very worthwhile. Make Sauce Espagnole as above, but stir 150ml/¼pt Sauce Demi-Glace (see below) into sauce in step 4 of the above recipe.

SAUCE DEMI-GLACE

MAKES ABOUT 300ml/½pt

600ml/1pt Sauce espagnole (see page 82)
peelings and chopped stems of 6 mushrooms
90ml/ 6 tbls dry sherry, or Madeira
15-30ml/1-2 tbls meat glaze (see page 88)

1. Boil SAUCE ESPAGNOLE until reduced to half of the original quantity, about 20 minutes.
2. Simmer mushroom peelings and chopped stems in dry sherry, or Madeira, in a thick-bottomed saucepan until the liquid is reduced to 45ml/3 tbls. Add this together with meat glaze to reduce sauce and simmer gently over a low heat for 15 minutes. Strain sauce.

MADEIRA SAUCE

Reduce 600ml/1pt sauce espagnole (see page 82) or rich sauce espagnole (see above) until it is half the original quantity. Add 90ml/6 tbls Madeira. Heat the sauce well, but do not let it boil or the flavour of the wine will be lost.

SAUCE PERIGUEUX

MAKES ABOUT 300ml/½pt

600ml/1pt Sauce espagnole (see page 82) or Rich
*   sauce espagnole (see this page)*
60ml/4 tbls Madeira
30ml/2 tbls finely diced truffles
15ml/1 tbls truffle liquor
30ml/2 tbls butter

1. Reduce SAUCE ESPAGNOLE or RICH SAUCE ESPAGNOLE in a thick-bottomed saucepan to half the original quantity. Add 45ml/3 tbls Madeira and bring slowly to the boil, stirring occasionally.
2. Take the pan off heat and stir in finely diced truffles and truffle liquor. Return to heat and add butter to the sauce, melting it in by moving the saucepan in a circular motion until butter is completely absorbed. Remove from heat and whisk in remaining 15ml/1 tbls Madeira to intensify the flavour.
3. Serve a few spoonfuls with baked eggs, or eggs *en cocotte*. Excellent with roast or grilled beef, chicken and veal.

TOMATO SAUCE

MAKES ABOUT 600ml/1pt

1 Spanish onion, finely chopped
2 garlic cloves, finely chopped
30ml/2 tbls butter
60ml/4 tbls olive oil
90ml/6 tbls Italian tomato purée
800g/1lb 12oz can Italian peeled tomatoes
2 bay leaves
30ml/2 tbls finely chopped parsley
1.5ml/¼ tsp dried oregano
1 small strip lemon peel
90ml/6 tbls dry white wine
salt and freshly ground black pepper
15ml/1 tbls Worcestershire sauce

1. Sauté finely chopped onion and garlic in butter and olive oil in a large, thick-bottomed frying pan until transparent and soft, but not coloured.

2. Stir in tomato purée and continue to cook for a minute or two, stirring constantly. Pour in Italian peeled tomatoes; add bay leaves, finely chopped parsley, dried oregano and the small strip of lemon peel. Add dry white wine and an equal quantity of water. Season with salt and freshly ground black pepper to taste, and simmer gently, stirring from time to time for 1 to 2 hours. Strain.

3. Just before serving, stir in Worcestershire sauce. Good for pasta, meat, poultry and veal.

SAUCE BEARNAISE

MAKES ABOUT 300ml/½pt

2 sprigs of tarragon
2 sprigs of chervil
15ml/1 tbls chopped shallots
2 black peppercorns, crushed
30ml/2 tbls tarragon vinegar
150ml/¼pt dry white wine
3 egg yolks, beaten
225g/½lb butter, diced
salt
cayenne pepper

1. Chop leaves and stems of tarragon and chervil coarsely and combine with chopped shallot, crushed peppercorns, tarragon vinegar and dry white wine in a saucepan. Cook over a high heat until liquid is reduced to a syrupy 'glaze' just covering the bottom of your pan. Remove from heat and allow to cool slightly.

2. Place pan in a larger saucepan containing hot, but not boiling, water, add beaten egg yolks to glaze and stir briskly with a wire whisk until light and fluffy, Never let the water in the bottom pan begin to boil, or sauce will not 'take'.

3. Add butter gradually to egg mixture, stirring briskly all the time, as sauce begins to thicken. Continue adding butter and stirring until sauce is thick. Season with salt and a little cayenne pepper to taste. Strain sauce through a fine sieve and serve.

NOTE: I sometimes add 30ml/2 tbls of finely chopped fresh tarragon leaves to sauce after it has been strained.

If at any time in the making of this sauce, the mixture should curdle or separate, immediately add 1 ice cube to mixture and whisk rapidly to 'rebind' the emulsion. Remove ice cube as soon as sauce is smooth again.

SAUCE CHORON

Make a *Sauce Béarnaise* as above and flavour with tomato purée, to taste.

SAUCE HOLLANDAISE

MAKES ABOUT 300ml/½pt

5ml/1 tsp lemon juice
salt and white pepper
225g/½lb softened butter
4 egg yolks

1. Combine 5ml/1 tsp lemon juice, 15ml/1 tbls cold water, salt and white pepper in the top of a double saucepan.

2. Divide butter into 4 equal pieces.

3. Add egg yolks and quarter of the butter to the liquid in the saucepan. Stir the mixture rapidly and constantly with a wire whisk over hot, but not boiling, water until the butter is melted and the mixture begins to thicken. Add the second piece of butter and continue whisking. As the mixture thickens and the second piece of butter melts, add the third piece, stirring from the bottom of the pan until it is

melted. Be careful not to allow the water over which the sauce is cooking to boil at any time. Add rest of butter, whisking until it melts and is incorporated in the sauce.

4. Now remove top part of the saucepan from the heat and continue to whisk the sauce for 2 or 3 minutes longer. Replace saucepan over hot, but not boiling, water and whisk for 2 minutes more. By this time the emulsion should have formed and your sauce should be rich and creamy. 'Finish' sauce with a few drops of lemon juice. Strain sauce and serve.

NOTE: If at any time in the operation the mixture should curdle or separate, immediately add 1 ice cube to mixture and whisk rapidly to 'rebind' emulsion. Remove ice cube as soon as sauce is smooth again.

SAUCE MOUSSELINE

Make sauce in the same way as *Sauce Hollandaise* adding 60-90ml/4-6 tbls whipped cream just before serving.

MAYONNAISE

MAKES ABOUT 300ml/½pt

2 egg yolks
salt and freshly ground black pepper
1.5-2.5ml/¼-½ tsp dry mustard
lemon juice
300ml/½pt olive oil

1. Combine egg yolks (make sure gelatinous thread of the egg is removed), salt, freshly ground black pepper to taste and mustard in a bowl. Use a wire whisk, fork or wooden spoon, and beat the yolks to a smooth paste.
2. Add a squeeze of lemon juice (the acid helps the emulsion) and, drop by drop, beat in about a quarter of the olive oil. Add a little more

lemon juice to the mixture and next, a little more quickly now, add more olive oil, beating all the while. Continue adding olive oil and beating until the sauce is of a good thick consistency. Correct seasoning with more salt, freshly ground black pepper and lemon juice, as desired.

NOTE: If you are going to make the mayonnaise a day before using, stir in 15ml/1 tbls boiling water when it is of the desired consistency. This will keep the mayonnaise from turning, or separating.
If the mayonnaise should curdle, break another egg yolk into a clean bowl and gradually beat the curdled mayonnaise into it. Your mayonnaise will begin to 'take' immediately.

SAUCE LOUIS

MAKES ABOUT 450ml/¾pt

*300ml/½pt well-flavoured **Mayonnaise***
(see this page)
45ml/3 tbls American chilli sauce (or use tomato
ketchup flavoured with cayenne pepper or
Tabasco)
45ml/1 tbls olive oil
15ml/1 tbls red wine vinegar
30ml/2 tbls finely grated onion
30ml/2 tbls finely chopped parsley
150ml/¼pt double cream, whipped
salt and freshly ground black pepper
cayenne pepper
30-45ml/2-3 tbls finely chopped stuffed
or black olives

1. Blend together the MAYONNAISE, American chilli sauce (or flavoured ketchup), olive oil, red wine vinegar, finely grated onion, finely chopped parsley and whipped cream. Season to taste with salt, freshly ground black pepper and a dash of cayenne pepper.
2. Stir in chopped stuffed or black olives and

chill for 1 or 2 hours before serving. A delicious sauce for all seafood cocktails, but particularly good with crab salad.

SAUCE VERTE

MAKES ABOUT 300ml/½pt

*300ml/½pt well flavoured **Mayonnaise**
  (see page 85)
60ml/4 tbls finely chopped watercress leaves
30ml/2 tbls finely chopped chervil
30ml/2 tbls finely chopped parsley
30ml/2 tbls finely chopped tarragon leaves
lemon juice
salt and freshly ground black pepper*

1. Whirl MAYONNAISE, chopped watercress and herbs in an electric blender, or food processor, or blend well with a whisk. Season with lemon juice, salt and freshly ground black pepper to taste.
2. Serve this sauce chilled with all fish and shellfish. Especially good with poached or grilled salmon, fish pâtés or mousses, or as an accompaniment to hard-boiled eggs.

SAUCE REMOULADE

MAKES ABOUT 300ml/½pt

*300ml/½pt well flavoured **Mayonnaise**
  (see page 85)
30ml/2 tbls finely chopped fresh tarragon, basil or
  chervil
30ml/2 tbls finely chopped parsley
1 garlic clove, finely chopped
5ml/1 tsp dry mustard
10ml/2 tsp finely chopped capers
2 small pickles, finely chopped*

1. Combine ingredients and blend well. Chill.
2. Serve with grilled fish, prawns and lobster. Also excellent with cold pork chops.

GREEK GARLIC SAUCE *(Skordalia)*

MAKES ABOUT 300ml/½pt

*2-4 garlic cloves, chopped
30-45ml/2-3 tbls finely chopped parsley
1 large boiled potato, or an equal quantity of moist
  fresh breadcrumbs
50g/2oz blanched crushed almonds
30-60ml/2-4 tbls red wine vinegar
150ml/¼pt olive oil
salt and freshly ground black pepper*

1. Pound chopped garlic, finely chopped parsley, boiled potato or moist breadcrumbs and crushed almonds in a large mortar.
2. Add 15ml/1 tbls wine vinegar, and then add olive oil, little by little, pounding until mixture is a smooth paste. Season with salt and freshly ground black pepper to taste, and continue to add olive oil, little by little, beating briskly until sauce is of the consistency of a thick mayonnaise.

SAUCE GRIBICHE

MAKES ABOUT 300ml/½pt

*yolks and whites of 3 hard-boiled eggs
15ml/1 tbls Dijon mustard
30ml/2 tbls fines herbes: finely chopped parsley,
  chives and chervil
150ml/¼pt olive oil
wine vinegar or lemon juice
salt and freshly ground black pepper*

1. Pound egg yolks with Dijon mustard and *fines herbes* (parsley, chives and chervil) in a large mortar until smooth.
2. Add olive oil, little by little, stirring all the time, as for a mayonnaise. Season with wine vinegar or lemon juice and salt and freshly ground black pepper to taste.
3. Chop egg whites finely and add to sauce. Stir sauce just before serving.

ROUILLE

MAKES ABOUT 150ml/¼pt

1 slice of white bread, trimmed of crusts
2 fat garlic cloves, peeled
15ml/1 tbls paprika
cayenne pepper or crushed hot red pepper
30ml/2 tbls olive oil
*60ml/4 tbls **Mayonnaise** (see page 85)*

1. Dip bread in water and squeeze until almost dry.
2. Pound bread garlic cloves, paprika and a touch of cayenne pepper or crushed hot red peppers in a mortar until smooth.
3. Add olive oil and MAYONNAISE little by little and blend to a smooth aromatic paste.
4. This highly-flavoured sauce is excellent in SOUPE AIGO-SAU (see page 122) and BOUIL-LABAISSE (see page 120). Use it, too, to spike a MAYONNAISE (see page 85) to serve with poached or grilled fish or lobster.

PROVENCAL TAPENADE

MAKES ABOUT 150ml/¼pt

50g/2oz stoned black olives
25g/1oz anchovy fillets
25g/1oz tuna fish
5-10ml/1-2 tsp Dijon mustard
50g/2oz capers
60-90ml/4-6 tbls olive oil
cognac
freshly ground black pepper

1. Pound stoned olives, anchovy fillets and tuna fish to a smooth paste in a large mortar with Dijon mustard and capers.
2. Add olive oil, a little at a time, as you would for a mayonnaise. Season with cognac and freshly ground black pepper, to taste, and force mixture through a fine sieve. The *tapénade* mixture keeps well in a jar, and is ex-cellent with hard-boiled eggs, or as a highly flavoured *canapé* spread.

BEURRE NOISETTE

100g/¼lb butter
lemon juice

1. Melt butter and cook to a light hazelnut colour. Add lemon juice, to taste.
2. Serve heated butter with eggs, calf's brains and boiled or steamed vegetables.

GARLIC BUTTER

100/4oz softened butter
2-4 garlic cloves, crushed
30ml/2 tbls finely chopped parsley
15-30ml/1-2 tbls lemon juice
salt and freshly ground black pepper

1. Cream butter with crushed garlic cloves and finely chopped parsley. Season with lemon juice, salt and freshly ground black pepper to taste. Shape butter into a neat roll. Wrap tightly in cling film and chill in refrigerator until firm.
2. Slice butter into neat pats and serve with grilled beef or salmon steaks.

PARSLEY BUTTER

100g/4oz softened butter
45ml/3 tbls finely chopped parsley
5-10ml/1-2 tsp lemon juice
salt and freshly ground black pepper

1. Cream softened butter with finely chopped parsley.
2. Flavour butter with lemon juice, and season with salt and freshly ground black pepper, to

taste. Shape butter into a neat roll. Wrap tightly in cling film and chill in the refrigerator until firm.

CRAYFISH BUTTER

crushed crayfish shells
1 small onion, finely chopped
1 bay leaf
2.5ml/¹/₂ tsp dried thyme
butter

1. Dry the crushed crayfish shells in the oven for a few minutes.
2. Gently sauté finely chopped onion with bay leaf, dried thyme and crayfish shells in 60ml/ 4 tbls butter for 20 to 30 minutes. Cool.
3. Add 100g/4oz butter and pound in a mortar until creamy. Rub mixture through a fine sieve

and use as required in fish or shellfish soups, *bisques* and sauces.

SHRIMP OR PRAWN BUTTER
As *Crayfish butter* (see this page), but use shrimp or prawn shells.

LOBSTER BUTTER
As *Crayfish butter* (see this page), but use shells and coral of lobster.

MEAT GLAZE

150ml/5oz can good quality beef consommé

1. Pour canned consommé into a thick-bottomed saucepan and boil fast for about 20 minutes until it is reduced to just 45ml/3 tbls and is a syrupy glaze.

SWEET SAUCES

APRICOT SAUCE

MAKES ABOUT 300ml/¹/₂pt

300ml/¹/₂pt apricot jam
30ml/2 tbls kirsch

1. Combine apricot jam with 150ml/¹/₄pt water in a saucepan and bring to the boil. Reduce heat and simmer gently, stirring from time to time, for 5 to 10 minutes.
2. Strain through a fine sieve and stir in kirsch.
3. Serve sauce warm over cake, sweet soufflés or ice cream.

VANILLA CUSTARD SAUCE

MAKES ABOUT 450ml/³/₄pt

450ml/³/₄pt milk
2.5ml/¹/₂ tsp vanilla essence
60-90ml/4-6 tbls sugar
4 egg yolks
1.5ml/¹/₄ tsp salt

1. Simmer milk for 5 minutes. Stir in vanilla essence.
2. Combine sugar, egg yolks and salt in a bowl and beat until fluffy and lemon-coloured.

3. Pour a little of the hot vanilla-flavoured milk into the egg and sugar mixture; blend well. Then stir into the remaining hot milk. Heat slowly in the top of a double saucepan, stirring constantly, until the mixture coats the back of a wooden spoon thickly.
4. Serve sauce warm over cake, sweet soufflés, or ice cream.

ZABAGLIONE SAUCE

MAKES ABOUT 300ml/½pt

3 egg yolks
25g/1oz sugar
45-60ml/3-4 tbls Marsala or medium sherry
25ml/1½ tbls cognac

1. Combine egg yolks with sugar and a little Marsala or sherry in the top of a double saucepan. Whisk mixture over hot, but not boiling, water until sauce thickens enough to coat the back of a wooden spoon thickly.
2. Stir in the rest of the Marsala or sherry and the cognac. Serve sauce warm over cakes, puddings, sweet soufflés and ice cream.

CREME PATISSIERE

MAKES ABOUT 300ml/½pt

4 egg yolks
50g/2oz sugar
15ml/1 tbls flour
300ml/½pt warm milk
1.5ml/¼ tsp vanilla essence

1. Whisk egg yolks and sugar together until mixture is fluffy and lemon-coloured.
2. Stir in flour, then add warm milk and vanilla essence and mix thoroughly.
3. Place mixture in top of a double saucepan and cook over water, stirring constantly, until it reaches boiling point. Boil for 2 minutes. Re-move pan from heat; pass sauce through a fine sieve and allow to cool before using.

RUM SAUCE

MAKES ABOUT 450ml/¾pt

2 egg yolks
sugar
300ml/½pt double cream
60ml/4 tbls dark rum
2.5ml/½ tsp vanilla essence

1. Beat egg yolks with 60ml/4 tbls sugar until fluffy and lemon-coloured.
2. Whip double cream until stiff; add dark rum and vanilla essence, and whip until stiff again. Add more sugar to taste, if desired.
3. Fold egg yolks into whipped rum cream.

APPLE SAUCE

SERVES 6

450g/1lb cooking apples
1-2 slices lemon
castor sugar
1 clove
1.5-2.5ml/¼-½ tsp vanilla essence
30ml/2 tbls double cream (optional)
1 pinch of ground cinnamon (optional)

1. Wipe, core and quarter apples.
2. Cut quartered apples into thick slices and put them in a thick-bottomed saucepan to-gether with 30-60ml/2-4 tbls water, lemon slices, 15ml/1 tbls sugar and clove. Bring to the boil; cover pan tightly and simmer gently for 10 minutes, or until apples are fluffy.
3. Remove lemon slices and clove and purée sauce through a fine sieve.
4. Flavour with vanilla essence, to taste. Stir in double cream for a richer sauce and add a pinch of ground cinnamon, if desired.

CHAPTER 4

EGGS

— THE VERSATILE EGG —

I T WAS IN FRANCE that I first learned to treat eggs with the respect they deserve. Until then, I had always considered them as just another breakfast food or late-night snack. But in France, where an omelette can be a thing of fragile beauty and where the soufflé soars to gastronomic heights of gossamer distinction, the egg really comes into its own as *gourmet* fare for any occasion.

France also taught me to appreciate the egg in its hard-boiled state – eggs mayonnaise as the refreshing beginning to a meal on a sun-dappled terrace; eggs *en tonneaux,* whole hard-boiled eggs filled with anchovies and made to look like little caper-filled barrels; and stuffed and dressed eggs of every variety.

Eggs are good mixers. They go well with any meat, fish or sauce, are one of the most versatile of foods, and can be prepared in almost endless ways. To my mind, no single food is more essential to good cooking than the egg.

The most important thing to remember in cooking eggs is to use low heat. The making of an omelette is the outstanding exception, and here the higher heat is nullified by the short time the eggs are subjected to it.

Always store eggs in the refrigerator. Keep eggs broad end up and away from smells (the porous nature of the shell makes the contents particularly receptive to odours). Do not store them near highly-flavoured cheese or onions. For best cooking results, bring eggs to room temperature about 45 minutes before using them. Whites will beat up faster and to a larger volume and shells will not crack when you boil them. If they have just come from the refrigerator, run warm water over them for a minute or so to bring them to room temperature.

No single food is more versatile or more essential to good cooking than the egg.

BOILED EGGS This is a misnomer. Eggs should never be boiled. Doing so produces an unpalatable tough white and a yolk which is dull yellow and rubbery. For the best results, eggs in the shell should be cooked in water which is barely simmering.

Always take the eggs out of the refrigerator at least 45 minutes before cooking. Fill a pan with enough water to cover the eggs thoroughly. Bring the water to a rolling boil and lower the eggs into it gently, using a spoon. Then lower heat until the water is just barely bubbling; otherwise the eggs will bang against the side of the pan and the shells may break. Eggs boiled more gently seem to taste better too.

The classic soft-boiled egg – the white coagulated but still on the soft side and the golden yolk runny – is cooked for 3 to 4½ minutes. A 6-minute egg *(œuf mollet)* has a firm white and runny yolk. A true hard-boiled egg is cooked in simmering water for about 10 minutes.

Remove eggs from the water at once or they will go on cooking. Rinse them under cold water for a brief second to make handling easier.

POACHED EGGS For the best results it is essential to use fresh eggs, preferably not more than three or four days old. I always find that the whites of older eggs tend to go stringy and the yolks are much more apt to break than those of fresh ones. A large wide pan is a necessity, too, if you intend to poach more than one egg at a time. And be sure it is deep enough to allow at least an inch of water over the eggs to prevent them from sticking to the bottom of the pan.

Fill the pan with water; bring it to the boil and add 15ml/1 tbls of vinegar and a little salt to help eggs keep their shape. Have your eggs ready, each broken into a separate cup. Holding a cup in each hand, tip the eggs into the rapidly boiling water. Remove the pan from the heat; as the whites begin to set, turn eggs once or twice with a perforated spoon to give them a proper shape; cover pan and allow eggs to simmer gently, still off the heat, for about 3 minutes. Lift eggs out with a perforated spoon and, if you are not going to serve them immediately, slide them into a bowl of warm water. If you are serving them straight away, put them in cold water for a minute to stop cooking and to remove all taste of acidity; drain them dry on a clean towel and trim straggly bits of white with a pair of scissors.

ŒUFS MOLLETS Poached eggs are not easy, by any standards, to make successfully. I often prefer to use *œufs mollets* in recipes that call for poached eggs. An *œuf mollet* is the French culinary term for a shelled soft-boiled egg with the white delicately firm and the yolk deliciously runny. Cook *œufs mollets* as hard-boiled eggs, but for 6 minutes only. Shell carefully under cold water.

Any French chef will tell you that certain egg dishes served with a special sauce or garniture require a poached egg, and that there are others which require an *œuf mollet*. These are practically interchangeable. So if, as I do, you find difficulty in preparing poached eggs, then use shelled soft-boiled eggs instead.

BAKED EGGS Butter individual baking dishes or soufflé dishes with a 5ml/1 tsp of butter. Slide 1 or 2 eggs into each, being careful not to break the yolks. Sprinkle the top with salt and freshly ground black pepper, to taste, and add a small dab of butter.

Place baking dishes in a pan of hot water and bake in a preheated slow oven (170°C/325°F/gas 3) for about 8 minutes, or a little longer if a firmer egg is desired. And be sure to remove eggs from the oven before they are completely cooked. They will continue cooking from the heat of the baking dish.

BAKED EGGS WITH CREAM

SERVES 4

150ml/¼pt double cream
60ml/4 tbls freshly grated Gruyère cheese
30ml/2 tbls lemon juice
30ml/2 tbls dry white wine
10ml/2 tsp Dijon mustard
salt and freshly ground black pepper
8 eggs
butter
buttered breadcrumbs

1. Preheat oven to moderate (190°C/375°F/gas 5).
2. Combine double cream, freshly grated Gruyère cheese, lemon juice, dry white wine and mustard, and season with salt and freshly ground black pepper to taste.
3. Break eggs into 4 individual buttered ramekins or casseroles, 2 eggs in each. Cover the eggs with the sauce and sprinkle buttered breadcrumbs over the top.
4. Place ramekins or casseroles in a roasting pan and pour in boiling water to come halfway up the sides of dishes. Bake in preheated oven for about 15 minutes. Serve immediately.

BAKED EGGS EN SOUFFLE

SERVES 4

4 eggs
salt and white pepper
butter
60ml/4 tbls double cream
60ml/4 tbls freshly grated Parmesan cheese

1. Preheat oven to hot (230°C/450°F/gas 8).
2. Separate eggs. Beat whites until very stiff and season generously with salt and pepper.
3. Butter 4 individual ramekins or casseroles, and spoon egg whites evenly into each. Use large dishes as egg whites tend to rise like a

soufflé. Make a hollow depression with the back of your spoon for each egg yolk.
4. Place yolks in hollows (1 to each ramekin or casserole); cover each yolk with 15ml/1 tbls double cream and sprinkle with freshly grated Parmesan cheese. Bake in preheated oven for 8 –10 minutes. Serve immediately.

EGGS EN CASSEROLE

SERVES 4

4 hard-boiled eggs
15ml/1 tbls Dijon mustard
30ml/2 tbls olive oil
60ml/4 tbls finely chopped parsley
90ml/6 tbls freshly grated Parmesan cheese
salt and freshly ground black pepper
2 slices of white bread, crusts removed
30ml/2 tbls butter
300ml/½pt well-flavoured **Tomato sauce** *(see*
  page 83)
10ml/2 tsp grated onion
30ml/2 tbls chopped stuffed olives

1. Preheat oven to moderate (190°C/375°F/gas 5).
2. Cut eggs in half lengthways. Remove yolks carefully.
3. Mash yolks and mix with mustard, olive oil, half the parsley and half the Parmesan cheese. Season with salt and black pepper to taste. Stuff egg cavities with this mixture.
4. Dice bread and sauté in butter.
5. Place diced *croûtons* at the bottom of 4 individual ovenproof baking dishes and arrange 2 stuffed egg halves on top. Cover with TOMATO SAUCE to which you have added remaining finely chopped parsley, the grated onion and chopped stuffed olives. Sprinkle with remaining freshly grated Parmesan cheese and heat through in preheated oven for 15 minutes. Serve alone as a hot first course, or with boiled rice as a luncheon dish.

DEEP-FRIED STUFFED EGGS

SERVES 6

6 hard-boiled eggs
125g/4oz can sardines in oil, drained
15-30ml/1-2 tsp Dijon mustard
juice of 1 lemon
Worcestershire sauce
salt and freshly ground black pepper
30-60ml/2-4 tbls **Mayonnaise** *(see page 85)*
flour, egg and breadcrumbs, for coating
corn or olive oil, for deep-frying

1. Cut the eggs in half lengthways. Remove the yolks carefully.
2. Sieve the yolks; mash the sardines and mix well together. Add Dijon mustard, lemon juice, Worcestershire sauce, salt and freshly ground black pepper to taste, together with sufficient MAYONNAISE to make a firm mixture.
3. Mound each half of egg whites with the filling and re-form into the shape of a whole egg. Dip in flour, shaking off excess; then coat with egg and breadcrumbs and place in the refrigerator for at least 2 hours.
4. Heat corn or olive oil in a deep-fryer to 190°C/375°F. (A 2.5cm/1in cube of bread takes 60 seconds to turn crisp and golden brown.)
5. Fry stuffed eggs in preheated oil for about 2 minutes or until golden brown. Drain eggs on absorbent paper and serve immediately.

ŒUFS FARCIS AUX ANCHOIS

SERVES 4

4 hard-boiled eggs
4-6 anchovy fillets
4-6 capers
30ml/2 tbls finely chopped parsley
150ml/¼pt thick **Béchamel sauce** *(see page 80)*
salt and freshly ground black pepper
butter
fresh breadcrumbs

1. Preheat oven to moderate (190°C/375°F/ gas 5).
2. Cut each egg in half lengthways. Remove yolks carefully.
3. Mash yolks to a smooth paste in a mortar with anchovies, capers and finely chopped parsley. Add thick BECHAMEL SAUCE and season with salt and freshly ground black pepper to taste. Blend well together.
4. Mound each half of egg with the filling to re-form into a whole egg shape. Place the re-formed eggs in a well-buttered baking dish. Sprinkle each egg with breadcrumbs; dot with butter and heat through in preheated oven for 10 minutes. Serve immediately.

ŒUFS A LA TAPENADE

SERVES 4

50g/2oz black olives, stoned
25g/1oz anchovy fillets
25g/1oz tuna fish
5ml/1 tsp Dijon mustard
25g/1oz capers
60-90ml/4-6 tbls olive oil
15ml/1 tbls cognac
freshly ground black pepper
4 hard-boiled eggs
lettuce leaves

1. Pound black olives, anchovy fillets and tuna fish to a smooth paste in a mortar with mustard and capers (called *tapéno* in Provence, from which this dish gets it name).
2. When the mixture has been blended to a smooth paste, pass through a fine sieve. Whisk in olive oil; add cognac and season with freshly ground black pepper to taste.
3. Cut hard-boiled eggs in half lengthways and remove yolks carefully. Blend yolks with *tapénade* mixture, adding a little more olive oil, if necessary. Fill egg cavities, and serve on a bed of lettuce leaves.

EGGS AND MUSHROOMS AU GRATIN

SERVES 4

8 eggs
225g/¹/₂lb mushrooms, sliced
60ml/4 tbls butter
*300ml/¹/₂pt well-flavoured **Béchamel sauce** (see page 80)*
60ml/4 tbls freshly grated Parmesan cheese

1. Preheat grill to high.
2. Boil eggs gently for about 6 minutes, so that the yolk is still soft and the white not yet cooked hard. Shell eggs carefully and chop coarsely.
3. Sauté sliced mushrooms in butter, then add to BECHAMEL SAUCE. Stir in coarsely chopped eggs and spoon the mixture into 4 individual heatproof casseroles or soufflé dishes. Sprinkle each dish with freshly grated Parmesan cheese and brown under preheated grill. Serve immediately.

BOUILLABAISSE D'ŒUFS

SERVES 6

2 leeks, white parts only, finely chopped
1 Spanish onion, finely chopped
90ml/6 tbls olive oil
3 tomatoes, peeled, seeded and coarsely chopped
4 garlic cloves, mashed
a little finely chopped fennel, if available
1 bouquet garni (1 bay leaf, 2 sprigs of parsley and chervil)
1 piece of dried orange peel
6 new potatoes, peeled and sliced
ground saffron
salt and freshly ground black pepper
water, or water and stock
1 egg per person
1 piece of slightly stale French bread per person

1. In a large casserole, sauté finely chopped leeks and onion in olive oil until they are transparent, but not coloured. Add coarsely chopped tomatoes, garlic cloves, fennel, *bouquet garni,* dried orange peel and sliced potatoes. Season with saffron to taste, and generous amounts of salt and freshy ground black pepper. Cover with water or water and stock, and boil as for a BOUILLABAISSE (see page 120).
2. When potatoes are cooked, poach eggs in the *bouillon.*
3. To serve, pour *bouillon* over pieces of bread in individual soup plates. Serve the potatoes and eggs separately on a heated serving platter.

BAKED EGGS LORRAINE

SERVES 4

4 slices bacon
15ml/1 tbls butter
2 slices of Gruyère cheese, diced
4 eggs
salt and white pepper
120ml/8 tbls double cream

1. Preheat oven to moderately hot (200°C/400°F/gas 6).
2. Poach bacon slices in boiling water for 5 minutes. Drain and dry on absorbent paper.
3. Dice bacon and sauté in butter until golden.
4. Place diced bacon in the bottom of 4 individual baking dishes. Cover bacon with a layer of diced cheese. Break 1 egg into each dish; season with salt and white pepper to taste and cover with double cream. Bake in a preheated oven for 20 minutes, or until whites are set. Serve immediately.

STUFFED EGGS MORNAY

SERVES 8

8 hard-boiled eggs
100g/4oz cooked fish, flaked
16 capers, finely chopped
15-30ml/1-2 tbls olive oil
salt and freshly ground black pepper
butter
300ml/¹/2pt hot **Mornay sauce** *(see page 276)*

1. Preheat grill to high
2. Cut egg in half lengthways. Remove yolks.
3. Combine yolks in a bowl with the flaked cooked fish and finely chopped capers. Beat in enough olive oil to make a smooth paste. Season mixture with salt and freshly ground black pepper to taste.
4. Fill each half of egg white with mixture. Place stuffed eggs, filling side up, in heatproof dish, cover with hot well–flavoured MORNAY SAUCE and brown under preheated grill. Serve immediately.

ŒUFS AU FOIE GRAS LOUIS OLIVER

SERVES 4

50g/2oz pâté de foie gras, cut into 4 thin slices
freshly ground black pepper
cayenne pepper
15-30ml/1-2 tbls butter
8 eggs
salt
Madeira sauce *(see page 83)*

1. Lightly sprinkle slices of *pâté de foie gras* with freshly ground black pepper and cayenne pepper, and sauté gently in butter.
2. Place *foie gras* in 4 buttered baking dishes and break 2 eggs per person into each dish. Season with salt and freshly ground black pepper to taste, and cook gently over a low heat until eggs are set.

3. When the eggs are cooked, pour a spoonful or two of hot MADEIRA SAUCE over the eggs and serve immediately.

ŒUFS FLORENTINE

SERVES 4

8 eggs
vinegar
butter
450g/1lb cooked spinach, finely chopped
salt and freshly ground black pepper
freshly grated nutmeg
lemon juice
300ml/¹/2pt **Mornay sauce** *(see page 276)*
freshly grated Parmesan cheese

1. Preheat grill to high.
2. Poach eggs in salted water containing a little vinegar for added flavour and to help hold eggs together (see page 92).
3. Butter 4 heatproof ramekins or individual baking dishes, large enough to hold 2 eggs. Season finely chopped spinach with butter, salt and freshly ground black pepper to taste; spread a layer of seasoned spinach in each dish.
4. Sprinkle spinach with a little freshly grated nutmeg and lemon juice and dot with butter. Place 2 poached eggs in each dish on top of the spinach.
5. Cover with MORNAY SAUCE; dust with grated Parmesan cheese and place under preheated grill for a few minutes until nicely browned.

ŒUFS A LA TRIPE

SERVES 4

6 hard-boiled eggs, sliced
4 small-sized onions, sliced
60ml/4 tbls butter
300ml/¹/2pt hot **Béchamel sauce** *(see page 80)*
salt and freshly ground black pepper

1. Preheat oven to moderate (190°C/375°F/ gas 5).

2. Sauté the sliced onions in butter until they are soft and transparent, but not coloured; do not let them brown.

3. Add onions and the butter in which they were cooked to hot BECHAMEL SAUCE; stir well; fold in the egg slices and season with salt and freshly ground black pepper to taste. Transfer to an ovenproof baking dish and heat through in preheated oven. Serve hot.

STUFFED EGG AND TOMATO SALAD

SERVES 4

200g/7oz can tuna fish, drained
6 hard-boiled eggs
*90ml/6 tbls **Mayonnaise** (see page 85)*

juice of ½ lemon
salt and freshly ground black pepper
6 medium-sized tomatoes, sliced
***French dressing** (see page 304)*
30ml/2 tbls finely chopped parsley

1. Pound tuna fish in mortar until smooth.

2. Cut eggs in half lengthways. Remove yolks carefully.

3. Mash yolks and add to fish mixture. Stir in MAYONNAISE and lemon juice. Season with salt and freshly ground black pepper to taste; mix well. Taste and correct seasoning. Add a little more MAYONNAISE or lemon juice, if mixture is too thick.

4. Stuff egg cavities with this mixture. Toss tomatoes in FRENCH DRESSING and arrange in serving dish. Place stuffed eggs on top and sprinkle with finely chopped parsley.

SCRAMBLED EGGS

Use plenty of butter in the pan. It should be hot when the eggs are added, but not smoking or browned.

Allow 2 eggs per person and add an extra one for the pan. Mix eggs lightly, but do not beat them. Add 15ml/1 tbls water or double cream for each egg. Water will make exceedingly fluffy eggs; cream gives a richer, smoother mixture. I often add 15ml/1 tbls of freshly grated Gruyère cheese to scrambled eggs for a little extra flavour.

Butter a small saucepan generously; pour in the eggs and cook over hot, but not boiling, water.

For fluffy or creamy scrambled eggs, allow the eggs to set slightly after you put them in the pan and then stir constantly with a wooden spoon, being certain to run the edge of the spoon around the edges and into the centre of the pan. Good scrambled eggs need constant and careful attention.

You may add seasonings when mixing the eggs or while they are cooking, or you may prepare seasonings first – pour the eggs over them and scramble with the pre-cooked seasoning. Serve immediately on hot plates.

Scrambled eggs with herbs: Use fresh herbs; prepared herb mixtures for eggs are usually dry and tasteless. The most agreeable herbs are parsley, chives, chervil and tarragon, chopped finely and added to the egg mixture either before or during cooking. I like to sprinkle extra herbs over the eggs just before serving for added flavour.

Scrambled eggs with smoked salmon: Cut thin slices of smoked salmon *en julienne* and heat for a moment in butter. Add eggs (2 for each person and 1 for the pan), slightly beaten with a little water or double cream. Add salt and freshly ground black pepper, to taste. Just before removing from the heat, add a few drops of lemon juice and a little chopped parsley.

Rumbled eggs: Mix eggs lightly and season with salt and freshly ground black pepper to taste. Melt butter in a saucepan and, when butter is hot, pour in the eggs and stir over a gentle heat until soft and creamy. The moment the eggs cream, scoop out on to hot buttered toast spread with anchovy paste.

SCRAMBLED EGGS WITH OYSTERS

SERVES 4

45ml/3 tbls butter
5ml/1 tsp anchovy paste
6 eggs
dash of Tabasco
12 fresh oysters, shelled, drained and chopped
salt and freshly ground black pepper
30ml/2 tbls finely chopped parsley
fried croûtons

1. Melt butter with anchovy paste.
2. Whisk eggs with a dash of Tabasco. Pour into hot anchovy butter and scramble.
3. When eggs are just beginning to set, toss in 12 oysters and finish scrambling. Season with salt and freshly ground black pepper to taste. Sprinkle with finely chopped parsley and serve with *croûtons*.

SCRAMBLED EGGS WITH WHITE TRUFFLES

SERVES 4

½ garlic clove
6 eggs
salt and white pepper
45ml/3 tbls butter
2 canned white truffles or 1 fresh white truffle, thinly sliced
90ml/6 tbls double cream

1. Rub bowl in which you are going to beat the eggs with garlic.
2. Beat eggs lightly. Season with salt and white pepper to taste.
3. Melt butter in a thick-bottomed saucepan and, as soon as it is hot, add thinly sliced canned or fresh truffle slices and sauté for 2 minutes. Add beaten eggs and cook over a low heat so that the eggs do not set too quickly. When the eggs just begin to set and are still quite liquid, stir in cream and continue stirring until eggs are creamy. Serve immediately.

THE OMELETTE

So much has been said as well as written about the omelette's capricious nature that otherwise daring cooks often refuse to attempt it. In actual fact, most of omelette making is easier to do than to explain.

Omelettes can be infinitely varied in flavour, for no other dish so lends itself to the inventiveness of the cook. And once you learn to make a basic omelette, its count-less variations – *paysanne, Provençale, Parisienne, Parmentier, au caviare, aux fines herbes* – become child's play. An omelette is perfectly easy to make and yet so easy to spoil. One false move and the dish is ruined. It takes talent to make it right and you must be on the job every moment it is in preparation, for speed and efficiency count above all. Every omelette must be made to measure – let your guests wait for the omelette, never let the omelette wait for the guests.

The basic omelette: Small omelettes are much easier to make than big ones. Four eggs make an easily-handled omelette for two to three people. If you have more guests, it is best to make several omelettes, for they then come hotter to the table and have a much better con-sistency.

For each small omelette, break 4 eggs into a bowl and season with salt and freshly ground black pepper to taste. Add, if desired, 15ml/ 1 tbls of water, milk or double cream.

Heat the omelette pan gradually over medium heat until it is hot enough to make butter sizzle on contact. Beat egg with a fork or wire whisk for about 30 seconds, just enough to mix yolks and whites. Add 15ml/ 1 tbls of butter to heated pan and shake so that butter coats bottom evenly. When butter is sizzling, but before it has turned colour, pour in the beaten eggs, all at once.

Quickly stir eggs for a second or two in the pan to assure even cooking just as you would for scrambled eggs. Then, as eggs start to set,

lift edges with your fork so that the liquid can run under. Repeat until liquid is all used up but the eggs are still moist and soft. You can keep eggs 'slipping-free' by shaking pan during the above operation. Now, remove pan from flame and with one movement press the handle of the pan downwards and slide the omelette towards the handle. When a third of the omelette has slid up the rounded edge of the pan, fold this quickly toward the centre with a knife. Then raise the handle of the pan, and slide opposite edge of omelette one-third up the side farthest away from the handle. Hold a heated serving dish under it and, as the rim of the omelette touches the dish, raise the handle more and more until the pan is turned upside down and your oval-shaped, lightly-browned omelette rests on the dish. Rapidly 'finish' the omelette by piercing a piece of butter with the tip of a knife and skimming the surface lightly to leave a glistening trail.

Garnish with fresh parsley and serve immediately.

The omelette pan: Although some cooks claim that an omelette can be made in any pan, I keep a pan exclusively for eggs. It is a pan expressly designed for omelettes alone – one of good weight, with rounded sides so the eggs can slide easily onto the plate when cooked. And unless you want your omelette to stick, never wash the pan. Instead, just rub it clean with paper and a few drops of oil.

If the pan is new, you must 'season' it before using by slowly heating oil in it; then leave the oil to soak into the pan for at least 12 hours.

Your pan must not be too small or too large for the number of eggs used in the omelette. A pan 18-20cm/7-8in in diameter is just about right for a 4-egg omelette.

Variations on the theme: Practice makes perfect and once you have mastered the basic omelette to your satisfaction you are ready to try some of the many exciting variations on the omelette theme. Some of the most delicious are the easiest to prepare; but always remember to make the omelette filling before you make the actual omelette itself. In this way your omelettes can come to the table crisply cased with a wonderfully moist interior and filling.

Cheese omelette: Perhaps the easiest version of all. Make your omelette as above and, just as eggs begin to set, add 30ml/2 tbls freshly grated Parmesan cheese and, if you like, 30ml/2 tbls double cream.

Watercress omelette: Add 30ml/2 tbls finely chopped watercress to the egg mixture; cook as above, and serve omelette surrounded with fresh watercress.

Mushroom omelette: Marinate 100g/¼lb sliced mushrooms in 15ml/1 tbls brandy for 15 minutes. Add 15ml/1 tbls butter and stir over high heat until liquid evaporates. Add 30-60ml/2-4 tbls double cream and salt and freshly ground black pepper to taste, and keep warm while you make omelette as above. As omelette sets, spread with this mixture, fold and serve.

Omelette Parmentier: Brown 60ml/4 tbls diced boiled potatoes in butter. Add 2.5ml/½ tsp each of finely chopped parsley and chives to egg mixture and, just before pouring into pan, add lightly-browned potatoes. Prepare omelette as above.

Omelette Florentine: Warm 60ml/4 tbls freshly-cooked, well-drained spinach in butter. Rub omelette pan lightly with cut clove of garlic and make omelette as above. When eggs are just set, spread spinach in centre, fold and serve. Another version chops the spinach and adds it to the egg mixture before cooking.

FRENCH COUNTRY OMELETTE

SERVES 2

90ml/6 tbls diced fat salt pork, or green bacon
30ml/2 tbls olive oil
90ml/6 tbls diced boiled potato
6 eggs
10ml/2 tsp finely chopped parsley
10ml/2 tsp finely chopped chives
salt and freshly ground black pepper
60ml/4 tbls butter

1. Parboil diced fat salt pork, or green bacon in water for a few minutes. Drain.
2. Heat olive oil in a thick-bottomed frying pan and sauté fat salt pork or green bacon, until browned. Remove from pan and keep warm.
3. Sauté diced boiled potato in the fats until golden.
4. Lightly beat eggs in a bowl; add sautéed meat and finely chopped potato, parsley and chives. Season with salt and freshly ground black pepper to taste. Melt butter in an omelette pan; pour in omelette mixture and cook as for BASIC OMELETTE (see page 99). When the first odour of browning is evident, turn the omelette and brown it slightly on the other side. Slide omelette onto a heated platter and serve immediately.

LA PIPERADE DU PAYS BASQUE

SERVES 2

1 green pepper, seeded and sliced
pork fat or olive oil
4 tomatoes, peeled, seeded and chopped
1 Spanish onion, sliced
1/2 garlic clove, crushed
30ml-60ml/2-4 tbls diced jambon de Bayonne or
*   cooked ham*
salt and freshly ground black pepper
30ml/2 tbls butter
6 eggs

1. Sauté sliced green pepper very gently in a little pork fat or olive oil. Add peeled, seeded and chopped tomatoes, together with sliced onion, crushed garlic and diced ham. Season with salt and freshly ground black pepper to taste. Add butter and simmer mixture slowly for about 30 minutes, or until the vegetables turn into a rather soft purée.
2. Beat eggs lightly and season with salt and freshly ground black pepper to taste. Stir beaten eggs gently into the hot vegetable mixture. Be sure not to overcook, for this Basque omelette should be soft and wet, with almost the consistency of scrambled eggs. Slide omelette onto a heated platter and serve.

MADAME PRUNET'S OMELETTES

SERVES 4-6

45ml/3 tbls castor sugar
400ml/2/3pt milk
4 eggs, separated
45ml/3 tbls flour
peanut oil
butter
Jamaica rum, warmed
castor sugar, to serve

1. Preheat oven to hot (230°C/450°F/gas 8).

2. Mix sugar with half a glass of milk. Add flour and egg yolks and blend well. Pour in remaining milk and flavour with rum to taste.
3. Beat egg whites until stiff. Fold gently into omelette mixture.
4. Heat an omelette pan and oil it lightly. Pour a ladle of the omelette mixture into the pan and cook as you would a pancake (see page 340). When it is cooked, roll omelette tightly and transfer to a buttered baking dish. Oil pan again and continue cooking as above until the mixture is used up.
5. Cook omelettes in the preheated oven for 10 minutes. They will swell and become crisp. Sprinkle with sugar; flame with rum and serve immediately.

L'OMELETTE DU PERE JOSEPH

SERVES 4

6-8 eggs
90ml/6 tbls double cream, warmed
salt and freshly ground black pepper
100g/4oz butter
100g/4oz pâté de foie gras, diced
1-2 small truffles, diced
15-30ml/1-2 tbls dry sherry
90ml/6 tbls double cream, warmed
1 truffle, cut into thin strips
cooked tongue, cut into thin strips

1. Combine eggs and double cream in a bowl. Season with salt and freshly ground black pepper to taste, and whisk until mixture is frothy.
2. Melt butter in an omelette pan and make omelette in usual way (see page 99).
3. Meanwhile, heat diced *pâté de foie gras* and truffles through in dry sherry.
4. Just before rolling omelette, stuff it with *foie gras* and truffles. Transfer to a heated platter and pour warmed cream over omelette. Sprinkle with thin strips of truffle and tongue and serve immediately.

101

OMELETTE SURPRISE 'VALBERG'

SERVES 4-6

8 eggs, separated
sugar
45ml/3 tbls butter
15ml/1 tbls peanut oil
30-60ml/2-4 tbls Cointreau or Grand Marnier
orange or banana slices, or diced pineapple
60ml/4 tbls cognac, Armagnac or rum, warmed

1. Whisk yolks until frothy; whisk whites until very stiff. Fold yolks into beaten whites and add sugar to taste.
2. Preheat grill to high.
3. Heat 30ml/2 tbls butter and the peanut oil in an omelette pan and, when very hot, pour in omelette mixture. Spoon over Cointreau or Grand Marnier, and cook until omelette is done, but still moist.
4. Meanwhile, heat orange or banana slices or diced pineapple through in the remaining butter.
5. Place slices of heated orange or banana or diced pineapple in centre of egg mixture and fold omelette over. Transfer omelette to heated platter, sprinkle with 5-10ml/1-2 tsp sugar and glaze under preheated grill. Flame with cognac, Armagnac or rum and serve.

ITALIAN FRITTATA

SERVES 4

1/2 Spanish onion, finely chopped
olive oil
6-8 eggs, beaten
15ml/1 tbls each finely chopped fresh parsley, mint
   and basil
salt and freshly ground black pepper
butter

1. Sauté finely chopped onion in 30ml/2 tbls olive oil until soft and transparent.

2. Combine sautéed onion in a bowl with beaten eggs and finely chopped parsley, mint and basil. Season with salt and freshly ground black pepper to taste, and mix well.
3. Heat 15ml/1 tbls each butter and olive oil in an omelette pan and, when very hot, pour in mixture and cook slowly until brown. Add a little more butter before turning over *frittata* to cook the other side. Transfer *frittata* to a heated platter and serve immediately.

FIFINE'S PIPERADE

SERVES 4-6

60ml/4 tbls olive oil
1/2 Spanish onion, coarsely sliced
4 peppers (green, yellow or red), seeded and
   coarsely sliced
4 tomatoes, peeled and seeded
salt and freshly ground black pepper
8-10 eggs
30ml/2 tbls freshly grated Gruyère cheese
30ml/2 tbls freshly grated Parmesan cheese
30ml/2 tbls butter

1. Heat olive oil in an omelette pan; add coarsely sliced onion and sauté, stirring from time to time, until onion is transparent but not coloured. Add seeded and sliced peppers and cook over a low heat, stirring from time to time, until peppers are soft but not mushy. Turn flame higher and stir in tomatoes and salt and freshly ground black pepper, to taste.
2. Break eggs into a bowl and beat with a whisk until foamy.
3. Pour eggs over vegetables; allow to set for 2 to 3 minutes, then stir with a wooden spoon or spatula, as you would for scrambled eggs. Mix finely grated Gruyère and Parmesan cheese and sprinkle over *pipérade* to bind. Fold omelette into shape. Slide butter under omelette to add flavour, turn out onto a heated platter and serve immediately.

THE SAVOURY SOUFFLE

The soufflé – to many people one of the most awe-inspiring creations of French *haute cuisine* – is, in reality, nothing more than a simple airy mixture of eggs, butter, flour and a purée of vegetables, meat, fish or fowl.

Try the soufflé as a perfect beginning to a meal, whether it be a simple cheese affair (try a combination of Gruyère cheese and Parmesan cheese), a concoction of fish or shellfish, or one made with a well-seasoned base of puréed vegetables (endive, onion, or mushroom and cheese).

Savoury soufflés also make light-as-air *entrées* of distinction for luncheon or supper parties. And there you can always let your imagination run riot. What do you risk? The basic soufflé mixture stays just the same. Add a breakfastcupful of diced, grilled kippers to your basic soufflé mixture for an after-theatre supper for four. Or take the same basic mixture, flavour with a hint of cognac and, instead of poached eggs, bury a surprise catch of diced lobster meat which you have first flamed in cognac, or in a more sophisticated moment, in Pernod. It's as easy as that!

You will find that soufflés are quite easy to make if a few basic rules are followed. First and foremost: a soufflé must be eaten when ready. A soufflé will not wait for your guests: your guests must wait for this delicate and sometimes temperamental dish. A rich, smooth sauce is the base of all soufflés. Many French soufflé recipes simply require a well-flavoured Béchamel Sauce.

The egg yolks and egg whites must be beaten separately; the yolks until thick and lemon-coloured, the whites until stiff but not dry. In separating the eggs, be sure that there is no speck of yolk left in the whites, otherwise you will not be able to beat your whites stiff. Use an unbuttered soufflé dish for your first attempts so that the soufflé can cling to the sides of the dish and rise to its full height. For added flavour, when you butter the dish, sprinkle the buttered surface with fresh breadcrumbs or a little freshly grated Parmesan cheese.

A moderate oven (180°C/350°F/gas 4) is essential. If your oven is too hot, the soufflé will be well cooked on top and undercooked inside. As long as it remains in a warm oven a soufflé is pretty sturdy. The best way to determine when a soufflé is done is to open the door after 30 or 35 minutes and to give the dish a slight shove. If the top crust moves only very slightly, the soufflé is done. However, if it really trembles, leave it in a few minutes more.

BASIC SAVOURY SOUFFLE

SERVES 4

60ml/4 tbls butter
45ml/3 tbls flour
300ml/¹/2pt hot milk
5 egg yolks
75g/3oz Gruyère cheese, freshly grated
50g/2oz Parmesan cheese, freshly grated
salt and freshly ground black pepper
cayenne pepper
6 egg whites

1. Preheat oven to moderate (180°C/350°F/gas 4).
2. Melt 45ml/3 tbls butter in the top of a double saucepan; add flour gradually and mix to a smooth paste, stirring constantly. Add hot milk and cook until sauce is smooth and thick.
3. Remove pan from heat and add egg yolks, one by one, alternately with a mixture of freshly grated Gruyère cheese and Parmesan cheese. Mix well and return to heat. Cook until cheese has melted into the mixture. Add generous amounts of salt, freshly ground black pepper and cayenne pepper. Remove pan from heat and allow sauce to cool slightly.
4. Butter a 18cm/7in soufflé dish and tie a band of buttered greaseproof paper around dish to make a high collar.
5. Beat egg whites till they are stiff and fold gently into the warm cheese mixture.
6. Fill prepared soufflé dish about three-quarters full with mixture and bake in preheated oven for 30 to 35 minutes, or until soufflé is golden. Serve immediately.

CRAB SOUFFLE

SERVES 4-6

75ml/5 tbls butter
45ml/3 tbls flour
300ml/¹/2pt hot milk
120ml/8 tbls freshly grated Parmesan cheese
150g/6oz crabmeat, shredded
salt and cayenne pepper
4 egg yolks
6 egg whites

1. Preheat oven to moderate (180°C/350°F/gas 4).
2. Melt 60ml/4 tbls butter in the top of a double saucepan; add flour and stir until well blended. Add milk and continue cooking, stirring constantly, until the sauce is smooth and thick.
3. Stir in freshly grated Parmesan cheese and continue cooking until cheese has melted into the mixture. Add shredded crabmeat and heat through. Season with salt and cayenne pepper to taste.
4. Beat egg yolks slightly and add hot sauce to them.
5. Butter a 18cm/7in soufflé dish and tie a band of buttered greaseproof paper around the dish to make a high collar.
6. Whisk egg whites until stiff and gently fold mixture into them, a little at a time.
7. Fill prepared soufflé dish about three-quarters full with mixture and bake in the preheated oven for 30 to 35 minutes or until soufflé is golden. Serve immediately.

SUPPER SOUFFLE

SERVES 4

60ml/4 tbls butter
45ml/ 3 tbls flour
300ml/¹/2pt hot milk
30ml/2 tbls grated onion
60ml/4 tbls freshly grated Parmesan cheese
salt and freshly ground black pepper
pinch of dry mustard
225g/¹/2lb poached fillets of sole or turbot
4 egg yolks
6 egg whites

1. Preheat oven to moderate (180°C/350°F/gas 4).

2. Melt 45ml/3 tbls butter in the top of a double saucepan; add flour and stir until smooth. Add hot milk and continue to cook over low heat, stirring constantly, until thick. Remove from heat. Add grated onion and freshly grated Parmesan cheese. Season with salt, freshly ground black pepper to taste and a pinch of dry mustard.

3. Flake poached fish fillets and stir gently into hot sauce. Allow to cool.

4. Beat egg yolks lightly and stir into fish mixture.

5. Butter a 18cm/7in soufflé dish and tie a band of buttered greaseproof paper around the dish to make a high collar.

6. Beat egg whites until they are stiff but not dry, and fold gently into fish mixture.

7. Fill prepared soufflé dish about three-quarters full with mixture and and bake in the preheated oven for 30 to 35 minutes or until soufflé is golden. Serve immediately.

CHICKEN SOUFFLE

SERVES 4

60ml/4 tbls butter
45ml/3 tbls flour
300ml/½pt hot milk
30ml/2 tbls cognac
salt and white pepper
pinch of dry mustard
4 egg yolks
225g/½lb chicken, minced
6 egg whites

1. Preheat oven to moderate (180°C/350°F/gas 4).

2. Melt 45ml/3 tbls butter in the top of a double saucepan. Blend in flour. Add hot milk and stir over heat until mixture comes to the boil. Remove from heat and add cognac. Season with salt and white pepper to taste and a pinch of dry mustard.

3. Beat egg yolks, one at a time, into sauce. Add minced chicken.

4. Butter a 18cm/7in soufflé dish and tie a band of buttered greaseproof paper around dish to make a high collar.

5. Beat egg whites until stiff and fold gently into warm chicken mixture.

6. Fill prepared soufflé dish about three-quarters full with soufflé mixture and bake in the preheated oven for about 30 to 35 minutes, or until the top of the soufflé is slightly browned and feels firm to the touch. Serve immediately.

MUSHROOM SOUFFLE

SERVES 4

60ml/4 tbls butter
45ml/3 tbls flour
300ml/½pt hot milk
60ml/4 tbls freshly grated Parmesan cheese
salt
cayenne pepper
pinch of grated nutmeg
1-2 shallots, finely chopped
150g-225g/6-8oz mushrooms, finely sliced
4 egg yolks
6 egg whites

1. Preheat oven to moderate (180°C/350°F/gas 4).

2. Melt 45ml/3 tbls butter in the top of a double saucepan; add flour and cook until the flour just starts to turn golden. Add hot milk and cook, stirring constantly with a wire whisk, until the sauce is thick and smooth. Add freshly grated Parmesan cheese, salt and cayenne pepper to taste and a pinch of grated nutmeg. Remove from heat.

3. Sauté finely chopped shallots in 30ml/2 tbls butter until shallots are transparent but not coloured; add finely sliced mushrooms and cook

until all the moisture has evaporated. Add mushroom mixture to hot sauce.

4. Beat egg yolks until frothy. Fold into mixture.

5. Butter a 18cm/7in soufflé dish and tie a band of buttered greaseproof paper around dish to make a high collar.

6. Beat egg whites until stiff and fold gently into mixture. Fill prepared soufflé dish about three-quarters full with mixture and bake in preheated oven for 30 to 35 minutes or until soufflé is golden. Serve immediately.

CHEESE SOUFFLE WITH GARLIC CROUTONS

SERVES 6

60ml/4 tbls butter
45ml/3 tbls flour
300ml/¹/₂pt hot milk
5 egg yolks
100-150g/4-6oz grated cheese (a mixture of
 Gruyère and Parmesan)
salt and freshly ground black pepper
cayenne pepper
30ml/2 tbls olive oil (optional)
1 garlic clove, mashed
2 slices of white bread, trimmed of crusts and diced
6 egg whites

1. Preheat oven to moderate (180°C/350°F/ gas 4).

2. Melt 45ml/3 tbls butter in the top of a double saucepan; add flour gradually and mix to a smooth paste, stirring constantly. Add hot milk and cook until sauce is smooth and thick.

3. Remove from heat and add egg yolks, one by one alternately with grated cheese. Mix well and return to heat and cook until cheese melts. Add generous amounts of salt, freshly ground black pepper and a hint of cayenne pepper. Allow to cool slightly.

4. Heat 30ml/2 tbls butter or olive oil in a fry-

ing pan; add garlic and bread and sauté until golden. Drain *croûtons* on absorbent paper.

5. Butter a 18cm/7in soufflé dish and tie a band of buttered greaseproof paper around dish to make a high collar.

6. Beat egg whites until stiff and fold gently into warm cheese mixture. Fold in garlic *croûtons*.

7. Fill prepared soufflé dish about three-quarters full with mixture and bake in preheated oven for 30 to 35 minutes, or until soufflé is golden. Serve immediately.

BASIC SWEET SOUFFLE

SERVES 4

45ml/3 tbls butter
45ml/3 tbls flour
300ml/¹/₂ pt hot milk
pinch of salt
strip of orange peel
5 egg yolks
75ml/5 tbls castor sugar
2.5ml/¹/₂ tsp vanilla essence
6 egg whites

1. Preheat oven to moderate (180°C/350°F/ gas 4).

2. Melt 45ml/3 tbls butter in the top of a double saucepan; add flour and cook, stirring, until well blended. Add hot milk, pinch of salt and strip of orange peel. Cook the sauce, stirring constantly, until smooth and thick. Remove orange peel and let sauce cool slightly.

3. Beat egg yolks well with 60ml/4 tbls sugar and vanilla essence and combine with soufflé mixture.

4. Beat egg whites until they are stiff but not dry, and fold into the soufflé mixture.

5. Butter and lightly sugar a 18cm/7in soufflé dish and tie a band of buttered greaseproof paper around dish to make a high collar.

6. Fill prepared soufflé dish about three-quarters full with mixture and bake in preheated oven for 30 to 35 minutes, or until soufflé is golden. Serve immediately.

LEMON SOUFFLE

SERVES 4

45ml/3 tbls butter
30ml/2 tbls flour
300ml/¹/₂pt hot milk
pinch of salt
grated rind of 1 lemon
45ml/3 tbls lemon juice
5 egg yolks
75ml/5 tbls castor sugar
6 egg whites

1. Preheat oven to moderate (180°C/350°F/ gas 4).
2. Melt 30ml/2 tbls butter in the top of a double saucepan; add flour and cook, stirring, until well blended. Add hot milk and a pinch of salt. Cook the sauce, stirring contantly, until smooth and thick, and continue cooking, stirring constantly, for a few more minutes. Let sauce cool slightly. Stir in grated lemon rind and lemon juice.
3. Beat egg yolks well with 60ml/4 tbls sugar and combine them with soufflé mixture.
4. Beat egg whites until they are stiff but not dry, and fold gently into the soufflé mixture.
5. Butter and lightly sugar a 18cm/7in soufflé dish and tie a band of buttered greaseproof paper around dish to make a high collar.
6. Fill prepared soufflé dish about three-quarters full with mixture and bake in preheated oven for 30 to 35 minutes, or until soufflé is golden. Serve immediately.

SOUFFLE AU GRAND MARNIER

SERVES 4

60ml/4 tbls butter
45ml/3 tbls flour
300ml/¹/₂pt hot milk
pinch of salt
strip of orange peel
5 egg yolks
75ml/5 tbls castor sugar
2.5ml/¹/₂ tsp vanilla essence
30ml/2 tbls Grand Marnier
sponge fingers, halved lengthways
30ml/2 tbls cognac
6 egg whites

1. Preheat oven to moderate (180°C/350°F/ gas 4).
2. Melt 45ml/ 3 tbls butter in the top of a double saucepan; add flour and cook, stirring, until well blended. Add hot milk, pinch of salt and a strip of orange peel. Cook the sauce, stirring constantly, until smooth and thick, and continue cooking, stirring constantly, for a few more minutes. Remove orange peel and let sauce cool slightly.
3. Beat egg yolks well with 60ml/4 tbls sugar and vanilla essence and combine with soufflé mixture. Stir in Grand Marnier.
4. Sprinkle sponge fingers with cognac.
5. Beat egg whites until stiff, but not dry, and fold gently into the cooled soufflé mixture.
6. Butter and lightly sugar a 18cm/7in soufflé dish and tie a band of buttered greaseproof paper around dish to make a high collar. Line dish with sponge fingers.
7. Fill prepared soufflé dish about three-quarters full with mixture and bake in preheated oven for 30 to 35 minutes, or until soufflé is golden. Serve immediately with APRICOT SAUCE (see page 88) or VANILLA CUSTARD SAUCE (see page 88).

CHAPTER 5

FISH

POACHED SALMON IN ASPIC

COOKS IN BRITAIN mainly regard fish as something to fry. They seem afraid of its other propensities – why, I wonder, when there is such a variety of ways which exist for the preparation of fish . . .

'*C'est la sauce qui fait manger le poisson*' – 'it is the sauce which makes people eat fish', is the adage in France, and French culinary history is full of delicious recipes for grilled, poached and baked fish of all kinds, served with delicately flavoured sauces. Grilled fillets of sole or flounder with a shrimp sauce or a sauce Hollandaise; sole, flounder and turbot, marinated in a white wine marinade and simmered *en casserole* in their own juices; turbot cooked in red wine – these are but a few of the delights that French fish cookery can offer us.

The art of cooking with wine is made easier (but no cheaper) for us these days by the wonderful array of imported vintages at our disposal. Keep a good stock of Burgundies, both white and red. Yes, fish can be cooked in red wine – *rosé,* too, for that matter. This legend of white for fish and red for meat is old-fashioned nonsense! There are no rules for this sort of thing and, indeed, anything goes. So add dry sherry and vermouth to your cooking cellar; experiment with port and Madeira.

Of course, even the most superb wine sauce cannot transform fish that is stale or overcooked. Always buy fish with firm skin and scales and bright eyes and cook it carefully to the point when the moist, opaque flesh can be easily flaked with a fork. More crimes are committed in fish cookery by plain, simple overcooking than by any other means. Fish should be firm and moist, not an overboiled mush of watery tastlessness.

The ultimate in elegant dining— poached salmon in aspic decorated with cucumber, lemon and tomato flowers.

GRILLED FISH

In Provence, I learned to like my fish grilled on an outdoor fire that had been fed with aromatic herbs. Many are the midnight beach picnics enjoyed on the vast expanses of Pampelonne, at which barbecued fish, freshly caught from the gulf of Pampelonne, played the starring role, preceded by a cool salad of Mediterranean vegetables and cold *ratatouille,* a Provençal vegetable stew of tomatoes, aubergines and courgettes, served cold with French dressing. The fish would be accompanied by melted tarragon butter and plain boiled potatoes, and washed down by liberal quantities of chilled *vin blanc du Var.*

Basil, tarragon, parsley and rosemary have natural affinities for fish. Their fragrant perfume and the odorous smoke from the wood fire make barbecued fish a dish fit for a king. Try this on your own barbecue as the weather gets warmer. But be sure you use a hinged grill so that you can turn your fish easily without danger of breaking its tender flesh. Oil all fish lightly before grilling and, if you are using fish steaks or fish fillets, be sure to baste them frequently with olive oil during cooking time. Whole fish, with skins intact, require less attention. I like to stuff cavities of fish with herbs – a selection of fennel, parsley and thyme – before grilling them and then baste them with olive oil as they grill, often using a switch of bay leaves as a basting brush to give added flavour.

FLAMED FISH

Along the coast from Marseilles to St. Tropez, in the little sea towns on the way, it has long been the custom to serve grilled fish in a jacket of flaming herbs. This is a delicious way of dealing with any fresh fish. First grill your fish as above and remove it to a heated serving dish which has been covered with rosemary, fennel, parsley and thyme. The fish is then topped with additional herbs and 2 or 3 tablespoons of warm cognac are poured over it and ignited. The burning herbs give the fish a subtle flavour which, once you have tasted it, is irresistible.

FISH COURT-BOUILLONS AND FUMETS

When fish is to be served cold with a fish sauce, French dressing or mayonnaise, or, for a special occasion, in a cool coat of shimmering aspic, it is always best to cook it in a well-flavoured fish *court-bouillon* to give it the utmost in flavour. A fish *court-bouillon* does for fish what a good chicken stock does for chicken.

FISH COURT-BOUILLON

MAKES ABOUT 1L/2pt

45ml/3 tbls butter
45ml/3 tbls olive oil
2 small carrots, finely chopped
2 celery stalks, finely chopped
1 Spanish onion, finely chopped
600ml/1pt dry white wine
1kg/2lb fish trimmings (haddock, halibut, cod etc)
1 bouquet garni (celery stalk, 1 sprig of thyme and
  1 sprig of parsley)
2 bay leaves
6 black peppercorns, bruised
2 cloves
salt

1. Heat butter and olive oil in a fish kettle or thick-bottomed saucepan and sauté finely chopped carrots, celery and onion until onion is transparent, but not brown.
2. Add 600ml/1pt water, dry white wine and fish trimmings to pan and bring to the boil. Skim; add *bouquet garni,* bay leaves, bruised peppercorns and cloves. Season with salt, to taste. Cover and simmer for 30 minutes.
3. Strain the *court-bouillon* and use as required.

LIGHT FISH COURT-BOUILLON FOR A LARGE FISH

MAKES ABOUT 1.7L/3pt

1L/2pt cold water
1 bottle dry white wine
1 Spanish onion, sliced
4 carrots, sliced
2 celery stalks, sliced
2 bay leaves
1 bouquet garni
salt
8 black peppercorns, bruised

1. Combine first five ingredients in a fish kettle or thick-bottomed saucepan large enough to hold the fish to be poached, and bring to the boil. Skim; add *bouquet garni*, bay leaves and peppercorns; season with salt, to taste. Cover and simmer for 30 minutes.
2. Strain the *court-bouillon* and use as required.

FISH FUMET

MAKES ABOUT 1L/2pt

225g/¹/₂lb white fish, cleaned and gutted
1L/2pt cold water
150ml/¹/₄pt dry white wine
2 carrots, sliced
1 leek, sliced
1 Spanish onion, sliced
6 black peppercorns, bruised
1 bouquet garni
1 garlic clove
salt

1. Combine first 6 ingredients in a thick-bottomed saucepan and bring to the boil. Skim. Add peppercorns, *bouquet garni* and garlic; season with salt, to taste. Cover and simmer for 30 minutes.
2. Strain the FUMET and use as required.

CONCENTRATED FISH FUMET

MAKES 700ml/1¹/₄pt

60ml/4 tbls butter
450g/1lb bones and trimmings of sole
1 carrot, chopped
1 Spanish onion, chopped
60ml/4 tbls chopped parsley
300ml/¹/₂pt dry white wine
3 black peppercorns, bruised
salt

1. Melt butter in a thick-bottomed saucepan and sauté fish bones and trimmings with chopped carrot, onion and parsley for 10 minutes.
2. Add 450ml/³/₄pt water, wine, and peppercorns and bring to the boil. Skim. Season with salt, cover and simmer gently for 30 minutes.
3. Strain the *fumet* and use as required.

FISH ASPIC

MAKES ABOUT 900ml/1¹/₂pt

100g/¹/₄lb raw white fish, finely chopped
1 leek, white part only, finely chopped
1 egg white
1 crushed egg shell
900ml/1¹/₂pt **Fish fumet** *(see this page)*
30ml/2 tbls gelatine
60ml/4 tbls dry white wine

1. In a thick-bottomed saucepan, combine the white fish and leek with the egg white, crushed egg shell and FISH FUMET. Bring to the boil, stirring constantly, and simmer, uncovered, for 20 minutes. Strain hot stock through a fine sieve.
2. Soften gelatine in dry white wine and stir into the hot stock. Allow to cool and set. For moulds or glazing, use fish aspic as soon as it gets syrupy, but before it starts to set.
NOTE: To set aspic quickly, place bowl containing aspic in a larger bowl containing ice cubes.

SALMON POACHED IN COURT BOUILLON

SERVES 12

1 whole salmon about 2.7kg/6lb, cleaned and
*   gutted*
1.7L/3pt **Court-bouillon** *(see page 110)*
lemon slices
cucumber slices
sprigs of watercress or parsley

1. Put the COURT-BOUILLON in a fish kettle or thick-bottomed saucepan large enough to hold salmon and bring to the boil. Skim. Let COURT-BOUILLON cool slightly.
2. Wrap salmon in muslin and lower into the COURT-BOUILLON. Add more liquid if necessary. Simmer gently for 50 to 60 minutes, or until the fish flakes easily with a fork.
3. Remove fish carefully from the COURT-BOUILLON with the help of the muslin and carefully remove the skin. Arrange the salmon on a heated platter and garnish with lemon slices, cucumber slices, sprigs of watercress or parsley. Serve with a SAUCE MOUSSELINE (see page 85), SAUCE CHORON (see page 84) or a SAUCE VERTE (see page 86).

POACHED SALMON IN ASPIC

SERVES 12

2.7kg/6lb salmon poached in **Court-bouillon**
*   (see page 110)*
1 egg white
1 crushed egg shell
34ml/2¼ tbls gelatine
fresh tarragon leaves
thin strips of cucumber, or spring onion
thin small cut-outs of egg white, tomato and cooked
*   carrot, or turnip*

1. Reserve COURT-BOUILLON and let poached salmon cool on a large board, or platter. Re-move skin carefully, cutting it at the tail and stripping it to the head.
2. Reduce COURT-BOUILLON to 1L/2pt and clarify with the egg white and crushed egg shell (see page 29). Strain COURT-BOUILLON through a fine sieve. Reserve.
3. Soften gelatine in 60ml/4 tbls cold water and prepare an ASPIC using the strained hot COURT-BOUILLON.
4. Place salmon on a rack over a long dish and brush with cooled ASPIC. Decorate with fresh tarragon leaves, thin strips of cucumber or spring onion, and cut-outs of egg white, to-mato and cooked carrot, or turnip. Brush with ASPIC again and allow to set.
5. Transfer salmon to a serving platter and serve with MAYONNAISE (see page 85) or SAUCE VERTE (see page 86).

GRILLED SALMON STEAKS

SERVES 4

4 large salmon steaks
salt and freshly ground black pepper
olive oil
melted butter
lemon wedges

LEMON AND PARSLEY BUTTER
100g/4oz slightly softened butter
30ml/2 tbls finely chopped parsley
lemon juice
salt and freshly ground pepper

1. Season both sides of salmon steaks with salt and freshly ground black pepper to taste, and leave at room temperature for 30 minutes.
2. Preheat grill to high.
3. When ready to grill, brush grid of grill pan with a little olive oil. Place salmon steaks on grid; brush with a little melted butter and grill for 3-5 minutes, about 7cm/3in from heat. Turn steaks, brush with a little more melted

butter and continue to grill until fish flakes easily with a fork, 3-5 minutes.

4. Transfer salmon steaks to a heated serving platter; top each steak with a round of lemon and parsley butter and garnish each with lemon wedges. Serve immediately.

5. To make lemon and parsley butter, pound slightly softened butter in a mortar with finely chopped parsley; season with lemon juice, salt and freshly ground black pepper, to taste. Shape butter into a neat roll, 6mm/¼in in diameter. Wrap tightly in cling film and chill in the refrigerator until firm. Reserve remaining butter to serve with grilled lamb or veal chops.

FRENCH SALMON TOURTE

SERVES 4-6

Fingertip pastry for 2-crust pie (see page 347)
350g/¾lb fresh salmon
100g/4oz button mushroom caps
150g/6oz butter
150ml/¼pt double cream
150ml/¼pt dry white wine
freshly ground black pepper
freshly grated nutmeg
2 egg whites, beaten
100g/¼lb sliced smoked salmon, diced
salt

LEMON BUTTER SAUCE
60ml/4 tbls butter
5ml/1 tsp chopped tarragon
5ml/1 tsp chopped parsley
5ml/1 tsp chopped chives
juice of ½ lemon

1. Preheat oven to moderate (190°C/375°F/gas 5).
2. Skin and bone fresh salmon and slice fish thinly. Pound two-thirds of the salmon to a smooth paste in a mortar with button mushroom caps and butter. Add double cream and

dry white wine and beat again until smooth and well mixed.

3. Season mixture generously with freshly ground black pepper and freshly grated nutmeg. Fold in beaten egg whites.

4. Line a 1L/2pt pie dish with FINGERTIP PASTRY. Spoon half the salmon paste into pastry shell. Cover with a thin layer of raw salmon slices and diced smoked salmon. Season lightly with salt and ground black pepper.

5. Add remainder of salmon paste and cover with the second layer of pastry. Make a hole in the centre of pastry crust and bake in preheated oven for 30 to 40 minutes.

6. Just before serving, pour lemon butter sauce through hole in top crust. Serve immediately.

7. To make lemon butter sauce: melt butter in a small thick-bottomed saucepan. Stir in chopped tarragon, parsley and chives together with lemon juice. Mix well.

BARBECUED FISH WITH TARRAGON

SERVES 4

2 sea bass or grey mullet, cleaned and gutted
2 sprigs each of rosemary, fennel and sage
2 bay leaves
60ml/4 tbls dry white wine
90ml/6 tbls melted butter
salt and freshly ground black pepper
cayenne pepper

SERVING SAUCE
100g/¼lb melted butter
juice of 1 lemon
60ml/4 tbls fresh tarragon, finely chopped

1. Light fire at least 1 hour before you start cooking.
2. Stuff cleaned and scaled fish with fresh herbs – rosemary, fennel, sage and bay leaves.

Secure fish to the spit with thin wire or wet cord. Or, if using a hinged grill, place fish on bottom half of grill; lower top half of grill over fish and secure grill loosely with a thin wire.
3. Combine dry white wine and melted butter. Season generously with salt and freshly ground black pepper, and a pinch of cayenne.
4. Grill fish over hot coals for 20-25 minutes, depending on size, turning fish from time to time during cooking and brushing them with wine and butter sauce. When fish are done, they should flake easily when tested with a fork. Transfer fish to a heated platter and serve with plenty of melted butter flavoured with lemon juice and finely chopped fresh tarragon.

NOTE: Fish may be cooked in oven or under the grill.

MATELOTE A LA BOURGUIGNONNE

Fish and wine have always seemed to me to have natural affinities . . . ever since the memorable summer of '31, when I was eight, my favourite brother, fourteen, and we lived on the banks of the Hudson river just twenty-five miles from New York. It was Prohibition – a zany period in American political history, when to indulge in a quiet drink between friends was punishable by law – and my brother and I spent the summer 'fishing' along with other members of the local citizenry for cases of champagne and caviar hastily thrown overboard one evening by a boatload of bootleggers temporarily at grips with the law.

Introduced to the illicit pleasures of fish and wine at such a tender age, it is small wonder that today I prefer fish and shellfish served in generous quantities of my favourite potions.

And I am not alone. The art of cooking fish in wine is as old as the art of gastronomy. The Rhône valley was probably the first to have its forests cleared and planted with vines by the early Romans when they conquered Gaul. Vines still flourish practically all along the Rhône today, coming into greater prominence below Lyons in the wine-growing districts of Châteauneuf du Pape, Hermitage and Côte Rôtie. Some of the most exciting little restaurants in France are to be found in this region; small bistros and unknown cafés where the food-conscious traveller is sure to find some of the best wine-simmered dishes in the country; simple little places with sawdust-strewn floors, where the chef is known to make the finest *matelote* in the region. The *matelote,* like the *pochouse bourguignonne,* combines the delicate meats of carp, pike, eel, and other local fish, flamed in cognac, and then simmered in a rich, smooth sauce of red or white wine, according to the tastes of house or region.

114

MATELOTE A LA BOURGUIGNONNE

SERVES 8 generously

1kg/2lb fresh eel, cleaned and skinned
1kg/2lb carp, cleaned and gutted
1kg/2lb pike, cleaned and gutted
olive oil
butter
100g/4oz fat salt pork, diced
1 Spanish onion, chopped
4 carrots, chopped
8 shallots, finely chopped
2-4 garlic cloves, finely chopped
60ml/4 tbls cognac, warmed
1 bottle good red Burgundy
salt and freshly ground black pepper
1 bouquet garni (1 sprig of thyme, 1 bay leaf, 1 sprig
*   of parsley, celery stalk and 1 sprig of rosemary)*
1 strip of lemon peel
1.5ml/¼ tsp dried basil
12 button onions
12 button mushrooms
30ml/2 tbls flour
lemon juice
fried croûtons
finely chopped parsley

1. Clean and skin eel and cut into 5cm/2in serving pieces. Your fishmonger, from whom you will have to order the eel in advance, can do this for you. Cut cleaned carp and pike into 5cm/2in serving pieces. Sauté eel, carp and pike pieces separately in equal parts olive oil and butter until golden on all sides. Remove from pan.
2. In the same pan sauté diced fat salt pork, chopped onion and carrots, finely chopped shallots and garlic cloves in a little olive oil until vegetables begin to take on a little colour.
3. Return fish pieces to pan; add warmed cognac and flame, shaking pan gently until the flames die down. Transfer contents of pan to a thick-bottomed saucepan; add red Burgundy and enough water to just cover fish. Season with salt and freshly ground black pepper, to taste. Add *bouquet garni*, strip of lemon peel and dried basil and poach fish pieces gently until just tender. Remove fish pieces and diced salt pork from pan. Keep warm. Strain liquid through a fine sieve. Reserve.
4. Simmer onions in a little of the reserved cooking liquid. Sauté mushrooms in a little butter flavoured with lemon juice.
5. Meanwhile, melt 60ml/4 tbls butter in a thick-bottomed casserole and make a pale roux by adding the flour. Cook roux for a few minutes, stirring constantly, without allowing it to take on colour. Then add the remaining reserved cooking liquid and cook over a low heat, stirring from time to time, to make a slightly thickened sauce.
6. Add fish pieces and diced pork to casserole together with cooked button onions and mushrooms. To finish dish, stir in 30ml/2 tbls butter and serve very hot, garnished with fried *croûtons* and finely chopped parsley.

MATELOTE DE BROCHET AU VIN ROSÉ

SERVES 4-6

2 fresh pike, 700g/1½lb each, cleaned and gutted
butter
30ml/2 tbls olive oil
50ml/2 fl oz Mirabelle, warmed
4 shallots, finely chopped
1 bay leaf, crumbled
salt and freshly ground black pepper
½ bottle of dry vin rosé
1 bouquet garni (1 sprig of thyme, 1 bay leaf, 1 sprig
*   of parsley, celery stalk and 1 sprig of rosemary)*
30ml/2 tbls flour
150ml/¼pt double cream
100/4oz button mushrooms, finely sliced and
*   sautéed in butter*
fried croûtons

1. Cut pike into thick serving pieces. Heat 60ml/4 tbls butter and the olive oil in a thick-bottomed saucepan large enough to take fish pieces in one layer, and sauté until golden.
2. Pour Mirabelle over fish pieces and flame. When flames have died down, add finely chopped shallots and crumbled bay leaf. Season with salt and freshly ground black pepper, to taste. Cover and allow to 'sweat' over a low heat for a few minutes. Add dry *vin rosé*, *bouquet garni* and enough water to just cover fish pieces, and allow to simmer gently, uncovered, until fish flakes easily with a fork. Remove fish from stock to a heated serving dish. Reserve stock and vegetables.
3. Melt 30ml/2 tbls butter in a saucepan and make a pale roux by adding the flour. Cook for a few minutes, stirring constantly, without roux taking on colour. Add reserved stock and vegetables and cook for 15 minutes until sauce is reduced and has thickened.
4. Just before serving, add double cream to sauce and correct seasoning. Strain hot sauce over fish pieces and garnish with finely sliced sautéed mushrooms and fried *croûtons*.

TURBOT A LA MARINIERE

SERVES 4

4 turbot fillets, about 225g/¹/₂lb each, skinned
4 carrots, thinly sliced
1 Spanish onion, thinly sliced
60ml/4 tbls finely chopped parsley
2 bay leaves
1 pinch of ground cinnamon
1 pinch of dried thyme
150ml/¹/₄pt dry white wine
150ml/¹/₄pt **Basic chicken stock** *(see page 66)*
60ml/4 tbls olive oil
450g/1lb potatoes, peeled and sliced
salt and freshly ground black pepper
melted butter
lemon juice

1. Combine thinly sliced carrots and onion, finely chopped parsley, bay leaves, ground cinnamon and dried thyme in a thick-bottomed casserole large enough to take turbot fillets in one layer. Add dry white wine, CHICKEN STOCK, 150ml/¹/₄pt water, olive oil and sliced potatoes to casserole; season generously with salt and freshly ground black pepper and cook over a high heat for 15 minutes.
2. Place turbot fillets carefully in the *court-bouillon* and simmer over a high heat until fish flakes easily with a fork (about 15 to 20 minutes).
3. Just before serving, stir in a little melted butter and a squeeze of lemon juice.

TURBOT AU CHAMPAGNE

SERVES 4

4 turbot fillets about 225g/¹/₂lb each, skinned
100g/4oz butter
30ml/2 tbls olive oil
2 shallots, finely chopped
100g/4oz button mushrooms, sliced
90ml/6 tbls reduced **Fish court-bouillon,** *made from fish trimmings (see page 110)*
¹/₂ quarter bottle of champagne
salt and white pepper
150ml/¹/₄pt double cream
15ml/1 tbls cornflour

1. Heat half the butter together with the olive oil in a thick-bottomed saucepan large enough to take turbot fillets in one layer, and sauté finely chopped shallots until transparent; add sliced mushrooms and continue cooking until tender. Remove from pan.
2. Add remaining butter to pan and sauté turbot fillets until lightly coloured on both sides. Return sautéed mushrooms and shallots to

Fillets of sole Bistro de Paris.

pan, together with half the fish stock and half the champagne, adding more champagne, if necessary, to barely cover the turbot fillets. Season with salt and white pepper, to taste, and simmer very gently for a few minutes until fillets are tender. Transfer turbot fillets to a heated serving dish. Keep warm.

3. Add double cream to the liquid in the pan and simmer, without boiling, until cream is warm.

4. Mix cornflour with a small amount of water; add to the sauce and cook, stirring constantly, over a very low heat, until sauce is smooth and rich.

5. When ready to serve, pour in remaining champagne; stir and mix with the sauce until warm. If you prefer a thicker sauce, use less champagne. Pour sauce over turbot fillets and serve immediately.

BAKED FISH ALBERT

SERVES 6-8

2 sea bass, 1-1.4kg/2-3lb each, or the eqivalent
weight of turbot or halibut, cleaned and gutted
6 medium-sized onions, finely chopped
4 garlic cloves, finely chopped
60ml/4 tbls each finely chopped parsley, chervil and
tarragon
150ml/¼pt dry white wine
30-60ml/2-4 tbls Pernod
60ml/4 tbls olive oil
1 large lemon, sliced thinly
butter
salt and freshly ground black pepper

1. Preheat oven to hot (230°C/450°F/gas 8).
2. Combine finely chopped onions, garlic cloves, parsley, chervil and tarragon with dry white wine, 150ml/¼pt water and Pernod.
3. Place prepared fish in a lightly buttered ovenproof baking dish large enough to take fish in one layer and moisten with olive oil.

Pour over wine and vegetable mixture. Cover fish with thin slices of lemon; dot with butter and season with salt and freshly ground black pepper, to taste.

4. Cover and bake fish in a preheated oven for 30 to 40 minutes, or until fish flakes easily with a fork, basting from time to time. If fish becomes too dry, add a little water and wine. Transfer fish to a heated serving platter and serve immediately.

SUPREME OF RED MULLET NICOISE

SERVES 4

4 fresh red mullet, filleted
butter
salt
cayenne pepper
dry white wine
Fish fumet *(see page 111)*
1 leek, white part only cut en julienne
4 tomatoes, peeled, seeded and chopped
300ml/½pt double cream
30ml/2 tbls butter
pinch of ground saffron

1. Preheat oven to moderate (180°C/350°F/gas 4).
2. Put fillets of red mullet in a well-buttered ovenproof baking dish large enough to take fish in one layer. Add salt to taste and a pinch of cayenne pepper; pour over equal parts dry white wine and FISH FUMET to cover and bake in preheated oven for 10 to 15 minutes. When fish is flaky but still moist, remove to another dish and keep warm in several spoonfuls of the stock.
3. Meanwhile, saute *julienne* strips of leek in butter until softened. Cook peeled, seeded and chopped tomatoes in a little butter, stirring frequently, until tomatoes are reduced to a purée.
4. Reduce remaining fish stock to half the original quantity with the *julienne* of leeks to add flavour, then add the double cream and to-

mato purée. When this mixture forms a smooth creamy emulsion, just thick enough to coat the back of a spoon, stir in 30ml/2 tbls melted butter, flavoured with a pinch of ground saffron. Heat through.

5. Transfer red mullet fillets to a heated serving dish and mask with the sauce. Serve immediately.

BOUILLABAISSE

Along the southern reaches of Provence – along the rocky coast from Marseilles to Monte Carlo – fish soup reigns supreme. If a meal in Provence doesn't start off with a refreshing appetiser salad, or a chilled *ratatouille,* you can almost be sure it will begin with a delicious fish soup –each of these traditional Provençal dishes lightly touched by the twin fingers of garlic and olive oil.

Deliciously fragrant *soupe de poissons* is made of tiny multi-coloured rock fish from the shores of the Mediterranean, each no longer than your finger, cooked with tomatoes, fennel, onions, garlic, olive oil and saffron and then pressed through a fine sieve to make a transluscent golden *bouillon* of high savour. This amber-tinted saffron-scented *bouillon* is not only a justly famous soup when served on its own with garlic-rubbed toasted *croûtons,* a richly flavoured *rouille* and freshly grated cheese, but it is the starting point for two other more glamorous fish soups – *la bourride* and *bouillabaisse.*

It is difficult to make a true *soupe de poissons* in this country because we do not have the little fish whose tender flesh and multiple bones give this authentic fish *bouillon* its inimitable flavour. Indeed purists are unanimous in saying that this famous trio of soups can only be made on this stretch of coast – and they go even further to say that the nearer you get to Marseilles, the better the soup.

I suggest that in the following recipes you use whatever small bony fish you find available in your local markets to capture sone of the warmth and flavour of Provence for your menus. I always add mussels, or winkles, a tiny raw crab or two if I can find them and a thick slice or two of conger eel to give flavour and body to the mix of brill, sea bass, *rouget,* monk fish, cod, or fresh haddock which must – by the very nature of things – make up our catch. And, for special occasions a small live lobster and five or six small clams.

LA BOUILLABAISSE 'MERE TERRATS'

SERVES 6

1.1kg/2½lb assorted fish and shellfish (at Mère
* Terrats famous restaurant just outside Cannes*
* they use rascasses, girelles, patacles, sarans,*
* perches, cleaned, and gutted, and small, thickly*
* sliced crabs and a large piece of congre*
olive oil
3 Spanish onions, finely chopped
2 stalks dried fennel
2 garlic cloves
6 tomatoes, coarsely chopped
1 bouquet garni (bay leaf, 2 sprigs parsley and
* thyme and 1 sprig rosemary)*
2.5-5ml/½-1 tsp ground saffron
2-3 small hot red peppers, diced
salt
3 new potatoes per person, sliced
1.8-2.3kg/4-5lb more important fish and shellfish,
* (1 small chapon, 1 pageot, 2 rascasses,*
* 1 galinette and 1 langouste)*
stale French bread (optional)
freshly grated Gruyère cheese (optional)

1. To make fish stock for *bouillabaisse:* choose 1.1kg/2½lb of fish and shellfish. It is exactly this selection of fish and shellfish that gives the 'fond' its individual *saveur.*

2. Pour 30ml/2 tbls olive oil per person into a thick-bottomed casserole; add finely chopped onions and dried fennel stalks and sauté until onions are transparent. Add garlic cloves, coarsely chopped tomatoes and *bouquet garni* and simmer until lightly browned. Add chosen fish and shellfish and continue to cook, stirring constantly, until fish begins to disintegrate.

3. Add 1.4L/2½pt water, ground saffron, hot red peppers, salt, to taste, and sliced potatoes. Bring to the boil; lower heat and simmer for 20 minutes. Remove sliced potatoes from pan and reserve. Strain *bouillon.* Pass fish and shellfish through a fine sieve.

4. Return *bouillon* and sliced potatoes to a clean pan and add fish and shellfish which you intend to serve in your *bouillabaisse.* Poach fish and shellfish for about 10 minutes, or until tender. Transfer sliced potatoes to a long serving dish; place fish and shellfish on top and moisten with a little stock.

5. Serve soup separately in a heated soup tureen. At Mère Terrats they always moisten a few slices of stale French bread with 5-10ml/1-2 tsp of the soup, then cover bread with freshly grated Gruyère cheese and brown in preheated oven (220°C/425°F/gas 7). ROUILLE (see page 123) – the red-coloured mayonnaise – is always served with *bouillabaisse* to give it 'body'.

BOUILLABAISSE FOR NORTHERN SEAS

SERVES 4-6 generously

450g/1lb eel, cleaned, skinned and cut in 5cm/2in
* lengths*
1kg/2lb fish (cod, haddock, sea bass, etc.),
* cleaned, gutted and cut into 5cm/2in lengths*
4 carrots, sliced
2 Spanish onions, sliced
4 garlic cloves, crushed
2 leeks, sliced
150ml/¼pt olive oil
4-6 tomatoes, peeled, seeded and chopped
1 bouquet garni
4-6 potatoes, peeled and sliced
600ml/1pt **Fish court-bouillon,** *made from fish*
* trimmings (see page 110)*
2.5ml/½ tsp ground saffron
salt and freshly ground black pepper
cayenne pepper
24 fresh mussels, washed, scraped and bearded
* (see page 144)*
1 small lobster, cut into serving pieces (optional)
garlic-flavoured croûtons
Rouille sauce *(see page 123)*

A selection of fish that will give a bouillabaisse its wonderfully individual flavour.

1. Place prepared carrots, onions, garlic cloves and leeks in a large thick-bottomed saucepan. Add olive oil and sauté until vegetables just begin to turn golden.
2. Add peeled, seeded and chopped tomatoes to vegetables, together with *bouquet garni,* eel and fish pieces and potato slices. Cook for about 6 minutes, stirring gently from time to time.
3. Add fish stock and enough water to just

121

cover fish. Season with ground saffron, salt, freshly ground black pepper and cayenne pepper to taste, and bring to the boil. Cook for 15 minutes. Add mussels and lobster pieces (if desired) and continue cooking until mussels open. Discard any that do not open.

4. Serve this wonderful dish as two courses: the amber-tinted soup first in a heated soup tureen, accompanied by garlic-flavoured *croûtons* and ROUILLE SAUCE, and the fish and potatoes immediately after the soup.

SOUPE DE POISSONS

SERVES 4-6

1.4kg/3lb assorted fish and shellfish chosen from 2 or more of the following: brill, sea bass, rouget, monk fish, cod or fresh haddock, cleaned and gutted and thickly sliced plus 600ml/1pt mussels, washed, scraped and bearded (see page 144)
2 Spanish onions, sliced
3-4 garlic cloves, chopped
1 bouquet garni (2 sprigs thyme, 2 bay leaves and 2-4 stalks dried fennel)
6 tomatoes, chopped
30ml/2 tbls tomato purée
2.5ml/1/2 tsp ground saffron
salt and freshly ground black pepper
cayenne pepper
olive oil
*300ml/1/2pt **Fish court-bouillon** (see page 110), or canned clam juice*
30ml/2 tbls Pernod (optional)
French bread, about 1.2cm/1/2in thick
cut garlic clove
***Rouille** (see page 123)*

1. Place thickly sliced fish, prepared mussels and conger eel in a porcelain or earthenware bowl (not metal) together with sliced onions, chopped garlic cloves, *bouquet garni,* chopped tomatoes, tomato purée, ground saffron, and salt, freshly ground black pepper and cayenne

pepper, to taste. Stir in 120ml/8 tbls olive oil, FISH COURT-BOUILLON, or clam juice, and Pernod, if desired. Marinate fish and shellfish in this mixture in the refrigerator for 6 to 8 hours, stirring once or twice to allow flavours to permeate flesh.

2. Meanwhile, preheat oven to fairly hot (220°C/425°F/gas 7).

3. Sprinkle slices of French bread with olive oil and bake in preheated oven for 5 minutes, or until dry. Rub with cut garlic clove and place in the bottom of a heated soup tureen. Keep warm.

4. Pour fish, shellfish and marinade juices together with 1L/2pt water into a thick-bottomed pan and bring rapidly to the boil; boil for 5 to 6 minutes. Pass *bouillon* and fish through a fine sieve and return to a clean pan. Correct seasoning. Bring to the boil again. Remove from heat and serve *soupe* immediately over slices of French bread and accompanied by ROUILLE.

SOUPE AIGO-SAU (PROVENCAL FISH SOUP WITH ROUILLE)

SERVES 4-6

1kg/2lb any firm white fish, cleaned and gutted
1 leek, chopped
1 Spanish onion, chopped
4 tomatoes, peeled, seeded and chopped
6 potatoes, peeled and cut in thick slices
salt and freshly ground black pepper
2 garlic cloves, crushed
2 sprigs of parsley
1 sprig of fennel
1 bay leaf
1 piece of lemon peel
*boiling water, or **Fish court-bouillon** made from fish trimmings (see page 110)*
French bread, sliced and rubbed with a cut clove of garlic
olive oil

ROUILLE SAUCE

2 fat garlic cloves
2 small dried hot red peppers
1/4 slice white bread, crusts removed, dipped in water and squeezed dry
30ml/2 tbls olive oil
150ml/1/4pt hot **Fish court-bouillon** *(see page 110)*

1. Cut prepared white fish into pieces of the same size.
2. Place fish pieces in a large thick-bottomed saucepan with chopped leek, onion and tomatoes, and sliced potatoes. Season generously with salt and freshly ground black pepper; add crushed garlic clove, parsley and fennel sprigs, bay leaf and lemon peel. Cover with boiling water or fish stock and cook over a high heat for 20 minutes. Transfer fish pieces and vegetables to a heated serving dish. Keep warm.
3. To serve, place slices of French bread in a soup tureen and sprinkle with a very little olive oil and freshly ground black pepper. Strain FISH COURT-BOUILLON over and serve separately. Follow with fish pieces and vegetables, served with a pungent rouille sauce.
4. To make rouille sauce: pound garlic cloves and hot red peppers in a mortar with bread. Blend to a smooth paste with olive oil and then thin this *pommade* to the consistency of thick cream with hot fish *bouillon*. This sauce is often served with *bouillabaisse*. (You will find an alternative recipe for ROUILLE SAUCE on page 87).

CREOLE CRAB GUMBO

SERVES 4-6

350g/3/4lb crabmeat, flaked
12 large cooked prawns, sliced
30ml/2 tbls butter
30ml/2 tbls olive oil
1 Spanish onion, chopped
1 small green pepper, seeded and chopped
30ml/2 tbls flour
300ml/1/2pt **Basic chicken stock,** *(see page 66)*
salt and freshly ground black pepper
1 bouquet garni (celery stalk, 1 sprig of parsley and 1 sprig of thyme)
1 garlic clove, finely chopped
1 small thin strip of lemon peel
dash of Tabasco
225g/8oz can okra, drained
800g/1-3/4lb can Italian peeled tomatoes, drained
300ml/1/2pt double cream

1. Combine butter and olive oil in a thick-bottomed saucepan and heat until butter has melted. Add chopped onion and green pepper and sauté until vegetables are tender.
2. Blend in flour and cook, stirring continuously, until thickened. Stir in CHICKEN STOCK, *bouquet garni,* finely chopped garlic clove, lemon peel and Tabasco. Stir in flaked crabmeat, sliced prawns, drained *okra* and tomatoes, and heat to boiling point. Season with salt and freshly ground black pepper, to taste, and simmer gently for 20-25 minutes.
3. Gradually stir in double cream and cook for a few minutes more over a medium heat, stirring gently until *gumbo* is heated through. Correct seasoning and remove *bouquet garni* and lemon peel. Serve in a heated soup tureen, or individual serving bowls.

NEW ENGLAND OYSTER STEW

SERVES 4

1L/2pt oysters, freshly opened
300ml/1/2pt milk
60ml/4 tbls melted butter
300ml/1/2pt double cream
salt and freshly ground black pepper
paprika

1. Strain oyster liquor from opened oysters, (approximately 450ml/¾pt,) into a thick-bottomed saucepan.

2. Wash oysters thoroughly to remove sand and grit. Add milk to oyster liquor and heat thoroughly, but do not allow mixture to come to the boil. Add oysters to pan and simmer gently for 3 to 5 minutes, until oysters become slightly firm, but not tough.

3. Stir melted butter and double cream into stew and season with salt, freshly ground black pepper and paprika, to taste. Cook for a few minutes more over a medium heat, stirring gently, until stew is heated through. Transfer to a heated soup tureen and serve immediately.

HAWAIIAN FISH CHOWDER

SERVES 4-6

1kg/2lb white fish, cleaned, gutted and cut into
* 2.5cm/1in cubes*
30ml/2 tbls olive oil
100g/¼lb fat salt pork, diced

1 Spanish onion, finely chopped
450g/1lb new potatoes, sliced
6 tomatoes, peeled, seeded and chopped
*425ml/¾pt boiling water, or well-flavoured **Fish***
* **court-bouillon** made from fish trimmings (see*
* page 110)*
450g/1lb fresh spinach, blanched, chopped and
* wilted in butter*
300ml/½pt double cream
salt and freshly ground black pepper

1. Heat olive oil in a thick-bottomed saucepan and sauté fat salt pork until golden. Remove and discard.

2. Add finely chopped onion and sauté in resulting fats until transparent. Add fish cubes, sliced potatoes and chopped tomatoes, and sauté for a minute or two more. Then add water, or FISH COURT-BOUILLON, and simmer for ½ hour, or until potatoes are tender.

3. Add wilted spinach and double cream to pan and cook for 3 minutes more. Season with salt and black pepper, to taste. Serve in a heated soup tureen, or individual soup bowls.

PROVENCAL AIOLI

A strange, soaring elation always grips me as I drive along the winding coastal road from St. Raphaël and first catch sight of the pink-shaded towers of St. Tropez across the glittering bay. There are certain places in the world for each of us – magic places where we immediately feel at home at first meeting – as if somehow, sometime, we had been there before. St. Tropez holds this magic for me.

Sheer good luck – unearned and unadorned – is as satisfying as it is exciting. St. Tropez is a case in point. I have watched its legend grow since the war and have often pondered on the pure chance that made millionaires out of simple folk I had come to know so well. Today, summer visitors flock to St. Tropez like migratory birds. How many of them realise, I wonder, that one of the best cooks in Provence can be found practically within arm's reach of the port?

Chez Fifine is a tiny restaurant on rue Suffren, with a kitchen and one small room containing five tables on the ground floor, a slightly larger dining-room upstairs, and a few tables placed strategically outside for the inevitable overflow. Fifine does all the cooking herself, aided by a kitchen staff of one; the service is carried out by family and friends – Josef, ex-fisherman and famous local *pétanque* champion, sometimes directs the activities of a team of personable young 'cousins' who wait on table. For those who demand *la grande cuisine,* an impressive décor and impeccable service, my advice is to stay away. For here the service is friendly but often erratic; there is no *cave* of select vintage wines; no flaming *spécialitiés de la maison,* no fuss, no bother; but the simple rustic dishes of Provence, lovingly prepared by Fifine, are sublime. All Provence is her domaine: fennel comes from the mountains behind the coast, wild thyme and rosemary from the neighbouring hills; the town's best fishermen arrive at her door several times a day with their latest catch; tomatoes are selected with care from the open-air vegetable market, fresh *basilic* from another.

Fifine loves and excels in the rustic dishes of Provence and the fruits of her private sea, the Gulf of St. Tropez. It was she who taught me the pleasures of the unknown local wines; the special richness of the pure olive oil of Provence; what fish to put into *bouillabaisse;* how to make an *aioli,* a *rouille,* a *tapénade.*

Aïoli, sometimes referred to as *le beurre de Provence,* was originally a sauce made of olive oil and crushed garlic, thickened with fresh breadcrumbs and mashed boiled potato. Today, the *liaison* of this famous sauce is almost always made with raw egg yolk, and modern *aïoli* is really a mayonnaise with a pungent garlic base.

Chez Fifine, *aïoli,* served *sur commande* only, and a masterpiece of presentation and high savour, features salt codfish and a medley of boiled vegetables – carrots, potatoes, bay marrows, French beans – also hard-boiled eggs, raw tomatoes and fresh herbs, served with a strong *aïoli* sauce from which the dish gets its name.

FIFINE'S AIOLI

SERVES 4-6

450g/1lb salt codfish
6 medium-sized potatoes in their jackets
6 small potatoes in their jackets
6 courgettes, topped and tailed
450g/1lb small carrots, peeled
450g/1lb French beans, topped and tailed
6 hard-boiled eggs, in their shells
6 large tomatoes

lettuce leaves
sprigs of fresh herbs (parsley, flat-leafed parsley,
    coriander leaves, basil, etc.)

AIOLI SAUCE
4 fat garlic cloves per person
salt
1 egg yolk for each 2 persons
olive oil
freshly ground black pepper
lemon juice

125

1. Soak salt codfish overnight in cold water. Drain.

2. Place salt codfish in a thick-bottomed saucepan; cover with cold water and bring to the boil. Drain and return to pan; cover with cold water and bring to the boil again. Turn off heat and allow to steep in hot water for 10 minutes. Do not overcook, or fish will toughen. Strain fish. Remove skin and bones and dice. Keep warm.

3. In separate saucepans of boiling salted water, cook potatoes in their jackets for 10–12 minutes, prepared courgettes for 7 minutes, peeled carrots for 10 minutes and prepared French beans for 4 minutes. All vegetables should be tender, but still quite firm, and on no account overcooked. Drain well.

4. Serve hot vegetables, hard-boiled eggs and raw tomatoes on a large serving dish decorated with lettuce leaves and sprigs of fresh herbs. Arrange salt fish in the centre of dish. For best effect, group well-drained vegetables by colour. Serve with aïoli sauce, from which this famous dish gets it name.

5. To make aïoli sauce: Crush garlic cloves to a smooth paste in a mortar with a little salt. Transfer to a large bowl and blend in egg yolks until mixture is a smooth homogeneous mass. Then, take olive oil and proceed (drop by drop at first, a thin fine trickle later) to whisk the mixture as you would for a MAYONNAISE (see page 85). The *aïoli* will thicken gradually until it reaches the proper stiff consistency. The exact quantity of oil is, of course, determined by the number of egg yolks used. Season to taste with additional salt, a little freshly ground black pepper and lemon juice. Chill aïoli sauce in refrigerator until ready to use. This sauce is served chilled in a bowl. Guests help themselves.

PORTUGUESE CODFISH

SERVES 6

450g/1lb salt cod fillets
90ml/6 tbls olive oil
60ml/4 tbls wine vinegar

ONION DRESSING
1 Spanish onion, finely chopped
90ml/6 tbls finely chopped parsley
90ml/6 tbls olive oil
30ml/2 tbls lemon juice
salt and freshly ground black pepper

1. Soak salt cod fillets overnight in cold water.
2. Drain fillets. Place in a thick-bottomed saucepan; cover with cold water and bring to the boil, turn off heat and allow to steep in hot water for 10 minutes. Drain fillets.
3. Sauté fillets gently in olive oil until golden. Remove from heat, pour wine vinegar over fillets and allow to stand for 5 minutes.
4. Transfer fish fillets to a heated serving dish and pour over onion dressing.
5. To make onion dressing: combine finely chopped onion and parsley with olive oil and lemon juice. Season with salt and black pepper, to taste, and whisk until well blended.

BRANDADE DE MORUE

SERVES 4-6

450g/1lb salt cod fillets
2 garlic cloves, crushed
90ml/6 tbls double cream
90ml/6 tbls olive oil
juice and grated rind of 1/2 lemon
freshly ground black pepper
toast triangles, fried in olive oil, or butter

Fifine's Aïoli features salt codfish and a medley of boiled vegetables served with aïoli sauce.

1. Soak cod fillets in cold water for at least 12 hours.

2. Drain fillets and place in a thick-bottomed saucepan; cover with cold water and bring to the boil. Drain and return to pan; cover with cold water and bring to the boil again. Turn off heat and allow to steep in hot water for 10 minutes. Drain and flake fish with a fork.

3. Place cod flakes in an electric blender or food processor with crushed garlic, 45ml/ 3 tbls double cream and 45ml/3 tbls olive oil and blend, adding equal quantities of double cream and olive oil alternately from time to time until the cream and oil are completely absorbed and the *brandade* has the consistency of mashed potatoes.

4. Simmer *brandade* in a *bain-marie* or in the top of a double saucepan; stir in lemon juice and grated lemon rind and season with freshly ground black pepper, to taste. *Brandade de morue* may be served hot or cold. If hot, place in a mound on a warm serving dish and surround with fried toast triangles.

NOTE: If *brandade* is too salty, blend in 1 or 2 boiled potatoes.

DELICES DE SOLE LUCAS CARTON

SERVES 6

3 soles, 450/550g/1-1¼lb each
½ chicken stock cube, crumbled
½ Spanish onion, finely chopped
2 sprigs of parsley
150g/6oz butter
90-120ml/6-8 tbls dry white wine
salt and freshly ground black pepper
2-4 very ripe tomatoes, peeled, seeded and chopped
50g/2oz white button mushrooms, cut in slivers
90-120ml/6-8 tbls double cream

1. Ask the fishmonger to fillet the sole, but ask him for the bones, head and fish trimmings to make a *fish fumet*. Soak fillets and bones in cold water for 1 hour.

2. To make *fish fumet,* cut bones into 4 or 5 pieces and simmer gently for a few minutes with fish heads and trimmings, ½ chicken stock cube, finely chopped onion, parsley sprigs and 30ml/2 tbls butter. Moisten with dry white wine and 90-120ml/6-8 tbls water. Bring to the boil, skim and simmer gently for 10-12 minutes. Strain *fumet.* Reserve.

3. Preheat oven to moderate (190°C/375°F/ gas 5).

4. Butter an ovenproof dish large enough to take the fillets in one layer and place the fillets in it. Season with salt and freshly ground black pepper, to taste.

5. Scatter peeled, seeded and chopped tomatoes over fish fillets together with slivers of mushrooms. Bring the *fumet* to the boil and pour over fish. Bring to the boil over a high heat, cover with buttered paper and bake in preheated oven for about 8-10 minutes, or until fish flakes easily with a fork. Transfer fillets to a heated serving dish. Keep warm.

6. Strain *fumet* into a thick-bottomed saucepan; stir in double cream and reduce over a high heat until the sauce is of the desired consistency. Place sauce in the top of a double saucepan over hot, but not boiling, water and gradually add remaining butter in little pieces, whisking sauce constantly as you would for a SAUCE HOLLANDAISE (see page 84). Do not let water under the pan come to the boil or you will curdle the sauce. Cover fish fillets with this sauce and serve immediately.

NOTE: At the Lucas Carton restaurant in Paris where this dish was created, they used to glaze the dish under a very hot grill for a few seconds just before serving.

FILETS DE SOLE BONNE FEMME

SERVES 4

2 soles, about 450g/1lb each
salt and freshly ground black pepper
butter
45ml/3 tbls finely chopped shallots
45ml/3 tbls finely chopped mushrooms
150ml/¼pt dry white wine
Fish court-bouillon, *made from fish trimmings*
  (see page 110)
1 bouquet garni (1 bay leaf, 1 sprig of thyme and
  4 sprigs of parsley)
12 button mushroom caps
15-30ml/1-2 tbls lemon juice
15ml/1 tbls flour

1. Ask your fishmonger to fillet the sole but keep heads, bones and trimmings for stock. Season fillets generously with salt and freshly ground black pepper and put them in the bottom of a buttered ovenproof baking dish large enough to take them in one layer. Sprinkle with finely chopped shallots and mushrooms and add half the dry white wine and just enough fish stock to cover fish.
2. Preheat oven to moderate (190°C/375°F/ gas 5).
3. Add *bouquet garni* and bring to the boil over a high heat. Cover with buttered paper and bake in preheated oven for 8-10 minutes or until fish flakes easily with a fork.
4. Meanwhile, sauté mushroom caps in 30ml/ 2 tbls butter flavoured with lemon juice until tender.
5. Preheat grill to high.
6. Transfer poached fillets to a heated serving dish and keep warm. Pour remaining fish liquor into a small saucepan, add remaining dry white wine and reduce over a brisk flame to half the original quantity. Thicken the sauce, if necessary, by whisking in a *beurre manié* (made by kneading 15ml/1 tbls butter and 15ml/1 tbls flour to a smooth paste). Bring

sauce to the boil and cook until it has the consistency of double cream.
7. Place 3 sautéed mushroom caps on each portion of sole, pour sauce over and glaze for a minute or two under preheated grill before serving.

CASSEROLETTES DE FILET DE SOLE 'LASSERRE'

SERVES 4

4 individual pastry shells, approximately
  9-10cm/3½in in diameter, baked blind
  (see page 26)
2 soles, about 450g/1lb each
1 egg white, beaten
butter
2 shallots, finely chopped
4 mushrooms stalks, finely chopped
salt and freshly ground black pepper
16 asparagus tips
8 button mushrooms, finely chopped
600ml/1pt hot **Béchamel sauce**
  (see page 80)
1 egg yolk

1. Preheat oven to hot (230°C/450°F/gas 8).
2. Brush bottoms of the pastry shells with a little egg white.
3. Remove fillets from sole, reserving the bones, and cut each fillet into 3 equal pieces. Arrange fish pieces in a well-buttered gratin dish. Sprinkle with chopped shallots and mushroom stalks, and season with salt and freshly ground black pepper, to taste. Cover with the fish bones. Cover dish with buttered paper and cook in preheated oven for 10 minutes.
4. Meanwhile, sauté asparagus tips in 30ml/ 2 tbls butter in a frying pan until heated through. Remove from pan, add another 30ml/2 tbls butter, and sauté chopped mushroom until tender.

5. Garnish the bottom of each baked pastry shell with finely chopped mushrooms and 4 asparagus tips. Remove fish from gratin dish and arrange in the pastry shells. Strain cooking liquid into a thick-bottomed saucepan.
6. Preheat grill to high.
7. Reduce cooking liquid from the sole to a few tablespoonsful and add it to the well-flavoured BECHAMEL SAUCE together with the egg yolk and 15ml/1 tbls butter. Spoon this sauce over fish pieces in pastry shells, using just enough of the sauce to fill shells and glaze under preheated grill until golden.

NOTE: Lasserre tops each *casserolette* with a glazed slice of truffle, sprinkles the dish with parsley and fixes a small pastry 'handle' to each tart to form a *casserolette,* or little casserole.

TROUT AMANDINE

SERVES 4-6

4-6 fresh trout, cleaned and gutted
salt and freshly ground black pepper
milk
flour
100g/4oz butter
30ml/2 tbls olive oil
60-90ml/4-6 tbls blanched slivered almonds
juice of ½ lemon
30-60ml/2-4 tbls parsley, finely chopped

1. Season cleaned trout with a little salt and freshly ground black pepper; dip in milk and then in flour, shaking off excess.
2. Heat half the butter and 30ml/2 tbls oil in a thick-bottomed frying pan and sauté the trout until golden brown on both sides. Transfer cooked trout to a heated serving dish.
3. Drain fat from pan. Melt remaining butter; add blanched slivered almonds and cook, shaking pan continuously until almonds are golden brown. Stir in lemon juice and finely

chopped parsley and pour the sauce over trout. Serve immediately.

TROUT PERE LOUIS

SERVES 4

4 fresh trout, cleaned and gutted
60ml/4 tbls butter
30ml/2 tbls olive oil
90-120ml/6-8 tbls double cream
15ml/1 tbls Grand Marnier
45ml/3 tbls cognac
salt and freshly ground black pepper
60-90ml/4 tbls sliced toasted almonds

1. Heat butter and olive oil in thick-bottomed frying pan and sauté cleaned trout until tender.
2. Meanwhile, heat double cream, without letting it come to the boil, in a thick-bottomed saucepan. Stir in Grand Marnier and cognac, and season with salt and freshly ground pepper to taste.
3. Transfer trout to a heated serving dish; pour over the sauce and sprinkle with sliced toasted almonds. Serve immediately.

CREAMED FINNAN HADDIE

SERVES 4-6

1kg/2lb smoked haddock
milk
45ml/3 tbls butter
45ml/3 tbls flour
425ml/¾pt double cream
2.5ml/¼ tsp ground turmeric
freshly ground black pepper
freshly grated nutmeg
triangles of bread, sautéed in butter

1. Soak haddock in water for 2 hours. Drain.
2. Put drained haddock in a thick-bottomed saucepan; cover with equal amounts of milk

and water and bring to a fast boil. Turn off heat and allow to stand for 15 minutes. Drain haddock and reserve stock.

3. Melt 45ml/3 tbls butter in the top of a double saucepan; stir in flour and cook for 3 minutes, stirring continuously until smooth. Add double cream, turmeric (for colour) and reserved 300ml/½pt haddock stock, and continue to cook, stirring from time to time. Season with freshly ground black pepper, to taste, and a little freshly grated nutmeg.

4. Remove skin and bones from haddock and break into pieces. Fold haddock pieces into sauce and simmer gently until ready to use. Serve in a shallow casserole surrounded by triangles of bread sautéed in butter.

CHINESE STEAMED FISH

SERVES 2

2 whiting, about 350g/¾lb each cleaned and
  gutted
100g/4oz button mushrooms
1 garlic clove, finely chopped
2 coarsely chopped spring onions, or 30ml/2 tbls
  coarsely chopped onion, or shallots
60ml/4 tbls olive oil
30ml/2 tbls soy sauce
15ml/1 tbls cornflour
30ml/2 tbls dry white wine
salt and freshly ground black pepper
Accompaniments: **Boiled rice** *(see page 179),*
  or boiled sliced carrots and courgettes

1. Place cleaned fish in a flat dish large enough to hold them both.
2. Slice mushrooms thinly and add to dish.
3. Combine finely chopped garlic and coarsely chopped spring onion (or onion, or shallots) with olive oil, soy sauce, cornflour and dry white wine. Season with salt and freshly ground black pepper, to taste. Mix well and pour over fish.

4. Place dish in a large steamer, or on a rack in a thick-bottomed saucepan wide enough to hold it, with about 2 inches of rapidly boiling water. Cover and steam for 15 minutes.
5. Transfer fish to a hot platter and serve immediately. BOILED RICE, or steamed sliced carrots, and courgettes should accompany this dish.

TRUITE AU VIN ROSE

SERVES 4

4 fresh trout, cleaned and gutted
butter
Vin rosé
4 shallots, finely chopped
150ml/¼pt **Sauce Hollandaise** *(see page 84)*
60ml/4 tbls hot double cream
salt and freshly ground black pepper
8 triangles white bread, sautéed in butter

1. Preheat oven to very slow (150°C/300°F/gas 2).
2. Place cleaned trout in a well-buttered ovenproof baking dish. Pour in *vin rosé* to cover; add finely chopped shallots and cover dish with buttered paper. Poach the fish in preheated oven for about 20 minutes, or until they are cooked through but still firm. Lay trout on a dry cloth and carefully remove skins. Keep warm.
3. Reduce the liquid in which the fish were poached until there remains only a small amount of slightly thickened sauce. Strain the sauce into the top of a double saucepan and add SAUCE HOLLANDAISE. Whisk in hot double cream and season with salt and freshly ground black pepper, to taste. Keep warm over hot, but not bubbling water.
4. Arrange the trout on a heated serving dish; spoon the sauce over the fish and serve immediately garnished with triangles of bread sautéed in butter.

CHAPTER 6

SHELLFISH

LOBSTER A L'AMERICAINE

T HEY ARE FISHING the Mediterranean dry. Voracious hordes of tourists are taking their toll on the sea itself, as well as despoiling the coastline of Southern France. This year, even in the fishing ports, local fish cost more than those brought overland a thousand miles from the Atlantic.

At the end of the war the rocky coves of the Riviera were filled with lobsters. But year by year the French have had to go farther afield to catch them, until now they have virtually deserted the shores of metropolitan France and are to be found in great numbers only off the coast of Corsica.

I think the reason the French are eating up their sources of lobster so quickly is that they are not content just to boil them and serve them with mayonnaise or a *sauce verte* as we do in this country. The English have a fixation about the perfection of their raw materials which makes them shy of masking their true flavours. But even the most perfect raw material can be enhanced by skilful blending with other flavours that will develop its subtlety and draw out its delicacy. This is what the French have done with lobster *à l'américaine*, one of the truly great dishes of the world – sometimes described as lobster *à l'armoricaine*, on menus throughout France.

There are two schools of thought on the lobster argument: certain food snobs claim that the spelling is *à l'armoricaine*, because *armor* was the old Breton name for sea and Brittany was at one time called *Armorica;* according to them, there was no other part of France where you could get better lobsters and so France's greatest lobster dish was at once baptised *à l'armoricaine*. Any other version of this name, they decided, was only a mistake in spelling. The other school of purists claim that

Whether you like to term it Lobster à l'Américaine or à l'Armoricaine, you'll find this world-famous *dish is a culinary drama that is guaranteed to make your name as a cook/host or hostess.*

132

this dish could not be Breton because of its use of garlic, tomatoes and cognac in the recipe, and that it most nearly resembled lobster cooked in the Provençal manner of Southern France. They called the dish lobster *à l'américaine,* not because the dish was of American extraction, but because it was created by Pierre Graisse, a Parisian chef recently returned from America, who, following the current vogue for all things American, called his restaurant Peter's and named this dish, his creation, lobster *à l'américaine.*

Legend has it that one evening when the dinner hour was well and truly over, and Pierre-Peter was getting ready to close up for the night, a party of guests entered his restaurant and insisted that he serve them dinner. The chef decided that if they had soup and hors-d'oeuvre, he would just have time to prepare a fish dish for them. But on looking into the depleted stores of the restaurant, he discovered that there was no fish left, just some live lobsters ready for the following morning. He chopped some onions, garlic and shallots, sautéed them gently in butter and olive oil, added tomatoes, fish stock and some dry white wine and, when the sauce was bubbling, cut up the lobsters and cooked them in the highly-spiced sauce. The result surpassed all expectations and one of the world's most famous dishes was born . . . the product of a moment of necessity and the inspiration of a great cook.

LOBSTER A L'AMERICAINE

SERVES 4-6

2 live lobsters, 1kg/2lb each
135ml/9 tbls butter
150ml/¼pt olive oil
2 carrots, finely chopped
2 small onions, finely chopped
2 shallots, finely chopped
2 garlic cloves, finely chopped
150ml/¼pt dry white wine
60-90ml/4-6 tbls cognac, warmed
400g/14oz canned Italian tomatoes
30ml/2 tbls tomato purée
1 bay leaf
150ml/¼pt well-flavoured **Fish court-bouillon**
  (see page 110)

salt and freshly ground black pepper
15ml/1 tbls flour
lemon juice
cayenne pepper
finely chopped parsley, chives and tarragon
Boiled rice (see page 179) or **Rice pilaff**
  (see page 301)

1. Drop live lobsters into hot water and bring to the boil so that they lose consciousness and die painlessly. Boil for 1 minute. Drain. Allow to cool for a few minutes.
2. Working over a shallow bowl to catch juices, break off and crack claws. Cut each lobster tail into thick slices. Cut body shells in half; remove and discard the intestinal tube which is exposed when the body of the lobster

is cut open; reserve coral and all the juices left in the bowl.

3. Combine 45ml/3 tbls butter and 45ml/3 tbls olive oil in a thick-bottomed frying pan; add lobster pieces and sauté for 3 minutes, stirring occasionally. Reserve.

4. Heat 75ml/5 tbls butter and the remaining olive oil in a thick-bottomed saucepan and sauté finely chopped carrots, onions, shallots and garlic until onion is transparent. Place lobster pieces on the aromatic bed of vegetables, pour over the white wine and simmer for 3 minutes. Pour over warmed cognac and flame. Add canned tomatoes, tomato purée, bay leaf, reserved lobster liquids and FISH STOCK to the pan. Season with salt and freshly ground black pepper, to taste. Cover the pan and simmer for 15 minutes. Remove lobster pieces. Keep warm.

5. Simmer tomato sauce, uncovered, until slightly reduced.

6. Meanwhile, cream coral with a *beurre manié,* made by mashing together 15ml/1 tbls each flour and butter into a smooth paste. Whisk into the sauce and simmer until thickened. Strain sauce into a clean pan. Flavour with lemon juice, salt, freshly ground black pepper and cayenne pepper, to taste. Add lobster pieces and juices from pan in which lobsters were cooked and heat through.

7. Just before serving, sprinkle with finely chopped parsley, chives and tarragon. Serve hot with BOILED RICE or RICE PILAFF.

BOILED LOBSTER

One of the best ways to appreciate a sweet, firm lobster, full of the clean taste of the sea, is to eat it freshly boiled. So if a fresh, live lobster comes your way, the best method of cooking is to plunge it into a simple *court-bouillon* (water, salt, freshly ground black pepper, bay leaf and thyme) and poach it for 5 minutes per 450g/1lb. Remember that the most common error in preparing lobster, and all fish or

shellfish for that matter, is overcooking.

When the lobster is cooked, allow it to cool in the *court-bouillon;* then remove it, place it on its back on a chopping block and split it lengthwise down the middle with a heavy French knife, or kitchen cleaver. Give the knife, or cleaver, a quick blow with a hammer or mallet so that the shell and meat are severed at the same time; remove the stomach, intestines and the dark vein that runs through the body at the centre. But do not throw away the greyish-green liver or coral-coloured roe: they are delicacies. Crack the claws so that the meat can be easily extracted and serve the lobster hot with melted butter and lemon wedges, or cold with freshly-made MAYONNAISE (see page 85).

GRILLED LOBSTER

Grilling a lobster takes a delicate touch. Its succulence depends on many things: the freshness of the lobster, its size, the heat of the grill and above all, of course, your own judgement. Split the live lobster down through the middle of the body and the tail; remove the roe (black when it is uncooked) and the dark vein that runs through the tail. Grill lobster halves under a preheated grill for 8–10 minutes on the shell side; turn over, spread with softened butter and grill for 6–8 minutes on the flesh side.

Garnish with paprika and melted butter to which a little lemon juice has been added. Serve with additional melted butter.

GRILLED LOBSTER WITH SHERRY

SERVES 4

2 live lobsters, 700-900g/1 1/2-2lb each
salt and freshly ground black pepper
120ml/8 tbls butter
60ml/4 tbls dry sherry
cayenne pepper
paprika
olive oil

1. Plunge lobster in hot water to which you have added salt and a generous amount of freshly ground black pepper, and bring gently to the boil. Boil for 1 minute. Drain. Split lobster lengthwise down the middle.
2. Preheat grill to high.
3. Melt butter gently in a thick-bottomed saucepan, add dry sherry and season with cayenne and paprika, to taste.
4. When ready to grill, brush grid of grill pan with a little olive oil. Place lobster halves on grid and grill on the shell side for 8 to 10 minutes. Turn over, pour over sauce and grill for another 6 to 8 minutes. Transfer lobster halves to a heated platter and serve immediately.

LOBSTER NEWBURG

SERVES 4-6

*4 small **Boiled lobsters** (see page 135)*
60ml/4 tbls butter
60ml/4 tbls cognac, warmed
2 egg yolks, beaten
300ml/¹⁄₂pt double cream
salt and freshly ground black pepper
cayenne pepper and paprika
***Boiled rice** (see page 179) or individual*
   vol-au-vent cases

1. Split cooked lobsters in half lengthwise. Crack claws. Remove lobster meat from the shells and cut into large cubes. Reserve the shells.
2. Heat butter and sauté lobster cubes for a few minutes. Add warmed cognac and flame. Reserve.
3. Combine beaten egg yolks and double cream in the top of a double saucepan and cook, stirring continuously with a wooden spoon, until the mixture coats the back of the spoon. Add lobster cubes and pan juices and heat through, taking care that the sauce does not curdle. Season with salt and freshly ground black pepper,

cayenne pepper and paprika, to taste.
4. Serve lobster Newburg in the half shells, on a bed of BOILED RICE or in individual *vol-au-vent* cases.

QUICK LOBSTER THERMIDOR

SERVES 4

*4 small **Boiled lobsters** (see page 135)*
*450ml/³⁄₄pt rich **Cream sauce** (see page 80)*
dry sherry
5ml/1 tsp dry mustard
cayenne pepper
Worcestershire sauce
salt and freshly ground black pepper
60-90ml/4-6 tbls freshly grated Parmesan cheese
paprika
butter

1. Cut cooked lobsters in half lengthwise. Crack claws. Remove lobster meat from the shells and cut into large cubes. Reserve the shells.
2. Preheat grill to high.
3. Heat CREAM SAUCE; season with a little dry sherry, dry mustard, cayenne pepper, Worcestershire sauce, salt and freshly ground black pepper, to taste. Simmer gently for 2 minutes; add lobster cubes and heat through.
4. Fill half shells with mixture. Sprinkle with grated Parmesan cheese, dust with paprika, dot with butter and brown under grill. Transfer to a heated platter and serve immediately.

LOBSTER AU GRATIN

SERVES 4

2 live lobsters about 700-900g/1¹⁄₂-2lb each
45ml/3 tbls butter
30ml/2 tbls olive oil
1 carrot, finely chopped
1 Spanish onion, finely chopped

1 celery stalk, finely chopped
1 bay leaf
pinch of dried thyme
salt and freshly ground black pepper
90ml/6 tbls cognac, warmed
150ml/¼pt dry white wine
cayenne pepper
225ml/½lb button mushrooms, sliced
1 large truffle, diced
150ml/¼pt double cream
300ml/½pt **Béchamel sauce** *(see page 80)*
30-60ml/2-4 tbls freshly grated Gruyère cheese
Crescents of flaky pastry *(see page 347)*

1. Split lobsters in half lengthwise and remove creamy parts.
2. Heat 30ml/2 tbls butter and olive oil in a thick-bottomed frying pan, sauté lobster halves for 3 minutes on each side, then remove from pan.
3. Add 15ml/1 tbls butter to pan and sauté finely chopped carrot, onion and celery stalk, together with bay leaf and thyme, until soft. Season with salt and freshly ground black pepper, to taste. Place lobster halves on top of this mixture and sauté for 1 minute more. Flame with cognac, shaking pan until the flames die out.
4. Pour over the dry white wine. Season with salt, freshly ground black pepper and cayenne pepper, to taste. Cover pan and simmer gently for 20 minutes.
5. When cooked, remove lobster halves from pan; remove meat from shells and dice coarsely.
6. Add sliced mushrooms and diced truffle to vegetable mixture in pan. Stir in double cream and simmer over the lowest heat possible until well blended.
7. Preheat grill to high.
8. In another pan, combine BÉCHAMEL SAUCE with diced lobster; correct seasoning and bring to the boil. Remove from heat and combine with creamed vegetable mixture.

9. Pour lobster and vegetable mixture into a well-buttered gratin dish. Sprinkle with grated Gruyère cheese, dot with little knobs of the remaining butter and grill until golden. Serve very hot garnished with CRESCENTS OF FLAKY PASTRY.

GREEN LOBSTER SALAD

SERVES 6

1 **Boiled lobster,** *700-900g/1½lb-2lb (see page 135)*
150ml/¼pt well-flavoured **Mayonnaise** *(see page 85)*
90ml/6 tbls cold **Puréed spinach** *(see page 277)*
salt and freshly ground black pepper
cayenne pepper
juice of 2 lemons
3 ripe avocado pears
½ cucumber, peeled, seeded and diced
2 hard-boiled eggs, diced
finely chopped tarragon, chives and parsley

1. Split cooked lobster in half lengthwise. Remove lobster meat from shells and dice.
2. Make a *sauce verte* by combining well-flavoured MAYONNAISE with puréed spinach. Season with salt, freshly ground black pepper and cayenne pepper, to taste, and a little lemon juice. Strain mayonnaise through a fine sieve.
3. Slice avocado pears in half; score the flesh with a sharp knife in even-sized segments about 6mm/¼in square, cutting down to the skin. Be careful not to pierce avocado skin with knife while doing so. Remove avocado segments carefully with a spoon; dice segments, marinate in lemon juice for 30 minutes. Brush inside avocado shells with lemon juice and reserve.
4. Drain diced avocado and combine with peeled, seeded and diced cucumber, lobster and hard-boiled eggs. Add *sauce verte;* toss carefully and fill avocado shells with this mixture. Chill.

5. Just before serving, sprinkle each filled avocado shell with finely chopped tarragon, chives and parsley.

AMERICAN CRAB SALAD – I

SERVES 4

450g/1lb cold cooked crabmeat, flaked
150ml/¼pt double cream, whipped
30ml/2 tbls tomato ketchup, or American chilli
  sauce
30ml/2 tbls grated onion
½ medium green pepper, seeded and finely chopped
60ml/4 tbls finely chopped stoned green olives
30ml/2 tbls finely chopped parsley
15-30ml/1-2 tbls lemon juice
salt and freshly ground black pepper
cayenne pepper
4 large tomatoes, halved and seeded
crisp lettuce leaves, washed
2 sliced hard-boiled eggs

1. Combine double cream, tomato ketchup or chilli sauce, grated onion, finely chopped green pepper, green olives, parsley and lemon juice. Add flaked crabmeat and season with salt, freshly ground black pepper and cayenne pepper, to taste. Mix well.·
2. Place tomato halves on 4 individual plates; pile crab salad on tomatoes and garnish each dish with lettuce leaves and sliced hard-boiled eggs.

AMERICAN CRAB SALAD – II

SERVES 4

450g/1lb cold cooked crabmeat, flaked
2 celery stalks, finely chopped
30ml/2 tbls finely chopped canned pimento
juice of 1 lemon
dry mustard
salt and freshly ground black pepper

cayenne pepper
*150ml/¼pt well-flavoured **Mayonnaise** (see page 85)*
lettuce leaves
4 tomatoes, quartered
2 hard-boiled eggs, quartered
8 black olives
finely chopped parsley

1. Combine lightly the flaked crabmeat with finely chopped celery and pimento. Season with lemon juice, a little dry mustard, salt, freshly ground black pepper and cayenne pepper, to taste. Bind the salad with half the well-flavoured MAYONNAISE.
2. Arrange lettuce leaves on 4 individual plates; pile crab salad on lettuce leaves and garnish with quarters tomatoes, quartered hard-boiled eggs and black olives. Top with a little MAYONNAISE and dust with finely chopped parsley.

BAKED AVOCADO WITH CRAB AURORE

SERVES 4

450g/1lb cooked crabmeat, flaked
*600ml/1pt **Béchamel sauce** (see page 80)*
30-45ml/2-3 tbls tomato purée
30ml/2 tbls grated onion
30ml/2 tbls butter
15ml/1 tbls curry powder
2 ripe avocado pears
salt
juice of 1 lemon

1. Preheat oven to moderate (180°C/350°F/gas 4).
2. To the BECHAMEL SAUCE add 30ml/2 tbls tomato purée. Mix well then add 30ml/2 tbls each of grated onion and butter. Add curry powder, and a little more tomato purée, if sauce is not a light pink colour. Fold in flaked

crabmeat and heat mixture just to boiling point, but do not let it boil.

3. Halve 2 avocado pears lengthwise; remove the stones and score flesh with a knife. Sprinkle with salt and lemon juice to preserve colour.

4. Pile avocado halves high with crabmeat mixture and arrange in an ovenproof baking dish. Add 5cm/1in boiling water.

5. Cover dish with aluminium foil and bake in preheated oven for about 20 minutes. Serve immediately.

AVOCADO CRAB SALAD

SERVES 4

450g/1lb cooked crabmeat, flaked
*150ml/¼pt well-flavoured **Mayonnaise** (see page 85)*
150ml/¼pt double cream, whipped
15-30ml/1-2 tbls grated onion
60-90ml/4-6 tbls American chilli sauce, or tomato ketchup, flavoured with a little Tabasco
salt and freshly ground black pepper
2 ripe avocado pears
juice of 2 lemons

1. Combine flaked crabmeat with well-flavoured MAYONNAISE, whipped cream, grated onion and chilli sauce, or tomato ketchup. Season with salt and freshly ground black pepper, to taste. Chill.

2. Slice ripe avocado pears in half; remove the stones and score the flesh with a sharp knife in even-sized segments about 6mm/¼in square, cutting down to the skin. Be careful not to pierce avocado skins with the knife while doing so. Remove avocado segments carefully with a spoon; dice segments and marinate them in lemon juice for 30 minutes. Brush inside of avocado shells with lemon juice to preserve colour. Reserve.

3. Combine crabmeat salad with diced avocado segments, adding more MAYONNAISE, or

lemon juice, if necessary. Correct seasoning. Fill avocado shells with this mixture and serve.

DEVILLED CRAB

SERVES 4

450g/1lb cooked crabmeat, flaked
60ml/4 tbls butter
60ml/4 tbls flour
450ml/¾pt hot milk
4 hard-boiled eggs, chopped
15ml/1 tbls Dijon mustard
5ml/1 tsp dry mustard
15-30ml/1-2 tbls Worcestershire sauce
30ml/2 tbls finely chopped parsley
30ml/2 tbls finely chopped onion
30ml/2 tbls finely chopped green pepper
salt and freshly ground black pepper
cayenne pepper
30-60ml/2-4 tbls freshly grated Parmesan cheese

1. Preheat oven to hot (230°C/450°F/gas 8).

2. Melt butter in the top of a double saucepan and make a pale roux by adding flour. Cook roux for a few minutes, stirring continuously, without allowing it to take on colour. Then add hot milk gradually, stirring continuously, until sauce begins to thicken. Stir in chopped hard-boiled eggs, mustards, Worcestershire sauce, finely chopped parsley, onion and green pepper. Simmer sauce, stirring from time to time, until thickened.

3. Add flaked crabmeat to sauce, stirring gently so as not to break meat. Season with salt, freshly ground black pepper and cayenne pepper, to taste.

4. Fill 4 crab shells or individual ovenproof dishes, with crab mixture. Sprinkle tops with freshly grated Parmesan cheese and bake in preheated oven for 20 minutes. Serve immediately.

CRAB TART

SERVES 4-6

Fingertip pastry for 20cm/8in pastry case (see page 347)
1 egg white, beaten
30ml/2 tbls butter
225g/¹/₂lb cooked crabmeat, flaked
30ml/2 tbls finely chopped parsley
30ml/2 tbls dry sherry
4 egg yolks
300ml/¹/₂pt single cream
salt and freshly ground black pepper
freshly grated nutmeg

1. Preheat oven to moderately hot (200°C/ 400°F/gas 6).
2. Line pie tin with FINGERTIP PASTRY. Prick bottom with a fork and chill in the refrigerator for 30 minutes. Bake blind (see page 26) in preheated oven for 10 minutes. Remove from oven and allow to cool. Brush bottom of pastry case with beaten egg white. Lower oven temperature to moderate (190°C/375°F/gas 5).
3. Melt the butter in a thick-bottomed pan and sauté crabmeat and finely chopped parsley. Sprinkle with dry sherry and spoon mixture over the bottom of pastry shell.
4. Whisk egg yolks; add cream and whisk again until thick and lemon-coloured. Season with salt and black pepper, to taste, and a little nutmeg. Pour mixture over the crabmeat and bake for about 30 minutes, or until set.

CURRIED CRAB PANCAKES

SERVES 8

PANCAKES
100g/4oz flour
15ml/1 tbls sugar
generous pinch of salt
2 eggs
2 egg yolks

450ml/³/₄pt milk
30ml/2 tbls melted butter
30ml/2 tbls cognac
butter, for frying

CRAB FILLING
450g/1lb cooked crabmeat, flaked
100g/4oz butter
1 apple, peeled, cored and sliced
4 shallots, finely chopped
15ml/1 tbls curry powder
5 ml/1 tsp crushed coriander seeds
15ml/1 tbls flour
milk
450ml/³/₄pt well-flavoured **Béchamel sauce** (see page 80)
lemon juice
salt and freshly ground black pepper

FOR THE GLAZE
butter
grated Parmesan cheese

1. To make pancake batter, sift together flour, sugar and salt. Beat together whole eggs and egg yolks and add them to the dry ingredients. Mix in the milk, melted butter and cognac until smooth. Strain through a fine sieve and let batter stand for at least 2 hours before cooking the pancakes. Batter should be as thin as cream.
2. For each pancake, melt 5ml/1 tsp butter in a small, thick-bottomed frying pan 15-20cm/ 6-8in in diameter; add about 30ml/2 tbls batter, swirling pan to allow batter to cover entire bottom of pan thinly; brush a piece of butter around edge of hot pan with the point of a knife and cook pancake over a medium heat until just golden, not brown – about 1 minute

What could be more delicious than a succulent fresh grilled lobster, surely one of the simplest, yet most luxurious dishes in the world.

on each side. This mixture makes 20 to 24 thin golden pancakes.

3. Preheat grill to high.

4. To make filling, melt butter in a thick-bottomed saucepan and sauté sliced apple and chopped shallots until they are soft. Add curry powder, coriander and flour. Mix well. Add just enough milk to make a thick paste. Stir well-flavoured BECHAMEL SAUCE into mixture

and season with lemon juice, salt and freshly ground black pepper, to taste. Add crabmeat to mixture, stirring gently, and heat through.

5. Fill pancakes with crabmeat mixture and place in a buttered baking dish; dot with butter and sprinkle with a little grated Parmesan cheese. Glaze pancakes under preheated grill for a few minutes.

OYSTERS

The Roman Emperor Tiberius is said to have lived on oysters practically all his life. Now I am not suggesting you follow suit, but a plate of fresh oysters from Colchester or Whitstable, served on ice with freshly ground black pepper and a wedge or two of lemon, is hard to beat.

It is very easy to tell a good oyster from a bad one. The shells of live oysters are tightly closed; those of dead oysters are usually, though not always, a little open. If tapping the shell produces a hollow sound within, it is very likely dead.

Oysters are a fine choice for a late-night supper party, either served on ice with piping hot tiny sausages as they do in Northern France; deep-fried in hot oil and butter and served with wedges of lemon, or, if you must, a little *sauce tartare;* or, perhaps my favourite of all, the New Orleans recipe for oysters Rockefeller, so named because the luscious Pernod and herb-flavoured butter sauce makes them 'as rich as Rockefeller'.

OYSTERS ROCKEFELLER

SERVES 4

24 freshly opened oysters
225g/½lb butter
90ml/6 tbls finely chopped shallots
60ml/4 tbls fresh breadcrumbs
1 bunch watercress, washed and stemmed

60ml/4 tbls finely chopped celery leaves
60ml/4 tbls finely chopped parsley
5ml/1 tsp finely chopped chervil
5 ml/1 tsp finely chopped tarragon
60ml/4 tbls Pernod
salt and freshly ground black pepper
cayenne pepper
rock salt

1. Preheat oven to hot (230°C/450°F/gas 8).

2. Heat 60ml/4 tbls butter and sauté finely chopped shallots until transparent; add breadcrumbs and stir over a low heat until lightly browned.

3. Finely chop watercress leaves, add chopped celery leaves and parsley, and combine with shallots and breadcrumb mixture in a large bowl, or mortar. Add finely chopped chervil and tarragon and Pernod. Season with salt, freshly ground black pepper and cayenne pepper, to taste. Add the remaining butter to bowl or mortar and pound to a smooth paste. Keep cool until ready to use.

4. Place a bed of rock salt in an ovenproof baking dish large enough to hold the oysters comfortably, or in 4 small ovenproof dishes; damp salt slightly and placed open oysters on this bed. Place 15ml/1 tbls green herb butter on each oyster and bake in preheated oven for 4–5 minutes or until butter has melted and oysters are heated through. Serve immediately.

FRIED OYSTERS

SERVES 4-6

2-3 dozen oysters
2 eggs, beaten
120ml/8 tbls double cream
salt and freshly ground black pepper
cornmeal, biscuit crumbs, or fresh breadcrumbs
100g/4oz butter
150ml/¹/4pt olive oil
lemon wedges

1. Shell oysters.

2. In a bowl, combine beaten eggs and cream. Add salt and freshly ground black pepper, to taste.

3. Dip oysters in egg and cream mixture, then in cornmeal or crumbs, shaking off excess, and allow to set on aluminium foil for about 10 minutes before cooking.

4. Melt butter in thick-bottomed frying pan, or deep-fryer. Add olive oil; bring to frying temperature and cook oysters in fats until they are golden brown. Drain oysters on absorbent paper and serve immediately with wedges of lemon.

OLD ENGLISH STEW'D OYSTERS

SERVES 4

600ml/1pt shelled oysters and their liquor
1 bay leaf
60ml/4 tbls butter
5ml/1 tsp Worcestershire sauce
salt
cayenne pepper
1.5ml/¹/4 tsp ground paprika
300ml/¹/2pt hot milk
300 ml/¹/2pt double cream, warmed
30-60ml/2-4 tbls dry sherry
freshly grated nutmeg

1. Place shelled oysters and their liquor in a thick-bottomed saucepan with bay leaf, butter and Worcestershire sauce. Season with salt and cayenne pepper, to taste; add paprika and simmer gently until oyster edges just begin to curl.

2. Remove bay leaf from pan and add heated milk and cream. Stir once; bring to simmering point again and add dry sherry. Correct seasoning and pour stewed oysters into individual serving bowls. Dust each bowl with a little freshly grated nutmeg and serve immediately.

MOULES MARINIERE

I have never seen a mussel growing on the Mediterranean coast, yet I can hardly remember a restaurant there that does not make a speciality of some delicious way of serving mussels. There are vast quantities of mussels along the cliffs of Cornwall, but how many of the local restaurants serve even the simplest mussel dish?

Moules marinière – one of the world's great dishes – makes the most of mussels, simmered for 10 minutes only in dry white wine with finely chopped shallots or a small onion or two and a little parsley and thyme. Make this simple and inexpensive dish your own. And then, using this same basic recipe, prepare mussels in any number of ways for a delicious first course or for a light luncheon or supper dish.

Try mussels *en brochette,* first simmered in dry white wine with aromatics, then stripped of their shells, rolled in egg yolk and breadcrumbs, slipped on metal skewers alternately with cubes of fat green bacon, and grilled until delicately brown. Or, more simply, fry egg-and-breadcrumbed mussels in deep fat until golden, and serve with lemon wedges or *sauce tartare.* I like mussels, too, prepared as above and folded into a creamy omelette; as the sea-rich savour of an Italian spaghetti sauce; or served in the half-shell with a cheese or garlic butter dressing.

TO CLEAN MUSSELS Always buy more mussels than the recipe calls for, in case some have to be discarded. Wash mussels well under running water. Scrape each shell with a knife, removing all traces of mud, seaweed and barnacles. Discard any mussels with cracked, broken or opened shells; they are dangerous. Rinse again in running water and remove 'beards' from mussels with a sharp knife.

TO KEEP COOKED MUSSELS Wrap mussels in a damp towel and put them on one of the lower shelves of your refrigerator. Strained, the mussel liquor can also be kept in the refrigerator to use the following day for a *sauce veloute* or a *soupe aux moules.*

MOULES MARINIERE

SERVES 4

48 mussels, washed, scraped and bearded (see above)
45ml/3 tbls butter
4 shallots, finely chopped
300ml/½pt dry white wine
30-45ml/2-3 tbls finely chopped parsley
2 sprigs of thyme
1 bay leaf
freshly ground black pepper
15ml/1 tbls flour

A delicious serving of Moules Marinière.

1. Melt 30ml/2 tbls butter in a thick-bottomed saucepan and sauté finely chopped shallots until transparent, but not coloured. Add dry white wine, finely chopped parsley, thyme and bay leaf; season with freshly ground black pepper, to taste. Simmer gently for 10 minutes.

2. Add prepared mussels to wine and herb mixture; cover and simmer, shaking constantly until shells open.

3. Drain mussels, discarding any unopened ones. Strain cooking liquor and reserve. Remove top shells from mussels and arrange mussels on a heated serving platter. Keep warm.

4. Reduce reserved cooking liquor to half the original quantity over a high heat and thicken by whisking in, bit by bit, a *beurre manié,* made by mashing 15ml/1 tbls each butter and flour together to form a smooth paste. Correct seasoning and pour sauce over mussels. Sprinkle with a little finely chopped parsley and serve immediately.

NOTE: Ring the changes on this basic mussel recipe for any of the following recipes by simply following Steps 1 and 2 and reducing the quantity of wine by half.

MUSSELS A L'AIL

SERVES 4

*Ingredients as for Steps 1 and 2 of **Moules**
 marinière (see page 144)*
50g/2oz butter
1 shallot, finely chopped
4 garlic cloves, finely chopped
60ml/4tbls finely chopped parsley
fresh breadcrumbs

1. Preheat oven to moderately hot (200°C/ 400°F/gas 6).

2. Prepare mussels. Remove top shells and ar-

range in an ovenproof gratin dish.

3. Heat butter and sauté finely chopped shallots and garlic cloves until soft. Do not let butter take on colour. Add finely chopped parsley and spoon mixture over mussels. Allow to cool; sprinkle with fresh breadcrumbs and bake in preheated oven until the sauce is melted and delicately browned. Serve immediately.

MOUCLADE

SERVES 4

*Ingredients as for Steps 1 and 2 of **Moules**
 marinière (see page 144)*
150ml/¼pt double cream
fresh breadcrumbs

1. Preheat oven to moderately hot (200°C/ 400°F/gas 6).

2. Prepare mussels and reserve cooking liquor. Remove shells completely and place mussels in a shallow ovenproof gratin dish.

3. Strain reserved cooking liquor and reduce over a high heat for 2-3 minutes. Add 150ml/ ¼pt cream and simmer for 10-15 minutes, stirring from time to time. Pour sauce over mussels, sprinkle lightly with fresh breadcrumbs and bake in preheated oven until heated through. Serve immediately.

MUSSELS MAYONNAISE

SERVES 4

*Ingredients as for steps 1 and 2 of **Moules**
 marinière (see page 144)*
Mayonnaise (see page 85)
finely chopped parsley

1. Prepare mussels, strain, and reserve cooking liquor. Remove shells completely and allow mussels to drain in a colander placed over a bowl to catch the juices.

2. Flavour MAYONNAISE with 30–45ml/2-3 tbls reserved cooking liquor. Combine with mussels in a serving dish; sprinkle with finely chopped parsley and chill for at least 30 minutes before serving.

DEEP-FRIED MUSSELS BEARNAISE

SERVES 4

*48 mussels, washed, scraped and bearded (see
  page 144)*
60ml/4 tbls finely chopped shallots
2 sprigs of thyme
2 sprigs of parsley
1 bay leaf
salt
150ml/¹/4pt dry white wine
olive oil, for deep frying
225g/¹/2lb green bacon, cut into squares
freshly ground black pepper
flour
1 egg, beaten
fresh breadcrumbs
Sauce Béarnaise *(see page 84)*

1. Place prepared mussels in a thick-bottomed saucepan together with finely chopped shallots, thyme, parsley and bay leaf. Season lightly with salt and moisten with dry white wine. Cover pan and steam for 4-5 minutes, or until shells are well opened.
2. Remove mussels from their shells, discarding any unopened ones.
3. Heat olive oil in a deep-fryer to 190°C/375°F (see page 94)
4. Place mussels onto 8 small skewers with squares of bacon between them. Season skewers of mussels and bacon with freshly ground black pepper to taste. Roll in flour, shaking off excess. Dip in beaten egg and then toss in breadcrumbs.
5. Thread skewers on a piece of string and fry in preheated oil until golden. Drain skewers on absorbent paper and serve with SAUCE BEARNAISE.

MUSSELS IN SNAIL BUTTER

SERVES 4

*48 large mussels, washed, scraped and bearded
  (see page 144)*
60ml/4 tbls finely chopped shallots
2 sprigs of thyme
2 sprigs of parsley
1 bay leaf
salt
150ml/¹/4pt dry white wine

SNAIL BUTTER
225g/¹/2lb butter
3 garlic cloves, finely chopped
120ml/8tbls finely chopped parsley
60ml/4tbls finely chopped chives

1. Place prepared mussels in a thick-bottomed saucepan together with finely chopped shallots, thyme, parsley and bay leaf. Season lightly with salt and moisten with dry white wine. Cover pan and steam for 4-5 minutes, or until the shells are well opened. Throw away any unopened mussels.
2. Make snail butter by kneading together butter, finely chopped garlic cloves, parsley and chives. If chives are unavailable, use more parsley.
3. Remove top shells from mussels and spread with snail butter. Then place stuffed mussels in the refrigerator until ready to serve.
4. Preheat oven to hot (230°C/450°F/gas 8).
5. When ready to serve, place stuffed mussels in 4 individual ovenproof dishes and bake in preheated oven for 2-3 minutes, or until sauce is melted and mussels are piping hot. Serve immediately.

SALADE DE MOULES

SERVES 4

*48 mussels, washed, scraped and bearded (see page
  144)*
30ml/2 tbls finely chopped shallots
2 sprigs of thyme
2 sprigs of parsley
1 bay leaf
salt
150ml/¼pt very dry white wine
red wine vinegar
olive oil
freshly ground black pepper
60ml/4 tbls finely chopped parsley

1. Place prepared mussels in a thick-bottomed
saucepan, together with chopped shallots,
thyme, parsley and bay leaf. Season lightly
with salt and moisten with dry white wine.
Cover and steam for 4-5 minutes, or until the
mussels are well opened. Throw away any unopened mussels. Remove shells completely
and arrange mussels in a serving dish. Strain
cooking liquor and reserve.
2. Prepare a dressing made of one part reserved cooking liquor, one part wine vinegar
and one part olive oil. Season with salt and
freshly ground black pepper, to taste, and pour
over mussels while they are still warm. Allow
to cool. Mussels should be moist, but without
excess dressing. Sprinkle mussels with chopped parsley and chill for at least 30 minutes before serving.

STEAMED MUSSELS IN CROCK 'FOUR SEASONS'

SERVES 4

*48 mussels, washed, scraped and bearded (see page
  144)*
3 shallots, finely chopped
15ml/1 tbls butter

150ml/¼pt dry white wine
150ml/¼pt canned clam juice
4 sprigs of parsley, finely chopped
150ml/¼pt double cream
salt and freshly ground black pepper
lemon juice

1. Place prepared mussels in a heatproof crock
with finely chopped shallots, butter, dry white
wine, clam juice and finely chopped parsley.
Cover and steam for 4-5 minutes, or until
mussels are all open. Discard any unopened
mussels.
2. Add double cream to crock and season with
salt, freshly ground black pepper and lemon
juice, to taste. Bring to boil again and serve immediately.

GRILLED SCALLOPS

SERVES 4

8 scallops
butter
salt and freshly ground black pepper
4 slices hot buttered toast
30ml/2 tbls finely chopped parsley
lemon juice

1. Preheat grill to high.
2. Wash and trim scallops; dry carefully. Slice
each scallop in half.
3. Place sliced scallops in a well-buttered
ovenproof baking dish. Brush scallops generously with melted butter and season with salt
and freshly ground black pepper, to taste.
Place scallops under preheated grill, about
7.5cm/3in from heat, and grill for 4-6
minutes, or until scallops become delicately
browned.
4. Spoon grilled scallops onto slices of hot
buttered toast; sprinkle with a little finely
chopped parsley and lemon juice and serve
immediately.

FRIED SCALLOPS

SERVES 4

8 scallops
2 eggs, beaten
90ml/6 tbls double cream
salt and freshly ground black pepper
cornmeal, biscuit crumbs, or fresh breadcrumbs
100g/¼lb butter
150ml/¼pt olive oil
lemon wedges

1. Wash and trim scallops, dry them carefully and slice each scallop in half.
2. In a small bowl, combine beaten eggs and double cream, and season with salt and freshly ground black pepper, to taste. Dip scallops in egg mixture. Toss in cornmeal, or crumbs, shaking off excess and allow to set on aluminium foil for about 10 minutes before cooking.
3. Melt butter in a thick-bottomed frying pan, or deep-fryer. Add olive oil; bring to frying temperature (see page 94) and cook scallops in fats until they are golden brown. Drain scallops on absorbent paper and serve immediately with wedges of lemon.

BASIC POACHED SCALLOPS

SERVES 4

8 scallops
300ml/½pt dry white wine
½ Spanish onion, finely chopped
1 bouquet garni (parsley, thyme and bay leaf)
salt and freshly ground black pepper

1. Wash and trim scallops; dry carefully.
2. Place dried scallops in a thick-bottomed saucepan, together with dry white wine and enough water barely to cover scallops. Add finely chopped onion and *bouquet garni;* season with salt and freshly ground black pepper, to

taste. Bring slowly to the boil; reduce heat and simmer gently for 5 minutes, or until scallops are tender. Drain scallops. Strain cooking liquor and reserve. Use scallops as directed in any of the following recipes.

BAKED SCALLOPS PROVENCAL

SERVES 4

Basic poached scallops (see page 149)
30ml/2 tbls butter
30ml/2 tbls olive oil
1 garlic clove, finely chopped
30ml/2 tbls finely chopped parsley
30ml/2 tbls fresh breadcrumbs
salt and freshly ground black pepper

1. Prepare scallops.
2. Preheat grill to high.
3. Heat butter and olive oil in a heatproof baking dish until butter sizzles.
4. Slice scallops in half and toss in dish, together with finely chopped garlic clove, parsley and breadcrumbs. Season with salt and freshly ground black pepper, to taste, and bake under preheated grill until scallops are golden. Serve immediately.

SCALLOP SALAD

SERVES 4

Basic poached scallops (see this page)
45ml/3 tbls olive oil
15ml/1 tbls red wine vinegar
salt and freshly ground black pepper
*150ml/¼pt **Mayonnaise** (see page 85)*
lettuce leaves

1. Prepare scallops.
2. In a bowl, mix olive oil and wine vinegar. Season with salt and black pepper, to taste.
3. Slice scallops in half and, while still warm,

toss in a bowl with olive oil and wine vinegar dressing. Chill.

4. Just before serving, add well-flavoured MAYONNAISE to scallop salad and toss. Serve in a lettuce-lined bowl.

CURRIED SCALLOPS

SERVES 4

Basic poached scallops (see page 149)
30ml/2 tbls butter
30ml/2 tbls flour
1.5-2.5ml/¼-½ tsp curry powder
90-120ml/6-8 tbls double cream
salt and freshly ground black pepper
finely chopped parsley

1. Prepare scallops, reserving the cooking liquor, and slice them in half.
2. Melt butter in the top of a double saucepan; stir in flour and curry powder and cook for a few minutes, stirring continuously, until roux is well blended. Add enough reserved scallop liquor, about 300ml/½pt, to make a smooth rich sauce. Add double cream and sliced scallops to sauce. Season with salt and freshly ground black pepper, to taste. Heat through.
3. Fill 4 scallop shells, or individual ovenproof dishes with curried scallops; sprinkle with chopped parsley and serve immediately.

SCALLOPS MORNAY

SERVES 4

Basic poached scallops (see page 149)
45ml/3 tbls butter
30ml/2 tbls flour
150ml/¼pt double cream
120ml/8 tbls freshly grated Gruyère cheese
salt and freshly ground black pepper
freshly grated nutmeg
60ml/4 tbls fresh breadcrumbs

1. Prepare scallops, reserving cooking liquor. Slice scallops in half.
2. Melt 30ml/2 tbls butter in the top of a double saucepan and make a pale roux by adding the flour. Cook roux for a few minutes stirring continuously, without allowing it to take on colour. Add double cream and enough reserved scallop liquor, about 150ml/¼pt, to make a smooth rich sauce. Stir in half the freshly grated Gruyère cheese and continue to cook until cheese has melted. Season sauce with salt, freshly ground black pepper and freshly grated nutmeg, to taste. Add poached sliced scallops to sauce and heat through.
3. Preheat grill to high.
4. Fill 4 scallop shells, or individual ovenproof dishes, with the scallop mixture. Sprinkle each dish with breadcrumbs and remaining Gruyère cheese. Dot with butter and put under preheated grill for a few minutes to glaze top.

SCALLOPS AND MUSHROOMS IN WHITE WINE

SERVES 4

Basic poached scallops (see page 149)
75ml/5 tbls butter
12 button mushrooms, thinly sliced
4 shallots, finely chopped
30ml/2 tbls finely chopped parsley
30ml/2 tbls flour
90ml/6 tbls double cream
fresh breadcrumbs

1. Prepare scallops and slice in half. Reserve liquor.
2. Melt 60ml/4 tbls butter in a thick-bottomed saucepan and sauté the mushrooms, shallots and parsley until golden.
3. Blend flour into pan and add the reserved scallop liquor very slowly, stirring constantly. Cook for a few minutes, stirring constantly. Stir in double cream.

150

4. Preheat grill to high.

5. Combine scallops with the sauce in a heat-proof gratin dish. Sprinkle dish with bread-crumbs; dot with butter and brown under pre-heated grill. Serve immediately.

SCALLOPS AU GRATIN

SERVES 4

8 small scallops
300ml/¹/2pt dry white wine
60ml/4 tbls finely chopped shallots
90ml/6 tbls double cream
salt and freshly ground black pepper
10ml/2 tsp butter
10ml/2 tsp flour
*30ml/2 tbls **Sauce Hollandaise** (see page 84)*
*   or 1 egg yolk*
4 button mushrooms, sliced and simmered in
*   acidulated water*

1. Wash scallops and dry carefully. Separate coral from scallops and remove any mem-branes still attached.

2. Place scallops in a thick-bottomed saucepan with dry white wine, finely chopped shallots and double cream. Season with salt and freshly ground black pepper, to taste. Bring to the boil, reduce heat quickly; cover pan and sim-mer for 3 minutes. Add coral and simmer for 2 minutes more.

3. Remove scallops and coral and keep warm. Mash butter and flour together to form a smooth *beurre manié* and whisk into the sauce. Simmer sauce until it is well blended and re-duced a little. To finish sauce, stir in SAUCE HOLLANDAISE, or if it is not available, egg yolk.

4. Preheat grill to high.

5. Fill 4 scallop shells, or individual heatproof dishes, with sliced scallops and coral; add a few slices of simmered mushrooms to each dish and pour the sauce over. Place under preheated grill until brown. Serve immediately.

SCALLOP KEBABS

SERVES 4

16 scallops
90ml/6 tbls fresh breadcrumbs
60ml/4 tbls parsley, finely chopped
2.5ml/¹/2 tsp dried marjoram
grated rind of ¹/2 lemon
salt and freshly ground black pepper
melted butter
4-8 rashers green bacon
olive oil
lemon juice

1. If barbecueing kebabs light fire at least 1 hour before cooking. If grilling kebabs, pre-heat grill to high.

2. Wash and trim scallops well in cold water; dry carefully.

3. Mix together breadcrumbs with finely chopped parsley, marjoram and grated lemon rind. Season with salt and freshly ground black pepper, to taste.

4. Dip scallops in melted butter and toss in breadcrumb mixture, shaking off excess.

5. Arrange 4 scallops on each skewer, with 1 or 2 rashers of green bacon, weaving the bacon slices around the scallops.

6. When ready to grill, brush grid with a little olive oil and grill scallops lightly over hot coals or under preheated grill for 5-7 minutes, basting with melted butter and turning skew-ers frequently during cooking time. Serve with melted butter seasoned with lemon juice.

COUPE 'CAPRICE'

SERVES 4

1 small melon
225g/¹/₂lb small frozen Norwegian prawns
*300ml/¹/₂pt well-flavoured **Mayonnaise** (see*
  page 85)
15-30ml/1-2 tbls tomato ketchup
60-90ml/4-6 tbls double cream
30ml/2 tbls finely chopped green pepper
30ml/2 tbls finely chopped red pepper
salt and freshly ground black pepper
dash of Tabasco
15-30ml/1-2 tbls finely chopped tarragon

1. Chill melon.
2. Combine MAYONNAISE, tomato ketchup and double cream, stir in finely chopped pepper and season with salt and freshly ground black pepper, to taste, and a dash of Tabasco. Chill.
3. Peel, seed and dice melon and combine with prawns and chilled sauce. Spoon into 4 individual salad bowls. Sprinkle with a little finely chopped tarragon and serve.

PRAWNS IN WHISKY

SERVES 4

450g/1lb large frozen prawns
60ml/4 tbls butter
60ml/4 tbls olive oil
30ml/2 tbls finely chopped shallots, or onion
1 garlic clove, finely chopped
2 tomatoes, peeled, seeded and chopped
salt and freshly ground black pepper
cayenne pepper
90ml/6 tbls whisky, warmed
90ml/6 tbls dry white wine
5ml/1 tsp cornflour
90ml/6 tbls double cream
1 pinch dried tarragon
1 egg yolk

1. Heat butter and olive oil in a thick-bottomed frying pan; add finely chopped shallots or onion, and garlic. Sauté until vegetables are transparent.
2. Add prawns and chopped tomatoes to pan. Season with salt, freshly ground black pepper and cayenne pepper to taste and continue to sauté gently for a few minutes more. Pour over 60ml/4 tbls warmed whisky and flame. Add dry white wine and simmer for 5 minutes. Remove prawns and keep warm in a heated serving dish.
3. Combine remaining whisky, cornflour and double cream; add to sauce and beat vigorously over a high heat until sauce comes to the boil. Boil for 1 minute. Remove pan from heat; add dried tarragon and pour a little of the hot sauce over egg yolk. Mix well and then stir egg mixture into sauce. Pour sauce over prawns and serve immediately.

HAWAIIAN PRAWNS WITH PINEAPPLE

SERVES 4

24 large frozen prawns
15ml/1 tbls cornflour
150ml/¹/₄pt pineapple juice (see below)
30ml/2 tbls soy sauce
15ml/1 tbls honey
15ml/1 tbls red wine vinegar
1.2ml/¹/₄ tsp ground ginger
olive oil
1 small can pineapple chunks, drained
  (reserving liquid)

1. Blend cornflour with a little pineapple liquid, then combine in a thick-bottomed saucepan with remaining pineapple juice, soy sauce, honey, wine vinegar and ginger. Cook over a low heat, stirring constantly, until sauce has thickened.
2. Preheat grill to high.

3. When ready to grill, brush grid of grill pan with a little olive oil. Thread prawns and pineapple chunks alternately on individual skewers. Dip skewers in sauce and grill under preheated grill turning skewers frequently during cooking time, until prawns are delicately brown on all sides. Serve immediately.

NOTE: Quartered button mushrooms, squares of green pepper, etc., can be threaded alternately with prawns and pineapple chunks, if desired.

CHINESE STEAMED PRAWNS

SERVES 4

700g/1½lb large frozen prawns
cornflour

4 shallots, finely chopped
100g/4oz mushrooms, finely sliced
50g/2oz cucumber, finely sliced
60ml/4 tbls soy sauce
60ml/4 tbls dry white wine
freshly ground black pepper
Boiled rice *(see page 179)*
small tomatoes

1. Roll prawns in cornflour and place on a platter in a steamer together with finely chopped shallots, sliced mushrooms and cucumber, soy sauce and dry white wine. Season with a little freshly ground black pepper and cook over 5cm/2in of fast-boiling water, covered, so that the platter is entirely confined in steam, until tender.

2. Serve prawns hot from the steamer on a bed of BOILED RICE garnished with tomatoes.

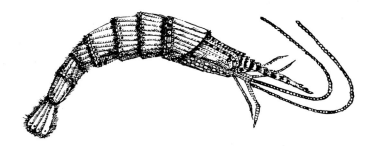

CHAPTER 7

BEEF

THE ROAST BEEF OF ENGLAND

W HEN ERASMUS DESCRIBED, more than four hundred years ago, the things upon which various nations of the world prided themselves – the Scots their nobility and logical sense, the French their breeding – he said of the English that they 'particularly challenge to themselves Beauty, Music and Feasting'. The excellence of English food had been a byword for centuries before Erasmus wrote, perhaps because the penalties for slapdash cooking were so severe, for Edward I once ordered all the cooks of the inns on the road between London and York to be executed because their dishes were not to his taste.

But even as early as the seventeenth century the English were looking back nostalgically to the good old days when 'poor boyes did turn the spitts and lick't the dripping-pan, and grew to be huge, lusty knaves'. The meat they were roasting, the meat of meats for the English, was Beef. The roast was brought to the table on a spit, a servant holding it while the guest cut off a piece, which was eaten with the fingers and often without a plate. Indeed, mediaeval directions for setting a table often referred to 'trencher pieces' of bread on which guests could lay down their portion of meat.

Nothing can compare with roast beef, charred on the outside, moistly tender within, served with King Edward potatoes baked in their jackets and a melting Yorkshire pudding, happy recipient of the noble juices of the roast.

Accompany this perfection with freshly grated horseradish beaten into whipped cream – a modern touch to an ancient recipe – and a green vegetable: topped and tailed green beans, a purée of green peas or new-born Brussels sprouts swathed in delicately browned, buttered breadcrumbs.

To the Englishman, nothing can quite compare with a roast of English beef, charred on the outside, moistly tender within, served with King Edward potatoes baked in their jackets.

Beef contains the highest form of protein for human consumption in the most palatable, stimulating and digestible form. Its juiciness is due to the presence of a certain proportion of fat both outside and inside the meat. It is the slow melting of this inside fat – the 'marbling', and its penetration into every cell of the roast – that is responsible for its savouriness.

FIVE TIPS FOR ROASTING BEEF

1. Only tender pieces of beef make good roasts.

2. A sirloin or rib roast, like all large pieces of meat, should stand for an hour or two at room temperature before roasting. So, if your beef has been stored in the refrigerator, be sure to take it out at least two hours before roasting.

3. Do not salt beef before putting it in the oven; the salt forms a crust which prevents meat from colouring uniformly. I like to prepare mine by rubbing it generously with fresh dripping or butter and then dusting it lightly with a mixture of dry mustard, freshly ground black pepper and browned flour, before leaving it to absorb these flavours for an hour or two at room temperature.

4. Remember to heat the serving dish and, especially, the sauceboat.

5. Do not put sliced beef to warm in the oven; it will dry out and become grey in colour.

ROAST BEEF

1 sirloin or rib roast of beef, 2.3-3.6kg/5-8lb
15ml/1 tbls dry mustard
freshly ground black pepper
30ml/2 tbls lightly browned flour
60-90ml/4-6 tbls dripping, or butter, softened
1 flattened piece beef suet
60-90ml/4-6 tbls red wine or water, warmed
salt

1. Preheat oven to fairly hot (220°C/425°F/gas 7).
2. Mix together dry mustard, freshly ground black pepper, to taste, and lightly browned flour.
3. Spread beef with dripping, or butter, and sprinkle with flour and mustard mixture. Tie a flattened layer of beef suet over the top of the beef.

4. When ready to roast, place beef on a rack over a roasting pan and brown in the preheated oven for 20 minutes. Reduce oven to slow (170°C/325°F/gas 3), add warmed red wine, or water, to the pan and continue to roast, basting frequently, allowing 15 to 18 minutes per 450g/1lb if you like your beef rare, 20 to 24 minutes per 450g/1lb for medium, and 25 to 30 minutes per 450g/1lb if you prefer it well done.
5. When meat is cooked to your liking, season with salt, to taste, and additional freshly ground black pepper. Transfer to a warm serving platter and let it stand for 15 to 20 minutes at the edge of the open oven before carving. During this time the beef sets, the cooking subsides, and the roast is ready for carving.

6. In the meantime, pour off the fat in the roasting pan and use the pink juices that pour from the roast as it sets; stir all the crusty bits into the juices to make a clear sauce. I sometimes add a little wine, a knob or two of butter and a dash of Worcestershire sauce. Bring to the boil, reduce heat and simmer for 1 or 2 minutes. Strain sauce and serve in a heated sauceboat with roast.

SLICED BEEF IN ASPIC

SERVES 4

8 slices rare roast beef
2.5ml/¹/₂ tsp dried thyme
2.5ml/¹/₂ tsp dried basil
salt and freshly ground black pepper
young carrot slices, cooked
button onions, boiled
leaves of chervil, tarragon or flat-leafed parsley
*600ml/1pt **Madeira aspic** (see page 67)*
5ml/1 tsp Worcestershire sauce
cayenne pepper

1. Arrange overlapping slices of cold rare beef in a shallow serving dish. Sprinkle with dried thyme and basil and season with salt and freshly ground black pepper, to taste. Garnish beef with rows of cooked carrot slices and button onions and decorate with leaves of chervil, tarragon or flat-leafed parsley.
2. Heat MADEIRA ASPIC; add Worcestershire sauce and a few grains of cayenne pepper. Cool until the aspic is syrupy.
3. Pour aspic over the beef slices and chill in the refrigerator for at least 2 hours, or until the aspic has set.

SUMMER BEEF SALAD

MAKES AN HORS-D'OEUVRE SALAD FOR 4-6

550g/1¹/₄lb cold roast beef
2 eating apples
2 celery stalks
4 shallots, finely chopped
1 small garlic clove, finely chopped
60ml/4 tbls finely chopped parsley
90-120ml/6-8 tbls olive oil
30ml/2 tbls red wine vinegar
salt and freshly ground black pepper

1. Trim fat from roast beef and cut into 6mm/¹/₄in cubes.
2. Peel and core apples and cut into 1.2cm/¹/₂in cubes. Dice celery stalks into 1.2cm/¹/₂in cubes.
3. Combine beef, apple and celery cubes with finely chopped shallots, garlic clove and parsley in a salad bowl.
4. Make a dressing by combining olive oil and red wine vinegar (3 to 4 parts olive oil to 1 part red wine vinegar). Season with salt and freshly ground black pepper, to taste, and pour over beef salad. Chill before serving.

GRILLED STEAK

SERVES 2

1kg/2lb rump steak, about 4cm/1¹/₂ in thick
450g/1lb beef fat
freshly ground black pepper
30-60ml/2-4 tbls softened butter
salt

1. Remove steak from refrigerator at least 30 minutes before cooking, and slit fat in several places around sides to prevent meat from curling up during cooking.
2. Preheat grill to high.
3. When ready to grill, rub grid of grill pan with a piece of beef fat. Sprinkle both sides of

steak with freshly ground black pepper and spread with butter. Grill steak 7.5cm/3in from heat, for 3 minutes on each side at a high heat. Reduce heat and cook for a further 3 minutes on each side for a rare steak. Grill for a minute or two more if you prefer medium rare steak. Sprinkle with salt to taste and serve.

STEAK A LA BORDELAISE

SERVES 2

450g/1lb rump steak, 4cm/1¹/2in thick
¹/2 Spanish onion, finely chopped
2 shallots, finely chopped
60ml/4 tbls finely chopped parsley
30ml/2 tbls olive oil
15ml/1 tbls flour
150ml/¹/4pt red wine
beef marrow from a 5-7.5cm/2-3in bone

1. Prepare steak as above.
2. In the meantime, prepare a Bordelaise sauce: sauté finely chopped onion, shallots and parsley in olive oil until onion is transparent. Stir in flour, add red wine and cook over a high flame, stirring continuously, until wine bubbles. Then lower flame and simmer, stirring continuously, until sauce thickens a little. Poach beef marrow for 1 minute in hot water, slice and add to sauce. Pour sauce over steak and serve immediately.

STEAK ALLA PIZZAIOLA

Prepare steak as above. In the meantime, prepare a *pizzaiola* sauce. Sauté 1 sliced garlic clove in 30ml/2 tbls olive oil until transparent. Add 1 400g/14oz can Italian peeled tomatoes and salt and freshly ground black pepper, to taste, and cook over a high flame for 15 minutes. Stir in 30ml/2 tbls finely chopped parsley and 1.5ml/¹/4 tsp dried oregano. Pour sauce over steak and serve immediately.

BEEFSTEAK AU ROQUEFORT

SERVES 2

450g/1lb rump steak, about 4cm/1¹/2in thick
olive oil
salt and freshly ground black pepper
25g/1oz Roquefort cheese
50g/2 oz butter
juice of ¹/2 lemon
30ml/2 tbls finely chopped parsley, chervil, or
  chives

1. Remove steak from refrigerator at least 30 minutes before cooking and slit fat in several places around sides to prevent meat from curling up during cooking.
2. Preheat grill to high.
3. When ready to grill, brush grid of grill pan with a little olive oil. Sprinkle both sides of steak with freshly ground black pepper and grill to your liking (see opposite column).
4. While steak is grilling, cream Roquefort cheese and butter with lemon juice and finely chopped parsley, chervil, or chives. Season with salt and freshly ground black pepper.
5. Serve steak immediately, topped with Roquefort butter.

ENTRECOTE A LA MIRABEAU

SERVES 4

1kg/2lb super rump steak, about 5cm/2in thick
butter
15ml/1 tbls flour
5ml/1 tsp anchovy paste
olive oil
freshly ground black pepper
45g/1³/4oz can anchovy fillets, drained
sliced stuffed olives

1. Remove steak from refrigerator at least 30 minutes before cooking and slit fat in several places around the sides to prevent meat from

curling during cooking.
2. Preheat grill to high.
3. Mash 30ml/2 tbls butter and the flour to a smooth paste, add anchovy paste and blend well.
4. When ready to grill, brush grid of grill pan with a little olive oil. Spread anchovy paste over steak; season with freshly ground black pepper, to taste, and grill under preheated grill for 7 minutes, 12.5cm/5in from the heat. If you prefer steak to be medium rare, grill for 1 minute more. Turn steak over and make a latticework of anchovy fillets on the uncooked side. Fill each square with a slice of olive; brush with melted butter, or olive oil, and continue grilling for 7 to 8 minutes, according to taste. Serve immediately with melted butter.

STEAK AU POIVRE

SERVES 4

1kg/2lb super rump steak, about 4cm/1½in thick
30ml/2 tbls black peppercorns
olive oil
salt
Parsley butter *(see page 87) or* **Garlic butter**
   (see page 87)
watercress

1. Crush peppercorns coarsely with a rolling pin, or with a mortar and pestle.
2. Slit fat in several places around the sides to prevent the meat from curling up during cooking. Sprinkle one side of the steak with half the peppercorns, pressing them into the meat with the flat of your hand. Repeat with other side. Let steak stand at room temperature for at least 30 minutes to absorb flavours.
3. Preheat grill to high.
4. When ready to grill, brush grid of grill pan with a little olive oil, then grill steak to your liking.
5. Transfer steak to a heated serving dish;

sprinkle with salt, to taste, and top with PARSLEY BUTTER or GARLIC BUTTER. Garnish with watercress and serve immediately.

TOURNEDOS

SERVES 4

4 tournedos, 125-175g/4-6oz each and
   5cm/2in thick
freshly ground black pepper
butter
30ml/2 tbls olive oil
4 rounds of bread
lemon juice

1. Ask your butcher to prepare 4 tournedos for you – slices cut from fillet, usually encased in a thin layer of fat.
2. Remove steaks from refrigerator at least 30 minutes before cooking. Season steaks with freshly ground black pepper, to taste, and sauté in 30ml/2 tbls each butter and olive oil until well browned (5 to 6 minutes on each side), but still pink and moist in the centre. Remove from pan and keep warm.
3. Sauté bread in butter until golden on both sides; sprinkle lightly with lemon juice and place a tournedos on each slice. Season tournedos with salt, to taste, and serve immediately with one of the following sauces.

TOURNEDOS A LA BEARNAISE
Prepare steak as above and spoon 30-45ml/2-3 tbls SAUCE BEARNAISE (see page 84) over each tournedos.

TOURNEDOS BEAUHARNAIS
Prepare steak as above and set a small cooked artichoke heart filled with SAUCE BEARNAISE (see page 84) on each tournedos. Sprinkle with finely chopped parsley and tarragon. Pour MADEIRA SAUCE (see page 83) around tournedos.

TOURNEDOS ROSSINI

Prepare steak as before, but place a slice of *pâté de foie gras* on each fried *croûton* before topping with tournedos. Pour MADEIRA SAUCE (see page 83) around tournedos.

BOEUF STROGANOFF – I

SERVES 4-6

1kg/2lb rump or fillet of beef
freshly ground black pepper
45ml/3 tbls finely chopped onion
90ml/6 tbls butter
225g/1/2lb button mushrooms, sliced
salt
freshly grated nutmeg
ground mace
1/2pt soured cream

1. Cut steak across the grain into slices 1.2cm/1/2in thick. Flatten each slice with a wooden mallet, and season with freshly ground black pepper, to taste.
2. Sauté onion in half the butter in a thick-bottomed casserole until it just begins to turn colour; add sliced beef and sauté for about 5 minutes more, turning pieces so that all sides are browned. Remove from casserole and keep warm.
3. Add remaining butter to casserole and sauté sliced mushrooms. Return beef to casserole and season with salt, nutmeg and mace, to taste. Add soured cream and heat through. Serve from casserole.

BOEUF STROGANOFF – II

As above, but simmer beef, after browning, for 10 to 15 minutes in a sauce made of 300ml/1/2pt well-flavoured BASIC BEEF STOCK (see page 65) mixed with 15-30ml/1-2 tbls tomato purée, and thickened with a *beurre manié* made of 30ml/2 tbls each flour and butter which you have mashed together to form a smooth paste.

SWISS STEAK

SERVES 4-6

1kg/2lb beef, rump, round, or chuck
salt and freshly ground black pepper
60ml/4 tbls flour
60ml/4 tbls olive oil
1/2 Spanish onion, finely chopped
400g/14oz can tomatoes

1. Season beef with salt and freshly ground black pepper, to taste. Rub well with flour.
2. Heat olive oil in a thick-bottomed casserole and sauté finely chopped onion until soft and transparent. Add beef and brown on both sides.
3. Pour tomatoes into casserole, cover and cook very slowly on top of the stove until the meat is tender, about 2 hours, adding a little water from time to time if necessary. Serve from casserole.

CARBONNADE DE BOEUF

SERVES 4

1kg/2lb braising steak
30ml/2 tbls olive oil
salt and freshly ground black pepper
30ml/2 tbls butter
4 Spanish onions, thinly sliced
15ml/1 tbls flour
1 bottle Guinness

1. Season beef with salt and freshly ground black pepper, to taste.
2. Heat olive oil in a thick-bottomed frying pan and brown beef on both sides. Transfer beef to a thick-bottomed ovenproof casserole large enough to hold the steak in one layer.
3. Add butter to frying pan and sauté thinly sliced onions, stirring constantly, until onions are golden brown. Sprinkle with flour, stir well and add to casserole.

4. Add Guinness, cover and cook over low heat for about 2 hours, or until beef is tender. Correct seasoning. Serve directly from casserole.

FILLET OF BEEF 'EN CHEMISE'

1 fillet of beef, approximately 1.1kg/2¹/₂lb
cognac
100g/4oz mushrooms, finely chopped
¹/₂ Spanish onion, finely chopped
softened butter
salt and freshly ground black pepper
60ml/4 tbls pâté de foie gras
Puff pastry (see page 348)
1 egg yolk, slightly beaten

1. Brush fillet of beef with brandy; trim neatly, removing ends, and let stand at room temperature for at least 30 minutes.
2. Preheat oven to moderate (190°C/375°F/gas 5).
3. Meanwhile, sauté finely chopped mushrooms and onion in 30ml/2 tbls butter until soft. Season with salt and freshly ground black pepper, to taste, and reserve.
4. Roast in preheated oven for 15 to 20 minutes, or until half cooked. Allow beef to cool slightly. Increase oven temperature to hot (230°C/450°F/gas 8).
5. Mix together *foie gras* and 60ml/4 tbls softened butter and season with salt and freshly ground black pepper, to taste.
6. Remove skewers, cords and fat from beef. Spread with pâté mixture and then with mushroom and onion mixture.
7. Roll out PUFF PASTRY into a thin sheet and wrap beef in it, securing it neatly. Place on a baking tin, brush pastry with cold water and bake in preheated oven for 12 to 15 minutes. Finally, brush pastry with slightly beaten egg yolk and continue baking until the crust is browned.

FILLET OF BEEF 'EN COCHONAILLES'

1 fillet of beef, approximately 1.1kg/2¹/₂lb
cognac
225g/¹/₂lb mushrooms, finely chopped
1 Spanish onion, finely chopped
butter
salt and freshly ground black pepper
11 slices cooked ham, or boiled bacon
Puff pastry (see page 348)
1 egg yolk, slightly beaten
Sauce Béarnaise (see page 84)

1. Brush fillet of beef with brandy; trim neatly, removing ends, and let beef stand at room temperature for a least 30 minutes.
2. Preheat oven to moderate (190°C/375°F/gas 5).
3. Sauté finely chopped mushrooms and onion in 60ml/4 tbls butter until soft. Season with salt and freshly ground black pepper, to taste.
4. Slice beef into 12 equal parts without completely cutting through the slices. Place a thin slice of cooked ham, or boiled bacon, cut to fit the beef, between each slice and spread with mushroom and onion mixture.
5. Re-form the fillet, fasten with metal skewers and roast in preheated oven for 15 to 20 minutes, or until half cooked. Allow beef to cool slightly. Increase oven temperature to hot (230°C/450°F/gas 8).
6. Remove skewers, cords and fat from beef. Spread with 60ml/4 tbls softened butter, season with salt and freshly ground black pepper, to taste, then spread thinly with remaining mushroom and onion mixture.
7. Roll out PUFF PASTRY into a thin sheet and wrap beef in it, securing it neatly. Place on a baking tin, brush pastry with cold water and bake in preheated oven for 12 to 15 minutes. Brush pastry with slightly beaten egg yolk and continue baking until the crust is browned. Serve with SAUCE BEARNAISE.

BEEF STEAK AND KIDNEY PIE

SERVES 4-6

1kg/2lb braising steak, cut into large bite-sized
  pieces
350g/³/4lb calf's kidney
flour
salt
freshly ground black pepper
60ml/4 tbls butter, or suet in equal quantity
4 shallots, finely chopped
300ml/¹/2pt **Basic beef stock** *(see page 65)*
1 bay leaf
15ml/1 tbls chopped parsley
pinch each of ground cloves and marjoram
butter, for pie dish
Flaky pastry *(see page 346)*
15-30ml/1-2 tbls dry sherry
5ml/1 tsp Worcestershire sauce

1. Clean kidney, split, remove fat and large tubes, and soak in salted water for 1 hour. Dry kidney and cut into 6mm/¹/4in slices.
2. Mix 45ml/3 tbls flour, 5ml/1 tsp salt and 2.5ml/¹/2 tsp freshly ground black pepper, and roll beef and kidney in this mixture shaking off excess.
3. Melt butter, or suet, in a thick-bottomed saucepan and sauté finely chopped shallots until golden. When shallots have taken on a little colour, add the beef and kidney and brown them thoroughly, stirring almost constantly. Moisten with BEEF STOCK. Add 1.5ml/¹/4 tsp freshly ground black pepper, bay leaf, chopped parsley, ground cloves and marjoram; stir, cover, and simmer over a low flame for 1 to 1³/4 hours, or until meat is tender. If liquid is too thin, thicken with a little flour mixed to a smooth paste with water.
4. Preheat oven to hot (230°C/450°F/gas 8).
5. Butter a 1L/2pt pie dish. Place a pie funnel in centre of dish; add meats and liquid and allow to cool.
6. Place FLAKY PASTRY over meat, moistening

and pinching edges to dish. Make vents in the pastry to allow steam to escape and bake in preheated oven for 10 minutes. Lower heat to moderate (190°C/375°C/gas 5) and continue baking for 15 minutes, or until pastry crust is golden brown.
7. Just before serving the pie, insert a small funnel into centre vent and pour in a mixture of dry sherry and Worcestershire sauce.

STEAK AND KIDNEY PUDDING

SERVES 4-6

700g-1kg/1¹/2-2lb braising steak
225g/¹/2lb calf's kidney
flour
freshly ground black pepper
salt
175g/6oz freshly grated or packaged suet, finely
  chopped
350g/12oz self-raising flour
dripping or butter
90ml/6 tbls finely chopped shallot, or onion
150ml/¹/4pt rich **Basic beef stock** *(see page 85)*
150ml/¹/4pt port
10ml/2 tsp soy sauce
grated rind of ¹/4 lemon

1. Cut steak and kidney into rather small pieces.
2. Mix together 30ml/2 tbls flour, 2.5ml/¹/2 tsp freshly ground black pepper and 2.5ml/¹/2 tsp salt, and roll steak and kidney pieces in this mixture, shaking off excess.
3. Combine finely chopped suet with flour, adding salt and freshly ground black pepper, to taste, to make a light suet crust. Roll out suet crust.
4. Grease a 1L/2pt basin with dripping or butter, line it with suet crust, reserving some for the lid, and put in the seasoned meat and finely chopped shallot, or onion.
5. Combine BEEF STOCK, port, soy sauce and

lemon rind, and fill up the basin with this mixture to near the top; put on a suet lid, making sure that the edges are well sealed to keep in the steam. Cover the whole pudding with a floured cloth and simmer, or steam, for 3 to 4 hours. Crust should be rather damp. Serve immediately.

BEEF OLIVES

SERVES 4-6

1kg/2lb topside of beef, thinly sliced
1 Spanish onion, finely chopped
100g/4oz mushrooms, finely chopped
75ml/5 tbls butter
olive oil (optional)
150ml/¼pt **Basic beef stock** *(see page 65)*
15ml/1 tbls flour

FORCEMEAT STUFFING

100g/4oz fresh breadcrumbs
50g/2oz freshly grated suet
60g/4 tbls finely chopped parsley
5ml/1 tsp dried marjoram, thyme, or winter savory
2.5ml/½ tsp grated lemon rind
2 eggs
freshly grated nutmeg

salt and freshly ground black pepper
dry white wine (optional)

1. To prepare Forcemeat stuffing: mix together breadcrumbs, freshly grated suet, finely chopped parsley, dried marjoram, thyme, or winter savory, lemon rind and eggs. Season generously with grated nutmeg, salt and freshly ground black pepper. If mixture seems too dry, add a little water or dry white wine.

2. Trim thin slices of beef into rectangles approximately 7.5 x 10cm/3 x 4in and beat well with a rolling pin to flatten and tenderize meat. Spread Forcemeat stuffing on each piece of meat; roll up and secure with very fine string. Makes about 12 beef olives.

3. Sauté finely chopped onion and mushrooms in 60ml/4 tbls butter, or olive oil, or a combination of the two, in a thick-bottomed casserole until onion is transparent. Add beef olives and brown on all sides. Pour over BEEF STOCK; cover and simmer very gently until tender, 1½ to 2 hours.

4. Just before serving, remove strings and thicken gravy by whisking in *beurre manié* (made by mashing 15ml/1 tbls butter with 15ml/1 tbls flour) bit by bit. Correct seasoning and serve immediately.

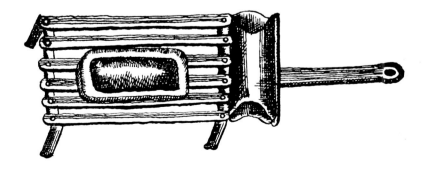

BOEUF A LA BOURGUIGNONNE

If one gave stars to the regions of France – as well as to their better restaurants – for the excellence of their cooking, Burgundy would have an unchallenged 'three'. The high quality of its native beef and poultry, allied to the fame of its vintages, makes this one of the most distinctive – if one of the richest – cuisines of France.

Most Burgundian dishes are of the long, slow-cooking variety – superb casseroles of meat, fish and game – guaranteed to make even the least expensive cuts of meat taste delicious. Indeed, food and wine are so closely linked together in Burgundy that it is a toss-up whether it is the famous vintages of the region or *boeuf à la Bourguignonne* that has brought Burgundy the greater international fame. For *boeuf à la Bourguignonne* – or *boeuf Bourguignonne* as it is sometimes more simply called – is one of the truly great dishes of the world. Combining tender nuggets of beef bathed in a rich wine-flavoured sauce with crisp *lardons* of fat salt pork or green bacon, tiny white onions cooked to *al dente* tenderness, and button mushrooms sautéed in butter and lemon juice, this dish is as delicious to eat as it is easy to prepare.

Like many wine-based dishes, *boeuf à la Bourguignonne* is better when reheated and served on the following day. Make this world-famous casserole one of your regular party dishes, preceded by a hot clear soup or a cold or hot hors-d'oeuvre and followed by a crisp green salad, cheese or fruit.

BOEUF A LA BOURGUIGNONNE

SERVES 4-6

1.4kg/3lb topside, or top rump of beef
flour
salt and freshly ground black pepper
60ml/4 tbls olive oil
90ml/6 tbls butter
100g/4oz fat salt pork or green bacon, cut into strips
60ml/4 tbls cognac, warmed
2 carrots
1 leek
4 shallots
1 Spanish onion

1 garlic clove
1 calf's foot, split (optional)
bouquet garni (sprig of thyme, bay leaf, celery stalk, and 2 sprigs of parsley)
1/2 bottle good red Burgundy
Basic beef stock *(see page 85) (optional)*
18 button onions
sugar
12 button mushrooms
lemon juice
finely chopped parsley

Boeuf à la Bourguignonne — a dish that is as delicious to eat as it is easy to prepare.

1. Preheat oven to very slow (140°C/275°F/gas 1 to 150°C/300°F/gas 2).

2. Cut beef into large cubes and remove fat. Roll cubes in flour seasoned generously with salt and freshly ground black pepper, shaking off excess.

3. Heat 30ml/2 tbls olive oil and butter in a large thick-bottomed frying pan and sauté fat salt pork or bacon until crisp and brown. Remove from pan and transfer to a large thick-bottomed ovenproof casserole.

4. Brown beef well on all sides in remaining fats; season with salt and freshly ground black pepper, to taste, and moisten with warmed cognac. Ignite cognac, let flames die down and add meat to casserole.

5. Coarsely chop carrots, leek, shallots, onion and garlic clove, and cook vegetables in fat remaining in frying pan, stirring occasionally, until they are lightly browned, adding a little more butter and olive oil, if necessary. Transfer vegetables to casserole; add calf's foot, if available, and *bouquet garni*. Pour over all but 4 tbls of the wine, and just enough good BEEF STOCK or hot water, to cover contents of casserole. Cover and cook in preheated oven for 1½ to 2 hours.

6. Skim fat from sauce, whisk in *beurre manié* (made by mashing 15ml/1 tbls butter with 15ml/1 tbls flour) bit by bit; cover and continue to cook gently in the oven until tender.

7. Brown button onions in 30ml/2 tbls butter in a thick-bottomed saucepan with a little sugar. Add remaining red wine, cover and cook over low heat until onions are almost tender. Keep warm.

8. Sauté mushrooms in 30ml/2 tbls olive oil and 15ml/1 tbls butter flavoured with a little lemon juice. Keep warm.

9. When meat is tender, remove calf's foot and *bouquet garni* from casserole. Correct seasoning; add glazed onions and sautéed mushrooms; sprinkle lavishly with finely chopped parsley and serve directly from casserole.

BOEUF A LA MODE

1 boned joint of beef (about 1.8-2.3kg/4-5lb)
salt and freshly ground black pepper
300ml/½pt red or white wine
1 Spanish onion, sliced
2 large carrots, sliced
2 celery stalks, sliced
1 garlic clove
2 bay leaves
4 sprigs of parsley
60ml/4 tbls cognac
pinch of dried thyme
45ml/3 tbls lard, or dripping
butter
30ml/2 tbls flour
*300ml/½pt **Basic beef stock** (see page 65)*
1 or 2 beef or veal bones
225g/8oz can tomatoes
6 whole carrots
24 button onions
sugar

1. If using oven, preheat to very slow (140°C/275°F/gas 1 to 150°C/300°F/gas 2).

2. Ask your butcher to lard beef (silverside or top rump of beef is best) with strips of larding pork. Season with salt and freshly ground black pepper, to taste, and put beef in porcelain or earthenware bowl (not metal) with red or white wine, sliced onion, carrots, and celery, garlic, bay leaves and parsley. Add cognac and a pinch of thyme. Let beef marinate in a cold place in this mixture for 6 hours or more, turning several times to allow it to absorb the flavour of the wine and aromatics.

3. Remove meat from the marinade, reserving marinade; drain and dry thoroughly. Melt lard, or dripping, in a thick-bottomed ovenproof casserole just large enough to hold beef; add beef and brown it on all sides. Pour off excess fat.

4. Melt 30ml/2 tbls butter in a thick-bottomed saucepan and make a roux by adding flour.

Cook, stirring constantly, until it is browned. Gradually stir in the reserved marinade followed by BEEF STOCK. Bring the sauce to the boil, stirring constantly, and pour over beef. Add beef or veal bones and tomatoes. Cover casserole closely and braise on top of the stove, or in preheated oven for 2 hours.

5. Cut whole carrots into pieces and blanch; glaze button onions in a little butter and sugar.

6. Remove beef from gravy; skim off all fat and strain gravy. Clean casserole and put back meat with carrots, glazed onions and strained gravy. Bring back to the boil, reduce heat and simmer for 1½ to 2 hours longer, or until the meat is tender. Transfer to a heated platter.

7. Correct seasoning of gravy, which should have reduced to about half the original quantity. If it has not done so, reduce by boiling it over a high heat until you are left with the correct quantity. Skim off any remaining fat.

8. Slice beef thinly across the grain so that the larding will show. Serve gravy separately.

BOEUF EN DAUBE A LA PROVENCALE

SERVES 6-8

1.8kg/4lb lean beef
2 Spanish onions, sliced
2 carrots, sliced
bouquet garni (sprig of thyme, 2 sprigs of parsley and bay leaf)
salt and freshly ground black pepper
300ml/½pt red wine
60ml/4 tbls cognac
60ml/4 tbls olive oil
225g/½lb lean bacon, diced
1 Spanish onion, quartered
4 garlic cloves
1 strip orange peel
*300ml/½pt hot **Basic beef stock** (see page 65), or hot water*
100g/4oz ripe olives, stoned

1. Cut beef into 2.5cm/1in. cubes and place in an earthenware or porcelain bowl (not metal), together with sliced onions and carrots, *bouquet garni*, red wine and cognac. Season with salt and freshly ground black pepper to taste and marinate for 5 to 6 hours, stirring occasionally.

2. Preheat oven to very slow (140°C/275°F/ gas 1 to 150°C/300°F/gas 2).

3. Heat olive oil in a thick-bottomed flame-proof casserole. Add diced bacon and onion quarters and sauté until browned. Set aside.

4. Drain beef, reserving marinade, and sauté beef with diced bacon and onion quarters until browned, shaking the pan from time to time.

5. Meanwhile, reduce marinade to half the original quantity over high heat.

6. Add garlic cloves and orange peel to casserole, then moisten with reduced marinade. Pour over BEEF STOCK or hot water; cover with greaseproof paper, put on the lid and cook in preheated oven for 3 to 4 hours.

7. Skim fat from surface; add stoned olives and correct seasoning. Continue to cook for a further 30 minutes. Serve in the casserole.

ESTOUFFADE DE BOEUF

SERVES 4-6

1.4kg/3lb lean beef, diced
225g/½lb lean bacon
butter
30ml/2 tbls olive oil
30ml/2 tbls flour
6 medium-sized onions, quartered
salt and freshly ground black pepper
1 bottle red wine
***Basic beef stock** (see page 65)*
2 garlic cloves, crushed
1 bouquet garni (sprig of thyme, bay leaf, 2 sprigs of parsley and celery stalk)
225g/8oz mushrooms, sliced

1. Preheat oven to very slow (140°C/275°F/gas 1 – 150°C/300°F/gas 2).
2. Blanch diced bacon in boiling water.
3. Heat 30ml/2 tbls each butter and olive oil in a thick-bottomed ovenproof casserole and sauté blanched bacon until golden. Remove from pan.
4. Cut lean beef into good-sized chunks, sprinkle with flour and brown in the same fat. Add quartered onions and cook, stirring constantly, until they are well browned. Season with salt and freshly ground black pepper, to taste. Add red wine and enough BEEF STOCK to cover, crushed garlic and *bouquet garni*. Bring to the boil, cover and cook in preheated oven for 2½ to 3 hours.
5. Drain the *ragoût* through a fine sieve into a thick-bottomed saucepan. Place beef and diced bacon in a clean thick-bottomed casserole.
6. Sauté sliced mushrooms in a little butter and add to the casserole.
7. Skim fat from surface of sauce, reduce over high heat to the desired consistency and strain it over the meat and mushrooms. Cover and simmer gently for 30 minutes, or until tender. Serve from casserole.

OXTAIL RAGOUT

SERVES 4-6

1 medium-sized oxtail
30ml/2 tbls flour
salt and freshly ground black pepper
30ml/2 tbls butter
30ml/2 tbls olive oil
100g/4oz fat bacon, diced
2 Spanish onions, stuck with cloves
1 generous bouquet garni
2 fat garlic cloves
8 carrots
450ml/³/4pt tomato juice
450ml/³/4pt **Basic beef stock** *(see page 65)*
4 turnips
4 leeks, white parts only
4 celery stalks

1. Preheat oven to very slow (140°C/275°F/gas 1 – 150°C/300°F/gas 2).
2. Ask your butcher to cut oxtail into serving pieces. Soak oxtail pieces in cold water for 3 to 4 hours, then put them into fresh water and bring to the boil, skimming regularly. Drain and dry with clean cloth.
3. Put the flour, seasoned generously with salt and black pepper, into a paper bag; add blanched oxtail pieces and shake well to coat evenly.
4. Heat butter and olive oil in a thick-bottomed flameproof casserole; add bacon and sauté until golden. Remove bacon and brown oxtail pieces in resulting fats. Then return bacon to casserole; add onions stuck with cloves, *bouquet garni* and garlic. Thickly slice 4 of the carrots and add to casserole. Season with salt and freshly ground black pepper, to taste.
5. Combine tomato juice and BEEF STOCK, add to the meat and vegetables and bring slowly to the boil. Cover and cook in preheated oven for 3 to 4 hours. Cool and skim off fat.
6. Cut 4 carrots in half lengthwise, quarter turnips and add to casserole with leeks and celery. Cook for 45 minutes or until tender.

ITALIAN BEEF STEW

SERVES 4-6

1.1kg/2½lb lean beef, cut into bite-sized pieces
15ml/1 tbls lard
15ml/1 tbls olive oil
225g/½lb fat salt pork, diced
1 Spanish onion, sliced
2 garlic cloves, chopped
salt and freshly ground black pepper
generous pinch of ground marjoram
300ml/¼pt dry red Italian wine (one of the
  rougher ones)
60ml/4 tbls tomato purée, diluted in a little water

1. Combine lard and olive oil in a thick-bottomed casserole. When fats begin to bubble, add diced fat salt pork, sliced onion and chopped garlic and sauté until golden.
2. Season beef pieces with salt and freshly ground black pepper, to taste, and marjoram; add to casserole and cook, stirring frequently, until meat is well browned on all sides.
3. Now add dry red wine and contine cooking until the wine has been reduced to half the original quantity.
4. Add diluted tomato purée and enough boiling water to cover the meat. Cover casserole and simmer slowly for about 2 hours, or until the meat is tender and the savoury sauce is thick and richly coloured. 15ml-30ml/1-2 tbls of red wine added just before serving will add extra *bouquet* to the dish, which should be served directly from the casserole.

SAUERBRATEN

SERVES 4-6

1.8kg/4lb top round of beef
450ml/¾pt dry red wine
150ml/¼pt red wine vinegar
5ml/1 tsp salt
5ml/1 tsp crushed black peppercorns

2 Spanish onions, sliced
2 large carrots, sliced
2 celery stalks, chopped
½ lemon, sliced
2 bay leaves
4 sprigs of parsley
4 allspice berries
4 cloves
90ml/6 tbls butter
60ml/4 tbls flour
15ml/1 tbls brown sugar
Dumplings *(see page 210)*

1. Ask your butcher to roll the beef and tie it into a round. Wipe with damp cloth and place in a porcelain or earthenware bowl (not metal).
2. Make a marinade by combining in a saucepan the wine and wine vinegar with salt, peppercorns, onions, carrots, celery, lemon, bay leaves, parsley, allspice and cloves. Bring to the boil and pour over the beef; allow to cool, then cover and place in the refrigerator for 3 days, turning it once a day.
3. Remove beef from marinade and wipe dry. Heat the marinade.
4. Meanwhile, melt 60ml/4 tbls butter in a thick-bottomed casserole and sear the meat; sprinkle with 30ml/2 tbls flour and brown on all sides. Pour over the hot marinade and cover tightly; lower the heat and simmer gently for 2½ to 3 hours, or until beef is tender.
5. Pour liquid off the beef and allow to cool. Set casserole containing beef aside. Skim fat from cooking liquid and strain.
6. Melt remaining butter ina thick-bottomed saucepan; blend in remaining flour and the sugar and cook slowly until slightly browned. Gradually add the strained cooking liquid and continue cooking, stirring constantly, until sauce is thick and smooth. Pour sauce over meat, cover, and simmer for 30 minutes. Serve *sauerbraten* accompanied with DUMPLINGS, or BUTTERED NOODLES.

THE AMERICAN MEAT LOAF

Among the great dishes of the world, many American specialities take pride of place – New England boiled dinner, clam chowder and Boston baked beans, Southern fried chicken, prawn and chicken gumbo, Caesar salad, San Francisco's *cioppino,* Philadelphia's 'pepper pot', lobster Newburg and oysters Rockefeller – to name just a few. But none has captured the heart of the American people so completely as the all-American meat loaf . . . an easy-to-cook, easy-to-serve Sunday night supper that is famous the length and breadth of the land.

Try this interesting meat loaf pâté – first cousin of the hamburger – the next time you want an informal supper dish for the family. It will become a fast favourite, I know.

Shape your meat loaf into a loaf or round to bake on a flat baking tray, or press it into a loaf tin or ring mould and cook in the same fashion.

Ring the changes on the basic recipe. Cut ingredients by half for a 'young family' loaf. Use just beef, or pork and veal, or just veal in the basic recipe. Make a loaf of tinned corned beef or a combination of calf's liver and sausage meat. Try poached chicken, finely ground and blended with a spicy, curry-flavoured *Béchamel sauce* before baking.

Change the flavours at will. Almost anything goes in the world of the American meat loaf. Try dry mustard, Worcestershire sauce and finely chopped savory for a different flavour accent. Give your meat loaf body and softness with fresh bread-crumbs, diced white bread and even cornflakes. For a chunky texture, stir in finely chopped green pepper, celery, crisp bacon or water chestnuts. Onions, garlic, herbs and spices lend flavour. Red wine, dry white wine, brandy, lemon juice, tomato and chilli sauces give dash and accent. Eggs are used to bind the mixture together.

Serve with tomato sauce, chilli sauce, chilled soured cream, hot curry sauce or red wine *sauce à la bordelaise.*

AMERICAN MEAT LOAF

SERVES 8

450g/1lb beef, finely ground
225g/¹/₂lb veal, finely ground
225g/¹/₂lb pork, finely ground
30ml/2 tbls olive oil
30ml/2 tbls butter
90ml/6 tbls finely chopped onion
3 celery stalks, finely chopped
2 garlic cloves, finely chopped
150ml/¹/₄pt red wine
2-4 slices bread
5ml/1 tsp salt
2.5ml/¹/₂ tsp freshly ground black pepper
ground allspice
2.5ml/¹/₂ tsp rubbed thyme
2 bay leaves, crushed
2 eggs, well beaten
30-45ml/2-3 tbls red wine, warmed
Tomato sauce *(see page 83), or chilli sauce*
butter, for loaf tin

1. Preheat oven to slow (170°C/325°F/gas 3).
2. Heat olive oil and butter in a thick-bottomed saucepan and sauté onion, celery and garlic until transparent. Add 150ml/¹/₄pt red wine and simmer for 5 minutes.
3. Combine finely ground beef, veal and pork in a large mixing bowl.
4. Trim crusts from bread, dice and add to wine mixture. Pour mixture over ground meats. Mix well and season with salt, freshly ground black pepper, allspice, thyme and bay leaves. The final seasoning should taste rather sharp.
5. Stir well beaten eggs into meat mixtures and pack into a well-buttered 1.7L/3pt loaf tin or pat mixture into a loaf shape on a buttered baking sheet. Bake meat loaf in preheated oven for a minimum of 1 hour, basting from time to time with a few tablespoons of warmed wine. Serve meat loaf with TOMATO SAUCE or chilli sauce.

EASY BLENDER LOAF

SERVES 8

700g/1¹/₂lb beef, finely ground
225g/¹/₂lb pork, finely ground
2 eggs
90ml/6 tbls red wine
1 Spanish onion, sliced
1 garlic clove
6 sprigs of parsley, coarsely chopped
5ml/1 tsp salt
freshly ground black pepper
ground sage, or thyme
butter, for loaf tin

1. Preheat oven to slow (170°C/325°F/gas 3).
2. Place eggs, red wine, sliced onion, garlic and coarsely chopped parsley in container of electric blender or food processor. Blend until vegetables are finely chopped.
3. Combine ground beef and pork, add red wine mixture and mix well. Season with salt, freshly ground black pepper, and sage, or thyme, to taste. Seasoning should be rather sharp.
4. Pack loaf mixture into a buttered loaf tin and bake in preheated oven for 1 to 1¹/₄ hours. Serve immediately.

GRILLED BEEFBURGERS

SERVES 4

1kg/2lb lean beef, chopped
60ml/4 tbls chopped beef marrow
60ml/4 tbls double cream, or cold water
60ml/4 tbls finely chopped onion
salt and freshly ground black pepper
olive oil
30ml/2 tbls melted butter

1. Preheat grill to high.
2. Combine first 4 ingredients and season with salt and freshly ground black pepper, to

taste. Form beef mixture into 8 patties.

3. Brush grid with olive oil, brush patties with melted butter and grill 7.5cm/3in from heat for 4 to 5 minutes on each side. Serve immediately.

SHEPHERD'S PIE

SERVES 4

450g/1lb cooked roast beef, minced
1 Spanish onion, finely chopped
30ml/2 tbls olive oil
300ml/¹/₂pt rich beef gravy, or **Sauce espagnole**
  (see page 82)
10ml/2 tsp Worcestershire sauce
15ml/1 tbls finely chopped parsley
1.5ml/¹/₄ tsp mixed herbs
salt and freshly ground black pepper
90ml/6 tbls double cream
45ml/3 tbls melted butter
1 egg, lightly beaten
hot mashed potatoes

1. Preheat oven to moderately hot (200°C/400°F/gas 6).
2. Sauté finely chopped onion in olive oil until transparent and soft; add minced cooked beef, rich beef gravy, or SAUCE ESPAGNOLE, Worcestershire sauce, finely chopped parsley and mixed herbs. Season with salt and freshly ground black pepper, to taste. Keep warm.
3. Add cream, 30ml/2 tbls melted butter and beaten egg to hot mashed potatoes and season with salt and freshly ground black pepper, to taste.
4. Place meat mixture in the bottom of a well-buttered ovenproof baking dish. Top with mashed potatoes, brush with remaining melted butter and bake in preheated oven for 15 to 20 minutes, or until potatoes are golden brown. Serve immediately.

MEAT BALLS IN TOMATO SAUCE

SERVES 4

450g/1lb minced beef
¹/₂ Spanish onion, finely chopped
1 garlic clove, finely chopped
30ml/2 tbls finely chopped parsley
30ml/2 tbls freshly grated Parmesan cheese
4 slices white bread
milk
2 eggs
dry white wine
salt and freshly ground black pepper
30ml/2 tbls butter
30ml/2 tbls olive oil
Tomato sauce *(see page 83)*

1. Combine minced beef, finely chopped onion, garlic, parsley and grated Parmesan cheese in a bowl and mix thoroughly.
2. Trim crusts from bread, soak in milk, squeeze dry and shred into beef mixture.
3. Add eggs and mix to a smooth paste. Add a little dry white wine and season with salt and freshly ground black pepper, to taste. Form the mixture into small balls.
4. Heat butter and olive oil in a thick-bottomed frying pan and sauté meat balls until golden. Then simmer in TOMATO SAUCE for 1 to 2 hours. Serve with spaghetti.

CHILLI CON CARNE

SERVES 4

1kg/2lb lean beef
450g/1lb fresh pork
1 Spanish onion, finely chopped
4 garlic cloves, chopped
30ml/2 tbls bacon fat
600ml/1pt boiling **Basic beef stock** *(see page 65)*
60ml/4 tbls chilli powder
15ml/1 tbls flour
2 bay leaves

2.5ml/¹/₂ tsp ground cumin
2.5ml/¹/₂ tsp dried oregano
salt and freshly ground black pepper
Mexican beans *(see page 280)*
Boiled rice *(see page 179)*

1. Cut beef and pork into bite-sized cubes, trimming fat as you go.
2. Brown meat, chopped onion and chopped garlic in bacon fat in a thick-bottomed cas-serole. Cover meat with boiling BEEF STOCK; bring again to the boil; cover and simmer gently for about 1 hour.
3. Blend chilli powder with flour in a little of the hot pan juices and add to the casserole to-gether with the bay leaves, cumin and oregano. Season with salt and freshly ground black pepper, to taste. Simmer over low heat until meat is tender. Check seasoning and serve with MEXICAN BEANS and BOILED RICE.

NEW ENGLAND BOILED DINNER

New England, the group of Eastern states that formed the Federal Union – with New York, Pennsylvania and Virginia – in the days when the American flag had only thirteen stars, has given us many great dishes.

The Irish cooks of the great New England first families whose fortunes came from the four-masted sailing ships which plied the seven seas, prided themselves on their plain, good, substantial and nourishing fare. And this love of hearty food, with no frills or furbelows, has come down to us to this very day.

I like New England clam chowder made with native clams *(quahaugs)* so fresh that the salty tang of the sea is still with them, combined with crisp bits of bacon, potatoes and onions simmered to pale gold, and bathed in a rich soup of milk, cream and butter; Saturday night suppers of Boston baked beans, cooked with tender salt pork and a touch of dry mustard, sweet with dark molasses and brown sugar, some-times laced with Jamaica rum. This unctuous dish, Puritan cousin of the French *cassoulet,* is at its succulent best when served with its traditional partner, steamed Boston brown bread, rich and moist.

I like Sunday breakfasts of deep-fried codfish cakes; grilled Maine lobsters with prawn butter; the fabulous outdoor feast that is the New England clam bake – a mis-nomer really, for clams make up only one item of this outdoor dinner and 'bake' is a relative term, for the clams and their companions – corn on the cob, lobsters, saus-ages, frankfurters and sweet and white potatoes – are actually steamed between layers of fresh seaweed, heated on a base of white-hot stones.

But best of all, in my estimation, is the New England boiled dinner. There is no misnomer here, for this is indeed a complete meal, a transatlantic echo of the great country dish that has found its way into the cuisine of every great nation – the hot pot of cock and beef of old England, the *pot-au-feu royale* of France, the *olla podrida* of Spain, and the *bollito misto* of Italy. The New England boiled dinner is an earthy concoction of corned brisket of beef, plump boiling fowl and fat salt pork, simmered until fork-tender with a quartered cabbage, carrots, turnips, onions and potatoes, and served with boiled beetroot, horseradish sauce and pickles.

To make this country dish, ask your butcher to 'corn' or 'salt' a brisket of beef in brine and saltpetre for seven days. Silverside, too, makes for very good eating.

NEW ENGLAND BOILED DINNER

SERVES 8-10

1.8-2.3kg/4-5lb corned brisket of beef
450g/1lb fat salt pork
2 bay leaves
6 black peppercorns
1 boiling chicken
6 large carrots
6 medium onions
6 large potatoes, peeled
2 medium turnips, quartered
1 medium head cabbage, quartered
2 medium cooked beetroot, quartered
horseradish sauce
pickles

1. Wipe brisket of beef with a damp cloth; tie into shape and put into a large thick-bottomed casserole. Add enough cold water to cover and bring to the boil. Drain and rinse beef. Repeat.
2. Cover brisket with boiling water; add salt pork, bay leaves and black peppercorns; cover and simmer over low heat for 3 to 4 hours, or until meat is tender, adding chicken after the first hour.

3. Cool slightly; skim off excess fat and add carrots, onions, potatoes and turnips. Cook for about 20 minutes, then add cabbage wedges and cook until cabbage and vegetables are cooked but still crisp. Serve the meats on a heated platter garnished with the vegetables and cooked beetroot. Accompany with horseradish sauce and pickles.

BOILED BEEF AND CARROTS

SERVES 8-10

1.8-2.3kg/4-5lb round of beef
24 large carrots
2 turnips, quartered
2 Spanish onions, quartered
2 celery stalks, chopped
8 black peppercorns
salt
2 cloves
bouquet garni (bay leaf, 2 sprigs of celery
*   tops and 4 sprig of parsley)*

1. Tie beef securely. Place in a thick-bottomed casserole, cover with water and bring to the boil. Lower heat so that the water is barely simmering, cover and simmer for 20 minutes.

2. Skim off fat and add the vegetables together with black peppercorns, salt, to taste, cloves and *bouquet garni*. Cover and simmer gently for 3 to 4 hours, or until the beef is just tender and the vegetables are soft.

3. To serve: remove beef from broth; untie it and place in a heated serving dish. Serve the vegetables separately on another dish. Accompany with ONION SAUCE (see page 80) and DUM-PLINGS (see page 210).

CHINESE STEAMED BEEF

SERVES 4-6

1kg/2lb rump steak
225g/½lb button mushrooms, thinly sliced
30-60ml/2-4 tbls coarsely chopped onion
30ml/2 tbls soy sauce
60ml/4 tbls olive oil
15ml/1 tbls cornflour
30ml/2 tbls dry white wine
freshly ground black pepper
Boiled rice *(see page 179)*

1. Slice rump steak thinly across the grain.

2. Put thinly sliced beef in a shallow heatproof dish, together with thinly sliced mushrooms and coarsely chopped onion.

3. Combine soy sauce, olive oil, cornflour and dry white wine and pour over beef and vegetables. Season with freshly ground black pepper, to taste, and place dish in steamer, or on a rack in a large thick-bottomed saucepan over 5cm/2in rapidly boiling water. Cover and steam for 15 minutes. Serve beef and vegetables hot from steamer. Serve beef accompanied by BOILED RICE.

CHAPTER 8

LAMB

— MIDDLE EAST KEBABS —

KEBAB (KABAB OR KABOB) means 'to grill or broil' in most of the languages in which it appears. *Shish* (Turkish and Middle Eastern) or *sikh* or *seekh* (Indian) means 'skewer'. So any food skewered and grilled is a *shish* or *sikh kebab*. In Britain, kebab commonly means skewered bits of meat, or meat and vegetables, grilled over charcoal, or under a gas or electric grill.

On a recent trip to Morocco, I was fascinated by the little stalls in the streets, where cooks grilled small brochettes of meat – tiny cubes of beef, lamb or liver – over portable charcoal braziers in the open market-places. The tantalising aroma of these grilled meats with their pungent sauces and spices made my mouth water in every city I visited. The famous *saté* of Java is a similar version of this dish. Made of beef, pork, lamb or chicken, the *saté* consists of nothing but meat, marinated in soy sauce and spices, grilled on thin skewers of bamboo.

But of all the skewered meat dishes in the world, by far the best known – and the most easily translatable in our kitchens – is the Turkish *shish kebab*. I like to serve this dish with a rice pilaff; or on a bed of shredded lettuce lightly dressed with olive oil and lemon juice; or with skewered vegetables; or combine the two for a *shish kebab* with vegetables. Green peppers, tomatoes, poached onions, sliced baby marrows or aubergines and button mushrooms all lend their flavours and textures to this magnificent dish.

First marinate your meat – the Turks like lamb, cut from the leg; others prefer beef. Let it remain in the marinade for at least 12 hours, or overnight. Then thread the cubed meat on long skewers alternately with the vegetables of your choice. Do not push the pieces of meat and vegetables too closely together. Grill over charcoal,

Middle East Kebabs, cubes of spicy meat, threaded onto skewers with tomatoes, mushrooms and herbs, are not only mouth-wateringly delicious, but also easy to prepare. Serve kebabs with saffron rice.

or under a gas or electric grill, until the meat is medium brown, basting with the marinade juices from time to time.

Nothing beats a rotating spit for kebabs. This method ensures even cooking and self-basting with precious juices. And if the weather is too cool for outdoor cookery, kebabs can be grilled indoors with ease. Electric or gas-fired grills or rotisserie spits equipped with skewers approximate the outdoor fire. Simply arrange the skewers under the grill and brown the meat, fish, vegetables or fruit as you would a steak or chops.

When cooking on a skewer, be careful not to let the skewered meat touch the metal grill. If you do, some of the meat will stick to the hot metal. And when you attempt to turn the skewer, the meat or vegetables may stick to the grid and some pieces may fall into the fire. It is much wiser to suspend the skewers above the flames and away from the hot metal grid. When cooking outdoors, for instance, I usually place a brick on each end of the grid and place the ends of the skewers on the bricks so that they can be turned easily.

TURKISH LAMB KEBABS

SERVES 4

1kg/2lb lamb, cut from leg
2 small green peppers, seeded and quartered
4 small tomatoes, halved
8 small onions, poached in stock until tender
2 baby marrows, sliced thickly
8 mushroom caps

FOR THE MARINADE
90ml/6 tbls olive oil
60ml/4 tbls dry sherry
1-2 garlic cloves, finely chopped
¼ Spanish onion, finely chopped
30ml/2 tbls finely chopped parsley
5ml/1 tsp dried oregano
salt and freshly ground black pepper

1. Combine marinade ingredients in a porcelain or earthenware bowl (not metal).

2. Cut lamb into 2.5cm/1in squares and place in the marinade mixture, making sure each piece of meat is properly covered. Cover the bowl with a plate and put in the refrigerator for 12-24 hours, turning the meat several times during this period.

3. If you are barbecuing kebabs, light fire at least 1 hour before you start cooking; if you are grilling kebabs, preheat grill to high.

4. When ready to cook, drain the meat, reserving the marinade, and thread on 8 skewers alternately with green pepper, tomato, poached onion, sliced baby marrow and mushroom cap. Before grilling, brush grid with a little olive oil. Brush the meat and vegetables with the reserved marinade and grill kebabs over hot coals or under the preheated grill for 10-15 minutes, turning the skewers frequently and basting several times during cooking. Serve kebabs with RICE PILAFF (see page 301).

MOROCCAN SKEWERED LAMB

SERVES 4

350g/3/4lb lamb
350g/3/4lb lamb fat
1 leek, white part only
1/2 Spanish onion
15ml/1 tbls chopped chervil
5ml/1 tsp salt
5ml/1 tsp each ground cumin, ginger and crushed
  black pepper
cayenne pepper
paprika
olive oil

1. Cut lamb and lamb fat into equal-sized cubes about 2cm/3/4in square and place in a large porcelain or earthenware bowl (not metal).
2. Pound white part of leek with the onion, chopped chervil and salt in a mortar; add to the meat and sprinkle with ground cumin and ginger, crushed black pepper, cayenne pepper and paprika, to taste, and 30ml/2 tbls olive oil. Mix well and let the lamb marinate in this mixture for 12-24 hours.
3. If you are barbecuing kebabs, light fire at least 1 hour before you start cooking. If you are grilling kebabs, preheat grill to high.
4. When ready to cook, drain lamb, reserving the marinade. Thread lamb onto skewers and brush with reserved marinade. Brush grid with a little olive oil and grill lamb over hot coals, or under preheated grill, for 8-12 minutes, turning skewers frequently and basting several times during cooking. Serve immediately.

RUSSIAN SKEWERED LAMB

SERVES 4-6

700g/1 1/2lb boned lamb
225g/1/2lb green bacon (in one piece)
225g/1/2lb gammon (in one piece)
lemon juice
350g/3/4lb rice
salt and freshly ground pepper
olive oil
30ml/2 tbls finely chopped parsley

1. Cut lamb, bacon and gammon into bite-sized pieces. Blanch bacon and gammon; drain.
2. If you are barbecuing lamb, light fire at least 1 hour before you start cooking; if you are grilling lamb, preheat grill to high.
3. Bring a pan of salted water to the boil with lemon juice. When water is bubbling, dribble in rice gradually through your fingers so that water does not come off the boil. Stir once to dislodge any grains stuck to bottom of pan and boil rice for 15 to 18 minutes, or until tender but still moist. Drain rice in a colander and rinse thoroughly with hot water. Shake out all excess moisture. Keep warm.
4. When ready to cook, thread lamb, bacon and gammon pieces on skewers alternately. Season with salt and freshly ground black pepper, to taste, brush grid with olive oil and grill over hot coals or under preheated grill for 10 to 15 minutes, turning skewers from time to time. Serve skewers on a bed of BOILED RICE and sprinkle with finely chopped parsley.

179

MOUSSAKA

SERVES 6-8

1 Spanish onion, finely chopped
1-2 garlic cloves, finely chopped
60ml/4 tbls olive oil
450g/1lb cooked lamb, diced, chopped finely, or
*   minced*
225g/¹/₂lb mushrooms, chopped
4-6 tomatoes, peeled, seeded and chopped
30ml/2 tbls finely chopped parsley
salt and freshly ground black pepper
15-30ml/1-2 tbls tomato purée
*60-90ml/4-6 tbls **Basic beef stock** (see page*
*   65), or light stock*
4-6 aubergines
flour
olive oil, for frying
60-90ml/4-6 tbls freshly grated Parmesan cheese

1. Preheat oven to moderate (190°C/375°F/
gas 5).
2. Heat olive oil in a thick-bottomed saucepan
and sauté finely chopped onion and garlic until
transparent. Add the lamb and continue cooking, stirring from time to time, until brown.
Add chopped mushrooms, peeled, seeded and
chopped tomatoes and finely chopped parsley.
Season with salt and freshly ground black pepper to taste, and cook until onion is tender.
3. Dilute tomato purée in BEEF STOCK, add to
meat and vegetable mixture, and simmer for
10 minutes.
4. Slice unpeeled aubergines lengthways in
thin slices, dust with flour and fry on both sides
in hot olive oil. Drain on absorbent paper.
5. Line an ovenproof baking dish with slices
of aubergine, spread a layer of the lamb mixture on them, sprinkle lightly with freshly
grated Parmesan cheese and cover with a layer
of aubergines. Continue this process until the
baking dish is full, ending with a layer of aubergines. Sprinkle with grated Parmesan
cheese and bake in the preheated oven until the

top has browned nicely. Serve hot. It is also
very good cold and can be successfully reheated.

MOUSSAKA VARIATIONS
1. Add freshly grated Parmesan cheese and
fresh breadcrumbs to the meat and vegetable
mixture and proceed as above.
2. Add freshly grated Parmesan cheese and
fresh breadcrumbs to the meat and vegetable
mixture. Fill an aubergine-lined dish with
mixture, pour over a well-flavoured BECHAMEL
SAUCE (see page 80), top with aubergine slices
and freshly grated cheese and bake as above.
3. Beat 2 eggs, blend in 30ml/2 tbls flour, add
1 carton plain yoghourt and whisk to a creamy
sauce. Pour this sauce over the meat and vegetable mixture and proceed as above.
4. Dice 1 aubergine, dust with flour, sauté in
olive oil and combine with meat and vegetable
mixture in original recipe, or in any of the
variations above.

MOROCCAN KEFTA

SERVES 6-8

450g/1lb lamb, taken from the leg
100g/¹/₄lb lamb fat, or make up to this amount with
*   beef suet*
¹/₂ Spanish onion, finely chopped
6-8 sprigs parsley, or fresh coriander leaves,
*   finely chopped*
2.5ml/¹/₂ tsp dried marjoram
salt and freshly ground black pepper
1.2ml/¹/₄ tsp each ground cumin, cayenne pepper
*   and paprika*
1 generous pinch of 2 or more of the following:
*   grated nutmeg, ground cinnamon, cloves, ginger*
*   and cardamom*
45ml/3 tbls butter
45ml/3 tbls olive oil

KEFTA SAUCE

450g/1lb tomatoes, peeled, seeded and coarsely
  chopped
½ Spanish onion, finely chopped
30ml/2 tbls finely chopped parsley, or fresh
  coriander leaves
1 garlic clove, finely chopped
60ml/4 tbls olive oil
paprika
cayenne pepper
salt

1. To make kefta sauce, combine ingredients in a saucepan (sauce should be very highly flavoured) and simmer for 1 hour, uncovered.
2. Meanwhile, put lamb, lamb fat and finely chopped onion through the finest blade of your mincer 3 times.
3. Combine lamb mixture with finely chopped parsley, or coriander leaves, and dried marjoram. Season with salt and spices, to taste, freshly ground black pepper. Mix well. The kefta mixture should be very highly flavoured.
4. Form mixture into little balls the size of a marble and poach gently in water for 10 minutes. Then sauté gently in butter and olive oil until lightly browned.
5. Finally, simmer in Kefta sauce for at least 10 minutes before serving. Serve in sauce, or on a bed of BOILED RICE (see page 179) with sauce apart.

ROAST SADDLE OF LAMB

1 saddle of lamb, 2.3kg/5lb
60ml/4 tbls softened butter
salt and freshly ground black pepper
crushed rosemary
450ml/¾pt well-flavoured Basic beef stock (see
  page 65)
15ml/1 tbls flour
olive oil

1. Preheat oven to moderately hot (200°C/400°F/gas 6).
2. Spread saddle of lamb with 45ml/3 tbls softened butter and sprinkle with salt, freshly ground black pepper and crushed rosemary. Place lamb in preheated oven, pour 150ml/¼pt water into the roasting pan and roast for 1 hour, basting frequently.
3. Remove lamb from oven. Discard fat from roasting pan and add well-flavoured BEEF STOCK. Whisk in a *beurre manié,* made by mashing 15ml/1 tbls butter and 15ml/1 tbls flour together to form a smooth paste. Cook over a high heat, stirring all crusty bits from the sides of the pan into the sauce, until sauce is smooth and thick. Strain and reserve.
4. Place partially roasted saddle of lamb in a cleaned and oiled roasting pan. Continue to roast for 15 minutes for pink meat, or up to 30 minutes if you prefer your meat well done. Transfer the lamb to a heated serving platter and leave in a warm place to 'settle' before carving.
5. Heat sauce through. Pour into a heated sauceboat.
6. Serve lamb accompanied by puréed potatoes, peas and sauce.

ROAST SADDLE OF LAMB A L'ARLESIENNE

1 saddle of lamb, 2.3kg/5lb
60ml/4 tbls softened butter
salt and freshly ground black pepper
crushed rosemary
450ml/¾pt Basic beef stock (see page 65)
15ml/1 tbls flour
6 medium-sized baby marrows
6 tomatoes, sliced
olive oil
1 Spanish onion, finely chopped
sprigs of thyme
garlic cloves, unpeeled

FOR THE GARNISH
24 new potatoes, boiled and sautéed in butter
90ml/6 tbls finely chopped mushrooms and
30ml/2 tbls each finely chopped parsley and
truffles, sautéed in butter

1. Preheat oven to moderately hot (200°C/ 400°F/gas 6).
2. Spread saddle of lamb with 45ml/3 tbls softened butter and sprinkle with salt, freshly ground black pepper and crushed rosemary. Place lamb in preheated oven, pour 150ml/ ¼pt water into roasting pan and roast for 1 hour, basting frequently.
3. Remove lamb from oven. Discard fat from roasting pan and add well-flavoured BEEF STOCK. Whisk in a *beurre manié,* made by mashing 15ml/1 tbls butter and 15ml/1 tbls flour together to form a smooth paste. Cook over a high heat stirring all crusty bits from sides of pan into sauce, until sauce is smooth and thick. Strain and reserve.
4. Slice each baby marrow lengwise into 4 or 5 slices, without cutting all the way through, to make a fan shape. Place a thin slice of tomato in each opening.
5. Place partially roasted saddle of lamb in a cleaned and oiled roasting pan on which you have scattered finely chopped onion, sprigs of thyme, garlic cloves and salt and freshly ground black pepper, to taste. Surround lamb with stuffed marrows, sprinkle with a little olive oil and continue to roast for 15 minutes for pink meat, or up to 30 minutes if you prefer your meat well done. Transfer lamb to a heated platter and leave in a warm place to 'settle'.
6. Heat sauce through. Pour into a heated sauceboat.
7. Garnish lamb with stuffed baby marrows at one end of the dish and sautéed potatoes at the other. Sprinkle vegetables with finely chopped mushrooms, parsley and truffles, which you have sautéed in butter. Serve accompanied by sauce.

BARBECUED SADDLE OF LAMB

1 saddle of lamb, 2.3kg/5lb
2 garlic cloves, finely chopped
60ml/4 tbls olive oil
60ml/4 tbls soy sauce
30ml/2 tbls dry white wine
salt and freshly ground black pepper

1. Wipe saddle of lamb with a damp cloth.
2. Combine the finely chopped garlic, olive oil, soy sauce and dry white wine and season with salt and freshly ground black pepper. Rub half of this mixture into the saddle of lamb and allow the flavour to penetrate for at least 1 hour.
3. Preheat oven to moderately hot (200°C/ 400°F/gas 6).
4. Just before cooking, rub more of the mixture into the lamb, reserving some for basting. Place the lamb in the preheated oven and roast for 15 minutes per 450g/1lb, basting from time to time, or until the lamb is pink and rare. Transfer lamb to a heated serving platter and leave in a warm place to 'settle' before carving.

ROAST SHOULDER OF LAMB WITH HERBS

1 shoulder of lamb, 1.4kg/3lb when boned
30ml/2 tbls olive oil
salt and freshly ground black pepper
6 sprigs each of thyme, bay leaves and rosemary

1. Preheat oven to slow (170°C/325°F/gas 3).
2. Ask your butcher to bone and trim a shoulder of lamb ready for rolling, but do not let him roll it. Lay the lamb out flat, brush with olive oil and sprinkle with salt and freshly ground black pepper, to taste. Place 2 sprigs each of thyme, bay leaves and rosemary on the lamb, roll it up neatly and tie securely.
3. Place 4 sprigs each of thyme, bay leaves and rosemary around the lamb. Brush with olive

oil and roast in the preheated oven for 1¼ hours for pink meat, or up to 1¾ hours for well done. 30 minutes before end of cooking time, increase oven temperature to moderately hot (200°C/400°F/gas 6) and cook until golden brown and cooked through. Transfer lamb to a heated serving platter and leave in a warm place to 'settle' before carving.

BARBECUED LAMB PROVENCAL

1 leg of lamb, 2.7-3.2kg/6-7lb
6 garlic cloves, finely chopped
90ml/6 tbls finely chopped parsley
90ml/6 tbls fresh breadcrumbs
90ml/6 tbls softened butter
juice of 1 lemon
salt and freshly ground black pepper

1. Make a smooth paste of the finely chopped garlic cloves and parsley, fresh breadcrumbs, softened butter and lemon juice. Season with salt and freshly ground black pepper, to taste.
2. Wipe lamb with a damp cloth and spread with the paste, pressing it well in so that the seasonings do not fall off during the cooking. Allow flavour to penetrate for at least 1 hour.
3. Light fire at least 1 hour before cooking time.
4. When ready to cook, balance lamb on the spit, inserting the spit in line with the bone so it can rotate freely and easily. Roast for 1½ to 2 hours for a leg of lamb as pink and juicy as I like it, longer if you like it less rare. Allow the meat to rest on the spit for 10 minutes to retain juices before removing spit.

NOTE: A leg of lamb may be roasted in a slow oven (170°C/325°F/gas 3) for 20 to 25 minutes per 450g/1lb. Provençal dressing will give the same wonderful flavour.

CHUMP CHOPS STUFFED WITH CHICKEN LIVERS

SERVES 4

4 lamb chump chops, 2cm/¾in thick
4 chicken livers, chopped
2 shallots, finely chopped
45ml/3 tbls butter
15ml/1 tbls lemon juice
salt and freshly ground black pepper
1 pinch of curry powder
4 large mushroom caps
olive oil
watercress

1. Trim chump chops and slash remaining fat with a sharp knife at intervals to to prevent it curling up during cooking. Slit a pocket in each chop.
2. Preheat grill to high.
3. Sauté chopped chicken livers and finely chopped shallots in 30ml/2 tbls butter until livers are cooked. Mash livers to a smooth paste with lemon juice and season with salt and freshly ground black pepper, to taste, and a pinch of curry powder. Stuff chops with this mixture.
4. When ready to grill: brush grid of grill pan with a little olive oil and grill under preheated grill, 7.5cm/3in from heat, for 3 minutes on each side for pink meat, or 5 minutes each side if you prefer your meat well done.
5. Meanwhile, sauté mushroom caps in remaining butter until tender.
6. To serve: transfer stuffed chops to a heated platter. Set 1 mushroom cap on each chop, garnish with fresh watercress and serve.

ROAST LEG OF LAMB PROVENCAL

1 leg of lamb, about 2.7kg/6lb
15ml/1 tbls butter
6 garlic cloves
700g/1½lb potatoes
salt and freshly ground black pepper
60-90ml/4-6 tbls finely chopped parsley
300ml/½pt **Basic chicken stock** *(see page 66)*

1. Ask your butcher to trim and tie a leg of lamb.
2. Preheat oven to slow (170°C/325°F/gas 3).
3. Butter a shallow thick-bottomed oven-proof casserole or gratin dish, just large enough to hold leg of lamb comfortably, and rub it lightly with a cut clove of garlic.
4. Peel potatoes, cut in thick slices and arrange in the bottom of the dish in overlapping rows. Season generously with salt and freshly ground black pepper. Chop the remaining garlic finely and sprinkle over the potatoes together with finely chopped parsley.
5. Place lamb on the potatoes and moisten with the BASIC CHICKEN STOCK. Roast in pre-heated oven for 1¼ hours, or until the lamb is pink and tender. If you prefer lamb less pink, increase cooking time to 1¾ hours.

MOROCCAN STEAMED LAMB

2.3kg/5lb lamb (cut from the shoulder)
coarse salt
large pinch of ground saffron
ground cumin
freshly ground black pepper
60ml/4 tbls butter
Boiled rice *(see page 179)*
Steamed couscous *(see page 281)*

1. Combine 15ml/1 tbls salt, ground saffron and 1.5ml/¼ tsp ground cumin and rub lamb

with this mixture. Season with freshly ground black pepper, to taste.
2. Wrap meat in a tea towel and place in the top section of a large double steamer over boiling water. (Bottom section of steamer should be three quarters full.) Close steamer hermetically with damp towels and steam lamb over a high flame for 3 hours with lifting cover.
3. Just before serving, sauté lamb in butter until golden. Serve with BOILED RICE or STEAMED COUSCOUS, and separate little pots of ground cumin and coarse salt.

LAMB CHOPS 'EN CUIRASSE'

SERVES 6

6 loin lamb chops
90ml/6 tbls butter
225g/½lb mushrooms, finely chopped
1 Spanish onion, finely chopped
2 slices ham, finely chopped
salt and freshly ground black pepper
Flaky pastry *(see page 346)*
1 egg, beaten
Tomato sauce *(see page 83)*

1. Preheat oven to hot (230°C/450°F/gas 8).
2. Trim all fat from lamb chops and sauté in a little butter until golden. Remove and allow to cool.
3. Add remaining butter to pan and sauté finely chopped mushrooms, onion and ham until vegetables are soft. Season with salt and freshly ground black pepper to taste. Allow to cool.
4. Spread mushroom mixture on both sides of each chop.
5. Roll out FLAKY PASTRY into 6 circles (big enough to encase chops) and place 1 chop on each. Wrap in pastry, leaving the bone sticking out, moisten join with water and seal securely. Place pastry-wrapped chops on baking sheet, join side down, brush with beaten egg and

bake in preheated oven for 15 to 20 minutes. Serve with TOMATO SAUCE.

ITALIAN BREADED LAMB CHOPS

SERVES 4

4-6 baby lamb chops
olive oil
salt and freshly ground black pepper
flour
1 egg, beaten
fresh breadcrumbs
60-90ml/4-6 tbls butter
watercress

1. Trim lamb chops, brush with olive oil and season with salt and freshly ground black pepper, to taste. Dust chops with flour, shaking off excess, dip in beaten egg and roll in breadcrumbs.
2. Saute chops in 60-90ml/4-6 tbls olive oil and butter until golden brown. Garnish with watercress and serve.

GRILLED MARINATED LAMB CHOPS

SERVES 4-6

8-10 loin lamb chops
salt and freshly ground black pepper
2 bay leaves, crumbled
2 garlic cloves, finely chopped
90ml/6 tbls olive oil
90ml/6 tbls dry white wine
suet pieces

1. Ask your butcher to trim a loin of lamb into 8 or 10 chops. Arrange them in a large flat dish and season with salt and freshly ground black pepper to taste. Add the crumbled bay leaves, finely chopped garlic cloves, olive oil and dry white wine and marinate chops in this mix-ture, turning them once or twice, for at least 2 hours.
2. Meanwhile, preheat grill to high.
3. When ready to grill, drain chops. Rub grid with the pieces of suet and grill chops 7.5cm/3in from heat for 4 minutes on each side for pink meat, 5 minutes on each side if you prefer your meat well done. Serve immediately.

ROGNONS FLAMBES 'LASSERRE'

SERVES 4

4 lambs' kidneys
60ml/4 tbls butter
5-10ml/1-2 tsp Dijon mustard
salt and freshly ground black pepper
30-60ml/2-4 tbls port
Armagnac, warmed
30-60ml/2-4 tbls pâté de foie gras
15-30ml/1-2 tbls lemon juice

1. Skin kidneys and sauté quickly in half the butter to allow them to stiffen and brown while still remaining practically raw. Dice kidneys.
2. Melt remaining butter in a thick-bottomed frying pan. Add diced kidneys and Dijon mustard and season with salt and freshly ground black pepper, to taste. Stir well over a high heat for a minute or two before adding the port. Sprinkle kidneys with the Armagnac and flame. Allow the flames to die down and the alcohol to evaporate, stirring continuously.
3. Mash *pâté de foie gras* with a fork until well blended, stir into the sauce and cook for a minute or two more until the sauce is smooth and the kidneys are tender. Do not allow sauce to boil at any time during its preparation.
4. Just before serving, stir in lemon juice, to taste. Serve kidneys with boiled new potatoes.

185

— NAVARIN DE MOUTON —

I FIRST BECAME INTERESTED in French casserole cookery when I lived in Paris, and Naomi came from her native Burgundy in answer to my advertisement for a housekeeper in the daily press. As soon as I saw her I knew that I must hire her. She was a trim, white-haired, little old lady with fat rosy cheeks, dressed in a strict blue suit and cream flannel blouse, with a narrow black tie that exactly matched the ribbon in her pince-nez.

Naomi had been a *cordon bleu* cook for a famous Marquis and as such was qualified for the highest of positions, but age and recurrent attacks of migraine had taught her to avoid the heavy responsibilities of *haute cuisine* and hire herself out as cook and maid of all work. I engaged her on the spot and for the five long years that I remained in Paris I never regretted the day. For Naomi proved to be a treasure such as I have rarely known, a superb cook, a wonderful housekeeper and a true friend.

Most of Naomi's dishes were of the long, slow-cooking variety – the superb casseroles of meat, fish and game for which France is famous. And she was an expert in the art of making even the least desirable cuts of meat taste delicious. Sometimes she would marinate the meat in wine, olive oil and herbs to tenderise it before it was cooked. Other times she would 'seize' it in a little butter or olive oil, flavour it with aromatic herbs and touch of garlic, and then simmer it for hours in a sauce made rich with stock, wine or cream.

I soon learned, however, that long cooking alone cannot ensure perfect results. Naomi taught me to watch the pot to make certain it cooked so gently that it hardly bubbled, for it was only in this way that meat could be kept from going stringy and tough; to add crisp *lardons* of green bacon or fat salt pork, along with tiny white onions parboiled to *al dente* tenderness, and button mushrooms sautéed in butter and lemon juice, to lend contrast in texture and flavour to my dishes. And she taught me to give casserole dinners. For Naomi had one failing only – a hangover from her days in the household of the Marquis – she disliked waiting on table, preferring the anonymity of her kitchen to facing the battery of guests in the dining-room. So together we evolved the perfect plan for easy entertaining: one superb casserole dish cooked to perfection, preceded by a cold or hot hors-d'oeuvre, and followed by a crisp green salad, cheese and fruit. Nothing could be simpler, or more delicious. And nothing moved my circle of Paris friends to more heartfelt thanks than one of Naomi's casseroles.

Navarin de mouton was one of her favourites — and to anyone who once tasted Naomi's version of this famous dish, no ordinary lamb stew would ever be the same again. A boned shoulder or breast of young lamb was the secret here, browned in butter and lard with a quartered onion, and simmered in a tomato-flavoured stock with a few quartered turnips.

Naomi always added glazed button onions, crisp golden bacon bits and tiny new potatoes and fresh peas to her *navarin* after the first hour of gentle cooking, so that the vegetables and diced bacon would offer texture and flavour contrast to the meltingly tender lamb.

NAVARIN DE MOUTON

SERVES 4-6

1.1kg/2½lb boned shoulder or breast of lamb
60ml/4 tbls butter
30ml/2 tbls lard
1 Spanish onion, quartered
30ml/2 tbls flour
granulated sugar
salt and freshly ground black pepper
1 garlic clove, finely chopped
4 small turnips, quartered
1 bouquet garni
450ml/¾pt **Basic chicken stock** *(see page 66)*
60ml/4 tbls tomato purée, diluted in a little water
12 small button onions
100g/4oz green bacon, diced
12 small potatoes, peeled
100g/4oz fresh peas, shelled
30ml/2 tbls finely chopped parsley

1. Preheat oven to moderate (180°C/350°F/gas 4).
2. Cut lamb shoulder or breast of lamb into 4cm/1½in cubes.
3. Melt 30ml/2 tbls each butter and lard in a thick-bottomed ovenproof casserole and brown lamb cubes with the quartered onion. Pour off some of the fat and blend in the flour, stirring over low heat until slightly thickened. Sprinkle with a generous pinch of sugar to give a deeper colour to the sauce and season with salt and freshly ground black pepper, to taste. Add the finely chopped garlic, quartered turnips and *bouquet garni*. Stir in 300ml/½pt CHICKEN STOCK and tomato purée diluted with a little water, and simmer, covered, in the preheated oven for 1 hour.
4. Meanwhile, melt 30ml/2 tbls butter in a thick-bottomed frying pan; add remaining sugar and the CHICKEN STOCK and glaze the button onions. Blanch and sauté the diced green bacon.
5. Remove lamb from casserole and strain sauce through a sieve, removing any skin or small bones. Allow the sauce to cool, skim fat from the surface and strain into a clean casserole. Add the lamb to the casserole with the glazed button onions, sautéed bacon, potatoes and fresh peas. Bring to the boil then return to the oven and simmer covered, for 30 to 40 minutes, or until the vegetables are cooked and lamb is tender. Sprinkle with finely chopped parsley just before serving.

SCOTS HOTCH POTCH

SERVES 4-6

1.4kg/3lb neck of lamb
2.3L/4pt light stock or water
2 Spanish onions, coarsely chopped
salt and freshly ground black pepper
celery salt
450g/1lb fresh peas, shelled
225g/¹/₂lb broad beans, shelled
4-6 young carrots, diced
4-6 young turnips, diced
1 small cauliflower
60ml/4 tbls finely chopped parsley

1. Place neck of lamb in a thick-bottomed cas-serole with the stock or water and coarsely chopped onions. Season with salt, freshly ground black pepper and celery salt, to taste. Bring slowly to the boil, skimming carefully.
2. Add half the fresh peas to the casserole to-gether with the broad beans, diced carrots and turnips. Bring to the boil again, skim care-fully, then lower heat and simmer slowly, co-vered, for 3 hours.
3. Separate cauliflower into flowerets.
4. Half an hour before serving, add prepared cauliflower and remaining peas to casserole and continue cooking until vegetables are ten-der.
5. Just before serving, remove lamb from cas-serole and cut into serving pieces. Return to casserole, sprinkle with finely chopped parsley, correct seasoning and serve.

IRISH STEW

SERVES 4-6

1.4kg/3lb shoulder of mutton
450g/1lb onions, thickly sliced
2 celery stalks, thickly sliced
225g/¹/₂lb carrots, thickly sliced
1kg/2lb potatoes, thickly sliced

salt and freshly ground black pepper
light stock or water
30-45ml/2-3 tbls finely chopped parsley

1. Cut the mutton into 6.5cm/2½in cubes.
2. Place a layer of sliced onions, celery and carrots in the bottom of a thick-bottomed cas-serole, cover with a layer of meat, and then a layer of potatoes. Continue filling casserole with alternate layers, seasoning each layer with salt and freshly ground black pepper. Finish with a layer of potatoes.
3. Add water or light stock to cover, and bring to the boil. Skim, lower heat and sim-mer, covered, until tender (almost 3 hours). Just before serving, sprinkle with finely chopped parsley.

BLANQUETTE D'AGNEAU

SERVES 4-6

1.1kg/2¹/₂lb shoulder or breast of lamb
lemon juice
light stock, or a mixture of stock and water
5ml/1 tsp salt
freshly ground black pepper
1 Spanish onion, studded with 1 clove
2 carrots
1 leek
1 bouquet garni (2 or 3 sprigs parsley, 1 sprig
*   thyme, 1 bay leaf and 1 celery stalk)*
12 button onions
12 button mushrooms
butter
30ml/2 tbls flour
2 egg yolks
125ml/4fl oz double cream
freshly grated nutmeg

1. Cut shoulder or breast of lamb, or a combi-nation of the two, into small pieces, and soak for 12 hours in cold water with a little lemon juice. Change the water 2 or 3 times.

2. Place blanched lamb pieces in a thick-bottomed casserole with enough light stock, or stock and water, to cover. Season with salt and freshly ground black pepper, to taste, and bring to the boil. Remove any scum that forms on the surface with a perforated spoon, as you would for a *pot-au-feu*. Add onion studded with 1 clove, carrots, leek and the *bouquet garni*. Cover and simmer gently over a very low heat for 1½ hours, or until tender.

3. Meanwhile, cook button onions in a little water until just firm. Drain and keep warm.

4. Simmer mushrooms in a little butter and lemon juice. Keep warm.

5. Make a white roux by melting 30ml/2 tbls butter in a thick-bottomed saucepan, add flour and cook for a few minutes, stirring constantly, without allowing it to take on colour. Then add 600ml/1pt stock from the casserole and stir well over a high heat until sauce is smooth and creamy. Lower heat and simmer for 15 minutes, stirring from time to time. Remove saucepan from heat and 'finish' sauce by stirring in egg yolks, double cream and the juice of half a lemon.

6. Drain lamb pieces from the remaining stock (removing bits of bone and fat which have separated from meat in cooking).

7. Clean casserole; return lamb pieces and strain sauce through a fine sieve over the meat. Stir cooked button onions and mushrooms carefully into the *blanquette;* season with a little freshly grated nutmeg and keep warm in oven, covered, until ready to serve. A little more cream and a squeeze of lemon may be added just before serving.

CARIBBEAN LAMB

SERVES 4-6

1.4kg/3lb shoulder of lamb
60ml/4 tbls butter
30ml/2 tbls olive oil

15ml/1 tbls curry powder
2.5ml/½ tsp ground turmeric
1 pinch ground ginger
1.5ml/¼ tsp cayenne pepper
coarse salt and freshly ground black pepper
30ml/2 tbls lemon juice
300ml/½ pint well-flavoured stock
Boiled rice (see page 179)
fried bananas
chutneys

1. Cut lamb into 6.5cm/2½in cubes.

2. Melt butter and olive oil in a thick-bottomed casserole and sauté lamb cubes until golden.

3. Combine curry powder, turmeric, ginger, cayenne pepper and coarse salt and freshly ground black pepper, to taste.

4. Stir curry mixture into casserole. Sprinkle with lemon juice, stir again and then add well-flavoured stock and enough water barely to cover. Cover casserole and simmer for 30 minutes, or until lamb is tender and sauce is reduced to the proper consistency. Serve with BOILED RICE, fried bananas and chutneys.

DAUBE DE MOUTON

SERVES 4-6

1.4kg/3lb boned shoulder of mutton
thin strips of pork fat
thin strips of green bacon
3 Spanish onions, sliced
4 carrots, sliced
1 bouquet garni (thyme, parsley and bay leaf)
salt and freshly ground black pepper
600ml/1pt red wine
60ml/4 tbls olive oil
100g/4oz green bacon, diced
600ml/1pt hot stock
30-60ml/2-4 tbls tomato purée
1 garlic clove, finely chopped
30ml/2 tbls finely chopped parsley

1. Cut mutton into 6.5cm/2½in cubes; lard each cube with thin strips of pork fat and green bacon and place in a porcelain or earthenware bowl (not metal), with 2 sliced onions and carrots, *bouquet garni,* salt and freshly ground black pepper to taste, and red wine. Marinate mutton in this mixture for 5 to 6 hours, stirring occasionally.

2. Preheat oven to slow (170°C/325°F/gas 3).

3. Remove mutton from marinade. Strain marinade into a thick-bottomed saucepan and reduce to half the original quantity.

4. Heat olive oil in a thick-bottomed ovenproof casserole and sauté diced green bacon and remaining sliced onion until onion is transparent. Add mutton and sauté with bacon and onion until browned, shaking casserole from time to time.

5. Meanwhile, combine hot stock and tomato purée.

6. Add finely chopped garlic to the casserole and moisten with the reduced marinade. Pour over the hot stock mixed with tomato purée. Cover casserole with greaseproof paper and the lid and cook in preheated oven for 3 to 4 hours.

7. Remove casserole from oven; skim fat from surface, sprinkle with finely chopped parsley and serve.

CURRIED LAMB LOAF

SERVES 4-6

1kg/2lb boned lamb, minced
15ml/1 tbls curry powder
1.5ml/¼ tsp each ground ginger, turmeric and
  coriander
generous pinch each of paprika and cayenne
  pepper
15ml/1 tbls flour
coarse salt and freshly ground black pepper
1 egg, lightly beaten
butter

FOR THE COURT BOUILLON
900ml/1½pts water
15ml/1 tbls ground coriander
generous pinch of dried thyme

FOR THE SAUCE
½ Spanish onion, finely chopped
30ml/2 tbls butter
salt and freshly ground black pepper
1.5ml/¼ tsp paprika
1.5ml/¼ tsp ground coriander
150ml/¼pt carton plain yoghourt

1. Combine minced lamb with curry powder, ginger, turmeric, coriander, paprika, cayenne pepper, flour and coarse salt and freshly ground black pepper, to taste. Add the egg; mix well and form meat mixture into a loaf. Place loaf in a buttered gratin dish just large enough to hold it.

2. To steam loaf: combine water, coriander and thyme; bring to the boil, place gratin dish in the top of a steamer and steam loaf for 20 to 30 minutes.

3. To make sauce: sauté finely chopped onion in butter until soft; sprinkle with salt and freshly ground black pepper to taste, paprika and ground coriander. Pour in juices from loaf, stir in yoghourt and heat through. Pour sauce over loaf and serve.

LAMB CURRY

SERVES 4-6

1.1kg/2½lb boned lamb
60ml/4 tbls butter
30ml/2 tbls olive oil
1 Spanish onion, finely chopped
1 garlic clove, finely chopped
1 green pepper, seeded and finely chopped
2 celery stalks, finely chopped
150ml/¼pt coconut milk (dried coconut, milk and
  butter) – see recipe

300ml/¹/₂pt well-flavoured stock
50g/2oz seedless raisins
90ml/6 tbls plain yoghourt
Boiled rice *(see page 179)*
poppadoms
curry condiments

KARI BLEND
30ml/2 tbls curry powder
2.5ml/¹/₂ tsp each ground ginger and turmeric
1.5ml/¹/₄ tsp each paprika and cayenne pepper
15ml/1 tbls flour
coarse salt
freshly ground black pepper

1. Cut lamb into 4cm/1¹/₂in cubes.
2. Melt butter in a thick-bottomed casserole and sauté lamb cubes, turning with a wooden spoon to preserve juices, until golden. Remove from casserole. Keep warm.
3. Add olive oil to casserole and sauté finely chopped onion, garlic, green pepper and celery until vegetables are soft.
4. Meanwhile, mix *kari* blend thoroughly in a bowl. (Note: If this is your first curry, stir in half the mixture; check flavour of sauce after you have added coconut milk and stock and add more *kari* until the sauce is of desired pungency.)
5. Stir *kari* blend into vegetable mixture.
6. Make coconut milk by simmering a handful of dried coconut in 150ml/¹/₄ pint milk with 15ml/1 tbls butter. Press this mixture through a fine sieve, combine with stock and add to vegetables and spices. Cover and simmer for 15 minutes.
7. Return lamb cubes to casserole together with raisins and continue cooking over a low heat until meat is tender, stirring occasionally.
8. Remove casserole from heat and stir in yoghourt; correct seasoning and serve curry with BOILED RICE, *poppadoms,* and traditional curry condiments: mango chutney, apple chutney, preserved *kumquats,* chopped cooked bacon, etc.

LAMB PROVENCAL

1 leg of lamb, about 2kg/4lb
15ml/1 tbls butter
1 cut garlic clove
30ml/2 tbls olive oil
1 bayleaf, crumbled
1.5ml/¹/₄ tsp dried thyme
150ml/¹/₄pt **Basic aspic** *(see page 67)*

PROVENCAL GLAZE
2-3 garlic cloves, finely chopped
90ml/6 tbls fresh breadcrumbs
120ml/8 tbls finely chopped parsley
90ml/6 tbls softened butter
¹/₂ small packet Philadelphia cream cheese
juice of 1 lemon
salt
freshly ground black pepper

1. Preheat oven to slow (170°C/325°F/gas 3).
2. Ask your butcher to trim and tie a leg of lamb. Butter a thick-bottomed ovenproof casserole, or *gratin* dish, just large enough to hold leg of lamb comfortably. Rub surface of lamb lightly with the cut garlic clove and sprinkle lightly with olive oil, crumbled bay leaf and dried thyme.
3. Roast lamb in the preheated oven for 1¹/₄ to 1³/₄ hours, or until lamb is pink and tender. If you prefer lamb less pink, increase cooking time. Remove lamb from oven and allow to become cold.
4. To prepare Provençal glaze: combine finely chopped garlic, fresh breadcrumbs, finely chopped parsley, softened butter, cream cheese and lemon juice. Mash to a smooth paste and season with salt and freshly ground black pepper, to taste.
5. Spread lamb with Provençal glaze, smoothing surface over with a spatula. Brush with several coats of well flavoured BASIC ASPIC and allow to set. Serve with individual glazed vegetable tarts.

LAMB COOKED LIKE GAME

SERVES 4-6

1.1kg/2½lb shoulder of lamb
olive oil
salt
2 Spanish onions, chopped
4 garlic cloves, chopped
red Burgundy
60ml/4 tbls cognac
peel of 1 orange
*150ml/¼pt **Basic chicken stock** (see page 66)*
45ml/3 tbls butter

AROMATIC SPICE MIXTURE

5ml/1 tsp salt
2.5ml/½ tsp ground nutmeg
1.5ml/¼ tsp ground cloves
2 bay leaves, crumbled
2.5ml/½ tsp dried thyme
6 juniper berries, crushed
12 black peppercorns, crushed
15ml/1 tbls sugar

1. Cut shoulder of lamb into even-sized cubes about 2.5cm/1in square.
2. Combine aromatic spice mixture.
3. Place lamb cubes in a porcelain or earthenware bowl (not metal); add 125ml/4fl oz olive oil and aromatic spice mixture and toss well. Season with salt, to taste. Add chopped onions and garlic cloves, 120ml/8 tbls red Burgundy and the cognac; toss well, cover and keep in the refrigerator for 2 to 3 days, tossing meats once or twice each day, to allow the rich flavours to permeate the lamb.
4. Remove lamb from the refrigerator and bring to room temperature. Add orange peel and CHICKEN STOCK.
5. Preheat oven to cool (110°C/225°F/gas ¼).
6. When ready to cook, drain the lamb, reserving marinade juices, and sauté in butter and olive oil until lightly browned.
7. Meanwhile, cook marinade juices over a high heat until reduced by one half; strain into a thick-bottomed ovenproof casserole; add lamb cubes and bring to the boil on top of the stove. Cover and cook in preheated oven for 1½ to 2 hours, or until tender, adding more red wine, from time to time, if necessary.

CARRE D'AGNEAU MICHAEL GUERARD

SERVES 2

1 small rack of lamb (about 6 chops)
1 cut garlic clove
softened butter, or olive oil
salt and freshly ground black pepper
crushed rosemary and thyme
*30ml/2 tbls reduced **Basic beef stock** (see page 65)*

1. Preheat oven to moderately hot (200°C/400°F/gas 6).
2. Rub rack of lamb with the cut garlic clove and then spread the meat generously with softened butter, or sprinkle with a little olive oil, before seasoning with salt and freshly ground black pepper, crushed rosemary and thyme, to taste. Cover rib bones with foil to prevent them burning during cooking.
3. Place lamb, fatty side down, on the rack of an open roasting pan and cook for 20 to 30 minutes for pink, leaving it a little longer if you prefer your lamb slightly less rare, or if the lamb is not as young as you would like.
4. Transfer lamb to a heated serving dish. Remove foil from rib bones and carve meat into chops. Keep warm.
5. Skim off excess fat from pan juices, add reduced BEEF STOCK to pan and cook over high heat, stirring briskly to dislodge crusty bits from bottom of pan. Strain the small quantity of juice over the meat and serve.

Lamb Cooked Like Game has a distinctive flavour.

CHAPTER 9

VEAL

OSSO BUCO

WHY CAN'T RESTAURANTS write menus that really help? First of all, most menus are too full. To offer a choice of 70 different dishes is not really helpful to the diner. Nobody's taste is so jaded that they cannot select a meal from a dozen or so alternatives. This *embarras du choix,* in fact, defeats all but the most practised, for the majority of people, if faced by too wide a selection (and this is proved by statistics) embarrassedly plump for shrimp cocktail and steak.

I cannot see why at least some of the main dishes on each menu should not be described in some detail. The White Tower in London and the Four Seasons in New York have made quite a thing out of their poetic descriptions of the day's specialities. But even a straightforward description of what is in a dish and how it is cooked would prove invaluable. So many people seem to be nervous of betraying their ignorance of what something is, particularly when they are young, that they stick to the same dreary things they have had every time before. And yet everyone, at some time or other, has to eat a dish for the first time.

I remember seeing a much travelled 60-year-old American – knowledgeable beyond belief about the intricacies of Russian and Chinese cooking – tripped by *osso buco.* Much to the scorn of the waiter, she left the marrow. To me, it was the waiter who showed his ignorance in not telling her that the marrow was the climax of the dish, instead of just whisking it away with a distinct sneer.

Because I am always trying something new, some dish I have only heard of before, I am never shy about asking. I discuss constantly with waiters what they mean by the international phrases they use so loosely (and to most waiters, remember, French is as foreign a language as it is to us). They never seem to mind this cross-

Osso Buco — veal marrow bones simmered in a rich tomato sauce and served with saffron rice.

This is definitely not a dish for dieters; it should be savoured to the very last mouthful.

examination; in fact, they seem rather to like it – at least you are showing an interest in their work.

But back to *osso buco:* what other dish hides its most succulent treats so secretly? How on earth, if you had not had it explained to you, could you be expected to know how to enjoy it? I like to serve *osso buco* accompanied by saffron rice as the main course for a summer luncheon with an Italian flavour. It is a sturdy country dish – rich and full-bodied – that fairly cries out to be eaten in the sun.

Serve the lightest of *antipasti* before it and follow with a tossed green salad and a choice of cheeses – Italian, of course – or perhaps a fresh fruit salad macerated in Chianti. Chianti or Bardolo Rosso is the perfect liquid accompaniment.

OSSO BUCO

SERVES 4

4 slices shin of veal
flour
salt and freshly ground black pepper
30ml/2 tbls olive oil
30ml/2 tbls butter
2 garlic cloves, finely chopped
1/2 Spanish onion, finely chopped
150ml/1/4pt light stock or boiling water
150ml/1/4pt dry white wine
30-60ml/2-4 tbls tomato purée
1 anchovy fillet, finely chopped
60ml/4 tbls finely chopped parsley
grated rind of 1/2 lemon
Saffron rice *(see page 297)*

1. Choose shin of veal with plenty of meat and have it sawn into pieces 5cm/2in thick. Dredge pieces with flour; season with salt and freshly ground black pepper, to taste.
2. Heat olive oil and butter in a thick-bottomed casserole and brown veal pieces. Add 1 finely chopped garlic clove and the onion; pour over light stock, boiling water or dry white wine and tomato purée; cover and simmer for about 1½ hours.

3. Add the anchovy fillet and the remaining garlic clove. Blend thoroughly, heat through and serve sprinkled with chopped parsley and grated lemon rind, and accompanied by SAFFRON RICE.

BLANQUETTE DE VEAU

SERVES 4-6

1.4kg/3 lb shoulder or breast of veal
lemon juice
light stock, or stock and water
5ml/1 tsp salt
freshly ground black pepper
1 Spanish onion, studded with 1 clove
2 carrots
1 leek
1 bouquet garni (2 or 3 sprigs parsley, 1 sprig thyme, 1 bay leaf and 1 celery stalk)
12 button onions
12 button mushroom caps
butter
30ml/2 tbls flour
2 egg yolks
150ml/1/4pt double cream
freshly grated nutmeg

1. Cut shoulder or breast of veal, or a combination of the two, into small pieces and soak for 12 hours in cold water with a little lemon juice. Change water 2 or 3 times.

2. Place blanched veal pieces in a deep thick-bottomed casserole with enough stock, or stock and water, to cover; season with salt and freshly ground black pepper to taste and bring to the boil. Remove any scum that forms on the surface with a perforated spoon as you would for a *pot-au-feu*. Add onion studded with clove, carrots, leek and the *bouquet garni*. Cover and simmer gently over a very low heat for about 1½ hours.

3. Meanwhile, cook button onions in a little water until just firm. Drain and keep warm.

4. Simmer mushrooms in a little butter and lemon juice. Keep warm.

5. Make a white roux by melting 30ml/2 tbls butter in a thick-bottomed saucepan; add flour and cook for a few minutes, stirring constantly, without allowing it to take on colour. Then add 600ml/1pt stock from the casserole and stir well over a high heat until sauce is smooth and creamy. Lower heat and simmer for 15 minutes, stirring from time to time. Remove casserole from heat and 'finish' sauce by stirring in egg yolks, cream and the juice of half a lemon.

6. Drain veal pieces from the remaining stock (removing bits of bone and fat which have separated from meat in cooking).

7. Clean casserole; return veal pieces and strain sauce through a fine sieve over the meat. Stir mushrooms and onions carefully into the *blanquette;* season with a little grated nutmeg and keep warm in oven, covered, until ready to serve. A little more cream and a squeeze of lemon may be added just before serving.

ZEPHIRES DE RIS DE VEAU 'PLANSON'

SERVES 6-8

3 pairs sweetbreads
dry white wine
450g/1lb fillet of veal, diced
salt and freshly ground black pepper
4 egg whites
600ml/1pt double cream
butter
Sauce béarnaise *(see page 84)*

1. Preheat oven to moderate (180°C/350°F/gas 4).

2. Soak sweetbreads in iced water then parboil for 15 minutes in equal quantities of dry white wine and water to cover. Drain, cool, slice them slantwise in 2 or 3 rather thick slices and arrange them in in the centre of a veal mousse made in the following manner.

3. Put diced veal through the finest blade of your mincer, then force through a fine sieve. Season with salt and freshly ground black pepper, to taste. Place minced veal in a bowl set in a bowl of ice and stir in egg whites, little by little. Then add the cream to this mixture, little by little, beating until mixture is light and smooth.

4. Butter a 1.4L/3pt ring mould and line it with veal mousse. Lay slices of sweetbread in centre of mould, filling up any empty spots with mousse, and top with remaining mousse mixture. Cover with buttered paper. Set the mould in a pan of water and bake in preheated oven for 20 to 30 minutes, or until firm. Unmould and serve with SAUCE BEARNAISE.

MAITRE PAUL'S 'BLANQUETTE DE VEAU MENAGERE'

SERVES 4-6

1.4kg/3lb shoulder or breast of veal
30-60ml/2-4 tbls butter
12 button onions
15ml/1 tbls flour
1 bouquet garni (2 or 3 sprigs of parsley,
  1 sprig thyme, 1 bay leaf and 1 celery stalk)
salt and freshly ground black pepper
2 egg yolks
juice of ½ lemon
30ml/2 tbls double cream
Boiled rice *(see page 197) or boiled new potatoes*

1. Cut veal into 5cm/2in cubes.
2. Melt butter in a thick-bottomed saucepan and sauté veal cubes with button onions until golden. Sprinkle with flour and add just enough water to cover. Add *bouquet garni* and season with salt and freshly ground black pepper, to taste. Simmer gently for about 1½ hours. Cool for a few minutes, then remove veal cubes and onions to a heated serving dish. Keep warm.
3. Thicken the sauce in the following manner: whisk together egg yolks, lemon juice and cream. Whisking vigorously, add a ladleful of boiling sauce from the pan. Pour this *liaison* into the sauce and bring to the boil, whisking well until thick and creamy.
4. Pass sauce through a fine sieve over the meat and onions and serve immediately accompanied by BOILED RICE or boiled new potatoes.

GOURMANDISE 'BRILLAT SAVARIN' LASSERRE

SERVES 4

4 slices fillet of veal, about 100g/4oz each
butter

salt and freshly ground black pepper
12 button mushrooms, sliced very thinly
10ml/2 tsp very finely chopped shallots
45-60ml/3-4 tbls dry sherry
4 thin pancakes, 15cm/6in in diameter (see
  page 339)
30-60ml/2-4 tbls grated Gruyère cheese

1. Preheat oven to hot (230°C/450°F/gas 8).
2. Melt 60ml/4 tbls butter in a thick-bottomed frying pan and sauté veal slices until well coloured and three-quarters cooked. Season with salt and freshly ground black pepper, to taste. Remove veal slices from pan and keep warm.
3. Sauté sliced mushrooms and shallots quickly in the same pan. Add sherry, season with salt and black pepper, to taste, and cook, stirring constantly, until sherry is reduced to half the original quantity.
4. Spoon one eighth of the mushroom and shallot mixture on to one side of each thin pancake; place a nearly-cooked veal slice on top and cover with remaining mushroom and shallot mixture. Close the pancake as if folding a package and place in a buttered baking dish; put a knob of butter on top of each pancake and sprinkle with a little freshly grated Gruyère cheese. Place in preheated oven for 5 minutes until heated through. Serve immediately.

ESCALOPES 'VISCAYENNES'

SERVES 4

4 veal escalopes
butter
30ml/2 tbls olive oil
1 Spanish onion, finely chopped
6 garlic cloves, finely chopped
4 green peppers, seeded and sliced
8 tomatoes, peeled, seeded and chopped
pinch of sugar
salt and freshly ground black pepper
60-90ml/4-6 tbls dry white wine

150ml/¼pt double cream
finely chopped parsley

1. Heat 30ml/2 tbls each butter and olive oil in a thick-bottomed frying pan and sauté finely chopped onion and garlic until transparent. Add sliced green peppers, then coarsely chopped tomatoes and cook, stirring continuously, for a minute or two. Season to taste with sugar, salt and freshly ground black pepper, and simmer for 30 minutes.
2. Sauté veal escalopes in a little butter in another frying pan until tender. Arrange on a heated serving platter and keep warm.
3. Stir dry white wine into pan juices and cook over a high heat until sauce is reduced by half. Add onion, pepper and tomato mixture; pour in cream and simmer sauce gently for 5 minutes. Whip 30ml/2 tbls butter into the sauce and pour sauce over veal escalopes. Sprinkle with finely chopped parsley and serve immediately.

COTE DE VEAU NORMANDE 'BOCAGE FLEURI'

SERVES 4

4 veal chops
salt and freshly ground black pepper
butter
100g/4oz mushrooms, sliced
60ml/4 tbls Calvados, warmed
175ml/6 fl oz double cream
2 tart eating apples, peeled and quartered

1. Season veal chops with salt and freshly ground black pepper, to taste.
2. Melt 30ml/2 tbls butter in a thick-bottomed frying pan and sauté veal chops until golden on both sides.
3. Add sliced mushrooms to pan and simmer gently for 10 minutes. Add Calvados and flame. As soon as the flames die down, stir in

cream. Reduce sauce, stirring continuously, until it is smooth and thick.
4. Meanwhile, sauté apples in a little butter.
5. Transfer veal chops in cream to a heated serving dish and serve garnished with quartered sautéed apples.

VEAL CHOPS 'EN PAPILLOTE'

SERVES 4

4 veal chops
salt and freshly ground black pepper
90ml/6 tbls butter
15ml/1 tbls lemon juice
1 garlic clove, crushed
30ml/2 tbls chopped shallots
225g/½lb mushrooms, finely chopped
150ml/¼pt dry white wine
30ml/2 tbls tomato purée
30ml/2 tbls fresh breadcrumbs
30ml/2 tbls finely chopped parsley
olive oil
8 thin slices prosciutto

1. Preheat oven to moderately hot (200°C/ 400°F/gas 6).
2. Season veal chops with salt and freshly ground black pepper to taste.
3. Melt 60ml/4 tbls butter in a thick-bottomed frying pan and sauté veal chops gently until golden on both sides. Remove from pan and keep warm.
4. Prepare a mushroom *duxelles* paste as follows: add remaining butter to pan together with lemon juice and crushed garlic clove and sauté finely chopped shallots and mushrooms gently until soft. Add dry white wine, tomato purée, salt and freshly ground black pepper to taste, breadcrumbs and chopped parsley, and cook until a soft paste results.
5. Cut 8 sheets of greaseproof paper into heart-shapes, big enough to enclose chops; oil them, and place hearts on the table in pairs.

Place a slice of *prosciutto* in the centre of 4 of the sheets. Coat *prosciutto* with *duxelles* paste; place veal chops on this; coat veal chops with *duxelles* paste and cover each chop with another piece of *prosciutto*. Cover with other paper hearts, oiled side down, and roll and pinch the edges together very firmly.

6. Sauté *papillotes* in olive oil until they swell up like balloons. Transfer to a baking sheet and bake in preheated oven until the meat is tender, about 20 to 25 minutes. Transfer *papillotes* to a heated serving dish and serve immediately.

VEAU AU VIN BLANC

SERVES 6-8

1 shoulder or loin of veal, 1.4-2.5kg/3-5lb
100g/4oz butter
2 Spanish onions, thinly sliced
4 large carrots, thinly sliced
4 tomatoes, peeled, seeded and coarsely chopped
salt and freshly ground black pepper
2 bay leaves
1 large garlic clove
4 large sprigs of parsley
300 ml/¹/₂pt dry white wine, warmed

1. Ask your butcher to bone, roll and tie the piece of veal.
2. Preheat oven to very slow (140°C/275°F/gas 1 to 150°C/300°F/gas 2).
3. Melt half the butter in a thick-bottomed ovenproof casserole and sauté thinly sliced onions and carrots with coarsely chopped tomatoes for about 3 minutes.
4. Remove vegetables from casserole and add remaining butter. Brown veal in juices until golden on all sides. Season thoroughly with salt and freshly ground black pepper.
5. Return vegetables to casserole, making them into a bed for the veal. Add bay leaves, garlic clove and sprigs of parsley. Place veal on this bed; moisten with warmed dry white wine; cover and roast in preheated oven for 2¹/₂-3 hours, or until tender. Transfer veal to a heated platter and keep warm.
6. Transfer vegetables to an electric blender, or food processor. Skim fat from pan juices. Moisten vegetables with a little of the pan juices and purée them. Stir in enough of the remaining juices to make a gravy of the consistency you require and serve with the veal.

COTE DE VEAU COUPOLE

SERVES 4

4 veal chops
salt and freshly ground black pepper
60ml/4 tbls butter
10ml/2 tsp finely chopped shallots
90ml/6 tbls double cream
60ml/4 tbls port
12-16 button mushrooms, sliced
60ml/4 tbls finely chopped ham
sautéed potatoes

1. Season veal chops with salt and freshly ground black pepper, to taste.
2. Melt butter in a thick-bottomed frying pan and sauté veal chops for 6 to 10 minutes on each side. Sprinkle with finely chopped shallots. Transfer veal chops to a heated serving dish and keep warm.
3. Stir cream and port into pan juices, add sliced mushrooms, heat through and pour sauce over veal chops. Sprinkle with finely chopped ham and serve with sautéed potatoes.

ESCALOPES DE VEAU A LA VALLEE D'AUGE

SERVES 4

4 veal escalopes
salt and freshly ground black pepper
30-60ml/2-4 tbls butter

30-60/2-4 tbls Calvados, warmed
30ml/2 tbls dry white wine
175g/6oz button mushroom, sliced and sautéed
  in butter
150ml/¼pt double cream

1. Season veal escalopes with salt and pepper.
2. Melt butter in a thick-bottomed frying pan
and sauté veal escalopes until tender. Pour over
warmed Calvados or brandy and flame. When
flames have died down remove veal escalopes
from pan and keep warm.
3. Stir dry white wine into pan juices and cook
over a high heat, stirring in all the crusty bits
from sides of pan. Add sautéed mushrooms
and cream. Season with salt and freshly
ground black pepper to taste and simmer for 2
to 3 minutes. Return veal escalopes to pan and
heat through in sauce. Serve immediately.

AILLADE DE VEAU

SERVES 6

1kg/2lb lean veal
60ml/4 tbls olive oil
30ml/2 tbls fresh breadcrumbs
10 fat garlic cloves
60ml/4 tbls tomato purée
salt and freshly ground black pepper
125ml/4 fl oz dry white wine
Boiled rice *(see page 179)*

1. Cut veal into 2.5cm/1in cubes.
2. Heat olive oil in a thick-bottomed casserole
and sauté veal cubes until golden. Add breadcrumbs, garlic and tomato purée. Cook over a
gentle heat, stirring continuously, for 5 to 7
minutes.
3. Season casserole with salt and freshly
ground black pepper, to taste. Moisten with
dry white wine and 50ml/2 fl oz water, cover
and simmer gently for 1 hour. Serve with
BOILED RICE.

SALTIMBOCCA ALLA ROMANA

SERVES 4

8 thin slices of veal
8 fresh sage leaves, or 2.5ml/½ tsp rubbed sage
freshly ground black pepper
8 thin slices prosciutto
90ml/6 tbls butter
30ml/2 tbls Marsala, or dry white wine
green beans, fresh peas, or croûtons of fried bread

1. Flatten veal into thin pieces about 10 x
12.5cm/4 x 5in; place 1 sage leaf, or pinch of
rubbed sage, on each slice and season with
freshly ground black pepper, to taste (no salt,
the *prosciutto* will flavour meat). Cover each
slice of veal with *prosciutto* cut to the same size;
make each into a small roll and secure with a
toothpick.
2. Cook these little rolls in melted butter until
they are golden on all sides, then add Marsala,
or dry white wine. Let them cook for a moment, then cover the pan and simmer gently
until the veal and ham rolls are quite tender.
3. Remove toothpicks and transfer *saltimbocca*
to a heated serving dish; surround with green
beans, fresh peas, or simply with *croûtons* of
fried bread and serve.

VITELLO TONNATO

It is almost impossible to eat badly in Rome. Italians have always regarded cooking as an art and you have only to visit a Roman street market in mid-morning to see some of the most beautiful raw foods in existence. Great platters of fish in all the colours of the rainbow; fruits and vegetables spilling from the stalls almost to the pavement; golden yellow cheeses; minute purple artichokes; milk-fed lamb and young kid no bigger than hares; tender young leaves of spinach, cabbage and red cabbage, picked when they are hardly more than sprouts, just right to be included raw, along with crisp pink radishes, in the salads so appreciated by the Romans.

Italian fishermen bring back a great variety of excellent fish and shellfish from the nearby sea. Fresh trout comes from the neighbouring hillside streams. And even the wines from the Alban hills – the famous *castelli romani,* which are not castles at all, but little mountain villages – even the wines are young.

You, like every visitor, will soon have your favourite little trattoria where on Fridays they make the most delicious *zuppa di pesce* in the world – one of those intimate little places where the inexpensive local wine has the warmth and colour of the sun – and where the company is as good as the food. These restaurants, scattered throughout the city, are for the most part quite inexpensive by our standards, serving meals with a smile and a bottle of *vino locale* from the hills behind Rome. They are small and usually crowded. The décor with few exceptions is modest, sometimes non-existent. But the food is uniformly excellent.

There are many Italian specialities that are particularly Roman in origin. Begin your meal with the famous *fettucine all'uove,* freshly made thin egg noodles served with country butter and freshly grated Parmesan cheese; or try *lasagne alla romana,* wide ribbons of pasta dough arranged in alternate layers with *ricotta* and *mozzarella* cheese, minced pork and veal, and slices of hard-boiled egg, the whole bathed with two unctuous sauces, a rich béchamel sauce and a special *ragù alla romana.*

Then there are the spaghettis: *alla carrettiera,* cooked *al dente* and served with an aromatic sauce of tuna fish, mushrooms and herbs; *alla matriciana,* with a sauce flavoured with chopped bacon and onions; *all'arrabbiata,* a special sauce made hot

Vitello tonnato makes a delicious summer dish. Lightly poached veal is bathed in a rich tuna fish sauce.

with chillis and flavoured with herbs and tomatoes; and *alla carbonara,* spaghetti or macaroni served with fried bacon or ham and a sauce of freshly grated Parmesan cheese, butter and the yolks of eggs.

Carciofi alla romana – fresh young artichokes cooked in Roman style – are also on the list of specialities not to be missed. They are utterly delicious in Rome, where they pick them early in the season when they are not much bigger than a baby's fist. The sharp tips of the leaves are cut off, the centre is opened and the whole is baked in oil and herbs. There's no need to remove the 'choke' in the Italian artichoke; all of the plant may be eaten, including the stem.

Romans are not, as a rule, overfond of roasts, steaks or chops. But Rome's own *abbacchio* – milk-fed lamb – is an exception. *Abbacchio* is wonderfully tender and delicate in flavour whether it is cooked *al forno,* in the oven with a breath of rosemary, or *alla cacciatora,* hunter's style with tomatoes, peppers, garlic, wine and herbs. *Saltimbocca alla romana* is a perfect way of giving much needed flavour to veal. Here the Roman cook combines thin pieces of tender veal with slices of *prosciutto,* flavours them with sage and sautés them in butter.

One of my favourite Italian summer dishes is *vitello tonnato,* lightly poached veal bathed in a rich tuna fish and anchovy sauce. Try Italian 'tunnied veal' as the cold first course for a company dinner, or as the refreshing main course for an outdoor luncheon in the sun. Serve a chilled white wine with it and follow with a green salad.

VITELLO TONNATO

SERVES 4

1 leg of veal, 1.1-1.4kg/2½-3lb when boned
  and trimmed
6 anchovy fillets
bay leaves
1 Spanish onion, sliced
2 carrots, sliced
2 celery stalks, sliced
2 sprigs of parsley
2 cloves
salt and freshly ground black pepper
300ml/½pt dry white wine (optional)
lemon slices

TUNA FISH SAUCE
175g/6oz can tuna fish, drained
6 anchovy fillets
5ml/1 tsp capers
30ml/2 tbls lemon juice
freshly ground black pepper
150ml/¼pt well-flavoured **Mayonnaise**
  (see page 85)

1. Ask your butcher to roll and tie a piece of leg of veal.
2. Cut anchovy fillets into small pieces; pierce holes in surface of veal and insert pieces of anchovy fillet into holes. Top veal with several bay leaves and place in a thick-bottomed cas-

serole with sliced onion, carrots, celery, parsley, cloves, and salt and freshly ground black pepper, to taste. Pour in dry white wine and add just enough water to cover meat (or use water only); bring it slowly to the boil, turn down heat, cover casserole and simmer for 1½ to 2 hours. When veal is tender, remove cord and skewers and allow to cool in the stock.

3. When cold, drain veal well reserving stock and place in a porcelain or earthware (not metal) bowl. Cover with tuna fish sauce; cover and let veal marinate overnight.

4. Three hours before serving, remove veal from sauce and slice thinly. Arrange slices on a serving dish; cover with sauce and refrigerate until ready to serve. Garnish veal dish with lemon slices.

5. To make tuna fish sauce: pound tuna fish, anchovy fillets and capers with lemon juice, and freshly ground black pepper, to taste, until smooth. Combine with MAYONNAISE in electric blender, or food processor, and blend (adding a little veal stock if too thick) until the sauce is smooth and creamy.

HUNGARIAN VEAL GULYAS

SERVES 6-8

1.1kg/2½lb boned veal, cut into 5cm/2in cubes
2 Spanish onions, finely chopped
2 garlic cloves, finely chopped
30ml/2 tbls lard
30ml/2 tbls paprika
1.5ml/¼ tsp caraway seeds
1 bay leaf
1 generous pinch each dried marjoram and thyme
salt and freshly ground black pepper
450g/1lb button mushrooms, sliced
2 red peppers, seeded and diced
2 green peppers, seeded and diced
400g/14oz can Italian peeled tomatoes
300ml/½pt soured cream

1. Preheat oven to very slow (140°C/275°F/gas 1 to 150°C/300°F/gas 2).

2. Sauté finely chopped onions and garlic cloves in lard in a thick-bottomed ovenproof casserole until transparent.

3. Add veal cubes to casserole and sauté until golden on all sides. Sprinkle with paprika and caraway seeds; add bay leaf and herbs and simmer gently for 10 minutes.

4. Season casserole with salt and freshly ground black pepper, to taste, and top with sliced mushrooms, diced peppers and canned tomatoes. Cover casserole, bring gently to the boil and simmer in preheated oven for at least 2 hours, or until tender. Serve from casserole with soured cream.

ROAST LOIN OF VEAL

1 loin of veal, 1.4kg/3lb
salt and freshly ground black pepper
crushed rosemary
30-60ml/2-4 tbls softened butter
150ml/¼pt dry white wine

1. Ask your butcher to bone and trim veal.

2. Preheat oven to moderately hot (200°C/400°F/gas 6).

3. Season veal with salt, freshly ground black pepper and crushed rosemary to taste. Spread with softened butter and roast veal in preheated oven for 15 minutes. Reduce oven temperature to slow (170°C/325°F/gas 3) and roast for a further 25 to 30 minutes per 450g/1lb, basting frequently.

4. Transfer veal to a heated serving platter and keep warm. Add dry white wine to roasting pan; bring to the boil, stirring, and scraping base and sides of pan to dislodge any crusty bits. Boil until sauce is reduced by about one-third. Correct seasoning, strain sauce into a heated sauceboat and serve as an accompaniment to the roast veal.

POACHED BREAST OF VEAL

1.4-1.8kg/3-4lb breast of veal

STUFFING INGREDIENTS
2 spanish onions, quartered
6 small leeks, cut into 1.2cm/1/2in segments
6 carrots, sliced
6 small turnips, quartered
bouquet garni
salt (optional)
light stock (optional)

1. Stuff breast of veal as in recipe above.
2. Combine veal with prepared vegetables – onions, leeks, carrots and turnips - in a thick-bottomed saucepan and poach gently with *bouquet garni* in enough salted water, or a light stock, to cover, until tender. Transfer veal and vegetables to a heated serving platter.

ROAST BREAST OF VEAL

1.4-1.8kg/3-4lb breast of veal
lemon juice
salt and freshly ground black pepper
flour
30ml/2 tbls olive oil

STUFFING INGREDIENTS
60ml/4 tbls butter
1/2 Spanish onion, finely chopped
225g/1/2lb sausage meat
15ml/1 tbls finely chopped parsley
1 egg, beaten
225g/1/2lb spinach, chopped and sautéed in butter
1.5ml/1/4 tsp ground allspice
1.5ml/1/4 tsp ground nutmeg
2.5ml/1/2 tsp dried thyme

1. Preheat oven to slow (170°C/325°F/gas 3).
2. Wipe breast of veal on both sides with a damp cloth; sprinkle with lemon juice and sea-son with salt and black pepper to taste.
3. Melt 30ml/2 tbls butter in a thick-bottomed frying pan and sauté finely chopped onion until it is transparent.
4. Combine the following ingredients in a large mixing bowl: sausage meat, sautéed onion, finely chopped parsley, beaten egg, sautéed spinach, allspice, nutmeg and thyme, and salt and pepper to taste. Mix well.
5. Lay sausage meat stuffing in the centre of the breast of veal, make into a neat roll and sew up with fine string. Dust veal with flour, place in a roasting pan with 30ml/2 tbls each butter and olive oil and roast in preheated oven for about 1½ to 1¾ hours, basting frequently.

VEAL PARMIGIANA

SERVES 4

4 thin veal escalopes
50g/2oz fresh breadcrumbs
45ml/3 tbls freshly grated Parmesan cheese
salt and freshly ground black pepper
1 egg, beaten
30ml/2 tbls olive oil
butter
300ml/1/2pt hot **Tomato sauce** *(see page 83)*
50g/2oz mozzarella cheese, cut into thin strips

1. Preheat oven to moderate (190°C/375°F/gas 5).
2. Mix together breadcrumbs and Parmesan cheese and season with salt and black pepper.
3. Dip veal escalopes in beaten egg, then in breadcrumb mixture. Let breaded escalopes stand for 10 minutes before cooking.
4. Heat olive oil in a thick-bottomed frying pan and sauté escalopes until tender.
5. Transfer escalopes to a well-buttered gratin dish. Pour over TOMATO SAUCE, top with thin strips of mozzarella cheese and bake in pre-heated oven for 10 to 15 minutes, or until cheese melts and browns. Serve immediately.

SAUTE DE VEAU MARENGO

SERVES 4-6

1.4kg/3lb boned shoulder of veal
flour
salt and freshly ground black pepper
butter
30ml/2 tbls olive oil
2 Spanish onions, finely chopped
1 garlic clove, finely chopped
300ml/½pt light stock
1 strip of orange peel
1 bouquet garni
30-45ml/2-3 tbls tomato purée
150ml/¼pt dry white wine
15ml/1 tbls flour
30ml/2 tbls finely chopped parsley

1. Cut boned veal into 5cm/2in cubes; dredge with flour and season with salt and pepper.
2. Heat 30ml/2 tbls each butter and olive oil in a thick-bottomed casserole and sauté veal cubes until browned on all sides.
3. Add finely chopped onions and garlic clove to casserole and simmer for a few minutes.
4. Bring light stock to the boil; add strip of orange peel, *bouquet garni,* tomato purée and dry white wine; allow to cook a little then pour over veal pieces. Cover and simmer until veal cubes are cooked through.
5. Whisk in a *beurre manié,* (made by mashing 15ml/1 tbls flour and 15ml/1 tbls butter together to form a smooth paste) bit by bit, until liquid is thick and smooth. Sprinkle with finely chopped parsley and serve from casserole.

MOROCCAN BROCHETTES

SERVES 4

450g/1lb calf's liver
225g/½lb beef fat
salt and freshly ground black pepper
ground cumin
cayenne pepper
olive oil

1. If you are going to barbecue brochettes, light fire at least 1 hour before cooking. If you are grilling brochettes, preheat grill to high.
2. Cut liver into cubes about 2cm/¾in square; cut fat into slightly smaller cubes.
3. Thread liver and fat cubes on skewers alternately. Sprinkle with salt and black pepper, ground cumin and cayenne pepper.
4. When ready to grill, brush grid of grill pan with a little olive oil and grill over hot coals or under preheated grill, for 3 to 4 minutes, turning skewers from time to time. Arrange kebabs on a heated platter and serve immediately.

RIS DE VEAU TRUFFES A LA CREME

SERVES 4

2 pairs calf's sweetbreads
juice of ½ lemon
court-bouillon (dry white wine, light stock
  and water)
*300ml/½pt hot **Béchamel sauce** (see page 80)*
15ml/1 tbls finely chopped truffle
15-30/1-2 tbls Madeira
salt and freshly ground black pepper
***Boiled rice** (see page 179)*

1. Soak sweetbreads in acidulated cold water (water and juice of ½ lemon) for 1 hour, changing water when it becomes tinged pink.
2. Blanch sweetbreads for 15 minutes in a simmering *court-bouillon.*
3. Allow to cool. Trim sweetbreads and cut into slices 5cm/2in thick.
4. Add sweetbreads to hot BECHAMEL SAUCE and heat thoroughly without letting the sauce boil. Add finely chopped truffle and a little Madeira to the sauce; season with salt and pepper, to taste, and serve in a ring of BOILED RICE.

CHAPTER 10

PORK

CHOUCROUTE GARNIE

Choucroute garnie is the beginning and end of all party meals: perfect for informal parties, beer gatherings and any other hospitable occasion when appetites are keen. Do not attempt to make this dish unless you know seven hearty trenchermen to share it with you. For *choucroûte* (sauerkraut) *garnie* (with all the trimmings) is not for the timid, for the wary or for the ubiquitous watchers of weight. This great country dish from Alsace is definitely for those who like to eat and prefer to wash down their hearty fare with generous quantities of chilled lager or dry white wine.

To me, making *choucroûte garnie* is as enjoyable as eating it. For when you cook sauerkraut you do not just lump it into a pot. You cook it in a very slow oven or over a gentle, low heat tossing it from time to time with a long fork until it is soft.

For flavour embellishments, you add a little onion, garlic and apple, perhaps a little grated potato, a few caraway seeds, or juniper berries if you have them, and instead of water, stock or dry white wine.

All sorts of changes can be rung upon the accessories cooked with or added to *choucroûte* just before serving. Build your *choucroûte garnie* on a flavoursome base of sauerkraut and add your choice of the following; salt pork, smoked ham, a wing or two of goose or partridge, a loin of pork or pork chops, and a combination of every type of sausage you can get your hands on . . . *bratwurst, knockwurst,* Frankfurt or Vienna sausages, *saucisses de Toulouse* or just plain 'bangers'. In France, a hot, spicy Lorraine sausage is one of the highlights of the feast. I often add a *cotechino* sausage stripped of its casing, cooked with the sauerkraut and then cut into fat slices just before serving.

Serve your sauerkraut on your largest platter and dress it with cooked meats and sausages and floury boiled potatoes. Serve, if desired, with mustard, pickles and lashings of chilled lager. *Choucroûte garnie* is a party feast you will remember for a very long time.

CHOUCROUTE GARNIE

SERVES 8 ROYALLY

pork fat, thinly sliced
2 Spanish onions, sliced
2 cooking apples, cored and sliced
4 garlic cloves, coarsely chopped
1.8kg/4lb sauerkraut, well washed
  and drained
225-350g/½-¾lb salt pork
freshly ground black pepper
6-8 juniper berries, crushed
dry white wine
1 boned loin of pork
1 large garlic sausage
8-16 sausages (bratwurst, Toulouse,
  knockwurst or frankfurters)
8 boiled potatoes
8 slices cooked ham (optional)

1. Preheat oven to very slow (140°C/275°F/ gas 1 to 150°C/300°F/gas 2).
2. Line a deep thick-bottomed ovenproof casserole with thinly sliced pork fat; add half the sliced onions, apples and chopped garlic. Place a thick layer of well-washed and drained sauerkraut on top with a piece of salt pork. Grind plenty of black pepper over salt pork; sprinkle with crushed juniper berries and add remaining onions, apples and garlic. Cover with remaining sauerkraut and add just enough dry white wine to cover the sauerkraut. Cover and cook in preheated oven for 4 to 6 hours. The longer it cooks the better.
3. A loin of pork, fresh or smoked, is excellent with *choucroûte*. Add pork to the *choucroûte* about 2½ hours before serving.
4. Half an hour later add a large garlic sausage and a selection of small sausages to the *choucroûte*, as available.
5. To serve: slice salt pork, loin of pork and garlic sausages. Heap the *choucroûte* in the middle of a heated platter and arrange slices of meat and garlic sausage and other sausages around it. Serve with boiled potatoes and, if desired, slices of cooked ham.

BAUERNSCHMAUS

In cooking, sometimes the simple things are best. When at home, Leon Lionedes, the celebrated owner of New York's Coach House restaurant, loves to serve black bean soup, a delicious purée of black beans and aromatics, a homely country dish which has made the restaurant famous. Peter Langan, the guiding light behind three famous London restaurants, Odins, Langan's Bistro and Langan's Brasserie, likes nothing better than a huge plate of German sausage and warmed potato salad, with champagne of course. René Hure, proprietor of the Hostellerie de la Poste in Avallon, one of France's greatest restaurants, prefers to serve an earthy *pot-au-feu* of beef,

Overleaf: Choucroûte Garnie is a flavourful combination of sauerkraut, pork and sausages.

pork, and chicken, simmered in beef stock, when he entertains special guests.

One of my favourite peasant dishes (worthy, I think, to take its place among the great dishes of the world) is *bauernschmaus* (a delectable concoction of boiled meats and sauerkraut, graced by the magisterial presence of a huge dumpling), an Austrian speciality famous from Salzburg to Vienna.

It was at the Vienna Culinary Festival held at the Carlton Tower that I renewed my happy acquaiantance with this homely dish. Master chef Karl Dutch and his team of Viennese experts prepared many delicious meals for us during his stay here: *leberknödelsuppe* (strong consommé with calf's liver dumplings), *tafelspitz 'alt weiner art* (the specially cut, slow-simmered beef so beloved by the Viennese) served with a chive and horseradish sauce and beetroot salad, and *paprikahuhn 'Franz Lehar'* (poached chicken in a paprika cream sauce, served with *spaetzle* (home-made Viennese egg noodles). But it was the *bauernschmaus* that I returned to sample time and time again.

BAUERNSCHMAUS

SERVES 6

1 loin of pork, cut into chops
2 x 450g/1lb sauerkraut, with juices
5ml/1 tsp cumin, or caraway seeds
1-2 garlic cloves
salt and freshly ground black pepper
beer (optional)
2 large raw potatoes, grated
2 Spanish onions, sliced
50g/2oz lard
1 piece back bacon, sliced
12 frankfurter sausages

DUMPLINGS

6 rolls
150ml/¼pt milk
2 eggs, beaten
30ml/2 tbls finely chopped parsley
salt and freshly ground black pepper
freshly grated nutmeg
sifted flour

1. In a deep thick-bottomed casserole combine pork chops with sauerkraut and juices, cumin or caraway seeds, garlic and salt and freshly ground black pepper, to taste. Pour over enough beer, or water, to cover chops and sauerkraut and simmer gently for 1½ hours. Stir in grated raw potatoes, moistened with a little cold water. Cook for 2 to 3 minutes more.

2. Sauté sliced onions in lard until transparent and add to sauerkraut together with sliced back bacon and frankfurters and simmer gently for 1 hour longer, adding water, or more beer, if necessary.

3. To serve: drain the sauerkraut, reserving juices, and pile on a large wooden platter. Surround with the 3 kinds of meat; garnish with large dumplings and serve with the gravy separately, which you have seasoned to taste.

4. To make dumplings: break up rolls into small pieces and soak in milk. Add beaten eggs, parsley, salt and freshly ground black pepper and nutmeg, to taste. Then add flour and work mixture into a dough with your hands, adding more flour if the dough is too moist to handle. Shape dough into 6 balls and drop them into a large saucepan of boiling salted water. Boil for 12 to 15 minutes, uncovered, until dumplings rise to the surface. Skim dumplings from water and drain well on absorbent kitchen paper.

SAUERKRAUT AND FRANKFURTERS

SERVES 4

60ml/4 tbls butter
2 medium-sized Spanish onions, sliced
1 garlic clove, finely chopped
450g/1lb sauerkraut, with juices
300ml/¹/₂pt beer
30ml/2 tbls brown sugar

1 bay leaf
2.5ml/¹/₂tsp celery salt or caraway seeds
salt and freshly ground black pepper
8 frankfurters
paprika
mustard

1. Melt 30ml/2 tbls butter in a thick-bottomed frying pan and sauté sliced onions and garlic until lightly browned.
2. Add sauerkraut and juices, beer, sugar, bay leaf, celery salt or caraway seeds, and season with salt and freshly ground black pepper, to taste. Stir well, cover and simmer for about ³/₄ hour, stirring from time to time.
3. Slash frankfurters diagonally to prevent bursting; dust with paprika and brown in remaining butter. Serve with sauerkraut and mustard.

ELIZA ACTON'S SUCKING PIG

'After the pig has been scalded and prepared for the spit, wipe it as dry as possible, and put into the body about half a pint of fine breadcrumbs, mixed with three heaped teaspoonsful of sage, minced very small, three ounces of good butter, a large saltspoonful of salt, and two thirds as much of pepper or some cayenne. Sew it up with soft, but strong cotton; truss it as a hare, with the forelegs skewered back, and the hind ones forward; lay it to a strong clear fire, but keep it at a moderate distance, as it would quickly blister or scorch if placed too near. So soon as it has become warm, rub it with a bit of butter tied in a fold of muslin or of thin cloth, and repeat this process constantly while it is roasting. When the gravy begins to drop from it, put basins or small deep tureens under to catch it in [a deep oblong dish of suitable size seems better adapted to this purpose]. As soon as the pig is of a fine light amber brown and the steam draws strongly towards the fire, wipe it quite dry with a clean cloth, and rub a bit of cold butter over it. When it is half done, a pig iron, or in lieu of this a large flat iron, should be hung in the centre of the grate, or the middle of the pig will be done long before the ends. When it is ready for table lay it into a very hot dish, and before the spit is withdrawn, take off and open the head and split the body in two; chop together quickly the stuffing and the brains, put them into half a pint of good veal gravy ready thickened, add a glass of Madeira or of sherry, and the gravy which has dropped from the pig; pour a small portion of this under the roast and serve the remainder as hot as possible in a tureen: a little pounded mace and cayenne with a squeeze of lemon juice, may be added, should the flavour require heightening. Fine bread sauce, and plain gravy should likewise be served with it. Some persons still prefer the old fashioned currant sauce to any other and many have the brains and stuffing stirred into rich melted butter, instead of gravy; but the receipt which we have given has usually been so much approved, that we can recommend it with some confidence, as it stands.' (1859)

ROAST SUCKLING PIG

1 suckling pig
olive oil
salt and freshly ground black pepper
60ml/4 tbls butter
60ml/4 tbls lemon juice
crushed thyme
1 small red apple
sprigs of watercress, or parsley
Sauce Béarnaise *(see page 84)*

1. Preheat oven to hot (230°C/450°F/gas 8).
2. Scald and prepare suckling pig for roasting; brush pig inside and out with olive oil. Season interior generously with salt and freshly ground black pepper.
3. Roast pig in preheated oven for 1½ to 2 hours, basting frequently with a mixture of the olive oil, butter and lemon juice, to taste. If skin starts to bubble, prick bubbles immediately. Fifteen minutes before end of cooking time season well with salt and freshly ground black pepper and crushed thyme.
4. When cooked, remove pig from oven; sprinkle with lemon juice; place a small red

apple in its mouth and garnish its ears with sprigs of watercress, or parsley. Place pig on a bed of watercress and serve accompanied by SAUCE BEARNAISE.

ROAST LOIN OF PORK

1 loin of pork, 6 chops
butter
crumbled thyme and bay leaf
30ml/2 tbls Dijon mustard
salt and freshly ground black pepper
flour
sprig of watercress
puréed potatoes

1. Ask your butcher to remove rind from loin of pork without removing fat.
2. Mix 60ml/4 tbls softened butter to a smooth paste with crumbled thyme and bay leaf and Dijon mustard to taste and rub well into pork several hours before roasting. Sprinkle with salt and freshly ground black pepper and let pork stand at room temperature to absorb flavours.

3. Preheat oven to hot (230°C/450°F/gas 8).
4. Place pork, fat side up, in a roasting pan and brown in a preheated oven for 20 minutes. Reduce temperature to very slow (150°C/300°F/gas 2), and continue to roast pork for 16 to 18 minutes per 450g/1lb.
5. Remove excess fat from pan and thicken pan drippings with a little flour mashed together with an equal amount of butter. Garnish pork with sprigs of watercress and serve with gravy and puréed potatoes.

CARRE DE PORC A LA BONNE FEMME

1 loin of pork, 6 chops
60ml/4 tbls softened butter
crumbled thyme and bay leaf
salt and freshly ground black pepper
30ml/2 tbls olive oil
18 peeled small new potatoes
*12 **Glazed button onions** (see page 253)*
*18 **Sautéed mushroom caps** (see page 253)*
bouquet garni
30ml/2 tbls finely chopped parsley

1. Ask your butcher to remove the rind from loin of pork, leaving the fat.
2. Mix softened butter to a smooth paste with crumbled thyme and bay leaf and rub well into pork several hours before roasting. Sprinkle with salt and freshly ground black pepper and let pork stand at room temperature to absorb flavours.
3. Preheat oven to hot (230°C/450°F/gas 8).
4. Place pork, fat side up, in a roasting pan; add olive oil and roast in preheated oven for 15 minutes. Reduce oven temperature to slow (170°325°F/gas 3) and continue to roast for 16 to 18 minutes per 450g/1lb.
5. Halfway through cooking time, surround pork with peeled new potatoes, GLAZED BUT-TON ONIONS and SAUTEED MUSHROOM CAPS. Add *bouquet garni* and continue cooking, basting frequently. Transfer to heated serving platter and sprinkle with parsley.

BOILED SALT PORK WITH PEASE PUDDING

SERVES 6-8

1 shoulder or breast of salt pork
6 large carrots
2 Spanish onions, stuck with 2 cloves
6 small leeks
6 parsnips

PEASE PUDDING
450g/1lb split peas
1 Spanish onion, thinly sliced
butter
3 eggs, beaten
salt and freshly ground black pepper
freshly grated nutmeg
flour

1. Place salt pork in water; bring to the boil; skim; add vegetables; bring to the boil and skim again. Then lower heat and simmer pork and vegetables gently until tender.
2. Place the pork on a heated serving platter; surround with accompanying vegetables and serve with pease pudding.
3. To make pease pudding: soak peas in cold water overnight. Strain. Place in a thick-bottomed saucepan with sliced onion; cover with water and simmer gently for 2 to 4 hours, or until cooked. Purée peas in electric blender, or food processor. Combine purée of peas with 100g/4oz butter and beaten eggs. Season with salt, black pepper and grated nutmeg, to taste. Mix well; put into a buttered pudding basin and cook in the oven, in water until done, or place in a scalded, buttered and floured cloth; tie up and cook in the pot with the pork.

CARRE DE PORC A LA PROVENCALE

1 loin of pork, 6 chops
8-12 sage leaves
salt and freshly ground black pepper
crumbled thyme and bay leaf
olive oil
90ml/6 tbls dry white wine
2-3 garlic cloves

1. Ask your butcher to bone and tie loin of pork.
2. Pierce pork with the point of sharp knife and insert sage leaves. Sprinkle with salt and freshly ground black pepper, crumbled thyme and bay leaf and a little olive oil and allow to stand at room temperature to absorb flavours.
3. Preheat oven to hot (230°C/450°F/ gas 8).
4. Place pork in a roasting pan; add 90ml/6tbls each water, dry white wine and olive oil; crush garlic cloves with the flat of your hand and add them to the cooking liquid. Roast pork in preheated oven for 15 minutes. Reduce oven temperature to slow (170°C/325°F/gas 3) and continue to roast for 16 to 18 minutes per 450g/ 1lb, basting frequently. Serve immediately.

PORK CHOPS A LA CHARCUTIERE

SERVES 4

4 loin pork chops, 2.5cm/1in thick
30-60ml/2-4 tbls melted butter
fresh breadcrumbs
salt and freshly ground black pepper
olive oil
puréed potatoes

CHARCUTIERE SAUCE

¼ Spanish onion, finely chopped
15ml/1 tbls butter
60ml/4 tbls dry white wine
15ml/1 tbls red wine vinegar

*300ml/½pt **Sauce espagnole** (see page 82)*
15ml/1 tbls tomato purée
Dijon mustard
15ml/1 tbls finely chopped pickles
15ml/1 tbls finely chopped parsley

1. Preheat grill to high.
2. Trim excess fat from pork chops; brush with melted butter; dip in breadcrumbs, pressing them well in, and season with salt and freshly ground black pepper, to taste.
3. When ready to grill, brush grid of grill pan with a little olive oil and grill pork chops 7.5cm/3in from heat, for 8 minutes, turning chops once during cooking. Transfer to a heated serving dish and serve with puréed potatoes and a charcutière sauce.
4. To make charcutière sauce: melt butter in a thick-bottomed saucepan and sauté finely chopped onion until golden. Add wine and red wine vinegar and cook until sauce is reduced to half the original quantity. Add SAUCE ESPAGNOLE; stir in tomato purée and simmer, uncovered, stirring from time to time, for 15 minutes. When ready to serve, stir in mustard, to taste, and finely chopped pickle and parsley.

PORK CHOPS BAKED IN CREAM

SERVES 4

4 thick loin pork chops
30ml/2 tbls butter
225g/½lb mushrooms, finely chopped
15ml/1 tbls lemon juice
15ml/1 tbls flour
salt and freshly ground black pepper
dried thyme, or oregano
olive oil
60ml/4 tbls double cream
finely chopped parsley

1. Preheat oven to slow (170°C/325°F/gas 3).
2. Trim excess fat from pork chops. Melt but-

ter in a thick-bottomed frying pan and sauté pork chops until golden on both sides, then remove from pan.

3. Spoon off all but 30ml/2 tbls fat from pan and sauté finely chopped mushrooms in remaining fat until soft; stir in lemon juice; sprinkle with flour and cook until slightly thickened and almost dry. Season with salt and freshly ground black pepper, to taste.

4. Rub pork chops with a little dried thyme, or oregano, and season with salt and freshly ground black pepper, to taste.

5. Cut 4 pieces of aluminium foil into heart shapes large enough to wrap a pork chop completely. Brush hearts with olive oil; place pork chop on one half; cover with mushroom mixture and pour over 15ml/1 tbls double cream. Sprinkle with parsley; fold the foil shape over and seal edges well by crimping them together. Place foil shapes on a baking sheet and bake in preheated oven until the chops are tender, 45 to 60 minutes. Transfer *papillotes* to a heated serving dish and serve immediately.

COTELETTES DE PORC AU SAUGE

SERVES 4

4 thick loin pork chops
5ml/1 tsp finely chopped onion
5ml/1 tsp finely chopped parsley
generous pinch of crumbled sage, about 2 leaves
1 egg
salt and freshly ground black pepper
fresh breadcrumbs
60ml/4 tbls olive oil or lard
sautéed sliced apples
sautéed sliced potatoes

1. Combine finely chopped onion, parsley, crumbled sage and egg in a bowl. Beat well and season with salt and freshly ground black pepper, to taste.

2. Trim excess fat from pork chops and dip in onion mixture several times. Drain well. Dip in breadcrumbs, pressing them well in. Allow to stand for 30 minutes.

3. Heat olive oil, or lard in a thick-bottomed frying pan and sauté breaded chops over a high heat for 2 minutes on each side: reduce heat and cook each side for a further 5 to 6 minutes until cooked through and crisp and golden on the outside. Transfer breaded chops to a heated serving dish and serve immediately accompanied by sautéed apples and potatoes.

PORK CHOPS 'AUBERGE DU GRAND SAINT PIERRE'

SERVES 4

4 thick loin pork chops
15ml/1 tbls olive oil
15ml/1 tbls butter
salt and freshly ground black pepper
100g/4oz Gruyère cheese, freshly grated
5-10ml/1-2 tsp strong mustard
double cream

1. Trim excess fat from pork chops.

2. Heat oil and butter in a thick-bottomed frying pan and sauté pork chops at a high heat for 2 minutes on each side. Reduce heat and cook each side for a further 5 to 6 minutes until cooked through and golden. Season with salt and freshly ground black pepper, to taste.

3. Meanwhile, preheat grill to high.

4. Make a *pommade* by combining freshly grated Gruyère cheese with strong mustard and just enough double cream to make a smooth mixture of spreading consistency.

5. Spread pork chops generously with cheese *pommade* and glaze quickly under preheated grill until sauce is golden. Transfer to a heated serving dish and serve immediately.

PORK CHOPS IN WINE

SERVES 4

4 thick loin pork chops
90ml/6 tbls butter
5ml/1 tsp coarse salt
1.5ml/¼ tsp freshly ground black pepper
2.5ml/½ tsp dry mustard
1 Spanish onion, finely chopped
150ml/¼pt dry white wine
30ml/2 tbls finely chopped parsley

1. Trim excess fat from pork chops.
2. Pound 30ml/2 tbls butter, salt, freshly ground black pepper and mustard to a smooth paste and spread on both sides of each chop.
3. Melt 60ml/4 tbls butter in a thick-bottomed casserole large enough to take chops in one layer and sauté finely chopped onion until transparent. Add pork chops to casserole and sauté until golden on both sides. Pour over dry white wine and simmer gently, covered, until tender, about 45 minutes. Correct seasoning; sprinkle with finely chopped parsley and serve.

COLD GAMMON OF BACON

1 gammon of bacon (4.5-5.4kg/10-12lb)
2 Spanish onions, stuck with cloves
4 large carrots
2 leeks
2 turnips, quartered
2 bay leaves
6 black peppercorns
toasted breadcrumbs (optional)
cloves, brown sugar, dry mustard and cider, or
*   fruit juice (optional)*

1. Wash gammon well; do not take off rind; soak for 24 to 48 hours to remove salt, changing water several times. Drain.
2. Put gammon in a thick-bottomed sauce-pan; cover completely with cold water and bring slowly to the boil. Change water; add vegetables, bay leaves and black peppercorns and bring slowly to boiling point again; reduce heat immediately; cover and simmer until cooking is complete, about 20 minutes per 450g/1lb for an average-sized gammon. Allow gammon to cool in its cooking water.
3. Do not remove rind until well set if you are going to serve gammon cold. I leave mine overnight. Then remove skin and sprinkle fat with toasted breadcrumbs; or, if you prefer, score fat criss-cross; stud with cloves; sprinkle with brown sugar and a little dry mustard and brown in a preheated moderately hot 200°C/400°F/gas 6 oven for 20 to 30 minutes, basting from time to time with cider, or fruit juice.

JAMBON CHAUD MODE D'ICI

SERVES 4

4 shallots, finely chopped
150ml/¼pt dry white Chablis
4 tarragon leaves, finely chopped
*150ml/¼pt **Basic beef stock** (see page 65)*
60ml/4 tbls tomato purée
150ml/¼pt double cream
butter
4 thick ham slices

1. Make a good *sauce piquante* with a reduction of finely chopped shallots, dry white Chablis and finely chopped tarragon leaves. Moisten with BEEF STOCK; add tomato purée, cover and simmer gently for an hour over a very low heat.
2. Add an equal quantity of cream to this sauce and simmer for a further 10 minutes.
3. Meanwhile, melt a little butter in a thick-bottomed frying pan and heat ham slices through, turning once.
4. Pass sauce through a fine sieve, stir in 30ml/2 tbls butter and pour over hot ham slices. Serve very hot.

JAMBON CHAUD A LA CHABLISIENNE 'HOSTELLERIE DE LA POSTE'

1 York ham (about 4.5kg/10lb)
6 large carrots
2 Spanish onions
1 bouquet garni (1 celery stalk, sprig thyme,
*   1 bay leaf and 2 sprigs parsley)*
2 medium-sized onions
4 shallots
60ml/4 tbls butter
2 sprigs of thyme
2 sprigs of parsley
2 bay leaves
1/2 bottle dry white Chablis

SAUCE
2-3 sprigs tarragon, finely chopped
750ml/1 1/4pt well-flavoured light stock
45ml/3 tbls tomato purée
salt and freshly ground black pepper
425ml/3/4pt double cream

1. Soak ham in cold water overnight. Drain.
2. Put ham in a thick-bottomed saucepan; cover completely in cold water and bring to the boil. Simmer gently for 2½ to 3 hours with 4 large carrots, Spanish onions and the *bouquet garni*. Allow ham to cool in its own liquid; then take off rind and some of the fat.
3. Meanwhile, preheat oven to moderate (180°C/350°F/gas 4).
4. To braise ham: chop the onions, remaining carrots and shallots coarsely, and sauté in butter until golden. Spread vegetables in the bottom of a roasting pan just large enough to hold ham; add thyme, parsley, and bay leaves. Place ham on vegetables, moisten with equal quantities of dry white Chablis and water and braise in preheated oven until ham is tender. Remove ham from roasting pan and keep warm. Sieve braising liquid and reserve.
5. To make sauce: reduce reserved braising liquids over a high heat until almost dry. Add finely chopped tarragon, light stock and tomato purée. Season with salt and freshly ground black pepper, to taste, and simmer sauce for 1 hour, skimming from time to time. Strain sauce; add double cream, correct seasoning and heat through.
6. To serve: slice braised ham; arrange on a heated platter and serve with sauce separately. Ham prepared in this way is delicious either served cold or used in any number of other recipes.

CHINESE PORK AND LOBSTER BALLS

Just how far back good cooking actually goes in China is hard to determine, but the Chinese were early discoverers of fire, and have been farmers for well over four thousand years. In the course of their long history they have evolved a high sense of harmony in the delicate blending of tastes and textures.

Some cooks believe that Chinese food is too exotic to be attempted in the home kitchen, but nothing could be further from the truth, for no special utensils are needed and the few special extras – soy sauce, bean sprouts, bamboo shoots and water chestnuts – can now be bought, bottled or canned, throughout the country.

Chinese dishes are inexpensive, quick to prepare and fun to cook. Using an electric frying pan, or a more traditional chafing dish, you can even cook Chinese food right in the dining room in front of your guests. A Chinese dinner served in true Oriental fashion assures a pleasant evening. And for those who like an authentic atmosphere, Chinese serving dishes and chopsticks are inexpensive and easily obtainable.

SERVING A CHINESE MEAL

Rice is the staple food of the Chinese but it is a mistake to think that the Chinese eat nothing but rice. Rice is the centre, the focal point, but ringed with a dozen different dishes, each blending perfectly with it and with each other. According to Chinese food authority Kenneth H. C. Lo, an average Chinese meal consists of one or two soups – vegetable soup and a chicken or beef-based soup – one or two meat dishes, an egg or fish dish and one or two vegetable dishes, served in conjunction with the rice. In wealthier families, when up to a dozen separate dishes are served during each meal, rice merely acts as a 'buffer' to the rich and tasty dishes, which may be served course by course or all at the same time.

The one supreme meat for the Chinese is pork. Those Chinese who can afford it eat it almost every day, poorer Chinese dream about it, and even the poorest try to save up a few coins to buy some with which to celebrate the New Year.

Sweet and sour conveys the Orient to our Western palates. Here are two classic recipes for serving pork and lobster balls with this favourite sauce.

PORK IN SWEET AND SOUR SAUCE

SERVES 4

550g/1¼lb ground pork
1 small garlic clove, minced
5ml/1 tsp salt
15ml/1 tbls dry sherry
15ml/1 tbls soy sauce
melted butter
60-90ml/4-6 tbls olive oil
Sweet and sour sauce *(see page 221)*

1. Combine ground pork and garlic. Season with salt, sherry and soy sauce and form mixture into small balls the size of a walnut. Roll in melted butter.

2. Heat olive oil in a thick-bottomed frying pan; toss pork balls in hot oil for 6 to 10 minutes.
3. Meanwhile, heat SWEET AND SOUR SAUCE through.
4. Transfer pork balls to a heated serving dish. Pour over SWEET AND SOUR SAUCE and serve.

LOBSTER IN SWEET AND SOUR SAUCE

SERVES 4

450g/1lb lobster, or shrimps, prawns, or fish
100g/4oz pork, not too lean
15ml/1 tbls cornflour

15ml/1 tbls dry sherry
15ml/1 tbls soy sauce
1.5ml/¼ tsp salt
5ml/1 tsp sugar
60-90ml/4-6 tbls lard, or olive oil
Sweet and sour sauce (see below)

BATTER
1 egg
120ml/8 tbls ice-cold water
120ml/8 tbls sifted flour

1. Shell and clean lobster, shrimps or prawns, or skin and bone fish, and grind finely. Grind pork.
2. Pound ground fish and pork to a smooth paste with cornflour, sherry, soy sauce, salt, sugar and 30ml/2 tbls water. Form mixture into balls the size of large walnuts.
3. To make batter: stir egg in a small bowl, but do not whip or beat. Add ice-cold water and mix well; then sprinkle with sifted flour. Do not beat, just stir lightly to mix the ingredients. Do not worry about lumps in batter. If you stir too much, the batter becomes sticky and will not react properly.
4. Heat lard, or olive oil in a thick-bottomed frying pan until very hot. Then reduce heat; dip balls in batter and place in hot oil. Fry for about 5 minutes, turning from time to time so they are cooked to a golden brown on all sides.
5. Meanwhile, heat SWEET AND SOUR SAUCE through.
6. This dish is best when served hot from the pan with SWEET AND SOUR SAUCE poured over, but may be put in an oven to crisp for 5 minutes before serving.

SWEET AND SOUR SAUCE

MAKES 300ml/½pt

1 small can pineapple chunks
2 small carrots, thinly sliced

1 green pepper, seeded and thinly sliced
15ml/1 tbls cornflour
15ml/1 tbls brown sugar
10-15ml/2-3 tsp soy sauce
30ml/2 tbls olive oil
30-45ml/2-3 tbls red wine vinegar
3-4 sweet pickles, sliced

1. Drain canned pineapple chunks and reserve juice.
2. Simmer thinly sliced carrots and pepper gently in reserved pineapple juice for 5 minutes, or until tender.
3. Mix cornflour, brown sugar, soy sauce, olive oil and wine vinegar together smoothly and stir into the vegetable stock. Cook for 3 minutes. Add pineapple chunks and sliced pickles to the sauce and continue cooking until heated through.

CHINESE SWEET AND SOUR PORK

SERVES 4

1kg/2lb boned pork, cut into 2.5cm/1in cubes
15ml/1 tbls soy sauce
45ml/3 tbls cornflour
15ml/1 tbls sake, or dry sherry
lard, or olive oil
1 garlic clove, finely chopped
1 small onion, finely sliced
2 small carrots, finely sliced
7ml/½ tbls finely sliced ginger root
1 green pepper, seeded and cut in thin strips
15ml/1 tbls brown sugar
45ml/3 tbls red wine vinegar
salt

1. Combine soy sauce, 30ml/2 tbls cornflour and *sake*, or dry sherry; add pork cubes and mix well. Let stand for 10 minutes.
2. Heat 60-90ml/4-6 tbls lard or olive oil and fry pork cubes until golden brown. Drain on absorbent paper.

3. Heat 30ml/2 tbls lard, or olive oil in a thick-bottomed frying pan and sauté garlic, onion, green pepper, carrots and ginger root for 2 minutes.

4. Mix together sugar, wine vinegar, 90ml/ 6tbls water, 15ml/1 tbls cornflour and salt, to taste. Add to the vegetables, stirring steadily until the mixture comes to the boil. Add pork cubes and cook over a low heat for 3 minutes. Transfer to a heated serving dish and serve immediately.

CHINESE BRAISED PORK

SERVES 6-8

1kg/2lb boned pork, cut in 2.5cm/1in cubes
30-60ml/2-4 tbls lard
90ml/6 tbls soy sauce
45ml/3 tbls sake, or dry sherry

5ml/1 tsp finely chopped ginger root
1 garlic clove, finely chopped
generous pinch of sugar
freshly ground black pepper
30ml/2 tbls olive oil
450g/1lb spinach, washed and drained

1. Heat lard in a deep thick-bottomed saucepan; add pork cubes and sauté, stirring constantly, until golden brown.

2. Combine soy sauce, *sake,* or dry sherry, 90ml/6 tbls water, finely chopped ginger, garlic, sugar and freshly ground black pepper, to taste; pour over pork cubes. Bring mixture to the boil; cover and then simmer gently for 1 hour.

3. Heat olive oil in a another saucepan; add washed and drained spinach and cook, stirring constantly, for 5 minutes. Drain well and serve with the braised pork.

ITALIAN SAUSAGE

The humble sausage – esteemed worthy meat only for a country breakfast or a family supper of 'bangers and mash' in Britain today – was considered a great delicacy by the early Greeks and Romans. The very word sausage comes from the Latin *salsus,* salty proof indeed that the sausage was a method of preserving as well as a type of food, a very necessary adjunct to good living in the days before refrigerators. And Italians today are as fond of the sausage as they were in Pliny's time.

A well-known Italian sausage, now so popular throughout the world that it is also produced in Germany, Hungary and the United States, is *salame,* generally made of lean pork, fat pork and beef, finely ground and highly seasoned, coloured with red wine and pickled in brine before it is air-dried. There is seemingly no end to the varieties of *salame* to be found in Italy today. Some are highly flavoured with garlic, others are mild, some are eaten fresh and others are considered to be at their best when they are most mature. A visit to any busy, crowded little *salumeria* in

Rome – pungent-smelling shops with sausages of all sorts piled high in the windows and hung in stacks like church candles from the ceiling – will give you an immediate idea of the immense variety of *salami,* smoked and raw hams and sausages available.

Perhaps the most familiar to us in this country are the *crespone* or *salame de Milano,* about 6.5cm/2½in in diameter, red-hued and granite-grained, with a very spicy flavour, and the *salame de Cremona,* a larger slightly coarser-grained version of the Milan sausage. Try, too, the *salame casalinga,* a rough marbled sausage with a more distinctive flavour; look for the deep cherry-red of the meat and the white waxiness of the fat which indicate that it is fresh.

Salame fiorentian – and its *anise*-flavoured brother, *salame finocchiono* – I have only had in Italy, but I am assured that they are available in this country from time to time. Both these sausages, specialities of Tuscany, are larger than the Milan sausage and made of pure lean pork and fat. Good, too, for the *antipasti* platter are the silver-wrapped *cacciatora* and *turisto* sausages on sale here.

One of my favourite Italian sausages is the large, round, rosy-fleshed *mortadella,* a smooth-tasting sausage studded with square white chunks of fat. *Mortadella* is made in Florence and Bologna from the flesh of pigs which feed on the chestnuts and acorns in the surrounding forests. Seasoned with wine, garlic and spices, it is very good for cooking.

The best sausages for culinary purposes are, of course, the ones specially made for this purpose . . . the *cotechino* sausage, a large sausage made of lean pork, fat salt pork, white wine and spices, is often served in Italy with brown lentils or white beans, the robust, country flavour and fat juiciness of this sausage providing the perfect complement to the mealy vegetables. Try slices of *cotechino,* too, with cooked spinach, a speciality of the Cotechino restaurant in Rome. *Cotechino* and the sausage-stuffed pig's trotter from Modena called *zampone* are often used interchangeably in the famous Italian dish, *bollito misto,* mixed boiled meats. This noble dish, served at Rome's glamorous Capriccio restaurant just off the Via Veneto, combines lean beef, fat beef, veal, chicken, a calf's head and a *cotechino* sausage, simmered in salted boiling water with onions, celery, carrots and parsley. Very much like the French *pot-au-feu, bollito misto* is served with a *salsa verde* or a spicy tomato sauce.

Other Italian culinary sausages available in this country are the *salsicce negroni,* fat mottled sausages with a rustic flavour, and the thinner, finer *chipolate* sausages. The *negroni* are best poached in water until tender; make sure you prick several holes in each before placing in water; then dry them carefully and sauté gently in oil and butter until done. This method keeps sausages from splitting and yet assures that they are cooked through without taking on too much colour. The *chipolate* are cooked in the usual manner.

COTECHINO WITH LENTILS

SERVES 4

1 cotechino sausage
350g/³⁄₄lb brown lentils
½ Spanish onion
2 celery stalks
15ml/1 tbls olive oil
15ml/1 tbls butter
50g/2oz fat salt pork, diced
salt and freshly ground black pepper

1. Prick holes in the skin of the *cotechino* with a fine skewer, or the point of a sharp knife. Put *cotechino* in cold water in a thick-bottomed saucepan just large enough to hold it and bring slowly to the boil. Turn down heat and let the water barely bubble for about 2 hours. While still hot, remove skin gently and allow sausage to cool. Reserve liquid. When sausage is cool, cut it into fairly thick slices.
2. Meanwhile, wash brown lentils well, picking out any impurities. Cook lentils in boiling salted water with onion and celery for 1½ hours. When lentils are soft, drain thoroughly.
3. Heat olive oil and butter in a thick-bottomed casserole and sauté diced fat salt pork until golden.
4. Add drained lentils to casserole and moisten with a little of the reserved liquid from the *cotechino*. Season with salt and black pepper, to taste; bring to the boil and then simmer gently for a few minutes until the lentils have absorbed all the liquid. Place *cotechino* slices on top; heat through and serve from casserole.

SAUCISSES CHIPOLATA EN CHEMISE

SERVES 4-6

450g/1lb chipolata sausages
30ml/2 tbls olive oil
Flaky pastry *(see page 346)*

flour
tarragon mustard
milk
Tomato sauce *(see page 83)*

1. Preheat oven to moderately hot (200°C/ 400°F/gas 6).
2. Heat olive oil in a thick-bottomed frying pan and sauté sausages until golden brown.
3. Roll out FLAKY PASTRY thinly on a floured pastry board. Cut rectangles in the pastry large enough to fold over each sausage; spread rectangles with tarragon mustard, and place a sausage on each.
4. Roll up pastry like a little package. Brush top of each with milk and bake in preheated oven for 15 minutes. Transfer sausage packets to a heated serving dish and serve with TOMATO SAUCE and a salad of your choice.

SAUCISSES AU VIN ROUGE

SERVES 4-6

450g/1lb Toulouse sausages
25g/1oz butter
30ml/2 tbls fresh breadcrumbs
300ml/½pt good red wine
salt and freshly ground black pepper
pinch of ground thyme
bay leaf

1. Melt butter in a thick-bottomed frying pan and sauté sausages over a low heat until they are golden on all sides, turning occasionally.
2. Add breadcrumbs, turn up heat and let breadcrumbs take on colour. Add red wine; bring to the boil; lower heat and simmer gently for 10 minutes. Add salt and freshly ground black pepper, to taste, a pinch of ground thyme and a bay leaf, and simmer for 5 to 10 minutes more. Transfer sausages to a heated serving dish. Pour over sauce and serve immediately.

SAUSAGES AND SAUERKRAUT CASEROLE

SERVES 4

4 Toulouse sausages
olive oil
350g/12oz cooked sauerkraut
4 mushroom caps, chopped
15ml/1 tbls butter
300ml/¹/₂pt **Sauce espagnole** *(see page 82)*

1. Preheat grill to high.
2. Place sausages in a thick-bottomed saucepan and cover with hot water. Bring to the boil; remove from heat and let stand for 5 minutes. Drain sausages.
3. When ready to grill, brush grid of grill pan with a little olive oil; reduce heat to medium and grill sausages lightly until golden.
4. Place cooked sauerkraut in a heatproof baking dish; top with sausages.
5. Sauté chopped mushrooms caps in butter for 3 minutes. Spoon sautéed mushrooms over sausages and sauerkraut; top with SAUCE ESPAGNOLE and heat under grill until bubbling. Serve immediately.

SAUSAGE PATTIES

SERVES 4-6

700g/1¹/₂lb lean pork
350g/³/₄lb fat salt pork
1 garlic clove
5ml/1 tsp salt
1 bay leaf, crushed
ground allspice
ground coriander
5ml/1 tsp coarsely ground black pepper
1 egg
1 Spanish onion, finely chopped
15ml/1 tbls finely chopped parsley
5ml/1 tsp rubbed thyme
30ml/2 tbls butter
30ml/2 tbls olive oil

1. Put meats through finest blade of mincer, or have it ground by your butcher.
2. Combine garlic, salt, crushed bay leaf, ground allspice and coriander, to taste, with coarsely ground black pepper in mortar, and pound to a smooth paste.
3. Add this mixture to ground meats together with egg, finely chopped onion, and finely chopped parsley. Mix thoroughly and form into patties.
4. Heat butter and olive oil in a thick-bottomed frying pan and sauté patties until cooked through, but not dry. Transfer to a heated serving dish and serve with soft scrambled eggs.

CHAPTER 11

POULTRY & GAME

— COQ AU VIN —

I MADE MY FIRST contact with *coq-au-vin,* one of the undisputed glories of French cuisine, when I was eighteen. The place – a little French restaurant on New York's West Side, one of those little bistros run by a French family, where you could eat inexpensively yet wonderfully well.

Maman served smilingly behind the bar in the small front room with its three or four tables. Papa cooked the specialities of France in the back dining room-cum-kitchen, separated from his clients by only a low counter, and their daughter served at table. Each night had Papa's favourite speciality: Monday was a creamy *blanquette de veau;* Tuesday, a hearty sausage-and-game filled *cassoulet;* Wednesday, a majestic *pot-au-feu;* Thursday, *navarin de mouton,* garnished with papa's own vegetables; Friday was *bouillabaisse* night. But best of all, for me at least, was Saturday, for that was the night they served *coq-au-vin.*

Papa's *coq-au-vin* was a simple affair – chicken simmered in Burgundy and chicken stock, with *lardons* of fat salt pork, tiny white onions and small new potatoes – and I returned there as often as I could after that first visit to enjoy this great country dish.

If that *coq-au-vin* was my first, it was certainly not my last, for this famous dish has travelled from its native Burgundy throughout the length and breadth of France. I

Some of the ingredients you will need for Coq au Vin —the great, classic dish from Burgundy, which can *be found in all its variations in almost every restaurant in France and throughout the world.*

226

do not know of a restaurant in all France that at some time does not feature a version of it. I have enjoyed chicken cooked in red wine, white wine, and even in champagne; I have had it garnished with button mushrooms, tiny white onions, *lardons* of fat salt pork or green bacon, *croûtons* of fried bread or golden pastry crescents, and even with soft-textured cockscombs as it is served today at the Restaurant La Bourgogne in Paris.

Here is my favourite recipe for this famous dish.

COQ-AU-VIN

SERVES 4

1.4kg/3lb chicken, dressed weight
60ml/4 tbls butter
30ml/2 tbls olive oil
100g/4oz green bacon, cut into cubes
12 button onions
12 button mushrooms
salt and freshly ground black pepper
45ml/3 tbls flour
2 garlic cloves, finely chopped
sprig of thyme
2 sprigs of parsley
2 bay leaves
60ml/4 tbls cognac, warmed
1/2 bottle good red wine
1 sugar lump
30ml/2 tbls finely chopped parsley

1. Cut the chicken into serving pieces.
2. Preheat oven to slow (170°C/325°F/gas 3).
3. Heat 45ml/3 tbls butter and the olive oil in a thick-bottomed ovenproof casserole and sauté green bacon cubes. When bacon begins to turn golden, add onions and cook for a minute or two, then add mushrooms. Sauté this mixture gently until the onions begin to turn transparent and the mushrooms brown. Remove bacon, onions and mushrooms from casserole and keep warm.
4. Roll chicken pieces in seasoned flour and

sauté in the same fats for about 5 minutes, or until they turn golden on one side. Then, without piercing the skin, turn chicken pieces over to brown on the other side. As each of the chicken pieces begins to 'stiffen', transfer to a covered dish and keep warm.
5. Return bacon, onions, mushrooms and chicken pieces with their juices to the casserole. Add salt and freshly ground black pepper, to taste, finely chopped garlic, sprigs of thyme, and parsley and bay leaves; cover casserole and cook in preheated oven for 35 to 45 minutes, or until chicken pieces are almost tender. Remove chicken pieces, bacon and vegetables from casserole and keep warm. Reduce oven temperature to very slow (140°C/275°F/gas 1-150°C/300°F/gas 2).
6. Skim off excess fat from the juices in casserole. Set casserole on a high heat, pour in warmed cognac and ignite. Allow to burn for a minute or two and then extinguish by pouring in the red wine. Add a lump of sugar; bring to the boil and reduce sauce over a quick heat to half the original quantity. Thicken by whisking in a *beurre manié* (made by mashing 15ml/1 tbls each butter and flour together to form a smooth paste). Correct seasoning.
7. Strain sauce into a clean casserole; return chicken pieces, bacon and vegetables; cover and allow to simmer in preheated oven until ready to serve. Just before serving, garnish with finely chopped parsley.

CHICKEN EN COCOTTE

SERVES 4

1.4kg/3lb chicken, dressed weight
salt and freshly ground black pepper
30ml/2 tbls butter
30ml/2 tbls olive oil
100g/4oz fat bacon, diced
4 shallots, coarsely chopped
2 carrots, coarsely chopped
50ml/2fl oz cognac, warmed
4 tomatoes, peeled, seeded and chopped
bouquet garni (2 sprigs parsley, bay leaf,
    1 sprig of thyme)
300ml/½pt red wine
Basic chicken stock (see page 66) (optional)

1. Cut chicken into serving pieces and season with salt and freshly ground black pepper, to taste.
2. Heat butter and olive oil in an iron *cocotte,* or thick-bottomed casserole and sauté diced bacon until golden. Remove bacon; add coarsely chopped shallots and carrots and cook, stirring constantly, until vegetables soften; then add chicken pieces and brown them on all sides.
3. Return bacon bits to *cocotte,* or casserole; pour over warmed cognac and ignite. When flames have died down, add peeled, seeded and chopped tomatoes, *bouquet garni* and red wine. Cover and simmer over a low heat for 35 to 45 minutes, or until chicken pieces are very tender. Add more wine or CHICKEN STOCK if the sauce reduces too quickly while cooking. Correct seasoning and serve immediately from *cocotte* or casserole.

POULET FRANCOIS ler

SERVES 4

1.6kg/3½lb chicken, drerssed weight
60ml/4 tbls butter

225g/½lb button mushrooms, cut into quarters
225g/½lb small white onions, peeled
60ml/4 tbls Calvados, warmed
150ml/½pt double cream
bouquet garni (2 sprigs parsley, 1 sprig thyme
    and 1 celery stalk)
salt and freshly ground black pepper
fried bread triangles

1. Preheat oven to slow (170°C/325°F/gas 3).
2. Cut chicken into serving pieces.
3. Melt butter in a thick-bottomed ovenproof casserole and sauté chicken until golden.
4. Add mushroom quarters and small onions to casserole and simmer gently for 5 minutes. Pour over warmed Calvados and ignite, shaking the pan until flames die out. Moisten with cream; add *bouquet garni* and season with salt and freshly ground black pepper. Cover and cook in preheated oven for 35 to 45 minutes, or until chicken pieces are tender.
5. To serve: place chicken pieces in a heated serving dish, remove *bouquet garni,* correct sauce for seasoning and pour over chicken pieces. Garnish with fried bread triangles and serve immediately.

MEDITERRANEAN CHICKEN

SERVES 4

1.6kg/3½lb chicken, dressed weight, trussed
30ml/2 tbls butter
30ml/2 tbls olive oil
225g/½lb fat green bacon, diced
225g/½lb green olives, pitted
225g/½lb button mushrooms
salt and freshly ground black pepper
90ml/6 tbls cognac
450g/1lb potatoes, diced and sautéed
4 tomatoes, peeled, seeded and chopped

1. Preheat oven to slow (170°C/325°F/gas 3).
2. Heat butter and olive oil in a thick-bot-

tomed ovenproof casserole and sauté chicken and diced green bacon until chicken is golden.
3. Meanwhile, soak pitted green olives in hot water to remove excess salt. Drain.
4. Add pitted green olives and button mushrooms to casserole. Season with a little salt and freshly ground black pepper. Moisten with cognac; cover and cook in preheated oven for 45 minutes.
5. Add diced sautéed potatoes and tomatoes and simmer gently for another 15 minutes, or until chicken is tender. Correct seasoning and serve from casserole or heated serving dish.

ITALIAN CHICKEN CASSEROLE

SERVES 4

1.6kg/3½lb chicken, dressed weight
225g/½lb cooked ham, diced
60ml/4 tbls fresh breadcrumbs
2 garlic cloves, finely chopped
finely chopped parsley
1 egg, beaten
freshly ground black pepper
30ml/2 tbls butter
30ml/2 tbls olive oil
*150-300ml/¼-½pt **Basic chicken stock** (see page 66)*
30ml/2 tbls tomato purée
salt
***Boiled rice** (see page 179)*

1. If using, preheat oven to slow (170°C/325°F/gas 3).
2. Combine diced cooked ham, breadcrumbs, finely chopped garlic and 30ml/2 tbls finely chopped parsley. Moisten with beaten egg; season with freshly ground black pepper, to taste, and stuff chicken with this mixture. Truss chicken.
3. Melt butter and olive oil in thick-bottomed ovenproof casserole and sauté chicken until it has turned golden on all sides.

4. Combine CHICKEN STOCK and tomato purée and pour over chicken. Cover casserole and simmer gently on top of the stove, or in preheated oven for 1 hour, or until chicken is tender. Correct seasoning; garnish with finely chopped parsley and serve from casserole with BOILED RICE.

CHICKEN A LA GRECQUE

SERVES 4

1.6kg/3½lb chicken, dressed weight
1 Spanish onion
2 large carrots
2 celery stalks
30ml/2 tbls butter
30ml/2 tbls olive oil
salt and freshly ground black pepper
*150-300ml/¼-½pt **Basic chicken stock** (see page 66)*
***Boiled rice** (see page 179)*
90ml/6 tbls dry white wine

STUFFING

90ml/6 tbls finely chopped shallots
30ml/2 tbls butter
100g/4oz toasted breadcrumbs
2 garlic cloves
1 celery stalk, finely chopped
30ml/2 tbls finely chopped parsley
grated rind of ½ lemon
salt and freshly ground black pepper
pinch of dried rosemary
30ml/4 tbls cognac

1. Preheat oven to slow (170°C/325°F/gas 3).
2. Cut onion, carrots and celery stalks into thin strips.
3. Heat butter and olive oil in a thick-bottomed saucepan; add vegetables and salt and pepper to taste, and cook, stirring continuously, until soft, about 5 minutes. Transfer vegetables to an ovenproof casserole.

4. To prepare stuffing: cook finely chopped shallots in butter until transparent. Mix with remaining stuffing ingredients.

5. Fill cavity of chicken with stuffing and truss. Place chicken on top of vegetables and cook in preheated oven for 30 minutes.

6. Pour CHICKEN STOCK over chicken and vegetables; cover casserole and continue to cook for a further 30 minutes or until tender.

7. To serve: arrange drained chicken and vegetables in a heated serving dish and garnish with BOILED RICE. Pour dry white wine into casserole and cook rapidly for several minutes to reduce liquid slightly. Correct seasoning, strain sauce and serve with chicken and vegetables.

CHICKEN IN CHAMPAGNE OASIS

SERVES 4

1.4kg/3lb chicken, dressed weight
60-90ml/4-6 tbls butter
30ml/2 tbls finely chopped onion
salt and freshly ground black pepper
15ml/1 tbls flour
½ bottle champagne
300ml/½pt double cream
4 egg yolks

1. Cut chicken into serving pieces.

2. Melt butter in a thick-bottomed saucepan and simmer chicken pieces together with finely chopped onion and salt and freshly ground black pepper, to taste. Turn chicken pieces several times; cover and steam at the lowest posible heat for 10 to 15 minutes. The chicken should not take on colour.

3. Sprinkle chicken pieces with flour; turn several times and then pour over champagne. Cover casserole and simmer gently for 25 to 35 minutes more, or until the chicken pieces are tender. Arrange chicken pieces on a heated serving dish; cover and keep warm.

4. Reduce pan juices in which chicken was cooked to a quarter of the original quantity over a brisk flame. Add all but 30ml/2 tbls double cream and continue cooking, stirring from time to time, until sauce is reduced by half.

5. Whisk egg yolks and remaining cream until well blended; add a little of the hot sauce to this mixture; blend well and pour mixture into hot sauce. Simmer sauce over a very low heat, or over water, until sauce is thick and smooth. Do not allow sauce to boil. Correct seasoning and strain sauce over chicken pieces through a fine sieve. Serve immediately.

SUMMER CHICKEN CASSEROLE

SERVES 4

1.4kg/3lb chicken, dressed weight
60ml/4 tbls butter
30ml/2 tbls olive oil
12 button onions
15ml/1 tbls flour
salt and freshly ground black pepper
bouquet garni (2 sprigs parsley, 1 sprig of thyme
*   and 1 bay leaf)*
24 button mushrooms
juice of 2 lemons
2 egg yolks
300ml/½pt double cream

1. Cut chicken into serving pieces.

2. Heat 30ml/2 tbls each butter and olive oil in a thick-bottomed saucepan and sauté chicken pieces together with onions until they just begin to turn colour.

3. Sprinkle chicken pieces with flour and add just enough water to cover. Season with salt and freshly ground black pepper, to taste; add *bouquet garni*, cover casserole and cook for 35 to 45 minutes, or until chicken pieces are tender. Arrange chicken pieces and onions in a serving dish and allow to cool. Strain and reserve stock.

4. Sauté button mushrooms in 30ml/2 tbls butter, to which you have added the juice of 1 lemon, until tender. Add to chicken pieces and onions.

5. Whisk together egg yolks, juice of 1 lemon and 150ml/¼pt double cream. Bring reserved stock to the boil, and, whisking vigorously, add a ladle of boiling stock to the cream and egg mixture. Pour mixture into the hot stock and bring gently to the boil, whisking well, until sauce is thick and creamy.

6. Strain sauce through a fine sieve and allow to cool. When cool, whisk in remaining cream; correct seasoning and pour over chicken and vegetables. Toss well. Chill before serving.

OLD ENGLISH CHICKEN PIE

1.4kg/3lb chicken, dressed weight
salt and freshly ground black pepper
90ml/6 tbls flour
90ml/6 tbls butter
Fingertip pastry *for 20cm/8in pie dish (see*
page 347)
2 hard-boiled eggs, quartered

WHITE FORCEMEAT
100g/4oz stale bread
grated rind of ½ lemon
5ml/1 tsp finely chopped parsley
1.5ml/¼ tsp finely chopped thyme
pinch of ground nutmeg
2.5ml/½ tsp salt
freshly ground black pepper
50g/2oz butter
1 egg yolk

SAUSAGE FORCEMEAT
liver and heart of chicken
100g/4oz sausage-meat
5ml/1 tsp finely chopped parsley
5ml/1 tsp finely chopped chives, or green parts of
spring onions

1. Bone chicken and simmer wings, neck and bones in a little seasoned water to make a light stock. Strain and reserve.

2. Reform the boned pieces of chicken and roll lightly in flour.

3. Melt 45ml/3 tbls butter in a thick-bottomed saucepan and sauté chicken pieces until they are a light golden colour on all sides. Season well with salt and freshly ground black pepper; cover pan and cook over a low heat for 20 minutes, turning occasionally. Set aside.

4. Meanwhile, preheat oven to moderate (190°C/375°F/gas 5).

5. To prepare white forcemeat: grate stale bread and mix thoroughly with grated lemon rind, finely chopped parsley and thyme and a pinch of ground nutmeg. Season with salt and freshly ground black pepper, to taste. Dice butter; add to mixture together with egg yolk and work to a smooth paste with your fingers.

6. To prepare sausage forcemeat: put liver and heart of chicken through mincer with sausage-meat and combine this paste with finely chopped parsley and chives, or green parts of spring onions.

7. Form small balls the size of walnuts from these 2 forcemeat mixtures by rolling them between your hands, or on a board (there should be enough mixture for 12 to 16 balls). Brown balls lightly in 45ml/3 tbls butter.

8. Line a 20cm/8in pie dish with FINGERTIP PASTRY and place chicken pieces in dish. Garnish with forcemeat balls and quartered hard-boiled eggs.

9. Stir 90ml/6 tbls of the reserved light stock into the pan in which the chicken was cooked, blending well with butter and remaining juices. Pour sauce over contents of pie dish and cover with a top layer of pastry. Moisten edges of pastry with water; pinch them together and cut one or two slits in the centre of the crust. Bake in preheated oven for 30 minutes, or until done. This pie is excellent served with CHICKEN VELOUTE SAUCE (see page 236).

MOROCCAN ROAST CHICKEN

1.4-1.6kg/3-3½lb chicken, dressed weight
15ml/1 tbls chopped parsley
15ml/1 tbls chopped chervil
½ Spanish onion, chopped
60-90ml/4-6 tbls butter
5ml/1 tsp ground cumin
2.5ml/½ tsp salt
generous pinch of cayenne pepper

1. Preheat oven to fairly hot (220°C/425°F/ gas 7).
2. Pound chopped parsley, chervil and onion in a mortar. Add butter, ground cumin, salt and a generous pinch of pepper and pound to a smooth paste.
3. Using a damp cloth or absorbent paper, wipe chicken clean both inside and out. Truss chicken; spread with herb mixture and roast in preheated oven for 35 to 40 minutes. Reduce oven temperature to moderate (180°C/350°F/ gas 4) and roast for a further 30 to 35 minutes, basting with sauce from time to time. Serve with sauce separately.

MOROCCAN CHICKEN

1.8-2.3kg/4-5lb chicken, dressed weight
1.5ml/¼ tsp paprika
1.5ml/¼ tsp ground cumin
salt and freshly ground black pepper
350g/¾lb onions, sliced
90ml/6 tbls butter
1.5ml/¼ tsp ground saffron
100g/4oz chick peas, soaked overnight
  and drained
*well-flavoured **Basic chicken stock***
  (see page 66)
60ml/4 tbls finely chopped parsley
sprig of fresh coriander, or lemon thyme
***Boiled rice** (see page 179) (optional)*
lemon juice

1. Cut chicken into serving pieces and season with paprika, ground cumin and salt and freshly ground black pepper, to taste.
2. Melt butter in a thick-bottomed saucepan and sauté chicken pieces together with sliced onions until golden.
3. Sprinkle chicken pieces with ground saffron; add chick peas and enough well-flavoured CHICKEN STOCK to cover and simmer gently for 35 to 45 minutes, or until chicken pieces and chick peas are tender.
4. Just before serving, stir in finely chopped parsley and sprig of coriander, or lemon thyme.
5. To serve: spoon half of the BOILED RICE into a heated serving dish. Place chicken pieces and chick peas on top of rice and pour over saffron sauce. Add remaining rice to dish; sprinkle with lemon juice and serve immediately.

CHICKEN BRAISED IN WINE

SERVES 4-6

1.8kg/4lb chicken, dressed weight, trussed
butter
30ml/2 tbls olive oil
100g/4oz fat bacon, diced
4 shallots, coarsely chopped
2 carrots, coarsely chopped
30ml/2 tbls cognac, warmed
1 bouquet garni (1 bay leaf, 1 sprig of thyme,
  2 sprigs of parsley)
dry white wine
***Basic chicken stock** (see page 66)*
salt and freshly ground black pepper

1. Heat 30ml/2 tbls butter and olive oil in an iron *cocotte* or thick-bottomed casserole just large enough to hold chicken. Sauté diced bacon in fats until golden. Remove bacon; add coarsely chopped shallots and carrots and cook, stirring constantly, until vegetables soften; then add chicken and brown on all sides.

233

2. Return bacon bits to casserole; pour over warmed cognac and ignite. When flames have died down add *bouquet garni,* 300ml/½pt dry white wine and 150ml/¼pt CHICKEN STOCK and season with salt and black pepper.

3. Cover chicken with a piece of buttered greaseproof paper cut to fit the casserole, with a small hole in the centre to allow steam to escape. Cover casserole and simmer gently over a very low heat for 35 to 45 minutes, or until chicken is tender. Add more wine or a little more CHICKEN STOCK if the sauce reduces too quickly during the cooking. Remove *bouquet garni* and serve from casserole.

CHICKEN PUDDING IN BUTTER CRUST

SERVES 4

1.4kg/3lb chicken, dressed weight
butter
flour
4 egg yolks, well beaten
100g/4oz ham (in one piece)
100g/4oz button mushrooms, quartered
30ml/2 tbls finely chopped parsley
salt and freshly ground black pepper
2.5ml/½ tsp each dried rosemary and tarragon
5ml/1 tsp freshly grated lemon rind
300ml/½pt well-flavoured **Basic chicken stock**
   (see page 66)

1. Grease a 1.4L/2½pt basin and line it with a crust made from 175g/6oz butter and 450g/1lb flour moistened with well beaten egg yolks and, if necessary, a little water. Reserve enough crust for the lid.

2. Cut chicken into small serving pieces and dust lightly with flour.

3. Melt 45ml/3 tbls butter in a thick-bottomed saucepan and sauté chicken pieces until they are a light golden colour on all sides. Transfer chicken pieces to basin.

4. Cut the ham into strips about 1.2cm/½in thick and 5cm/2in long.

5. Scatter ham, quartered mushrooms and finely chopped parsley among chicken pieces. Season with salt and black pepper, to taste, dried rosemary, tarragon and lemon rind.

6. Pour well-flavoured CHICKEN STOCK into basin. Cover with remaining crust and pinch edges together; cover with a piece of buttered paper, then with a cloth. Tie up securely and boil for 2½ to 3 hours. Serve from basin.

OVEN FRIED CHICKEN

SERVES 4

1.1kg/2½lb chicken, dressed weight
50g/2oz flour
5ml/1 tsp salt
2.5ml/½ tsp black pepper, crushed
15ml/1 tbls finely chopped parsley
5ml/1 tsp dried tarragon, crushed
5ml/1 tsp dried rosemary, crushed
grated rind of 1 lemon
1 egg, beaten
milk
butter
60ml/4 tbls olive oil
thin triangles of bread, sautéed in butter

1. Preheat oven to moderately hot (200°C/400°F/gas 6).

2. Cut chicken into serving pieces.

3. Combine flour, salt, crushed black pepper, finely chopped parsley, crushed tarragon and rosemary and grated lemon rind in a bowl.

4. Combine beaten egg and a little milk in a bowl.

5. Dip chicken pieces into egg and milk mixture and then into seasoned flour, shaking off excess. Chill.

6. Place 60ml/4tbls butter and olive oil in an ovenproof baking dish and heat in preheated oven until butter sizzles.

7. Place chicken pieces in dish, spoon butter and olive oil over them and cook for 30 to 35 minutes, or until chicken is tender and brown, turning pieces once or twice during cooking time.

8. Serve chicken pieces on thin slices of toast which you have sautéed in butter until crisp, accompanied by the cooking juices.

POULET AU BLANC

SERVES 4

1.4kg/3lb chicken, dressed weight
600ml/1pt good light stock
60ml/4 tbls butter
12 mushroom caps
juice of 1 lemon
30ml/2 tbls flour
2 egg yolks
salt and freshly ground black pepper

1. Preheat oven to moderate (180°C/350°F/gas 4).
2. Place chicken in a thick-bottomed oven-proof casserole and add enough light stock to half cover it. Cover exposed part of chicken with a piece of buttered paper; cover casserole and simmer in preheated oven for about 1 hour, or until chicken is tender.
3. Meanwhile simmer mushroom caps in 30ml/2 tbls butter and the lemon juice until tender. Keep warm.
4. Remove chicken from casserole, reserving cooking liquid. Keep warm.
5. Melt 30ml/2 tbls butter in a thick-bottomed saucepan, then add flour to make a white roux. Cook for a few minutes, stirring constantly, without allowing roux to take on colour. Strain 600ml/1pt of reserved cooking liquid into roux to make a VELOUTE SAUCE (see page 81). Remove sauce from heat and stir in egg yolks. Correct seasoning.
6. Carve chicken into serving pieces and put

into a clean casserole; add VELOUTE SAUCE and mushroom caps. Season with salt and freshly ground black pepper, to taste; warm through and serve from casserole.

POULE-AU-POT HENRI IV
Good King Henry's chicken in the pot

SERVES 4-6

1.6-2kg/3½-4½lb chicken, dressed weight

COURT BOUILLON
gizzard, heart, wing tips, neck and feet of chicken
1 veal knuckle
5ml/1 tsp salt
freshly ground black pepper
2 carrots
2 leeks
2 turnips
2 potatoes
1 Spanish onion, stuck with 2 cloves
bouquet garni (1 celery stalk, 2 sprigs of parsley and 1 bay leaf)
few cabbage leaves (optional)

STUFFING
chicken liver
100g/4oz green bacon
100g/4oz fresh pork
2-3 garlic cloves
100g/4oz fresh breadcrumbs
milk
30-45ml/2-3 tbls finely chopped parsley
2.5ml/½ tsp dried tarragon, or chervil
generous pinch of mixed spice
2 eggs
salt and freshly ground black pepper

1. To make *court-bouillon*: combine gizzard, heart, wing tips, neck and feet of the chicken in a thick-bottomed saucepan together with veal knuckle, salt, freshly ground black pepper, to taste, carrots, leeks, turnips,

235

potatoes, onion stuck with cloves and *bouquet garni*. Add 3.4L/6pts water and bring to the boil. Skim, lower heat and simmer, covered, for 1 hour.

2. To make stuffing: put chicken liver, green bacon, fresh pork and garlic through the finest blade of the mincer. Moisten breadcrumbs with milk and combine with minced meats. Add finely chopped parsley, dried tarragon, or chervil, a generous pinch of mixed spice and eggs. Season with salt and freshly ground black pepper. Mix well, adding more milk, if necessary, to make a fairly loose mixture.

3. Stuff chicken and truss. Poach, covered, in *court-bouillon* for approximately 1 hour, or until chicken is tender. If there is any stuffing left over, place 15-30ml/1-2 tbls in a cabbage leaf, fold up like a parcel, tie securely and poach with chicken for last 20 minutes of cooking time.

4. To serve: for a family luncheon, the hot broth is served first, followed by the chicken surrounded by freshly poached vegetables . . . choose among carrots, turnips, onions, green beans and potatoes. Add stuffed cabbage parcels. For a company dinner, place chicken on a heated serving dish and surround with individual pastry shells filled with GLAZED CARROTS (see page 279), GLAZED BUTTON ONIONS (see page 279), or FRENCH-STYLE PEAS (see page 280). Just before serving, spoon a little CHICKEN VELOUTE SAUCE (see this page) over chicken and serve remaining sauce separately.

POULET A LA CREME

SERVES 4

1.6kg/3¹/₂lb chicken, dressed weight
100g/4oz butter
1 medium onion, finely chopped
salt and freshly ground black pepper
300ml/¹/₂pt double cream
4 egg yolks

1. Cut chicken into serving pieces.

2. Melt butter in a thick-bottomed saucepan and sauté chicken pieces gently without letting them colour. Add finely chopped onion and season with salt and freshly ground black pepper, to taste. Cover with hot water and simmer gently, covered, for 30 to 40 minutes or until chicken pieces are tender.

3. Just before serving, combine double cream and egg yolks and pour over chicken pieces. Heat through, without boiling for 5 minutes, stirring continuously. Correct seasoning. Transfer to a heated serving dish and serve.

POULET AU RIZ AU SAFRAN

SERVES 4

1.4kg/3lb chicken, dressed weight, trussed
1 Spanish onion, stuck with 2 cloves
2 large carrots
bouquet garni (1 bay leaf, 1 sprig of thyme,
    2 sprigs of parsley)
1 celery stalk
2 garlic cloves
1 glass dry white wine
1L/2pt light stock
salt
black peppercorns

SAFFRON RICE

15ml/1 tbls butter
1 Spanish onion, finely chopped
225g/¹/₂lb long-grain rice
salt and freshly ground black pepper
freshly grated nutmeg
generous pinch of ground saffron

CHICKEN VELOUTE SAUCE

30ml/2 tbls butter
30ml/2 tbls flour
salt and freshly ground black pepper
2 egg yolks
juice of 1 lemon

1. Place chicken in a thick-bottomed saucepan together with onion stuck with cloves, carrots, *bouquet garni,* celery stalk and garlic cloves. Add dry white wine and light stock. Season with salt, to taste, and a few black peppercorns and simmer gently, covered, for about 1 hour, or until chicken is tender.

2. Remove chicken from saucepan. Keep warm. Strain chicken stock and use for saffron rice and chicken veloute sauce.

3. To make saffron rice: melt butter in a thick-bottomed saucepan; add finely chopped onion and stir for a minute over the heat until transparent. Stir in rice and add half of the reserved chicken stock. Season with salt and freshly ground black pepper, to taste, a little freshly grated nutmeg and a generous pinch of ground saffron. Simmer very gently, covered, for about 20 minutes, or until rice is tender but still moist. Drain.

4. To make chicken veloute sauce: melt butter in a thick-bottomed saucepan and make a white roux by stirring in flour. Cook roux for a few minutes, stirring constantly, without allowing it to take on colour. Add remaining reserved chicken stock and bring slowly to the boil, stirring constantly. Simmer, stirring from time to time, until sauce is thick and smooth. Correct seasoning and just before serving, stir in egg yolks and lemon juice.

5. To serve: line bottom of a heated serving dish with saffron rice; arrange chicken on the rice and pour over chicken velouté sauce. Serve immediately.

THE FESTIVE DUCK

The duck is a festive bird. It is ideal for a special occasion. I am always disappointed when I hear cooks in this country recommending that it should be served 'plain roast with green peas and sauce'. I far prefer the Continental method – French, Italian and Greek – of dealing with this delicious bird, half-way in flavour between poultry and game. It is rich, meltingly tender when young and fairly cries out to be simmered with wine, herbs and brandy in the Provençal manner. It can be filleted raw, marinated in Madeira and herbs and encased with the remainder of the meat, pounded and mixed with truffles and fat salt pork in a terrine or *pâté en croûte:* or stuffed with rice or wheat and pine nuts and herbs *à la grecque,* before being roasted.

I remember delicious country meals in France at which duck was the star performer: duck *en gelée,* the duck simmered in a rich stock with carrots, onions and celery, cooled in its own liquids and then served whole in its own jelly, surrounded by young vegetables: duck *en casserole,* the duck cut into serving pieces and marinated overnight in wine and brandy, flavoured with garlic, herbs, onions and car-

Overleaf: the flavour of duck is complemented by oranges in Duckling with Oranges.

237

rots, and then simmered in the marinated juices until tender. I also remember duck stuffed with diced green bacon, sauerkraut and diced green apples and roasted in the oven, bathed in dry white wine and its own juices.

But perhaps best of all, I like to roast my ducks to the half-way mark and then finish them with a variety of sweet and savoury ingredients. Duck goes wonderfully with oranges, olives, apples, cherries, herbs and spices, sauerkraut, wild rice, wines, cognac and gin.

Be imaginative with duck at your next dinner party. One 2.3-2.7kg/5-6lb duck, or two smaller ones, will serve 4 to 6 people easily.

DUCK NOTES

Ducks mature rapidly and reach their prime about 9 to 12 weeks after they hatch, when they weigh about 5 to 6 pounds.

You can judge the age of a duck by pressing its beak with your finger. A young duck's beak should be soft and flexible, while an older bird's beak will be hard and firm. A duck is a very fat bird so you will not need to add additional fat when roasting. I usually cut all visible fat from openings before cooking and pour off excess fat occasionally as it accumulates in the pan.

ROAST DUCKLING

1. To prepare: trim wing tips and cut off the neck of a 2.3-2.7kg/5-6lb duckling. Wipe with a damp cloth, or absorbent paper, inside and out, and sprinkle the cavity with salt and freshly ground black pepper. Rub the cavity with lemon juice, or brandy, and fill with half an onion, sliced, half an apple, peeled and sliced and a few celery leaves. Truss duckling.
2. Preliminary roasting: prick the skin of duckling with a fork; rub with a cut garlic clove and sprinkle with salt and freshly ground black pepper. Place the duckling, breast side up, on a rack in a roasting pan and cook in a preheated moderate oven (180°C/350°F/gas 4) for ½ hour.
3. To finish: skim fat from the pan juices; add 300ml/½pt dry white wine and continue to roast the duckling until tender, basting fre-

quently and pricking skin every 30 minutes to allow fat to escape. Allow about 20 minutes cooking time to the pound.

DUCKLING WITH OLIVES

1. To prepare: trim wing tips and cut off the neck of a 2.3-2.7kg/5-6lb duckling. Wipe with a damp cloth, or absorbent paper, inside and out, and sprinkle the cavity with salt and freshly ground black pepper. Rub the cavity with lemon juice, or brandy, and fill with half an onion, sliced, half an apple, peeled and sliced, and a few celery leaves. Truss duckling.
2. Prick the skin of duckling with a fork; rub with a cut garlic clove and sprinkle with salt and freshly ground black pepper. Place the duckling, breast side up, on a rack in a roasting pan and cook in a preheated moderate oven

(180°C/350°F/gas 4) for ½ hour. Keep warm.
3. To finish: pour off all but 30ml/2 tbls fat from the pan. Stir in 15ml/1 tbls flour and cook, stirring continuously, until flour is golden. Add 150ml/¼pt CHICKEN STOCK (see page 66) and 150ml/¼pt dry white wine and cook, stirring, until the sauce is smooth and slightly thickened. Transfer sauce to a thick-bottomed ovenproof casserole large enough to hold duck; season sauce with salt and freshly ground black pepper, to taste; and add *bouquet garni* (3 sprigs of parsley, 1 bay leaf, 1 celery stalk and 1 sprig of thyme). Place duckling in the casserole and simmer, covered, for about 1 hour, or until duckling is tender.
4. To serve: pit 24 green olives and poach them in water for 5 minutes to remove excess salt; drain. Place duckling on a heated serving platter; add the olives to the sauce and pour sauce over the duckling. Serve immediately.

DUCKLING WITH ORANGES

1. To prepare: trim wing tips and cut off the neck of a 2.3-2.7kg/5-6lb duckling. Wipe the duckling with a damp cloth, or absorbent paper inside and out, and sprinkle the cavity with salt and freshly ground black pepper. Rub the cavity with lemon juice, or brandy, and fill with half an onion, sliced, half an apple, peeled and sliced, and a few celery leaves. Truss duckling.
2. Prick the skin of duckling with a fork; rub with a cut garlic clove and sprinkle with salt and freshly ground black pepper. Place the duckling, breast side up, on a rack in a roasting pan and cook in a preheated oven (180°C/350°F/gas 4) until duckling is tender, basting frequently and pricking skin every 30 minutes to allow fat to escape. Allow about 20 minutes minutes cooking time to the pound. Remove duckling from pan. Keep warm.
3. To finish: skim fat from pan juices and add

150ml/¼pt CHICKEN STOCK (see page 66) to the pan, scraping in all the crusty bits from bottom and sides of pan. Stir in the juice of 2 oranges and 1 lemon, and 30ml/2 tbls cognac. Blend 30ml/2 tbls sugar and water in a thick-bottomed saucepan and cook until sugar turns to caramel. Add this to the sauce and simmer gently until sauce is reduced by half.
4. To serve: carve the duckling; place on a heated serving platter; pour over sauce and sprinkle with the rinds of 2 Seville oranges cut into thin strips and blanched in boiling water. Garnish with fresh orange segments and sprigs of watercress.

DUCK EN DAUBE

SERVES 4

1.8-2.3kg/4-5lb duck, dressed weight
salt and freshly ground black pepper
1 celery stalk, chopped
2 carrots, sliced
2 Spanish onions, sliced
120ml/8 tbls cognac
425ml/¾pt dry red wine
100g/4oz fat bacon, diced
15ml/1 tbls olive oil
bouquet garni (1 bay leaf, 1 sprig of thyme,
*   2 sprigs of parsley)*
1 garlic clove
225g/½lb mushrooms, sliced

1. Cut duck into serving pieces and place in a porcelain or earthenware bowl (not metal). Add salt and freshly ground black pepper, to taste, celery, carrots, onions, cognac and red wine, and marinate the duck in this mixture for at least 2 hours.
2. Remove duck from marinade; drain and dry with a clean cloth, or absorbent paper. Reserve marinade.
3. Sauté diced bacon in olive oil until golden, then remove bacon and brown duck pieces in

the resulting fats.

4. Place bacon and duck pieces together with pan juices in a thick-bottomed casserole and simmer, covered, for 20 minutes.

5. Add reserved marinade, *bouquet garni*, garlic and mushrooms. Continue cooking over a low heat for about 1 hour, or until duck is tender. Remove *bouquet garni*, skim fat; correct seasoning and serve from casserole.

PINEAPPLE DUCK

SERVES 4

1.8-2.3kg/4-5lb duck, dressed weight
olive oil
juice of canned pineapple slices (see below)
1 glass of red wine
1 garlic clove, finely chopped
salt and freshly ground black pepper

PINEAPPLE AND ORANGE SAUCE

15g/¹/₂oz cornflour
juice and rind of 1 orange
pan juices from the duck, skimmed of fat and made
  up to 300ml/¹/₂pt with water
225g/8oz can pineapple slices, drained and
  chopped, juice reserved
50g/2oz seedless raisins

1. Preheat oven to moderate (180°C/350°F/ gas 4).

2. Cut duck into serving pieces; place in a roasting pan and brush well with olive oil.

3. Pour the juice from canned pineapple into the pan together with the red wine, finely chopped garlic clove and salt and freshly ground black pepper, to taste. Cook duck in the preheated oven for 1 to 1½ hours, until tender, basting frequently with pan juices. Transfer to a heated serving dish and serve with pineapple and orange sauce.

4. To make pineapple and orange sauce: mix cornflour to a smooth paste with orange juice.

Skim fat from pan juices and make up to 300ml/¹/₂pt with water. Strain into a small thick-bottomed saucepan and add the cornflour mixture. Stir vigorously over moderate heat until sauce has thickened. Add chopped pineapple slices, raisins and grated orange rind and heat through. Pour into a heated sauceboat.

DUCK WITH SAUERKRAUT AND APPLE STUFFING

1.8-2.3kg/4-5lb duck, dressed weight
175g/6oz fat salt pork
1 Spanish onion, coarsely chopped
2 cooking apples, peeled, cored and diced
30ml/2 tbls brown sugar
salt and freshly ground black pepper
dried thyme
5ml/1 tsp caraway seeds
700g/1¹/₂lb sauerkraut

1. Preheat oven to moderate (180°C/350°F/ gas 4).

2. Dice fat salt pork and heat in a thick-bottomed frying pan until transparent. Add chopped onion and fry until transparent.

3. Add peeled, cored and diced apples and toss with onion and salt pork. When apple and onion are golden add brown sugar, salt and freshly ground black pepper and thyme, to taste, and caraway seeds. Remove from heat.

4. Drain sauerkraut and toss with apple and onion mixture.

5. Wipe duck inside and out with a damp cloth, or absorbent paper. Rub cavity with a little salt and freshly ground black pepper and stuff with apple, onion and sauerkraut mixture. Truss duck; prick well with a fork and place on rack over a roasting pan. Roast in preheated oven for about 2 to 2½ hours, basting frequently and pricking skin every 30 minutes to allow fat to escape.

ROAST GOOSE

3.6-4.5kg/8-10lb goose, dressed weight
Austrian stuffing *(see below)*
15ml/1 tbls flour
salt and freshly ground black pepper
fresh breadcrumbs

1. Preheat oven to moderately hot (200°C/400°F/gas 6).
2. Using a damp cloth, or absorbent paper, wipe goose inside and out and season generously inside and out with salt and pepper. Stuff goose, truss, and sprinkle lightly with flour. Roast in preheated oven for 15 minutes, then reduce heat to slow (170°C/325°F/gas 3) and continue roasting for 1¼ to 2 hours, or until goose is tender. Do not baste goose during cooking time as it is already fatty enough. Prick skin occasionally during cooking to allow fat to escape and remove fat from pan several times during cooking. The fat will keep indefinitely in a cool place.
3. Fifteen minutes before the end of cooking time, sprinkle goose lightly with breadcrumbs; raise oven heat again to moderately hot and cook for the final 15 minutes.

AUSTRIAN STUFFING FOR GOOSE OR TURKEY

1 Spanish onion, finely chopped
60ml/4 tbls lard
225g/½lb sausage-meat
30ml/2 tbls finely chopped parsley
4 anchovy fillets, finely chopped
2 eggs
juice of ½ lemon
dried thyme
dried marjoram
salt and freshly ground black pepper
225g/½lb poultry livers, chopped
50-75g/2-3oz fresh breadcrumbs

1. Sauté finely chopped onion in lard until transparent. Add sausage-meat and sauté until the onion is golden.
2. Remove onion and sausage-meat mixture from pan and combine with finely chopped parsley and anchovy fillets, eggs, lemon juice, dried thyme and marjoram and salt and freshly ground black pepper, to taste.
3. Sauté chopped poultry livers in remaining fat; add breadcrumbs and toss until golden. Combine with sausage-meat mixture.

CONFIT D'OIE *(Preserved goose)*

3.6-4.5kg/8-10lb goose, dressed weight
salt
5ml/1 tsp mixed spices
1.5ml/¼ tsp crushed thyme
lard (optional)

1. Cut goose into 8 or 10 pieces, reserving all goose fat.
2. Pound 5ml/1 tsp salt, mixed spices and crushed thyme in a mortar; mix well and rub goose pieces with this mixture. Place goose pieces in a large casserole and add 20g/¾oz salt per 450g/1lb of goose. Mix well and leave in a cool place for 24 to 36 hours.
3. Dice goose fat, combine with 1L/2pt water in a thick-bottomed saucepan and melt fat gently over a low heat. Brush salt off the goose pieces. When fat is melted, add goose pieces and simmer gently for 2½ hours, or until goose pieces are tender. Remove goose pieces from pan.
4. Wash out earthenware containers with boiling water; dry well and arrange pieces of preserved goose in containers.
5. Continue to simmer the fat until froth forms on the surface; skim thoroughly, remove from heat and allow to cool for 10 minutes. Pour fat through a fine sieve to cover goose pieces. If there is not enough fat to cover

all the pieces completely, melt some fresh lard. Allow to cool, seal containers with grease-proof paper and tie securely. *Confit* will keep in a cool place several months. Serve hot with puréed potatoes, or in a *cassoulet*.

ROAST TURKEY

4.5-5.4kg/10-12lb turkey, dressed weight
strips of pork fat, or green bacon
salt and freshly ground black pepper
225g/¹⁄₂lb butter, melted
juice of 1 lemon

1. Preheat oven to fairly hot (220°C/425°F/gas 7).
2. Using a damp cloth, or absorbent paper, wipe turkey inside and out and truss. Place turkey, breast side up, in a roasting pan and cover breast with thin strips of pork fat, or green bacon. Season generously with salt and freshly ground black pepper and roast in preheated oven for 15 minutes; then reduce temperature to moderate (180°C/350°F/gas 4) and cook for 15 to 20 minutes per 450g/1lb. To test if the turkey is cooked, stick in a skewer at the leg joint – the juices should run clear. Baste frequently with melted butter flavoured with lemon juice.
3. If turkey has not become golden towards the end of cooking time, bring heat up to fairly hot (220°C/425°F/gas 7) again and roast for 10 to 15 minutes more.

PINTADEAU ROTI ET FLAMBE A LA RICHE

SERVES 4-6

2 guinea fowl, 1kg/2lb each, dressed weight
300ml/¹⁄₂pt red Burgundy
grated rind of 1 lemon
60-90ml/4-6 tbls cognac, warmed
Dijon mustard
100g/4oz butter
100/4oz pâté de foie gras
15-30ml/1-2 tbls lemon juice
salt and freshly ground black pepper

1. Preheat oven to hot (230°C/450°F/gas 8).
2. Using a damp cloth, or absorbent paper, wipe guinea fowl inside and out and truss. Roast guinea fowl in preheated oven for 25 to 30 minutes, or until almost cooked. Cut into serving pieces.
3. In a thick-bottomed casserole reduce wine with grated lemon rind to one third of the original quantity. Add guinea fowl pieces to pan and heat through. Pour over the warmed cognac and ignite. When flames have died down stir in Dijon mustard, to taste, and continue to simmer for a few minutes, turning guinea fowl pieces from time to time.
4. Mix butter and *foie gras* to a smooth paste and add to casserole, stirring in all the juices. Add lemon juice. Stir pieces of guinea fowl into sauce, making sure they are well covered. Season with salt and freshly ground black pepper to taste and serve from the casserole.

MAGDALEN VENISON

MOST OF US imagine that a medieval banquet would have consisted of a series of great set pieces like Sir Osbert Sitwell's recipe: 'You first captured a swan – having previously been granted, of course, the necessary royal permission – and then stuffed it with a peacock, inside which you have placed a pheasant, which contained a partridge, and so *ad infinitum*.' But the first written recipes in English, produced by Richard II's cooks in 1391, have an amazingly modern ring about them. I was surprised by the variety of fruits and vegetables available; the numbers of ways of preparing fish, both salt and 'green'; the different recipes for meat and game; the imaginative use of seasonings, wine and herbs; and the great variety of the recipes themselves. One, for example, advocates the use of grapes to stuff a chicken, together with garlic, parsley and sage.

But the modern ring of these ancient dishes is not so surprising. The High Tables of the Plantagenet kings and of the great houses of the Tudor nobility have their direct descendants today in the High Tables at Oxford and Cambridge, where the rulers of the college still dine on a raised dais, separated from the commoners below them.

Famous feasts linger long in the memory of a place like Oxford. Gaudies and Bump Suppers, banquets to royalty and to visiting statesmen, even ordinary fish and flesh days, all have given rise to recipes that are handed down throughout the years from chef to chef in the college kitchens . . . the Christmas Boar's Head at Queen's, the legendary Cherry Pie at All Souls, the superb Meringues of Christ Church, and at Magdalen, the seventeen-day ritual of Magdalen venison.

One of Oxford's greatest dishes, Magdalen venison, which has been served for two and a half centuries at the yearly Restoration Dinner, is a saddle of venison from the College's own herd, marinated for days, braised in château-bottled wine, garnished with glazed chestnuts, glazed onions and sautéed mushrooms, and served with a heady port wine sauce. Tradition has it that there should be only as many deer in the park as there are Fellows in College . . . and so every year at the Restoration Dinner venison is served.

According to a centuries-old recipe, 'second year' beasts are selected from the herd, killed, blooded and stripped, dusted with rock salt and powdered ginger, and allowed to hang for at least ten days. Then the choicest parts – the saddle, leg or haunch – are cut for High Table and marinated for three days to one week to improve the flavour and tenderise the meat.

MAGDALEN VENISON

2.7-3.2kg/6-7lb saddle of venison
60ml/4 tbls butter
60ml/4 tbls olive oil
225g/½lb fat salt pork, diced

MARINADE
1 Spanish onion
2 carrots
30ml/2 tbls butter or olive oil
1 bottle red wine, either Burgundy or claret
3 sprigs of parsley
1 sprig of thyme
1 bay leaf
2 garlic cloves
4-5 black peppercorns
1-2 juniper berries, crushed

SAUCE
15ml/1 tbls butter (optional)
15ml/1 tbls flour (optional)
1 wine glass of port
30ml/2 tbls redcurrant jelly

GARNISH
400g/14oz can whole chestnuts in syrup, drained
Glazed button onions *(see page 253)*
sautéed button mushrooms

1. To make marinade: slice onion and carrots and sweat them gently in a little butter or olive oil. Place vegetables in a porcelain or earthenware bowl (not metal) and add red wine, parsley, thyme, bay leaf, garlic, peppercorns and crushed juniper berries.

2. Soak venison in the marinade, covered, for 3 days to a week in a cool place, turning 3 or 4 times a day so that all surfaces of the meat are evenly exposed to the marinade and keep well moistened. The longer the meat is marinated, the gamier the flavour. Drain venison, reserving the marinade.

3. Preheat oven to moderate (180°C/350°F/gas 4).

4. Boil down the marinade until reduced to half the original quantity.

5. To cook meat: heat butter and olive oil in a thick-bottomed ovenproof casserole with a tight cover. Add diced fat salt pork and sauté until crisp and golden. Add venison to casserole. Strain reduced marinade over venison, cover and cook in preheated oven for 1 hour. Increase oven temperature to fairly hot (220°C/425°F/gas 7) and continue cooking for a further 10 minutes. Transfer venison to a heated serving platter and keep warm.

6. To make sauce: skim fat from sauce in which venison was cooked and reduce to half the original quantity by cooking over a high heat. Thicken, if necessary, by whisking in a *beurre manié* (made by mashing 15ml/1 tbls each butter and flour together to form a smooth paste.). Add port and redcurrant jelly and blend all together, taking care to stir in all the crusty bits. Correct the seasoning.

7. Strain the sauce, which should be dark and rich, over the venison and serve garnished with alternate clusters of chestnuts, GLAZED BUTTON ONIONS and button mushrooms.

At Magdalen College, Oxford, the preparation for Magdalen Venison lasts 17 days!

VENISON IN PORT

2.7-3.2kg/6-7lb saddle of venison
150ml/¹/₄pt olive oil
100g/4oz butter
2 carrots, sliced
1 Spanish onion, sliced
2 garlic cloves
1 sprig of thyme
1 bay leaf
salt and freshly ground black pepper
¹/₃ bottle port
15ml/1 tbls flour
15ml/1 tbls butter
15ml/1 tbls redcurrant jelly

GARNISH

400g/14oz can whole chestnuts in syrup, drained
Glazed button onions *(see page 253)*
Sautéed mushroom caps *(see page 253)*
fried croûtons

1. Preheat oven to moderate (180°C/350°F/gas 4).
2. Heat olive oil and 100g/4oz butter in a thick-bottomed ovenproof casserole. Add sliced carrots, onion, garlic, thyme and bay leaf and cook until vegetables soften.
3. Season saddle of venison generously with salt and freshly ground black pepper and place on the bed of aromatics. Cover casserole and cook in preheated oven for 1 hour. Increase oven temperature to fairly hot (220°C/425°F/gas 7) and continue cooking for a further 10 minutes. Pour over the port; Transfer venison to a heated serving platter and keep warm.
4. Skim fat from the casserole and strain the sauce into a thick-bottomed saucepan. Reduce the sauce by boiling down to half the original quantity. Thicken it by whisking in a *beurre manié* (made by mashing 15ml/1 tbls each butter and flour to form a smooth paste). Stir in redcurrant jelly. Correct seasoning.
5. Carve the saddle of venison and serve on the bone, surrounded with whole chestnuts, GLAZED BUTTON ONIONS, SAUTEED MUSHROOM CAPS.
6. Just before serving, strain the sauce over the venison and surround with fried *croûtons.*

VENISON STEAKS

SERVES 4

1.4kg/3lb leg or loin of venison, cut into 4 thick steaks
fat salt pork
100g/4oz butter
salt and freshly ground black pepper
8 juniper berries, crushed
dried rosemary
1 Spanish onion, grated
*150ml/¹/₄pt rich **Basic beef stock** (see page 65)*
150ml/¹/₄pt red Burgundy
150ml/¹/₄pt soured cream
100g/4oz mushrooms, sliced
redcurrant jelly

1. Lard venison steaks with thin strips of fat salt pork; trim off larding ends into a thick-bottomed frying pan. Add butter (reserving 15ml/1 tbls for later use), salt and freshly ground black pepper, to taste, crushed juniper berries and dried rosemary (a good pinch per steak) to the frying pan and place over moderate heat. Add steaks and cook for about 5 minutes each side, or until tender. Remove steaks from pan and keep warm.
2. Reduce heat to a simmer and add the grated onion, BEEF STOCK and red wine to the pan. Mix well, scraping in all crusty bits from sides of pan. Reduce gently until sauce is rich and thick; add soured cream and simmer gently until heated through. Strain sauce.
3. Clean pan and sauté sliced mushrooms in remaining butter until tender; add steaks to pan and pour over sauce. Heat through and serve with redcurrant jelly.

PIGEONS CONFITS AUX RAISINS

SERVES 4

4 pigeons, 150g/6oz each, dressed weight
salt and freshly ground black pepper
60-90ml/4-6 tbls cognac, warmed
150g/6oz chicken fat, or lard
*4 oval pastry cases of **Fingertip pastry** (see page*
  347) fully baked blind (see page 26), or
  rectangular canapés
1 small can mousse de foie gras
1 small can black truffles, drained
24 large white grapes, peeled and seeded
***Basic aspic** (see page 67)*

1. Using a damp cloth, or absorbent paper, wipe pigeons inside and out. Season pigeons generously with salt and freshly ground black pepper. Place in a frying pan, pour over warmed cognac and ignite.

2. Melt chicken fat or lard with a few drops of water in a thick-bottomed saucepan over a low heat. As soon as the fat is nearly melted, add pigeons, bring to a moderate boil and simmer, covered, for 45 minutes to 1 hour or until pigeons are tender.

3. Transfer pigeons to a stone or earthenware crock; Strain fat over pigeons and allow to cool.

4. Spread pastry cases, or rectangular *canapés* with *mousse de foie gras* and place 1 pigeon in the centre of each. Decorate pigeons with small pieces of black truffle; surround each bird with 6 large peeled and seeded white grapes and glaze with aspic.

VINTNER'S STEW OF RABBIT OR HARE

SERVES 4

1 rabbit or hare, skinned and cleaned
salt and freshly ground black pepper
30ml/2 tbls flour

60ml/4 tbls olive oil
***Basic beef stock** (see page 65)*
600ml/1pt red Burgundy

MARINADE MIXTURE
1 Spanish onion, sliced
2 carrots, sliced
2 garlic cloves
300ml/1/2pt red Burgundy
4 sprigs of parsley
1 sprig of thyme
600ml/4 tbls olive oil
salt and freshly ground black pepper

GARNISH
12 button mushrooms
*12 **Glazed button onions** (see page 253)*
100g/1/4lb fat salt pork, diced and sautéed
fried croûtons
30ml/2 tbls finely chopped parsley

1. Cut rabbit or hare into serving pieces.

2. Place sliced onion and carrots and garlic cloves in a porcelain or earthenware bowl (not metal); add wine, sprigs of parsley and thyme, olive oil and salt and freshly ground black pepper, to taste. Place rabbit or hare pieces in the marinade and leave for 2 days, turning them several times each day so that they will be well marinated. Drain rabbit pieces. Strain and reserve marinade.

3. Season rabbit pieces well with salt and freshly ground black pepper and sprinkle liberally with flour. Heat olive oil in a thick-bottomed saucepan and sauté rabbit pieces until golden; skim fat and add reserved marinade, red Burgundy and enough BEEF STOCK to cover. Bring to the boil, skim and allow to simmer slowly for about 1½ hours. Transfer rabbit pieces to a heated serving dish, and keep warm.

4. Strain sauce into a thick-bottomed casserole, skim fat and correct seasoning. Add rabbit pieces, button mushrooms, GLAZED

BUTTON ONIONS and sautéed, fat salt pork to the sauce and cook for ½ hour more, or until rabbit pieces are tender. Serve from casserole garnished with fried *croûtons* and finely chopped parsley.

RABBIT AUX DEUX MOUTARDES

SERVES 4

1 fat rabbit, skinned and cleaned
30ml/2 tbls flour
salt and freshly ground black pepper
30ml/2 tbls olive oil
30ml/2 tbls butter
100g/4oz fat bacon, diced and blanched
4 shallots, chopped
bouquet garni (1 bay leaf, 1 sprig of thyme,
   2 sprigs of parsley).
150ml/¼pt dry white wine
*150ml/¼pt **Basic chicken stock** (see page 66)*
5ml/1 tsp Dijon mustard
5ml/1 tsp prepared English mustard
300ml/½pt double cream

1. Cut rabbit into serving pieces. Roll pieces in flour and season with salt and freshly ground black pepper, to taste.
2. Heat olive oil and butter in a thick-bottomed casserole and sauté rabbit pieces together with diced bacon until golden.
3. Add chopped shallots and the *bouquet garni* to casserole; moisten with dry white wine and CHICKEN STOCK, and cook gently, covered, for about 2 hours, or until rabbit is tender. Transfer rabbit to a heated dish and keep warm.
4. Skim fat from the sauce and remove *bouquet garni*. Whisk Dijon mustard and prepared English mustard thoroughly with the double cream and add to the sauce. Correct seasoning, adding a little more mustard, salt and freshly ground black pepper, if desired. Return rabbit pieces to casserole; heat through and serve from casserole.

CASSEROLED PHEASANT

SERVES 6-8

2 pheasants, about 1kg/2lb each, dressed weight
pheasant livers, finely chopped
175g/6oz cooked ham, finely chopped
*90ml/6 tbls **Boiled rice** (see page 179)*
90ml/6 tbls cognac
1 egg
salt and freshly ground black pepper
ground thyme and marjoram
fat salt pork
60ml/4 tbls butter
60ml/4 tbls olive oil
2-4 shallots, finely chopped
30ml/2 tbls cognac, warmed
450g/1lb button mushrooms
2 garlic cloves
juice of ½ lemon

1. If using, preheat oven to slow (170°C/325°F/gas 3).
2. Combine chopped pheasant livers with finely chopped ham and BOILED RICE; moisten with cognac and egg and flavour with salt, black pepper, thyme and marjoram, to taste.
3. Wipe pheasants inside and out with a damp cloth, or absorbent paper. Stuff pheasants with liver mixture, truss firmly and wrap each one in fat salt pork.
4. Heat 30ml/2 tbls each butter and olive oil in a thick-bottomed, flameproof casserole and brown pheasants on all sides together with finely chopped shallots. Pour over warmed cognac and ignite. When flames have died down, cover casserole and simmer over a low heat, or in the preheated oven until almost done, adding a little more liquid, if necessary.
5. Sauté mushrooms and garlic cloves in remaining butter and olive oil. Season well and add to casserole.
6. Finish cooking casserole over a low heat or in a slow oven, and sprinkle with lemon juice just before serving.

Game birds like these have a marvellous flavour, which can be enhanced by marinades.

NORMANDY PHEASANT

SERVES 6-8

2 pheasants, about 1kg/2lb each, dressed weight
60ml/4 tbls butter
2 large tart apples
1 wine glass of Calvados
300ml/½pt double cream
juice of ½ lemon
salt and freshly ground black pepper

1. Preheat oven to moderate (190°C/375°F/ gas 5).

2. Wipe pheasants inside and out with a damp cloth, or absorbent paper, and truss them.

3. Melt 30ml/2 tbls butter in a thick-bottomed frying pan and sauté pheasants until they are nicely browned on all sides. Remove from pan and keep warm.

4. Peel, core and slice apples and sauté in remaining butter until golden.

5. Place apples in the bottom of a thick-bottomed ovenproof casserole; arrange pheasants on top; baste with the pan juices thinned down with Calvados and cook, covered, in preheated oven for about 30 minutes.

251

6. Add double cream and lemon juice and season with salt and freshly ground black pepper, to taste. Return the casserole to the oven and cook until pheasants are tender and the sauce is thick and creamy. Serve directly from casserole.

PHEASANT A LA CREME

SERVES 4

1 pheasant, about 1kg/2lb dressed weight
75ml/5 tbls butter
30ml/2 tbls olive oil
30ml/2 tbls carrot, finely chopped
30ml/2 tbls onion, finely chopped
1 good pinch of dried thyme
1 bay leaf, crumbled
30-60ml/2-4 tbls cognac, warmed
300ml/¹/₂pt double cream
pheasant liver
cognac
bread
salt and freshly ground black pepper

1. Wipe pheasant inside and out with a damp cloth, or absorbent paper, and truss it.
2. Heat 60ml/4 tbls butter and 30ml/2 tbls olive oil in a thick-bottomed casserole and brown pheasant on all sides. Add together with finely chopped carrot and onion, thyme and bay leaf. Cover casserole and simmer for 20 minutes.
3. Pour off excess fat from casserole, pour in warmed cognac and ignite. When flames have died down, moisten with cream; cover casserole and simmer for a further 10 to 20 minutes, or until pheasant is tender and sauce has reduced a little.
4. Meanwhile mash pheasant liver with a little butter and cognac and spread a *canapé* of white bread with this mixture.
5. Transfer pheasant to *canapé*. Pass the sauce through a fine sieve; correct seasoning and

cover pheasant with sauce, which should be quite thick. Serve immediately.

PHEASANT A LA SOUVAROFF

SERVES 4-6

2 pheasants, about 1kg/2lb each dressed weight
100g/4oz pâté de foie gras, diced
1 small can truffles, drained, juice reserved
45ml/3 tbls cognac
salt and freshly ground black pepper
butter
dry white wine
2-3 slices fat salt pork, or green bacon
60ml/4 tbls Madeira
*45ml/3 tbls **Sauce demi-glace** (see page 83)*
   (optional)
flour

1. Preheat oven to moderately hot (200°C/ 400°F/gas 6).
2. Combine diced *pâté de foie gras* with 1 thinly sliced truffle; moisten with cognac and season with salt and freshly ground black pepper, to taste.
3. Wipe pheasants inside and out with a damp cloth, or absorbent paper. Stuff pheasants with *foie gras* mixture and truss. Place pheasants in a roasting pan with a little butter and some dry white wine. To prevent pheasants from drying out in cooking, cover breasts with several slices of fat salt pork, or green bacon, and cook for about 40 minutes in the preheated oven.
4. Remove pork or bacon strips from breasts of pheasants; cut strings and place in thick-bottomed ovenproof casserole just large enough to hold them comfortably. Cover casserole. Set pan juices aside to cool. All the above can be done in advance.
5. Reheat oven temperature to hot (230°C/ 450°F/gas 8).
6. About 25 minutes before you wish to serve pheasants, dice remaining truffles and toss

them in a little melted butter to bring out their flavour.

7. Skim solidified fat from roasting pan and add Madeira, cognac, truffle juice, and, if available, SAUCE DEMI-GLACE, to the pan juices Stir this mixture over a low heat until it nearly reaches boiling point then strain over the pheasants. Cover casserole and seal the edges with a band of stiff dough made of flour and water. Bake in preheated oven for 20 minutes. Bring the sealed casserole to the table and break seal just before serving.

NOTE: Partridge and quail are also excellent cooked in this way, and I have often made a delicious casserole with a fine fat capon.

PHEASANT WITH GREEN APPLES

SERVES 4

1 pheasant, about 1kg/2lb dressed weight, trussed
100g/¼lb green bacon, diced
½ Spanish onion, finely chopped
1 garlic clove, finely chopped
30ml/2 tbls butter
30ml/2 tbls olive oil
4 small cooking apples
60ml/4 tbls Cointreau
300ml/½pt double cream
salt and freshly ground black pepper

1. Preheat oven to very slow (140°C/275°F/ gas 1-150°C/300°F/gas 2).
2. Sauté diced green bacon, finely chopped onion and garlic clove in butter and olive oil in a thick-bottomed flameproof casserole until golden. Remove bacon and vegetables from casserole and keep warm.
3. Brown pheasant on all sides in the resulting fats. Remove pheasant from casserole and keep warm.
4. Peel, core and slice apples thickly and sauté in remaining fats until they start to turn gol-

den. Pour over Cointreau. Remove apples from casserole and keep warm.
5. Skim fat from juices. Return pheasant to casserole; surround with apple slices, bacon bits, onion and garlic, and allow to simmer, covered, for 10 minutes.
6. Stir double cream into casserole and season with salt and freshly ground black pepper, to taste. Cover and cook in preheated oven until the pheasant is tender.
7. When ready to serve, remove the pheasant and bacon bits to a clean casserole and keep warm. Purée sauce and apples in an electric blender, or food processor. Correct seasoning; reheat sauce and pour over pheasant.

PHEASANT IN RED WINE

SERVES 4-6

2 pheasants, about 1kg/2lb dressed weight
pheasant livers
4 shallots, finely chopped
30ml/2 tbls olive oil
45ml/3 tbls butter
600ml/1pt red Burgundy
8 mushroom stalks
salt and freshly ground black pepper
15ml/1 tbls flour

GLAZED BUTTON ONIONS
12 small white onions
salt
15ml/1 tbls butter
15ml/1 tbls sugar

SAUTEED MUSHROOM CAPS
12 button mushroom caps
15ml/1 tbls butter
salt and freshly ground black pepper

1. Preheat oven to very slow (140°C/275°F/ gas 1-150°C/300°F/gas 2).
2. Put 2 finely chopped shallots and the pheas-

Roast game birds, like these pheasants, are traditionally served with game chips.

ant liver into the cavity of each bird and truss.
3. Heat olive oil and 30ml/2 tbls butter in a thick-bottomed saucepan and sauté pheasants gently until they are golden on all sides and almost tender. Transfer pheasants to a thick-bottomed ovenproof casserole and keep warm.
4. Pour red wine into the pan in which you have cooked pheasants and cook over a high heat, combining wine with the pan juices. Add mushroom stalks and salt and pepper to taste, and continue to cook until the liquid is reduced by half. Thicken sauce by whisking in a *beurre*

manié (made by mashing 15ml/1 tbls each butter and flour together to form a smooth paste). Simmer for a few minutes; strain through a fine sieve into a bowl and allow to cool slightly so that the grease can be skimmed off the surface.
5. Pour wine sauce over the pheasants; correct seasoning and add glazed button onions and sautéed mushroom caps. Cover casserole and cook in preheated oven for 50 to 60 minutes or until pheasants are tender. Serve from casserole.
6. To make glazed button onions: cook small

white onions in boiling salted water until they are tender; drain well. Melt butter in a thick-bottomed saucepan; add sugar and stir until well blended. Add drained onions and cook slowly until they are glazed.

7. To make sautéed mushroom caps: melt butter in a thick-bottomed frying pan and sauté button mushrooms until golden. Season with salt and freshly ground black pepper, to taste.

QUAIL WITH WHITE GRAPES

SERVES 4

4 quail, 100g/4oz each, dressed weight
salt and white pepper
30ml/2 tbls flour
60ml/4 tbls butter
150ml/¹/4pt dry white wine
30ml/2 tbls lemon juice
75g/3oz seedless grapes
30ml/2 tbls blanched almonds, sliced

1. Wipe quails inside and out with a damp cloth, or absorbent paper, and truss. Rub quail with a mixture of salt, white pepper and flour.
2. Melt butter in a thick-bottomed casserole and sauté quails until they are golden on all sides. Add wine and lemon juice; cover and cook over low heat for 15 to 20 minutes.
3. Add seedless grapes and sliced blanched almonds to casserole and cook for 5 to 10 minutes more, or until quails are tender. Serve from casserole.

PARTRIDGE WITH JUNIPER BERRIES

2 partridges, 450g/1lb each, dressed weight
60ml/4 tbls melted butter
salt and freshly ground black pepper
60ml/4 tbls shredded bread

30ml/2 tbls finely chopped ham
4-6 juniper berries, crushed
grated rind of ¹/2 lemon
dried marjoram
1 egg, beaten
fat salt pork
90ml/6 tbls dry white wine
*150ml/¹/4pt rich **Basic chicken stock** (see page 66)*
1 carrot, finely chopped
1 small onion, finely chopped

1. Preheat oven to fairly hot (220°C/425°F/gas 7).
2. Wipe partridges inside and out with a damp cloth, or absorbent paper. Brush cavities with a little melted butter and season liberally with salt and freshly ground black pepper.
3. Combine remaining melted butter, shredded breaded, chopped ham, crushed juniper berries and grated lemon rind; season with salt, freshly ground black pepper and dried marjoram, to taste; mix in beaten egg and stuff partridges with this mixture.
4. Truss partridges; wrap a thin piece of fat salt pork around each and roast in preheated oven for 25 to 35 minutes, or until tender, basting from time to time with dry white wine, CHICKEN STOCK and finely chopped carrot and onion. Serve with sauce separately.

VEAL AND PARTRIDGE PIE

225g/¹/2lb lean veal
1 partridge, 450g/1lb dressed weight
225g/¹/2lb lean pork
100g/¹/4lb fat salt pork
salt and freshly ground black pepper
finely chopped parsley, marjoram and thyme
100g/4oz bacon, cut into cubes
*150ml/¹/4pt **Basic beef stock** (see page 65)*
***Fingertip pastry** (see page 347)*
1 egg yolk

1. Preheat oven to moderate (190°C/375°F/ gas 5).

2. Pass veal, pork and fat salt pork twice through the finest blade of your mincer; season generously with salt and freshly ground black pepper and add generous amounts of finely chopped parsley, marjoram and thyme.

3. Cut partridge into serving pieces.

4. Butter a 1.8L/3pt pie dish and place a layer of minced meat mixture in bottom of dish. On this place a layer of partridge, then a few cubes of bacon and more minced meats. Continue to add layers of these until the dish is well filled

5. Moisten with BEEF STOCK: cover with FINGERTIP PASTRY; decorate and brush with egg yolk. Bake in preheated oven for 1 to 1½ hours. Serve hot or cold.

PARTRIDGE WITH LENTILS

SERVES 4

2 partridges, about 450g/1lb each, dressed weight
salt and freshly ground black pepper
30ml/2 tbls butter
30ml/2 tbls olive oil
100g/4oz fat salt pork, diced
1 Spanish onion, sliced
2 carrots, sliced
150ml/¼pt dry white wine
*150ml/¼pt **Basic chicken stock** (see page 66)*

LENTILS

350g/12oz green lentils
1 onion, stuck with 2 cloves
2 garlic cloves
sprig of thyme
2 sprigs of parsley
salt and freshly ground black pepper

1. Soak green lentils overnight. Drain.

2. Wipe partridges inside and out with a damp cloth, or absorbent paper. Sprinkle cavities with a little salt and freshly ground black

pepper. Truss partridges.

3. Heat butter and olive oil in a thick-bottomed casserole and sauté partridges with diced fat salt pork and sliced onion and carrots.

4. When birds are golden on all sides, add dry white wine and cook until wine is reduced by half. Add CHICKEN STOCK and season with salt and freshly ground black pepper, to taste. Cover casserole and cook over a low heat until partridges are tender, 25 to 35 minutes.

5. Meanwhile, place lentils in a thick-bottomed saucepan and cover with water. Add onion stuck with cloves, garlic, thyme, parsley, and salt and freshly ground black pepper, to taste. Bring to the boil; reduce heat and allow to simmer until tender, but not too soft. Each lentil should be separate, not mushy. When cooked, drain and remove onion, garlic cloves and herbs.

6. To serve: place partridges on a heated serving dish and surround with cooked lentils. Skim fat from pan juices; strain and pour over partridges. Serve immediately.

SALMIS OF WOODCOCK

SERVES 4

4 woodcock, 175g/6oz each, dressed weight
salt and freshly ground black pepper
livers and giblets, finely chopped
60ml/4 tbls dry white wine
*60ml/4 tbls **Basic beef stock** (see page 65)*
juice of 2 lemons
finely grated rind of 1 lemon
freshly grated nutmeg
15-30ml/1-2 tbls dry mustard
50-75g/2-3oz mushrooms, sliced
15ml/1 tbls butter
15ml/1 tbls flour
30ml/2 tbls finely chopped parsley

1. Preheat oven to fairly hot (220°C/425°F/ gas 7).

2. Wipe woodcock inside and out with a damp cloth, or absorbent paper. Season generously with salt and black pepper. Truss woodcock.

3. Roast woodcock in preheated oven for 15 minutes, basting frequently, until half cooked, then cut into serving pieces. Be sure to cut woodcock on a serving dish to catch blood and juices. Arrange pieces in the blazer pan of a chafing dish or a thick-bottomed casserole.

4. Crush livers and giblets into serving dish containing juices; add dry white wine, BEEF STOCK and juice of 2 lemons; stir in the finely grated peel of 1 lemon, and season with salt and freshly ground black pepper, freshly grated nutmeg to taste and dry mustard. Add sliced mushrooms and pour this mixture over woodcock; place chafing dish, or casserole over heat and cook for 20 minutes, stirring to moisten each piece of meat thoroughly and to prevent it from sticking to the dish. Do not let the *salmis* come to the boil.

5. Just before serving, whisk in a *beurre manié* (made by mashing 15ml/1 tbls each butter and flour together to form a smooth paste). Sprinkle entire dish with finely chopped parsley. Serve immediately.

SALMIS OF GROUSE

SERVES 6

3 young grouse, 450g/1lb each, dressed weight
butter
1 Spanish onion, finely chopped
2 small carrots, finely chopped
2 garlic cloves, finely chopped
175ml/6 fl oz red wine
30ml/2 tbls flour
425ml/¾pt well-flavoured light stock
2 sprigs of thyme
1 bay leaf
salt and freshly ground black pepper
225g/½lb button mushrooms, sliced
juice of ½ lemon

12 small bread triangles
45ml/3 tbls olive oil
finely chopped parsley

1. Preheat oven to fairly hot (220°C/425°F/gas 7).

2. Wipe grouse inside and out with a damp cloth, or absorbent paper. Season generously with salt and freshly ground black pepper. Truss grouse.

3. Spread grouse with a little softened butter and roast in preheated oven for 15 minutes until partially cooked, basting frequently. Cut grouse into serving pieces; be sure to cut grouse on a serving dish to catch blood and juices.

4. Melt 60ml/4 tbls butter in a thick-bottomed saucepan and sauté finely chopped onion, carrots and garlic until golden. Pour over red wine and simmer, stirring continuously, until wine reduces a little. Add flour and stir vigorously until sauce thickens; then add light stock, juices from birds, thyme, bay leaf, and salt and freshly ground black pepper, to taste. Cover pan and simmer gently for 1 hour.

5. Meanwhile, sauté sliced mushrooms in 30ml/2 tbls butter flavoured with lemon juice until tender. Remove from pan.

6. Strain sauce into a clean saucepan; add sautéed mushrooms and grouse pieces and simmer for 5 minutes, or until they are heated through and the flavour of the sauce has permeated the meat.

7. Fry bread triangles in 45ml/3 tbls butter and olive oil and place 6 in a heated serving dish; cover with *salmis*: sprinkle with finely chopped parsley and garnish with remaining bread triangles. Serve immediately.

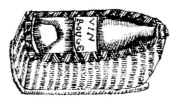

CHAPTER 12

VEGETABLES

RED CABBAGE NORMANDY

MANY MEN ARE known to be ardent, if furtive, members of the anti-vegetable school. And who can blame us if we are apt to recoil surreptitiously from the tasteless, soggy blobs of greenery that all too often masquerade on dinner plates throughout the country under the misleading names of 'peas', 'string beans', 'cauliflower' and 'cabbage'? Why, when the waiter offers us that old standby, 'a cut off the joint with two veg', do we instinctively know that the 'two veg' will almost certainly consist of boiled cabbage and potatoes, perhaps ennobled by the terminology 'boiled greens' or, more euphemistically, 'spring greens'?

I for one would like to start a counter-revolution against the habit of serving vegetables in their own water. Let us take courage in both hands and borrow from the cuisines of other lands to give vegetables a fighting chance on our dinner tables. Let us cook them – as do the Chinese – until they are just tender, not waterlogged and mushy. Let us serve them – like the French – as a fresh-tasting first course, or as a separate vegetable course to be served *after* the meat, so much easier on the cook and so much more inviting for the diner.

Of all vegetables, cabbage particularly seems to suffer from this lack of imagination. Yet the culinary potential of this year-round vegetable is as rich as its history. The ancient Greeks served cabbage with savoury stuffings of meat and rice, flavoured with pine nuts, currants, grated lemon rind and herbs. It was known and used in China as far back as the first century. Indeed, sour cabbage, known throughout the world today as sauerkraut, was, in fact, an early Chinese invention.

The Mediterraneans have used cabbage as the main ingredient for stews and soups for centuries; the Poles call it 'little pigeons' – braised cabbage leaves deliciously stuffed with finely chopped meat, onion, tomatoes and herbs. The Russians immortalise it in a superb peasant soup called *stchi,* made of cabbage, onions, tomatoes and beets simmered in stock; the Germans poach it until tender and stuff it with buttered noodles flavoured with caraway seed; and the Austrians even use this versatile vegetable in a sweet cabbage *strudel*.

There are three main varieties of cabbage. The common or green cabbage, sold everywhere, is bright green in the summer months, whiter, firmer and larger in the winter. The Savoy cabbage – a bright, deep green in colour with a curly leaf – is much more delicate in flavour. I like to use its tender leaves for stuffed cabbage recipes. White cabbage is used commercially for the preparation of sauerkraut and is also used extensively for salads and cole slaw.

Red cabbage is delicious either raw or cooked. Always add lemon juice or vinegar to water when cooking this attractive vegetable or it will turn purple in cooking. Red cabbage must be firm and the outer leaves must be bright in colour. Cut the head in quarters and remove the heavy veins, then shred the rest of the leaves on a coarse shredder. Often served as an *hors-d'oeuvre* salad in France, red cabbage is delicious when shredded in this way, drained to the last drop of the water in which it was soaked and then simmered gently in butter with diced apples and spices, a wonderful accompaniment to all pork dishes, goose and many forms of veal and hare.

Perhaps the most noble version of this dish is red cabbage cooked in the fashion of the Norman French.

RED CABBAGE WITH APPLES

SERVES 4-6

1 head red cabbage
60ml/4 tbls butter
450g/1lb cooking apples
225g/½lb onions
2 garlic cloves, finely chopped
1.5ml/¼ tsp each of ground nutmeg, allspice,
* cinnamon, thyme and caraway seed*
10ml/2 tsp grated orange rind
freshly ground black pepper
30-60ml/2-4 tbls brown sugar
300ml/½pt red wine
30ml/2 tbls red wine vinegar

1. Preheat oven to moderate (180°C/350°F/ gas 4).
2. Wash cabbage and remove central core and outer leaves. Shred cabbage, or cut into 6mm/ ¼in thick slices, removing ribs.
3. Soak cabbage in cold salted water for ½ hour then drain. Cook prepared cabbage in butter, in a covered thick-bottomed saucepan, for 5 minutes.
4. Peel and core apples and cut into quarters; slice onions.
5. Place these ingredients in a thick-bottomed casserole in layers, beginning with a layer of cabbage, then onions, then apples, and continue until casserole is full. Season each layer with finely chopped garlic, spices, grated orange rind and freshly ground black pepper, to taste. Sprinkle brown sugar over the top and add red wine, wine vinegar and a little hot water. Cover and simmer very slowly in preheated oven until tender, adding a little more wine if necessary. Serve immediately.

BUTTERED CABBAGE

SERVES 4-6

1. Remove and discard outer leaves from 1 head of green cabbage. Wash, core and cut into shreds, or wedges. Soak cabbage in cold salted water for ½ hour. Drain.

2. Cook cabbage, covered, in a very small amount of boiling salted water or well-flavoured light stock, until just tender. Drain. Transfer to a heated dish; season with salt and freshly ground black pepper, to taste, and serve with finely chopped parsley and melted butter.

SCALLOPED CABBAGE

SERVES 4-6

1 head cabbage
salt
60ml/4 tbls butter
300ml/½pt rich **Cream sauce** *(see page 80)*
freshly ground black pepper
60ml/4 tbls freshly grated Parmesan cheese

1. Preheat oven to moderate (180°C/350°F/gas 4).

2. Remove and discard outer leaves from cabbage. Wash, core and shred cabbage and soak in cold salted water for ½ hour. Drain.

3. Melt butter in a thick-bottomed saucepan; add shredded cabbage and simmer, covered until cabbage is just tender, but not browned.

4. Line a thick-bottomed ovenproof casserole with half the simmered cabbage. Add half of the CREAM SAUCE; sprinkle with freshly ground black pepper and half the freshly grated Parmesan cheese. Add remaining cabbage; pour remaining sauce over the top and add more pepper and remaining Parmesan cheese. Place casserole in preheated oven and cook until the casserole bubbles and the top is golden brown, about ½ hour. Serve immediately.

SAFFRON CABBAGE

SERVES 4-6

1 head cabbage
salt
Basic beef stock *(see page 65)*
1 generous pinch of ground saffron
90-120ml/6-8 tbls finely chopped ham
½ Spanish onion, thinly sliced
freshly ground black pepper
1 generous pinch of cayenne pepper

1. Remove and discard outer leaves from cabbage. Wash, core and shred cabbage and soak in cold salted water for ½ hour. Drain.

2. Combine cabbage in a thick-bottomed saucepan with 600ml/1pt BEEF STOCK and simmer for 15 minutes, or until half cooked.

3. Mix ground saffron with a little water and add to cabbage together with finely chopped ham, thinly sliced onion, salt and freshly ground black pepper, to taste, and cayenne pepper.

4. Stir well and simmer until cabbage is tender, adding a little more BEEF STOCK or water, if necessary. Serve immediately.

MY COLCANNON

SERVES 4-6

1 head cabbage
salt
4-6 potatoes, peeled
4-6 young carrots
4-6 young turnips
butter
90ml/6 tbls **Basic chicken stock**
(see page 66)
freshly ground black pepper
150ml/¼pt double cream
2 egg yolks
fresh breadcrumbs
freshly grated cheese (optional)

1. Preheat oven to (190°C/375°F/gas 4).

2. Remove and discard outer leaves from cabbage. Wash, core and quarter cabbage and soak in cold salted water for ½ hour. Drain.

3. Cook cabbage and potatoes in water until tender. Drain.

4. Slice carrots and turnips into thin strips; place in a thick-bottomed saucepan and blanch in sufficient water to cover. Pour off water; add 60ml/4 tbls butter and the CHICKEN STOCK to pan; cover and simmer until vegetables are tender. Season with freshly ground black pepper, to taste. Drain.

5. Chop cooked cabbage finely. Mash cooked potatoes until smooth. Combine chopped cabbage and mashed potatoes with double cream, egg yolks and 300ml/2 tbls butter and season with salt and freshly ground black pepper, to taste. Mix well.

6. Spread half of the cabbage and potato mixture in the bottom of a well-buttered ovenproof *gratin* dish. Arrange a layer of alternating strips of carrots and turnips down the centre of dish and cover with remaining cabbage and potato mixture. Sprinkle with breadcrumbs; top with a little freshly grated cheese, if desired, and dot with butter. Cook in preheated oven for 30 minutes, or until golden. Serve immediately.

CAULIFLOWER A LA POLONAISE

The cabbage family is a large and powerful clan which ranges from the earthy tones of cabbage and sprouts to the more sophisticated flavour of cauliflower, the undoubted aristocrat of the family. I like cauliflower steamed or simmered in salted water with a little lemon juice until it is just tender, not mushy, and then served with melted butter or a delicious sauce.

When buying cauliflower, choose heads that are very white and very firm, with small compact flowers squeezed tightly together. A yellow cauliflower has a very strong flavour and if the flowers are loosely separated from each other, this is usually a sign of excess maturity.

HOW TO COOK CAULIFLOWER

WHOLE: Cut off stem and remove outer green leaves from a medium-sized cauliflower. Soak the head for ½ hour in cold water to which you have added 2.5ml/½ tsp salt and the juice of ½ lemon to free it from insects. Fill a deep saucepan with enough water to cover cauliflower; add 2.5ml/½ tsp salt and bring to the boil. Put cauliflower into the boiling water; cover saucepan and simmer gently, about 20 minutes, or until the cauliflower is just tender when pierced at the stem end with a fork. Do not overcook. Drain well; arrange on a heated serving dish or in a

bowl and top with butter. Season to taste with salt and freshly ground black pepper.
FLOWERETS: If you do not intend to cook the head whole, break or cut cauliflower into flowerets. Prepare as on page 261, but cook for 10 to 15 minutes only, so that flowerets are just tender. Drain and serve as described, or with any of the sauces.

CAULIFLOWER VARIATIONS

Prepare cauliflower as above, either whole or cut into flowerets.
CAULIFLOWER HOLLANDAISE: Serve hot cauliflower with a *sauce Hollandaise*.
CAULIFLOWER AMANDINE: Sauté 60ml/4 tbls blanched slivered almonds in butter; pour sauce over hot cauliflower and season with salt and ground black pepper.
CHEESED CAULIFLOWER: Melt 60ml/4 tbls butter; add 60ml/4 tbls toasted bread-crumbs, 2.5ml/½ tsp grated onion, 60ml/4 tbls freshly grated Gruyère cheese, and salt and freshly ground black pepper, to taste. Cook over low heat, stirring continuously until cheese is melted. Pour over cooked hot cauliflower.

CAULIFLOWER A LA POLONAISE

SERVES 4

1 head cauliflower
salt
juice of ½ lemon

POLONAISE SAUCE
90ml/6 tbls butter
90ml/6 tbls fresh breadcrumbs
juice of ½ lemon
45ml/3 tbls finely chopped ham
1 hard-boiled egg, finely chopped
45ml/3 tbls finely chopped parsley
salt and freshly ground black pepper

1. Trim skim and remove and discard outer green leaves from cauliflower; wash and leave in cold salted water and lemon juice for ½ hour. Drain.
2. Measure enough water to cover cauliflower into a thick-bottomed saucepan; add salt to taste, and bring to the boil. Put cauliflower into the boiling water; cover saucepan and simmer gently for about 20 minutes, or until cauliflower is just tender when pierced at the stem end with a fork. Do not overcook. Drain. Arrange in a heated serving dish and top with Polonaise sauce. Serve immediately.
3. To make Polonaise sauce: melt butter in a thick-bottomed frying pan. Add breadcrumbs and cook until crumbs are a light brown. Stir in lemon juice, ham, hard-boiled egg and parsley. Season with salt and black pepper, to taste until heated through.

CAULIFLOWER AU GRATIN

SERVES 4

1 head cauliflower
juice of 1 lemon
butter
60ml/4 tbls flour
600ml/1pt hot milk
100g/4oz freshly grated Gruyère cheese
5ml/1 tsp Dijon mustard
salt and freshly ground black pepper
60ml/4 tbls whipped cream
60ml/4 tbls fresh breadcrumbs

Cauliflower is the aristocrat of the cabbage family.

1. Trim stem and remove and discard outer green leaves from cauliflower; wash and leave in cold salted water and half the lemon juice for ½ hour. Drain.

2. Preheat oven to moderate (190°C/375°F/gas 5).

3. Cut cauliflower into flowerets and cook in boiling salted water for 10 to 15 minutes, or until tender. Drain.

4. Meanwhile, make sauce: melt 60ml/4 tbls butter in the top of double saucepan; blend in flour and cook over hot water, stirring constantly, until smooth. Add hot milk gradually and cook, stirring constantly, until sauce comes to the boil. Add freshly grated Gruyère cheese and cook, stirring, until cheese melts. Season with Dijon mustard, lemon juice, and salt and freshly ground black pepper, to taste.

5. Arrange cauliflower in a buttered ovenproof baking dish. Pour sauce over; spread with whipped cream; sprinkle with breadcrumbs; dot with butter and bake in preheated oven for about 20 minutes, or until top is golden. Serve immediately.

FRENCH FRIED CAULIFLOWER

SERVES 4

1 head cauliflower
1 egg
150ml/¼pt milk
100g/4oz flour
salt
juice of ½ lemon
oil, for deep frying
Tomato sauce *(see page 83)*

1. To make batter: beat egg in a saucepan; add milk and heat. Add flour and 5ml/1 tsp salt and beat until smooth, then set aside.

2. Trim stem and remove and discard outer green leaves from cauliflower; wash and leave in cold salted water and lemon juice for ½ hour. Drain.

3. Separate cauliflower into small flowerets and cook in boiling salted water for 5 minutes. Drain and refresh under cold running water. Drain again.

4. Heat oil in a deep-fryer to 190°C/375°F (see page 94).

5. Dip cauliflowerets into batter. Deep-fry in hot oil until golden. Drain on absorbent paper and serve immediately with TOMATO SAUCE.

CAULIFLOWER A LA NICOISE

SERVES 4

1 head cauliflower
salt
juice of ½ lemon
1 Spanish onion, finely chopped
2 garlic cloves, finely chopped
45ml/3 tbls olive oil
45ml/3 tbls butter
6 large tomatoes, peeled, seeded and diced, or 1
*   400g/14oz can Italian peeled tomatoes, drained*
45ml/3 tbls finely chopped parsley
freshly ground black pepper
30ml/2 tbls fresh breadcrumbs

1. Trim stem and remove and discard outer green leaves from cauliflower; wash and leave in cold salted water and lemon juice for ½ hour. Drain.

2. Cut cauliflower into flowerets and cook in boiling salted water for about 5 minutes. Drain.

3. In a thick-bottomed saucepan sauté finely chopped onion and garlic in olive oil and butter until transparent. Add peeled and diced tomatoes, or canned tomatoes, and finely chopped parsley. Season with salt and freshly ground black pepper, to taste. Stir in breadcrumbs, add cauliflowerets and simmer for a further 10 minutes, or until tender. Transfer to a heated dish and serve immediately.

GRATIN DAUPHINOIS

'Let the sky rain potatoes', cried Sir John Falstaff deliriously as Mistress Ford appeared in the last scene of *The Merry Wives of Windsor*. For the sudden arrival of the potato from America had caused uproar throughout Europe. Denounced as an aphrodisiac from the pulpits of England, prohibited by the Parliament of Besançon as a cause of leprosy, the potato was stolidly ignored by the poor to whom it would have been so useful. But the rich seized on it as a new fad. Elizabeth Tudor feasted on potatoes from Raleigh's Irish estate. Louis XVI brought their flower into high fashion by accepting a bouquet of them from Parmentier – collectors know how widespread was the use of the potato flower as a decorative design for plates. Francis Bacon lauded them with stately phrases in his *History of Life and Death*.

This first excitement soon waned and as they became more common, potatoes slowly sank to the bottom of the menu, following all other vegetables. The problem? We eat them too much; they have become a necessity, not a pleasure. In this country we tend to look at them without imagination, without desire. But give a French chef a potato and he will create a hundred succulent dishes. So do not take the potato for granted. Give it a little credit. Treat it – as the French do – with *panache!*

Select potatoes best suited to your purpose:
BAKING POTATOES are large with a fine, mealy texture when cooked. Use floury potatoes for baking and for soups and purées.
NEW POTATOES range in size from tiny ones no bigger than a walnut to those the size of a regular potato. The smallest are delicious cooked whole with their skins left on and served with butter, or butter and lemon juice.

When SALAD POTATOES are hard to come by, larger new potatoes are good for potato salads, and cooked dishes such as *gratin dauphinois* for which you want potato slices to keep their shape. Never bake new potatoes.

Whenever possible, cook potatoes with their skins on. Most of the food value of a potato lies just under the skin and is lost if peeled away. After cooking, the skins will slip off easily enough if you prefer serving them without their jackets.

The major mistake in potato cookery – as with most vegetables – is overcooking. When you boil potatoes, test them with a fork. They are done when you can pierce them easily. Do not allow them to become watery and mushy.

265

On special occasions that call for a little more than the usual baked, sautéed or puréed potato, apply the Gallic touch and dress your potatoes for company. Cut them in slices or cubes; shape them with a knife to resemble olives. Parboil them for 5 minutes in salted water; drain, then sauté in clarified butter until they are soft and golden. Serve with finely chopped sautéed onions and parsley, crumbled cooked bacon, or a combination of finely chopped parsley, chervil and chives. To clarify butter, place as much butter as desired in a container over hot water until butter has melted. Pour off butter carefully and discard remaining sediment.

Follow on in the French tradition by serving thinly sliced potatoes paired off with the flavours of butter, cream, freshly grated Gruyère cheese or Parmesan cheese and finely chopped onions. *Gratin dauphinois* combines layers of thinly sliced potatoes with cream and freshly grated cheese, dots the whole with knobs of butter and bakes it in a gratin dish in the oven until bubbling and golden-crusted. Serve this delicious dish as a hot first course (as the Italians do *gnocchi* or pasta) or with a roast. Potatoes Lyonnaise sautées thin slices of boiled new potatoes in butter and serves them with gently-fried sliced onions. *Pommes de terre Anna* sets overlapping layers of sliced raw potatoes in a small buttered baking dish or round mould, each layer dotted with butter and the whole then baked in a hot oven until cooked through. The potatoes are turned out of the mould like a crisp, golden cake just before serving.

GRATIN DAUPHINOIS

SERVES 4

450g/1lb new potatoes
butter
120ml/8 tbls freshly grated Gruyère cheese
60ml/4 tbls freshly grated Parmesan cheese
150ml/¼ pt double cream
salt and freshly ground black pepper
freshly grated nutmeg

1. Preheat oven to moderate (180°C/350°F/gas 4).
2. Butter a shallow thick-bottomed oven-proof casserole, or *gratin* dish.
3. Peel and slice potatoes thinly and soak in cold water for a few minutes. Drain and dry thoroughly with a tea towel, or absorbent paper.
4. Combine freshly grated cheeses(Gruyère and Parmesan).
5. Place layer of sliced potatoes in bottom of casserole, or *gratin* dish, in overlapping rows; pour over a quarter of the cream; sprinkle with 45ml/3 tbls freshly grated cheeses: dot with butter and season with salt and freshly ground black pepper and freshly grated nutmeg, to taste. Continue this process until dish is full, finishing with a layer of cheese. Dot with butter and cook in preheated oven for 1 to 1¼ hours, or until potatoes are cooked through. If top becomes too brown, cover with aluminium foil. Serve very hot.

GRATIN SAVOYARD

SERVES 4

450g/1lb new potatoes
butter

150ml/¼pt **Basic beef stock**
  (see page 65)
90ml/6 tbls freshly grated Gruyère cheese
30ml/2 tbls freshly grated Parmesan cheese
salt and freshly ground black pepper

1. Preheat oven to moderate (180°C/350°F/gas 4).
2. Butter a shallow thick-bottomed oven-proof casserole, or *gratin* dish.
3. Peel and slice potatoes thinly and soak in cold water for a few minutes. Drain and dry thoroughly with a tea towel, or absorbent paper.
4. Combine freshly grated cheeses.
5. Place a layer of sliced potatoes in bottom of casserole, or *gratin* dish, in overlapping rows; pour over a quarter of the BEEF STOCK; sprinkle with 30ml/2 tbls freshly grated cheeses; dot with butter and season with salt and freshly ground black pepper, to taste (not too much salt). Continue this process until dish is full, finishing with a layer of cheese. Dot with butter and cook in preheated oven for about 1 to 1¼ hours, or until potatoes are cooked through. If top becomes too brown, cover with aluminium foil. Serve very hot.

POTATOES LYONNAISE

SERVES 4

450g/1lb boiled new potatoes, peeled and sliced
60ml/4 tbls butter
30ml/2 tbls olive oil
1 small onion, thinly sliced
salt and freshly ground black pepper
30ml/2 tbls finely chopped parsley

1. In a thick-bottomed frying pan, sauté sliced potatoes in butter and olive oil over a medium heat until golden on both sides. Remove potatoes from pan.
2. Sauté thinly sliced onion in remaining fats until golden.
3. Return potatoes to pan; season with salt and freshly ground black pepper, to taste, and continue cooking until potatoes are heated through. Transfer to a heated serving dish; sprinkle with chopped parsley and serve.

POMMES DE TERRE ANNA

SERVES 4

450g/1lb new potatoes
50-75g/2-3oz softened butter
salt and freshly ground black pepper

1. Preheat oven to fairly hot (220°C/425°F/gas 7).
2. Peel and slice potatoes thinly and soak in cold water for a few minutes. Drain and dry thoroughly with a tea towel, or absorbent paper.
3. Butter a shallow thick-bottomed oven-proof casserole, or *gratin* dish (one with almost straight sides gives the best results) and place in it a layer of sliced potatoes, overlapping around sides. Place a layer of sliced potatoes on bottom of casserole, or *gratin* dish, in overlapping rows; spread potatoes with 15ml/1 tbls softened butter and season with salt and freshly ground black pepper, to taste. Repeat layers as above with a final spreading of butter on top. Bake in preheated oven for about 1 hour, or until the potatoes are cooked through.
4. Just before serving, invert casserole, or *gratin* dish, on to a dish, to pour off any excess butter. Return casserole, or *gratin* dish, to its upright position. Lay a plate on top of the potatoes and press down firmly, to help potatoes form a solid cake. Return to the oven for 10 more minutes.
5. To serve: loosen potatoes from sides of dish with a spatula if necessary, invert potato cake onto a heated serving dish and serve.

LATKES *(Jewish potato pancakes)*

SERVES 4

4 large raw potatoes, peeled and grated
1 Spanish onion, grated
2 eggs, beaten
30ml/2 tbls flour
2.5ml/½ tsp baking powder
salt and freshly ground black pepper
butter and olive oil, for frying

1. Combine grated potatoes and onion; stir in beaten eggs, flour and baking powder and season with salt and freshly ground black pepper, to taste.
2. Heat a little butter and olive oil in a thick-bottomed frying pan; drop potato mixture into fats by spoonfuls and fry *latkes* until browned on both sides. Drain on absorbent paper. Transfer *latkes* to a heated serving dish and serve immediately.

HASH-BROWNED POTATOES

SERVES 4-6

6 large potatoes, baked in jackets
1 Spanish onion, coarsely grated
salt and freshly ground black pepper
45ml/3 tbls butter
45ml/3 tbls lard

1. Chill potatoes; peel and shred coarsely. Add coarsely grated onion and season with salt and freshly ground black pepper, to taste.
2. Melt butter and lard in a thick-bottomed frying pan. Put potatoes into pan, leaving 2cm/½in space around edge. Brown for 10 to 12 minutes. When crusty and hot, hold serving dish over pan and invert. Serve immediately.

NOTE. I sometimes brown top of hash-browned potatoes under the grill before serving.

ITALIAN POTATO BALLS

SERVES 6

700g/1½lb potatoes
salt
2 egg yolks
90ml/6 tbls freshly grated Parmesan cheese
30ml/2 tbls finely chopped onion
30ml/2 tbls butter
60ml/4 tbls finely chopped parsley
freshly ground black pepper
2 eggs
flour
fresh breadcrumbs
oil, for frying

1. Peel potatoes and boil in salted water until tender. Mash and combine with egg yolks and freshly grated Parmesan cheese.
2. Sauté finely chopped onion in butter until golden, but not brown. Add to potato mixture together with finely chopped parsley and generous amounts of salt and freshly ground black pepper. Mix to a smooth paste and form into small balls the size of a large walnut. Makes about 24 balls.
3. Beat eggs with a fork until well blended.
4. Roll potato balls in flour, shaking off excess, and then in beaten egg. Coat with breadcrumbs and chill until ready to use.
5. Heat oil in a deep-fryer to 190°C/375°F (see page 94). Fry a few potato balls at a time until they are golden in colour and heated through. Drain on absorbent paper. Transfer potato balls to a heated serving dish and serve.

LEMON DILL POTATOES

SERVES 4-6

700g/1½lb tiny new potatoes
salt
15ml/1 tbls olive oil
30ml/2 tbls butter

30ml/2 tbls flour
300ml/¹/₂pt milk
5ml/1 tsp dill seeds
30ml/2 tbls lemon juice
30ml/2 tbls finely chopped parsley
freshly ground black pepper

1. Peel or scrape new potatoes. Cook until just tender in boiling water to which you have added salt and olive oil. Drain. Transfer potatoes to a heated serving dish.

2. Melt butter in a thick-bottomed saucepan; blend in flour and gradually stir in milk. Add dill seeds and cook, stirring constantly, until sauce is smooth and thick.

3. Add lemon juice and finely chopped parsley to sauce and season with salt and freshly ground black pepper, to taste. Pour hot lemon dill sauce over the potatoes and serve immediately.

ARTICHOKES

The French believe that if you eat old vegetables you yourself become old. Not for them the jumbo carrots or the giant cabbages so beloved by English housewives. It is the infant vegetables they use. In Italy, too, where the artichoke is very popular, tiny raw artichokes no bigger than a baby's fist are eaten raw as an appetiser, preserved in olive oil as an integral part of an Italian *antipasto* platter, or dipped in batter and fried, either alone, or with tiny octopus and prawns in an Italian mixed fry called *fritto misto del mare.*

In Rome, tender young artichokes are often cooked in olive oil, lemon and herbs, *alla romana,* and served as a marvellously flavoured hot or cold hors-d'oeuvre. I like artichoke hearts done in this manner, too, flavoured with a little finely chopped garlic and oregano. In France, artichokes *au vin blanc* top the bill, the artichokes simmered in dry white wine with a little olive oil and seasonings. Artichokes *à la provençale, à la barigoule, à la grecque,* are all exalted variations on this basic theme.

There are so many ways to serve this delicate, nutty-flavoured vegetable – rich in iron, mineral salts and iodine – that I cannot understand why so many people consider it an acquired taste. I like them baked, fried, stuffed, puréed with rich cream as an accompanying vegetable, and even in a soup. But my favourite way of dealing with this sophisticated vegetable is to cook it in boiling water with a little salt, olive oil and lemon juice, and serve it cold with a French dressing as a first course, or hot as a separate vegetable course. Whole, halved or quartered, a hot artichoke served with a *sauce Hollandaise* or melted butter and lemon juice makes an unbeatable dish; each leaf should be pulled off separately, the large succulent end dipped in the sauce and the soft fleshy bit prised gently off with the teeth.

Artichoke hearts, found at the base of each vegetable, make one of the best garnishes for cold dishes imaginable if cooked and then chilled. They can be served as a vegetable, stuffed with various ingredients or used as the decorative base for a host of salads and *hors-d'oeuvre* dishes.

ITALIAN ARTICHOKES WITH MUSHROOM SAUCE

SERVES 4

4 small artichokes
salt
juice of 1/2 lemon
butter

MUSHROOM SAUCE
30ml/2 tbls butter
90ml/6 tbls finely chopped mushrooms
45ml/3 tbls finely chopped shallots
90ml/6 tbls dry white wine
30ml/2 tbls tomato purée
30ml/2 tbls finely chopped parsley
salt and freshly ground black pepper

1. Cut small artichokes into quarters; trim tough outer leaves and tips of tender leaves and remove chokes.
2. Poach artichokes for 5 minutes in boiling water to which you have added a little salt and the lemon juice. Drain. Arrange artichoke quarters in a buttered thick-bottomed casserole. Cook for 2 minutes over a high heat; spoon over mushroom sauce, cover and simmer until tender.
3. To make mushroom sauce: melt butter in a thick-bottomed frying pan and sauté finely chopped mushrooms and shallots until almost golden; moisten with dry white wine and simmer for 3 minutes. Add tomato purée and finely chopped parsley and season with salt and freshly ground black pepper, to taste. Continue cooking until heated through.

ARTICHOKE HEARTS WITH FOIE GRAS

SERVES 4

4 artichokes
juice and rind of 1 lemon
30ml/2 tbls olive oil
salt and freshly black pepper
60ml/4 tbls butter
4 slices canned pâté de foie gras
*60-120ml/4-8 tbls **Sauce Béarnaise** (see page 84)*

1. Choose tender artichokes. Cut the hearts out carefully. Brush each heart with lemon juice and place immediately in a bowl of cold water to keep colour fresh, adding squeezed rind and any remaining lemon juice to water.
2. Pour the acidulated water into a thick-bottomed saucepan and bring to the boil; add olive oil and salt and freshly ground black pepper, to taste, and poach artichoke hearts, covered, in this liquid until they are tender, about 15 to 20 minutes, according to their size. Drain.
3. Preheat grill to high.
4. Melt butter in a *gratin* dish, or shallow heatproof casserole; place artichoke hearts in *gratin* dish, or casserole, upside-down and let them simmer in the butter for a few minutes; turn them delicately and when done, place a round of *pâté de foie gras* in each heart; cover each heart with a spoonful or two of SAUCE BEARNAISE and grill for a few seconds to brown the sauce.

There are many ways to serve the delicate, nutty flavoured artichoke rich in iron, mineral salts and iodine.

ARTICHOKES AU VIN BLANC

SERVES 4

4 medium artichokes
30ml/2 tbls olive oil
150ml/¼ pt dry white wine
2 garlic cloves, finely chopped
1 small onion, finely chopped
30ml/2 tbls finely chopped parsley
pinch of dried savory
salt and freshly ground black pepper

1. Cut off tops of artichokes. Trim tough outer leaves and tips of tender leaves and remove chokes. Trim the base and stems with a sharp knife.
2. Combine olive oil, dry white wine, finely chopped garlic, onion, parsley, savory, and salt and freshly ground black pepper, to taste.
3. Place trimmed artichokes in a thick-bottomed saucepan just large enough to hold

them and pour wine mixture over them. Cover and simmer slowly for 45 minutes, adding a little more wine and olive oil, if necessary. When tender, transfer artichokes to a heated serving dish; spoon over hot juices and serve immediately.

ARTICHOKES VINAIGRETTE

SERVES 4

4 artichokes
salt
juice of ½ lemon
French dressing *(see page 304)*

1. Trim tough outer leaves of artichokes and tips of tender leaves. Trim the base and stem with a sharp knife.
2. Cook artichokes until tender, 30 to 40 minutes, in a large quantity of boiling salted

271

water to which you have added the lemon juice. Artichokes are cooked when a leaf pulls out easily. Turn artichokes upside-down to drain.

3. Serve artichokes cold with a well-flavoured FRENCH DRESSING. Pull off a leaf at a time; eat tender base of each leaf. Remove choke and eat artichoke heart.

STUFFED PEPPERS

SERVES 4

4 green peppers
45ml/3 tbls olive oil
50g/2oz butter
salt and freshly ground black pepper
100g/4oz rice
*hot **Basic chicken stock** (see page 66)*
1/2 Spanish onion, finely chopped
50g/2oz chopped mushrooms
100g/4oz finely chopped ham
30-45ml/2-3 tbls tomato purée
*300ml/1/2pt hot **Basic beef stock** (see page 65)*
30-45ml/2-3 tbls chopped parsley

1. Preheat oven to moderate (180°C/350°F/ gas 4).
2. Remove the tops of peppers and reserve. Remove pith and seeds. Place peppers in boiling water to which you have added 15ml/1 tbls olive oil and cook for 5 minutes. Drain and dry with a tea towel, or absorbent paper. Place a small piece of butter in bottom of each pepper (using half the butter), and season well with salt and freshly ground black pepper.
3. Melt remaining butter in a thick-bottomed saucepan. Add rice and sauté until golden. Cover with hot CHICKEN STOCK and cook, stirring constantly, until mixture comes to the boil; reduce heat; cover and cook slowly for about 30 minutes, adding a little more CHICKEN STOCK if necessary.
4. Meanwhile sauté finely chopped onion and

chopped mushrooms in 30ml/2 tbls olive oil and add to rice mixture.
5. Mix in finely chopped ham, season with salt and freshly ground black pepper, to taste, and fill the peppers. Replace pepper caps and arrange in an ovenproof baking dish.
6. Blend tomato purée with hot BEEF STOCK; pour over STUFFED PEPPERS and bake in preheated oven for 30 to 40 minutes, or until done, basting frequently. Sprinkle entire dish with chopped parsley and serve immediately.

CHILES RELLENOS *(cheese-stuffed green peppers)*

SERVES 4

4 large green peppers
225g/1/2lb Mozzarella cheese, finely grated
225g/1/2lb mild Cheddar cheese, finely grated
salt and freshly ground black pepper
Tabasco, or chilli sauce
60ml/4 tbls flour
4 eggs, separated
oil, for deep-frying

1. Preheat grill to high.
2. Roast green peppers under preheated grill, turning them from time to time, until skins are charred. Rub charred skins off under cold water; dry peppers with a tea towel, or absorbent paper, and make a small cut down the side without opening the pepper full length. With a spoon scrape out the seeds and all the pith.
3. Mix finely grated cheeses together and season with salt and freshly ground black pepper, to taste, and a little Tabasco, or chilli sauce. Fill peppers with cheese mixture. Reshape the peppers and roll them lightly in 30ml/2 tbls flour.
4. Beat egg whites until they are stiff. Lightly beat egg yolks and fold into egg whites together with 30ml/2 tbls flour.
5. Preheat oil in a deep-fryer to 190°C/375°F (see page 94).

6. Dip stuffed peppers in batter and fry them in deep hot fat until they are golden brown. Drain on absorbent paper. Transfer stuffed peppers to a heated serving dish and serve immediately.

RATATOUILLE

SERVES 4

120ml/8 tbls olive oil
2 Spanish onions, sliced
2 green peppers, seeded and diced
2 aubergines, diced
2 baby marrows, cut in 1.2cm/1½in slices
4-6 ripe tomatoes, peeled, seeded and chopped
salt and freshly ground black pepper
30ml/2 tbls parsley, chopped
1 pinch of dried marjoram, or oregano
1 pinch of basil
1 large garlic clove, crushed

1. Heat olive oil in a thick-bottomed saucepan; add sliced onions and sauté until transparent.
2. Add the diced green peppers to pan together with diced aubergines and, 5 minutes later, baby marrow slices and peeled, seeded and chopped tomatoes. The vegetables should not be fried but stewed in the oil, so simmer gently in pan, covered, for 30 minutes. Season with salt and freshly ground black pepper, to taste, chopped parsley, marjoram, basil and crushed garlic. Cook, uncovered, for about 10 to 15 minutes more, or until ratatouille is well mixed and has the appearance of a *ragoût* of vegetables – which it is. Serve hot from casserole, or cold as a delicious beginning to a summer meal.

PROVENCAL STUFFED VEGETABLES

SERVES 4

VEGETABLE CASES
4 courgettes
4 small aubergines
4 medium onions
salt
4 tomatoes
olive oil
butter

PROVENCAL STUFFING
175g/6oz ground veal
25g/1oz fat salt pork, diced
1 Spanish onion, finely chopped
60ml/4 tbls olive oil
1 garlic clove, crushed
finely chopped fresh tarragon
finely chopped fresh parsley
1 egg, beaten
30ml/2 tbls freshly grated Parmesan cheese
*90-120ml/6-8 tbls **Boiled rice** (see page 179)*
aubergine and courgette pulp
salt and freshly ground black pepper

1. Preheat oven to moderate (190°C/375°F/gas 5).
2. Poach courgettes, aubergines and onions whole for 1 minute in boiling salted water. Drain.
3. Cut tops off tomatoes, aubergines, courgettes and onions. Scoop out insides of vegetables, being careful not to damage the skins. Keep pulp of aubergines and courgettes for stuffing.
4. To make Provençal stuffing: in a thick-bottomed frying pan sauté ground veal, diced fat salt pork and finely chopped onion in olive oil. Combine next 7 ingredients and add them to meat and onion mixture. Season with salt and freshly ground black pepper, to taste, and sauté for a few minutes more, stirring continuously.

273

5. Stuff scooped-out vegetables with Provençal mixture. Place stuffed vegetables in an ovenproof baking dish to which you have added a little olive oil; place a knob of butter on top of each vegetable and bake in preheated oven for ½ hour. Serve one of each vegetable as a main course.

AUBERGINE CASSEROLE

SERVES 4

4-6 aubergines
salt
30ml/2 tbls olive oil
butter
freshly ground black pepper
120-150ml/8-10 tbls freshly grated Parmesan
 cheese
150ml/¼pt double cream
4-6 large tomatoes, thickly sliced
60-90ml/4-6 tbls fresh breadcrumbs

1. Peel the aubergines; cut in thin slices; sprinkle with salt and let them 'sweat' for 2 hours.
2. Preheat oven to moderate (180°C/350°F/ gas 4).
3. Drain aubergine slices and wipe them dry with a tea towel, or absorbent paper. Sauté aubergine slices lightly in olive oil until they are golden. Drain on absorbent paper.
4. Butter a thick-bottomed casserole; place a layer of aubergine slices in the bottom; season with black pepper, to taste, and sprinkle generously with Parmesan cheese and cream. Add a layer of thickly sliced tomatoes, then black pepper, to taste, and a little more cream and cheese, followed by another layer of aubergine slices and so on, until the dish is full, finishing with cream. Cover entire dish with breadcrumbs and Parmesan cheese; dot with butter and cook in preheated oven for approximately 45 minutes. Serve from casserole.

STUFFED AUBERGINES

SERVES 4-6

4 medium-sized aubergines
salt
olive oil
2 Spanish onions, sliced
2 garlic cloves, finely chopped
45ml/3 tbls finely chopped parsley
6 tomatoes, peeled, seeded and chopped
4 tomatoes
sugar
freshly ground black pepper

1. Trim aubergines; cut in half lengthwise and scoop out some of the aubergine flesh, leaving shell about 6mm/¼in thick. Make 4 incisions lengthwise in each half, being careful not to cut through the skin. Salt aubergine halves, making sure salt goes into incisions, and leave for 20 minutes.
2. Preheat oven to slow (170°C/325°F/gas 3).
3. Wash aubergines and squeeze dry. Heat 60ml/4 tbls oil in a thick-bottomed frying pan and sauté aubergines until soft and pliable. Remove from pan, reserving oil.
4. Sauté sliced onions in 45ml/3 tbls olive oil in another frying pan until transparent. Add finely chopped garlic, parsley and peeled seeded, chopped tomatoes, and sauté for a few minutes more, stirring from time to time. Allow to cool.
5. Place sautéed aubergines, cut side up, in a fairly deep ovenproof baking dish, or shallow ovenproof casserole. Stuff aubergines with onion and tomato mixture, spooning any left over around the sides.
6. Slice tomatoes and place 3 slices on top of each stuffed aubergine; sprinkle with a little sugar and season with salt and freshly ground black pepper, to taste. Pour over the reserved oil; add a little water to dish and cook in preheated oven for 1 hour, or until tender. Serve stuffed aubergines cold as an appetiser.

BOUILLABAISSE D'EPINARDS

1.4kg/3 lb fresh spinach
60ml/4 tbls butter
90ml/6 tbls olive oil
1 Spanish onion, finely chopped
2 garlic cloves, finely chopped
350g/³⁄4lb potatoes, peeled and thinly sliced
salt and freshly ground black pepper
1.5ml/¹⁄4 tsp ground saffron
1 bouquet garni (2 sprigs parsley, 1 sprig thyme,
 1 stalk fennel and 1 bay leaf)
strip of lemon peel
1 egg per person
1 fried toast triangle per person

1. Preheat oven to moderate (180°C/350°F/ gas 4).
2. Wash spinach well; drain and remove coarse stems and any yellowed leaves.
3. Melt butter in a thick-bottomed saucepan; add spinach leaves and cook, stirring continuously, until spinach has 'melted', then drain.
4. Heat olive oil in another pan and sauté finely chopped onion and garlic cloves until transparent but not golden.
5. Add thinly sliced potatoes to pan and let them sauté a minute on both sides without taking colour. Transfer potatoes and onion to a thick-bottomed ovenproof casserole; season with salt and freshly ground black pepper, to taste; pour over 425ml/³⁄4pt boiling water and stir in ground saffron.
6. Press cooked spinach between your hands to get rid of excess moisture; chop finely and stir into casserole, being careful not to break potato slices. Add the *bouquet garni* and strip of lemon peel; cover and allow to simmer in preheated oven for at least 1 hour, or until the potatoes are tender.
7. When ready to serve, remove casserole from the oven and make shallow depressions in the mixture with the back of a serving spoon (1 per person). Break 1 egg into each depres-sion, cover, and simmer gently until egg whites set. One toast triangle fried in butter for each guest accompanies this country dish.

SPINACI CON SALSICCIA

SERVES 4

1kg/2lb fresh spinach
60ml/4 tbls butter
¹⁄2 chicken stock cube, crumbled
freshly ground black pepper
60ml/4 tbls olive oil
1 small garlic clove
225g/¹⁄2lb dry Italian sausage, diced
salt
lemon wedges

1. Wash spinach several times in cold water. Drain; remove coarse stems and any yellowed leaves.
2. Melt butter in a thick-bottomed saucepan; add spinach leaves and chicken stock cube and cook, stirring continuously, until spinach has 'melted'. Season with freshly ground black pepper, to taste. Drain cooked spinach and press between your hands to get rid of excess moisture.
3. Heat olive oil in a thick-bottomed frying pan and sauté garlic in this mixture until golden, then remove garlic clove from pan and discard.
4. Add sausage to pan and sauté until thoroughly cooked. Stir in the cooked spinach and heat through. Season with salt and freshly ground black pepper, to taste. Transfer to a heated serving dish and serve accompanied by lemon wedges.

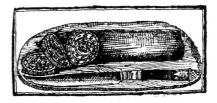

SAUTEED SPINACH

SERVES 4

1kg/2lb fresh spinach
butter
1/2 chicken stock cube, crumbled
freshly ground black pepper
30ml/2 tbls olive oil
1 Spanish onion, finely chopped
1 garlic clove, finely chopped
90ml/6 tbls double cream
90ml/6 tbls fresh breadcrumbs
90ml/6 tbls freshly grated Parmesan cheese
freshly grated nutmeg
2 slices white bread

1. Wash and cook spinach as in steps 1 and 2 of preceding recipe.
2. Heat 30ml/2 tbls each butter and olive oil in a thick-bottomed saucepan and sauté finely chopped onion and garlic clove until transparent.
3. Chop cooked spinach finely and add to vegetable mixture. Cook over a low heat, stirring constantly, until fats are absorbed.
4. Stir double cream into pan together with breadcrumbs and freshly grated Parmesan cheese; season with salt and freshly ground black pepper and freshly grated nutmeg, to taste, and heat thoroughly, but do not allow to boil.
5. Trim crusts from bread; cut into cubes and sauté in 60ml/4 tbls butter until golden. Just before serving, stir *croûtons* into spinach. Transfer to a heated serving dish and serve immediately.

BAKED SPINACH MORNAY

SERVES 4

2 small packets frozen spinach (about
*   225g/8oz), defrosted*
butter

salt and freshly ground black pepper
90ml/6 tbls double cream
3 slices of bread
15-30ml/1-2 tbls freshly grated Parmesan cheese

MORNAY SAUCE
30ml/2 tbls butter
30ml/2 tbls flour
300ml/1/2pt hot milk
2.5ml/1/2 tsp dry mustard
90ml/6 tbls freshly grated Parmesan cheese
pinch of cayenne pepper

1. Place defrosted spinach in thick-bottomed saucepan with 60ml/4 tbls butter and season with salt and freshly ground black pepper, to taste. Cook slowly for 3 to 6 minutes, stirring from time to time. Stir in double cream.
2. Trim crusts from bread; dice and sauté in 30ml/2 tbls butter until golden. Fold *croûtons* into spinach and spoon mixture into a buttered *gratin* dish. Keep warm.
3. Preheat grill to high.
4. To make sauce: melt butter in the top of a double saucepan; add flour and cook, stirring continuously, until the mixture is smooth. Pour in hot milk and stir over hot water until the mixture begins to thicken. Add dry mustard, freshly grated Parmesan cheese and a pinch of cayenne pepper and simmer gently for 5 minutes.
5. Pour sauce over spinach; sprinkle top with freshly grated Parmesan cheese; Dot with butter and brown quickly under preheated grill.

PUREED SPINACH

SERVES 4

1kg/2lb spinach
60ml/4 tbls butter
*60ml/4 tbls **Basic chicken stock** (see page 66)*
freshly ground black pepper
salt

1. Wash spinach several times in cold water, removing any yellowed or damaged leaves. Drain thoroughly and remove any tough stalks.

2. Combine spinach with butter and CHICKEN STOCK in a thick-bottomed saucepan; season with freshly ground black pepper, to taste, and cook over a high heat, stirring constantly, until spinach is tender, about 5 minutes. Drain and squeeze dry. Chop and then purée spinach in an electric blender, or food processor.

3. Return puréed spinach to a clean saucepan; correct seasoning, adding a little salt, if necessary, and reheat. Serve immediately.

MUSHROOMS A LA GRECQUE

SERVES 4-6

2 carrots, chopped
1 Spanish onion, chopped
olive oil
30ml/2 tbls corn oil
150ml/¼pt dry white wine
salt and freshly ground black pepper
1 bouquet garni (2 sprigs parsley, 2 sprigs thyme,
   2 bay leaves and 1 stalk celery)
8-12 coriander seeds
1 fat garlic clove
450g/1lb button mushrooms
225g/½lb tomatoes, peeled, seeded and chopped
30-45ml/2-3 tbls finely chopped parsley

1. In a thick-bottomed saucepan, sauté chopped carrots and onion in 30ml/2 tbls each olive oil and corn oil until they are soft and golden. Moisten with white wine: season with salt and freshly ground black pepper, to taste, and add the *bouquet garni,* coriander seeds and garlic clove.

2. Trim stems of button mushrooms and add to vegetables together with peeled, seeded and chopped tomatoes and a little more wine, if necessary. There should not be too much liquid at this stage as the mushrooms will add liquid in cooking. Cook, uncovered, for about 15 to 20 minutes.

3. Remove pan from heat and allow to cool. Remove *bouquet garni* and add 30ml/2 tbls olive oil. Transfer to a serving dish; sprinkle with parsley and serve cold as *hors-d'oeuvre*.

BAKED STUFFED MUSHROOMS

SERVES 4

12 large mushrooms
60ml/4 tbls olive oil
50g/2oz bacon, finely chopped
2 shallots, finely chopped
salt and freshly ground black pepper
1 egg
60ml/4 tbls double cream
15ml/1 tbls cognac
butter
30-45ml/2-3 tbls fresh breadcrumbs

1. Preheat oven to hot (230°C/450°F/gas 8).

2. Remove stems of mushrooms and reserve. Brush caps with olive oil and bake in preheated oven for 5 minutes or until they are half cooked.

3. Finely chop mushroom stems. Heat remaining olive oil in a thick-bottomed frying pan and gently sauté finely chopped mushroom stems, bacon and shallots for 10 minutes. Season with salt and freshly ground black pepper, to taste. Remove frying pan from heat.

4. Beat together the egg, double cream and cognac and stir into stuffing. Allow to cool.

5. Preheat grill to high.

6. Place mushroom caps in a buttered *gratin* dish and fill them with the stuffing, piling it up in the centre. Sprinkle with breadcrumbs, place a dab of butter on each mound and brown under preheated grill. Serve immediately.

CRAB-STUFFED MUSHROOMS

SERVES 4

16 large mushrooms
100g/4oz crabmeat, flaked
90ml/6 tbls fresh breadcrumbs
2 eggs, beaten
60ml/4 tbls double cream
60ml/4 tbls finely chopped parsley
30ml/2 tbls finely chopped onion
butter
salt and freshly ground black pepper
lemon juice

1. Preheat oven to moderate (190°C/375°F/gas 5).
2. Remove stems from mushrooms.
3. Combine crabmeat, breadcrumbs, eggs, cream and parsley.
4. Sauté finely chopped onion in 30ml/2 tbls butter until soft. Stir into crab mixture and season with salt and freshly ground black pepper and lemon juice, to taste.
5. Fill mushroom caps with crab mixture. Dot with butter; arrange stuffed mushroom caps in a lightly-buttered *gratin* dish and bake in preheated oven for 15 to 20 minutes, or until mushrooms are tender. Serve with MORNAY SAUCE (see page 276).

LEEKS AU GRATIN

SERVES 4-6

12 leeks
salt
butter
flour
425ml/³⁄₄pt hot milk
100g/4oz freshly grated Gruyère cheese
5ml/1 tsp Dijon mustard
juice of ¹⁄₂ lemon
freshly ground black pepper
45ml/3 tbls fresh breadcrumbs

1. Preheat oven to moderate (190°C/375°F/gas 5).
2. Wash leeks; cut off roots and green tops to within an inch of white. Split leeks from top almost to root end and wash thoroughly under running water. Simmer leeks in boiling salted water for 20 minutes, or until tender. Drain.
3. Melt 60ml/4 tbls butter in top of double saucepan; blend in flour and cook over water, stirring constantly, until smooth. Add hot milk gradually and cook, stirring constantly, until sauce comes to the boil. Add freshly grated Gruyère cheese and cook, stirring, until cheese melts. Flavour with mustard, lemon juice and salt and black pepper, to taste.
4. Place leeks in buttered *gratin* dish; pour sauce over them. Sprinkle with breadcrumbs; dot with butter and bake in preheated oven for about 20 minutes, or until top is golden. Serve immediately.

GARLIC-STUFFED ONIONS

SERVES 6

6 Spanish onions
12 fat garlic cloves
salt
olive oil
freshly ground black pepper
90ml/6 tbls finely chopped parsley
butter
fresh breadcrumbs

1. Preheat oven to moderate (190°C/375°F/gas 5).
2. Simmer whole, peeled onions and garlic cloves in boiling salted water until tender. Drain.
3. Scoop out centres of onions. Combine scooped-out flesh of onions with cooked garlic cloves; chop very finely then pound together until smooth with olive oil, salt and freshly ground black pepper, to taste, finely chopped

parsley and 90ml/6 tbls breadcrumbs.

4. Stuff scooped-out onions with mixture. Place in a buttered *gratin* dish; sprinkle with breadcrumbs; dot with butter and cook in pre-heated oven until onion shell is tender. Serve immediately.

GLAZED WHITE ONIONS

SERVES 4

450g/1lb small white onions, peeled
60ml/4 tbls butter
*60ml/4 tbls **Basic chicken stock** (see page 66)*
15ml/1 tbls sugar
salt and freshly ground black pepper

1. Place onions in a thick-bottomed saucepan; cover with cold water and cook over a high heat until the water boils. Drain.

2. Return blanched onions to pan; add butter and CHICKEN STOCK; season with the sugar, and salt and freshly ground black pepper, to taste, and simmer over a low heat until onions have absorbed the liquid without burning and have taken on a little colour. Transfer to a heated serving dish and serve immediately.

BRAISED CELERY

SERVES 4

2 heads celery
¼ Spanish onion, thinly sliced
2 small carrots, thinly sliced
*150ml/¼pt **Basic chicken stock** (see page 66)*
salt and freshly ground black pepper
15ml/1 tbls butter
10ml/2 tsp flour
finely chopped parsley

1. Cut each celery head in half lengthwise and trim off tops. Blanch in boiling water for 10 minutes. Drain.

2. Place celery lengths in a thick-bottomed saucepan together with thinly sliced onion, carrots and CHICKEN STOCK. Season with salt and freshly ground black pepper, to taste; cover and cook slowly until vegetables are tender, 30 to 40 minutes.

3. About 5 minutes before you remove vegetables from heat, stir in butter and flour, which you have mashed together to form a smooth paste. Transfer braised celery to a heated serving dish; sprinkle with finely chopped parsley and serve.

GLAZED CARROTS

SERVES 4

450g/1lb small carrots
60ml/4 tbls butter
*60ml/4 tbls **Basic chicken stock** (see page 66)*
15ml/1 tbls sugar
salt and freshly ground black pepper

1. Scrape carrots; slice thickly and place in a thick-bottomed saucepan; cover with cold water and bring to the boil. Drain.

2. Return blanched carrots to pan together with butter and CHICKEN STOCK; season with salt and freshly ground black pepper, to taste; add sugar and simmer over a low heat until carrots have absorbed the liquid without burning and have taken on a little colour. Transfer to a heated serving dish and serve immediately.

SLICED CARROTS AND MUSHROOMS

SERVES 4-6

1 bunch young carrots
30ml/2 tbls butter
15ml/1 tbls olive oil
1 small onion, finely chopped

½ garlic clove, finely chopped
6 button mushrooms, sliced
salt and freshly ground black pepper
pinch of crushed rosemary
pinch of crushed cardamom (optional)
90ml/6 tbls double cream
cognac, Madeira or lemon juice (optional)

1. Scrape carrots and slice diagonally.
2. Heat butter and olive oil in a thick-bottomed saucepan and sauté finely chopped onion and garlic clove for 1 minute.
3. Add sliced carrots and mushrooms to pan; season with salt and freshly ground black pepper, to taste, a pinch of crushed rosemary and a pinch of crushed cardamom, if desired. Cover and cook over a low heat for 10 minutes, or until vegetables are just tender. Stir in double cream and simmer gently for 5 minutes more. Just before serving, correct seasoning, adding a little more salt and freshly ground black pepper and a dash of cognac, Madeira or lemon juice, if desired. Transfer to a heated serving dish and serve immediately.

FRENCH-STYLE PEAS

SERVES 4

450g/1lb frozen peas
60ml/4 tbls butter
60ml/4 tbls **Basic chicken stock** *(see page 66)*
15ml/1 tbls sugar
salt and freshly ground black pepper

1. Place peas in a thick-bottomed saucepan; cover with cold water and bring to the boil. Drain.
2. Return blanched peas to pan together with butter and CHICKEN STOCK; season with salt and freshly ground black pepper, to taste; add sugar and simmer over a low heat until peas have absorbed the liquid and are tender. Transfer to a heated serving dish and serve.

PETITS POIS AU LARD

SERVES 6-8

100g/4oz salt pork, or bacon, in one piece
60ml/4 tbls butter
1kg/2lb fresh peas, shelled
12 tiny white onions, blanched
4 lettuce leaves, shredded
15ml/1 tbls sugar
salt and freshly ground black pepper

1. Parboil salt pork or bacon for 5 minutes in water to cover. Drain and dice.
2. Melt butter gently in a thick-bottomed saucepan and sauté diced salt pork, or bacon, until golden.
3. Add peas, blanched onions, shredded lettuce, 60ml/4 tbls water and sugar to pan. Season with salt and freshly ground black pepper, to taste. Cover and simmer gently for about 20 minutes, or until tender. Transfer to a heated serving dish and serve immediately.

MEXICAN BEANS

SERVES 4

225g/½lb red kidney beans, soaked overnight
1 Spanish onion, finely chopped
1 garlic clove, finely chopped
pinch of salt
30ml/2 tbls butter
10ml/2 tsp flour
1.5ml/¼ tsp ground cumin
15ml/1 tbls Mexican chilli powder
1 bouquet garni (2 sprigs thyme, 1 celery stalk,
    1 bay leaf)
150ml/¼pt **Basic beef stock** *(see page 65)*
freshly ground black pepper

1. Put beans in a thick-bottomed saucepan; cover with 600ml/1pt cold water and bring to the boil over a low heat. Remove pan from heat; cover and leave beans to soak for 1 hour.

2. Drain beans and transfer to a clean saucepan. Add onion and garlic, cover with a fresh pint of water and add a pinch of salt. Bring to the boil; boil for 10 minutes, then simmer, covered, for 50 to 60 minutes until beans are soft but still whole. Drain well and return to a clean saucepan.

3. Cream butter and flour to a smooth paste; add ground cumin and chilli powder and stir into beans in tiny pieces. Add *bouquet garni* and BEEF STOCK and season with salt and freshly ground black pepper, to taste. Bring to a simmer and cook, covered, for 45 minutes until sauce is smooth and rich, stirring occasionally. Serve immediately.

COUSCOUS AS A VEGETABLE

SERVES 4

BOUILLON
30ml/2 tbls olive oil
1 Spanish onion, quartered
4 carrots, scraped and cut into chunks
4 celery stalks, cut into chunks
2 fat garlic cloves, crushed
5ml/1 tsp ground ginger
1.5ml/¼ tsp cayenne pepper
1.5ml/¼ tsp ground cumin

COUSCOUS
450g/1lb couscous
60ml/4 tbls butter
60ml/4 tbls olive oil
90ml/6 tbls steaming **Bouillon** *(see recipe above)*
tiny pinch each of cayenne pepper, paprika, ground cumin, ginger and cinnamon
salt

1. For the *bouillon* heat olive oil in the bottom of a *couscousière*, or thick-bottomed saucepan. Add onion and carrot and celery chunks. Sauté vegetables for 15 minutes until browned.

2. Meanwhile prepare *couscous:* place the grains in a bowl and moisten with 90ml/6 tbls water, one spoonful at a time, working evenly with your fingertips. The grains will absorb the water without any trouble, and look and feel almost as it did when it came out of the packet.

3. Line steamer top with a clean tea towel (wrung out in boiling water, just in case any detergent remains) and wrap *couscous* in this.

4. Sprinkle browned vegetables with the crushed garlic and spices. Stir well and pour over 1L/2pt boiling water; stir again and bring to the boil. Fit steamer over top of pan containing steaming *bouillon* and allow to simmer for 45 minutes, uncovered, occasionally drawing a fork through the grains to aerate them and to prevent any lumps forming.

5. After 45 minutes cooking time, fluff *couscous* with a fork to separate grains and transfer to a bowl that will fit the steamer. Add butter and fluff *couscous* with a fork; do likewise with the olive oil and 60ml/4 tbls of the *bouillon*. Sprinkle over spices; season with salt, to taste.

6. Bring *bouillon* back to the boil and place bowl in the top half of the steamer; cover and steam for a further 45 minutes over simmering *bouillon*, adding 30ml/2 tbls *bouillon* after 15 minutes, fluffing it in with a fork.

7. When ready, toss *couscous* with a fork to separate grains and serve on a heated platter.

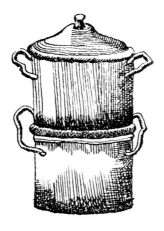

CHAPTER 13

PASTA & RICE

Inexpensive, easy to prepare, wonderfully filling and practically imperishable in storage, pasta – as typically Italian as Grand Opera and Chianti – has much to recommend it as one of the great dishes of the world.

Though all pasta is made of the same basic wheat flour dough, the different shapes and sizes it comes in are as varied as the different towns and regions of Italy. Some varieties – *pasta asciutta* – are eaten with sauce and freshly grated Parmesan cheese; others are stuffed with finely chopped meats, spinach, *ricotta* cheese and other ingredients. Still others – *pasta in brodo* – are meant to be served in soups.

Most of us are familiar with several varieties of pasta. Italians have more than a hundred different shapes and sizes to choose from – ranging from tiny golden specks called *pastine,* used mainly in light soups and invalid broths, to huge ribbed *rigatoni,* so large and hearty that they are individually stuffed with meat, cheese and tomatoes.

The delightful names the Italians give to these shapes are proof of their great affection for pasta. Spaghetti (which means little strings) and macaroni are, of course, best known to us, but they are just two of the immense pasta family: *amorini,* little cupids; *farfallette,* little bows or butterflies; *conchiglie,* little shells; *cappelletti,* little hats; *tirabaci,* kiss-bringers . . . are a few of the other delicious forms that pasta takes. And strange as it seems, the cut and shape of pasta, in one or another of these many forms, alters the taste of the finished dish, for it affects the cooking and the amount of sauce included with each mouthful.

Even more important than the size and shape of the pasta is the kind of sauce that accompanies it. Not all Italian pasta sauces are tomato-based. One of my favourite

Pasta—one of the world's great dishes—comes in even more shapes and sizes than there are regions of Italy. Italians have wonderful names for pasta— hats, little cupids and kiss-bringers are just a few.

recipes serves well-drained spaghetti with only butter and freshly grated Parmesan cheese; another adds one or two raw egg yolks and a little cream to this basic recipe for a really superb sauce. An 'emergency shelf' sauce that I find useful for pasta features finely chopped onions sautéed in butter and olive oil, and moistened with canned clam broth; the whole is simmered for 10 minutes and coarsely chopped canned clams and fresh cream are added just before serving. I like, too, a sauce made of pounded anchovies and finely chopped onion and garlic; or, when fresh basil is available, the famous *pesto* or 'green sauce' of Genoa, made by pounding fresh basil and parsley with pine nuts, garlic and olive oil. But best of all, perhaps, and certainly the most famous, is *spaghetti alla bolognese,* spaghetti served with a rich and delicious meat and tomato sauce.

One pint of sauce is enough for a pound of pasta, as there should be just enough to flavour, moisten and coat each strand or piece of pasta but not enough to leave a pool of sauce in the bottom of the serving dish.

HOW TO COOK PASTA PERFECTLY

One pound of pasta serves 4 people for a main course, 6 people for a first course. Cook pasta in boiling, salted water (1-2L/6-8pt water per 450g/1lb of pasta).

Let water boil briskly for a minute before adding pasta. Instead of breaking long spaghetti or macaroni, hold a handful at one end and dip the other into the boiling water. As the pasta softens, curl it round in the pan until the whole length goes in. Do not cover; use a kitchen fork or a long wooden spoon to stir at the start of the cooking to prevent spaghetti from sticking to the pan. Stir frequently during cooking.

Cook pasta until tender, but still firm – 'al dente', as the Italians say, which means just firm enough to bite comfortably but not so soft that it is mushy. And remember, cooking time varies with the shape, thickness and freshness of pasta. Dried pasta – the commercial variety available in this country – should be cooked for 12 to 15 minutes. *Pasta fatta in casa* – the home-made kind – takes only about 5 minutes to cook. Lift out one strand with a fork and bite it to test whether it is ready.

Be careful not to overcook pasta. When done, drain at once in a big colander, shaking it to remove as much water as possible. For best results, serve pasta immediately.

TO KEEP PASTA HOT

If it is impractical to serve pasta as soon as it is cooked, set the colander of drained pasta over a saucepan containing a small amount of boiling water. Cover with a damp towel until ready to serve.

BASIC HOME-MADE EGG PASTA

450g/1lb sifted flour   5ml/1 tsp salt   3 eggs, well beaten

1. Mix flour, salt and eggs and a little water with a fork until pasta dough is just soft enough to form into a ball, adding a little more water if mixture seems too dry.
2. Sprinkle a large pastry board with flour and knead the dough until smooth and elastic (about 15 minutes) on this board with the flat of your hand, sifting a little flour on hands and board from time to time.
3. Divide dough into 6 equal parts and, using a rolling pin, roll out a piece at a time into paper-thin sheets. To do this, roll out in one direction, stretching the pasta dough as you go, and then roll out in the opposite direction. Sprinkle with flour, fold over and repeat. The dough should be just dry enough not to stick to the rolling pin. Repeat this process of rolling, stretching and folding the dough another 2 or 3 times. Repeat with other pieces of pasta dough.

TO MAKE TAGLIATELLE
Prepare egg pasta as above. Dust liberally with flour. Fold loosely and cut into 6mm/¼in strips. Spread on a clean cloth to dry for at least 1 hour before cooking. *See recipe page 287.*

TO MAKE LASAGNE
Prepare egg pasta as above. Dust liberally with flour. Fold loosely and cut into 5cm/2in strips. Spread on a clean cloth to dry for at least 1 hour before cooking. *See recipe page 290.*

TO MAKE CANNELLONI
Prepare egg pasta as above. Dust liberally with flour. Cut into 7.5 x 10cm/3 x 4in rectangles. Spread on a clean cloth to dry for at least 1 hour before cooking. Drop rectangles into boiling salted water, 6 to 8 at a time, and boil for 5 minutes. Remove and drop immediately into cold water. Drain and spread on a clean cloth to dry. Fill as desired and bake until stuffing is cooked through. Serve with TOMATO SAUCE (see page 83) and freshly grated Parmesan cheese.

SPAGHETTI ALLA BOLOGNESE

SERVES 4

450g/1lb spaghetti
45ml/3 tbls butter
60ml/4 tbls olive oil
100g/4oz fat salt pork, or green bacon
*   finely chopped*
1 Spanish onion, finely chopped
2 carrots, finely chopped
1 celery stalk, finely chopped
225g/1/2lb sirloin of beef, minced
strip of lemon peel
bay leaf
60ml/4 tbls tomato purée
300ml/1/2pt **Basic beef stock** *(see page 65)*
150ml/1/4pt dry white wine
salt and freshly ground black pepper
freshly grated nutmeg
60ml/4 tbls double cream
freshly grated Parmesan cheese

1. Heat 30ml/2 tbls butter and the olive oil in a thick-bottomed saucepan; add finely chopped fat salt pork, or green bacon, onion, carrots and celery, and sauté over a medium heat, stirring occasionally, until meat browns.
2. Stir in minced beef and brown evenly, stirring continuously. Add strip of lemon peel, bay leaf, tomato purée, BEEF STOCK and dry white wine, and season with salt, freshly ground black pepper and nutmeg, to taste. Cover and simmer the sauce gently for ½ hour, stirring occasionally.
3. Remove lemon peel and bay leaf from sauce and simmer, uncovered, for ½ hour more, or until sauce has thickened slightly. Add double cream and simmer gently for 2 to 3 minutes more.
4. Meanwhile, cook spaghetti in boiling salted water until tender, but still *al dente*. Drain. Dot with remaining butter and serve immediately with Bolognese sauce and freshly grated Parmesan cheese.

SPAGHETTI SOUFFLE

SERVES 4

100g/4oz spaghetti
30ml/2 tbls butter
30ml/2 tbls flour
300ml/1/2pt milk
100g/4oz freshly grated Parmesan cheese
5ml/1 tsp Dijon mustard
cayenne pepper
salt
5 eggs
Tomato sauce *(see page 83)*

1. Preheat oven to moderate (180°C/350°F/gas 4).
2. Melt butter in the top of a double saucepan. Add flour and blend well. Add milk and stir until sauce begins to thicken, then add grated Parmesan cheese and stir until sauce is smooth and thick. Season with mustard, cayenne and salt, to taste. Allow to cool slightly.
3. Meanwhile, cook spaghetti in boiling salted water until tender, but still *al dente*. Drain.
4. Separate eggs and stir yolks, one by one, into slightly-cooled cheese mixture. Stir spaghetti into cheese mixture.
5. Beat egg whites until they are stiff, but not dry. Fold gently into spaghetti and cheese mixture and pour into a well-buttered 2-pint soufflé dish. Cook in a preheated oven for about 25 minutes, or until done. Serve immediately with well-flavoured TOMATO SAUCE.

SPAGHETTI ALLA MATRICIANA

SERVES 4

450g/1lb spaghetti
30ml/2 tbls olive oil
100g/4oz fat salt pork, diced
1 Spanish onion, finely chopped
2 garlic cloves, finely chopped
800g/1lb 12oz can Italian peeled tomatoes

30ml/2 tbls tomato purée
4 *large tomatoes, peeled, seeded and chopped*
salt and freshly ground black pepper
freshly grated Parmesan cheese
butter

1. Heat olive oil in a thick-bottomed saucepan and sauté diced fat salt pork, finely chopped onion and garlic until golden.
2. Add tomatoes, tomato purée and diced red pepper and season with salt and freshly ground black pepper, to taste. Simmer sauce gently for 1 hour.
3. Meanwhile, cook spaghetti in boiling salted water until tender but still *al dente*. Drain. Dot with butter and serve immediately with *matriciana* sauce and grated Parmesan cheese.

SPAGHETTI ALLA BERSAGLIERA

SERVES 4

450g/1lb spaghetti
60ml/4 tbls olive oil
1 *Spanish onion, finely chopped*
100g/4oz *salame*
60ml/4 tbls dry white wine
1kg/2lb *tomatoes, peeled, seeded and*
    coarsely chopped
salt and freshly ground black pepper
100g/4oz *provolone cheese*
freshly grated Parmesan cheese
butter

1. Heat olive oil in a thick-bottomed saucepan and sauté finely chopped onion until golden.
2. Cut *salame* in thin strips and add to onion mixture. Allow *salame* to take on colour, moisten with dry white wine and cook, stirring, until wine evaporates. Stir in coarsely chopped tomatoes and season with salt and freshly ground black pepper, to taste. Simmer sauce gently for at least 45 minutes.
3. Meanwhile, cook spaghetti in boiling salted

water until tender, but still *al dente*.
4. Cut *provolone* cheese into thin strips and when pasta is almost cooked, add it to the tomato and *salame* sauce and mix well.
5. Drain spaghetti, cover with *Bersagliera* sauce and sprinkle with grated Parmesan cheese. Serve with butter and additional Parmesan cheese.

TAGLIATELLE VERDI

SERVES 4

450g/1lb green noodles
salt
4 *egg yolks*
150ml/¼pt double cream
pinch of ground nutmeg
butter
1 *small can Italian white truffles, thinly sliced*
freshly grated Parmesan cheese

1. Cook green noodles in boiling salted water until tender, but still *al dente*. Drain
2. Meanwhile, beat together egg yolks, cream and a pinch of ground nutmeg.
3. Melt 45ml/3 tbls butter in a thick-bottomed saucepan and sauté thinly sliced truffles for a minute or two.
4. Add noodles to sautéed truffles and pour over the egg yolk and cream mixture. Stir for a minute, remove from heat and add a further 45ml/3 tbls butter. The sauce should be creamy and the eggs should not begin to solidify. Transfer *tagliatelle* to a heated serving dish and serve with additional quantities of butter and freshly grated Parmesan cheese.

SPAGHETTI WITH MUSHROOM SAUCE

SERVES 4

450g/1lb spaghetti
60ml/4 tbls olive oil
butter
2 Spanish onions, coarsely chopped
450g/1lb mushrooms, thinly sliced
2 garlic cloves, crushed
salt and freshly ground black pepper
550g/1¼lb tomatoes, peeled, seeded and coarsely chopped
2.5ml/½ tsp dried oregano, basil, or marjoram
freshly grated Parmesan cheese

1. Heat olive oil and 60ml/4 tbls butter in a thick-bottomed iron *cocotte* or casserole and sauté coarsely chopped onions until golden.
2. Add thinly sliced mushrooms, crushed garlic and 5ml/1 tsp salt to *cocotte,* or casserole, and season with freshly ground black pepper, to ₍aste. Simmer gently, stirring frequently, for 10 minutes. Add tomatoes and oregano, basil, or marjoram and continue to simmer for 30 minutes more.
3. While sauce is simmering, cook spaghetti in boiling salted water until tender, but still *al dente.* Drain. Pour over mushroom sauce and serve with a generous knob of butter and freshly grated Parmesan cheese.

SPAGHETTI ALLA MARINARA

SERVES 4

450g/1lb spaghetti
1 Spanish onion, finely chopped
2 garlic cloves, finely chopped
60ml/4 tbls olive oil
450g/1lb ripe tomatoes, peeled, seeded and coarsely chopped
salt and freshly ground black pepper
5-10ml/1-2 tsp brown sugar

2.5ml/½ tsp dried oregano, basil, or marjoram
450g/1lb prawns, shelled and, if large, chopped
150ml/¼pt dry white wine
60ml/4 tbls finely chopped parsley
butter

1. Heat olive oil in a thick-bottomed saucepan and sauté finely chopped onion and garlic until onion is transparent.
2. Add tomatoes to pan and season with salt and freshly ground black pepper, to taste, brown sugar, and dried oregano, basil, or marjoram. Simmer gently for 15 to 20 minutes.
3. Meanwhile, combine prawns and dry white wine in another saucepan and simmer gently for 5 minutes. Add prawns to tomato sauce together with finely chopped parsley and continue to simmer for 10 minutes more. Correct seasoning.
4. While sauce is simmering, cook spaghetti in boiling salted water until tender, but still *al dente.* Drain. Pour over tomato sauce and serve with a generous knob of butter.

SPAGHETTI AL TONNO

SERVES 4

450g/1lb spaghetti
1 garlic clove
60ml/4 tbls olive oil
90-120ml/6-8 tbls tomato purée
80g/3½oz can tuna fish, drained
4 anchovy fillets
salt and freshly ground black pepper
finely chopped parsley
butter

1. Heat olive oil in a thick-bottomed saucepan and sauté garlic clove until golden. Discard garlic clove.
2. Meanwhile, mix tomato purée with 300ml/½pt water. Add to the garlic oil and simmer gently for 30 minutes.

3. Chop tuna fish coarsely. Chop anchovies finely. Add chopped fish to tomato mixture and season with salt and freshly ground black pepper, to taste. Simmer gently for 15 minutes, stirring occasionally.

4. While sauce is simmering, cook spaghetti in boiling salted water until tender, but still *al dente*. Drain and mix with sauce. Transfer to a heated serving dish; sprinkle with finely chopped parsley; dot with butter and serve.

FETTUCINE WITH PESTO SAUCE

SERVES 4

450g/1lb fettucine
2-3 garlic cloves, finely chopped
60-90ml/4-6 tbls finely chopped basil
60-90ml/4-6 tbls finely chopped parsley
15ml/1 tbls pine nuts
90-120ml/6-8 tbls freshly grated cheese
  (Romano, pecorino or Parmesan)
6 tbls olive oil
salt and freshly ground black pepper
butter
freshly grated Parmesan cheese

1. Pound garlic, basil, parsley, pine nuts and cheese in a mortar until smooth. Gradually add olive oil and whisk until sauce is thick and smooth. Season with salt and black pepper.

2. Meanwhile cook *fettucine* in boiling salted water until tender, but still *al dente*. Drain. Pour over Pesto sauce and toss *fettucine* in sauce until the heat of the pasta 'cooks' the sauce. Serve with a generous knob of butter and freshly grated Parmesan cheese.

ITALIAN SPAGHETTI

SERVES 4

450g/1lb spaghetti
30-60ml/2-4 tbls olive oil

1 Spanish onion, finely chopped
1 garlic clove, finely chopped
212g/7½oz can mushrooms, sliced
800g/1lb 12oz can Italian peeled tomatoes
90ml/6 tbls tomato purée
bay leaf
small strip of lemon peel
1 beef stock cube
salt and freshly ground black pepper
15ml/1 tbls Worcestershire sauce
freshly grated Parmesan cheese
butter

1. Heat olive oil in a thick-bottomed saucepan and sauté finely chopped onion and garlic until onion is transparent.

2. Add sliced mushrooms and sauté for a minute or two more. Then add canned tomatoes, tomato purée, bay leaf, lemon peel, crumbled beef stock cube and season with salt and freshly ground black pepper, to taste. Simmer gently, covered, stirring from time to time, for 1 hour. Just before serving, stir in Worcestershire sauce.

3. Meanwhile cook spaghetti in boiling salted water until tender, but still *al dente*. Drain. Serve with tomato sauce and freshly grated Parmesan cheese and butter.

SPAGHETTI WITH OIL AND GARLIC SAUCE

SERVES 4

450g/1lb spaghetti
salt
butter
olive oil
4 garlic cloves, finely chopped
60ml/4 tbls finely chopped parsley
freshly ground black pepper
freshly grated Parmesan cheese

1. Cook spaghetti in boiling salted water until tender, but still *al dente*. Drain.

2. Meanwhile, heat 60ml/4 tbls butter and olive oil in a thick-bottomed saucepan and simmer finely chopped garlic cloves and parsley until sauce is hot, but do not allow garlic to take on colour.

3. Add drained spaghetti to sauce and stir until thoroughly moistened, adding a little more warm oil, if necessary. Season with salt and black pepper, to taste. Turn spahetti into a heated serving dish, sprinkle with grated Parmesan cheese, dot with butter and serve.

TAGLIATELLE CON TARTUFI

SERVES 4

450g/1lb tagliatelle
butter
2 egg yolks
freshly grated Parmesan cheese
90ml/6 tbls double cream
salt and freshly ground black pepper
1 small can white truffles, finely sliced

1. Cook *tagliatelle* in boiling water until tender, but still *al dente*. Drain.

2. Place noodles in a heated serving bowl, or chafing dish; add 60ml/4 tbls butter, egg yolks, 90ml/6 tbls freshly grated Parmesan cheese and double cream.

3. Toss *tagliatelle* in this mixture until the heat of the noodles 'cooks' the egg and cream sauce. Season with salt and freshly ground black pepper, to taste; sprinkle with finely sliced white truffles and serve immediately with additional quantities of butter and Parmesan cheese.

LASAGNE AL FORNO

SERVES 4

450g/1lb lasagne noodles
salt
butter

225g/¹/₂lb mozzarella cheese, diced
100g/4oz cooked Italian sausage, coarsely chopped
2 hard-boiled eggs, sliced
50g/2oz freshly grated Parmesan cheese
225g/¹/₂lb ricotta cheese, crumbled

TOMATO SAUCE
1.4kg/3lb tomatoes, coarsely chopped
45ml/3 tbls tomato purée
3 large carrots, coarsely chopped
1 Spanish onion, coarsely chopped
3 celery stalks, coarsely chopped
2 garlic cloves, chopped
30ml/2 tbls finely chopped parsley
grated rind of ¹/₂ lemon
salt and freshly ground black pepper
30ml/2 tbls olive oil
30ml/2 tbls butter

1. Preheat oven to moderate (190°C/375°F/gas 5).

2. Cook lasagne noodles, 6 or 8 at a time, in boiling salted water, until they are half done; drain carefully.

3. Line a well-buttered baking dish with a layer of lasagne. Add a layer of diced *mozzarella* cheese, a layer of coarsely chopped Italian sausage and a layer of sliced hard-boiled eggs. Sprinkle generously with freshly grated Parmesan cheese and crumbled *ricotta* cheese and moisten with well-seasoned tomato sauce. Repeat, using the same quantities, finishing with tomato sauce as before. Dot with butter and bake in preheated oven for about 30 minutes. Serve immediately.

4. To make tomato sauce: in a thick-bottomed saucepan combine tomatoes with tomato purée and onion and celery stalks. Stir in chopped garlic, parsley and grated lemon rind. Simmer this mixture for 1¹/₂ hours, then press through a fine sieve. Return sauce to pan; season with salt and black pepper and simmer until thick. Just before using, stir in 30ml/2 tbls each olive oil and butter.

CANNELLONI RIPIENI

SERVES 4

450g/1lb cannelloni
450g/1lb button mushrooms, chopped
225g/¹⁄₂lb cooked ham, or veal, diced
¹⁄₂ Spanish onion, chopped
butter
30ml/2 tbls olive oil
freshly grated Parmesan cheese
salt and freshly ground black pepper

CHEESE SAUCE
30ml/2 tbls butter
30ml/2 tbls flour
600ml/1pt hot milk
60ml/4 tbls freshly grated Parmesan cheese
salt and freshly ground black pepper

1. Preheat oven to moderate 180°C/350°F/gas 4.
2. Cook cannelloni (see page 285).
3. To make filling: sauté chopped mushrooms, diced ham, or veal, and chopped onion in 30ml/2 tbls butter and olive oil until vegetables are cooked. Allow to cool. Add 30ml/2 tbls freshly grated Parmesan cheese and season with salt and freshly ground black pepper, to taste.
4. Place 30ml/2 tbls mushroom filling on each rectangle of cannelloni and roll it carefully around filling. Arrange filled cannelloni in a buttered ovenproof baking dish; cover with cheese sauce; sprinkle generously with freshly grated Parmesan cheese and bake in preheated oven for about 30 minutes, or until golden brown. Serve immediately.
5. To make cheese sauce: melt butter in the top of a double saucepan; stir in flour and blend well. Add hot milk gradually, stirring continuously; season with Parmesan cheese and salt and freshly ground black pepper, to taste, and cook, stirring from time to time, until sauce is smooth and thick.

CHINESE SHO M'AI

MAKES ABOUT 3 DOZEN

450g/1lb sifted flour
225g/¹⁄₂lb minced raw pork
60ml/4 tbls finely chopped water chestnuts
4-6 Chinese mushrooms, soaked and finely chopped
1 slice fresh ginger root, finely chopped
2 spring onions, finely chopped
sake, or dry sherry
soy sauce
15ml/1 tbls corn or olive oil
freshly ground black pepper
*120ml/8 tbls **Basic chicken stock** (see page 66)*

1. To make thin pastry dough: mix flour and 300ml/¹⁄₂pt water. When well mixed, knead dough for 15 minutes. Cover with a damp cloth and leave for 30 minutes.
2. Combine minced pork with finely chopped water chestnuts, Chinese mushrooms, ginger root and spring onions, 15ml-30ml/1-2 tbls *sake,* or dry sherry, and soy sauce, oil and freshly ground black pepper, to taste.
3. When ready to serve: roll dough into a long roll, 2.5cm/1in in diameter. Slice roll thinly, flatten each piece with the palm of your hand and roll out on a floured board to a circle, 7.5-10cm/3-4in in diameter. Place a tablespoon of filling in the middle of each circle and bring edges up over filling, pinching top together to contain filling. Place *sho m'ai* in a wet towel and steam in a steamer for 15 minutes. Serve with a sauce made of 30ml/2 tbls soy sauce, *sake,* or dry sherry and CHICKEN STOCK heated through.

CREOLE JAMBALAYA

For me, one of the most romantic places in the United States, and perhaps the world, is the shadowy, unreal swampland of Louisiana where the grey streamers of Spanish moss trail heavily from the branches of oak trees, removing all sense of depth and turning the *bayoux* into a series of dreamy backdrops for some gigantic ballet.

The trees, growing straight out of the water, seem to float in space, balanced precariously over their own writhing reflections. Strange creatures of these wastes – alligators, raccoons and swimming snakes – contest possession of the dark waterways with men in canoes, Cajun Indians, who have lived in this area for centuries and yet (almost the strangest fact of all about this lost land) speak among themselves perfect seventeenth-century French.

It was from this magic country and its capital, New Orleans, where Indian, Spanish, Negro and French cultures have combined to produce the Creole, that I first discovered how foreign and exotic American regional food could be. It was here that I first tasted baked *pompano* with spicy Creole sauce, red snapper *court-bouillon,* fluffy oyster cutlets, feathery-light beaten biscuits and the heady delights of Creole *gumbos* (highly-flavoured soups of chicken, oysters, shrimps and crabs, seasoned with *okra* and powdered *sassafras*) and Creole *jambalaya,* my favourite of them all.

This great Creole speciality seems to sum up the troubled history of Louisiana, combining the subtlety of the French, the exoticism of the *Conquistadores* and the earthy magic of the Negro plantation cooks. Ham and shrimps or prawns are a necessity for this dish; hot Spanish sausage *(chorizo)* and cubed poached chicken are often added for festive occasions; and even chick-peas can go into the pot with the spices, herbs, rice and tomatoes that give such character and flavour to this great dish.

Creole *jambalaya* takes time to prepare and more time to cook, but the results make the operation more than worth the extra effort involved. I particularly like this dish for its easy stretchability. The recipe here feeds six lavishly, will stretch comfortably to eight, and can be doubled for twelve. Easily manageable with a fork, it is an admirable standby for buffet suppers.

CREOLE JAMBALAYA

SERVES 6

350g/³/4lb cooked ham
350g/³/4lb jumbo prawns
225g/¹/2lb chorizo sausage
60ml/4 tbls olive oil
30ml/2 tbls butter
30ml/2 tbls lard
1 Spanish onion, finely chopped
350g/³/4lb risotto rice
1 celery stalk, chopped
1 green pepper, seeded and chopped
6 tomatoes, peeled, seeded and chopped
65g/2¹/2oz can tomato purée
Basic chicken stock *(see page 66)*
1 small glass of dry white wine
60ml/4 tbls finely chopped parsley (optional)
pitted black olives (optional)

SEASONINGS

1 bay leaf, crumbled
2.5ml/¹/2 tsp dried oregano
large pinch of dried thyme
large pinch of ground cloves
2 garlic cloves
salt and freshly ground black pepper
cayenne pepper

1. If using, preheat oven to cool (110°C/ 225°F/gas ¹/4).
2. Cut ham into 2.5cm/1in squares; shell and clean prawns and cut into smaller pieces if they seem a little large; slice *chorizo* sausage (if not available, substitute pork or garlic sausage).
3. Heat olive oil in a thick-bottomed frying pan and sauté ham chunks, prawns and sausage until they are golden brown. Reserve.
4. Melt butter and lard in the bottom of a thick-bottomed ovenproof casserole and sauté finely chopped onion until transparent. Stir in risotto rice and cook over a low heat, stirring until the rice is golden.
5. Add ham, prawn and sausage mixture to rice, and stir in chopped celery, pepper, tomatoes, tomato purée and seasonings.
6. Bring 1.4L/2¹/2pt CHICKEN STOCK to the boil and pour over *jambalaya* mixture. Cover casserole and simmer over a low heat for 20 to 25 minutes, or until rice is tender, but still moist, adding a little more liquid if necessary.
7. Just before serving, stir in dry white wine and correct seasoning. A little finely chopped parsley, or a handful of pitted black olives, may be added if desired.

QUICK JAMBALAYA

SERVES 4

30ml/2 tbls butter
30ml/2 tbls olive oil
1 Spanish onion, finely chopped
1 green pepper, seeded and finely chopped
1 garlic clove, finely chopped
225g/¹/2lb cooked ham, diced
225g/¹/2lb jumbo prawns, shelled
100g/¹/4pt dry white wine
800g/1lb 12oz can Italian peeled tomatoes
2.5ml/¹/2 tsp dried thyme
1.5ml/¹/4 tsp dried basil, or oregano
1.5ml/¹/4 tsp Tabasco
salt and freshly ground black pepper
225g/¹/2lb risotto rice

1. Heat butter and olive oil in a thick-bottomed casserole and sauté onion, pepper and garlic until onion is transparent.
2. Stir diced ham and prawns into casserole and sauté for a few minutes longer. Add dry white wine and canned tomatoes and season with dried thyme and basil, or oregano, Tabasco and salt and freshly ground black pepper, to taste. Bring gently to the boil.
3. Stir in risotto rice gradually, reduce heat, cover casserole and simmer gently, adding more wine if necessary, for about 20 to 25 minutes. Serve immediately.

SPANISH PAELLA

One of the prime pleasures of travelling is the chance we have to sample foods that differ from our own. Spain is famous for its *empanados,* deep-fried 'little pies' of finely chopped seafood or meat, served in tiny pastry cases; its savoury *tortillas,* thick flat omelettes rich with vegetables and meats; and *gazpacho,* a cold tomato and garlic-based soup with finely chopped trimmings – spring onions, radishes, pimento, cucumber, green pepper, hard-boiled egg and ripe olives – served in individual bowls on the side so that *aficionados* may flavour it as they see fit.

Hearty soups – *cocida,* a knife-and-fork soup that blends the flavours of chicken, beef, smoked ham, chick-peas and other vegetables – and fragrant combinations of beans, beans and pork, chicken and rice, or lobster and rice, are intrinsic parts of this exotic fare, as rich in tradition as the country itself. But perhaps the most famous and most exciting of all is the famous *paella valenciana* – one of the great dishes of the world – which combines many of these ingredients in one delicious dish.

Paella gets its name from the flat, round frying pan with two handles in which this dish is traditionally cooked and served. In Spain these pans range from 15cm/6in in diameter for one portion to about 61cm/2ft for parties. I always think of *paella* as the perfect party dish – glamorous and attractive and as easy to make as it is easy to serve. It combines its four essential ingredients – saffron, pimentos, Spanish onion and rice – with a selection of the following: fried chicken, diced bacon, ham, veal or pork, *chorizo* sausage, mussels or cockles, prawns or shrimps, and (for gala occasions) a lobster.

SPANISH PAELLA

SERVES 4 to 6

12 mussels, washed, scraped and bearded
  (see page 144)
90ml/6 tbls dry white wine
30ml/2 tbls finely chopped onion
60ml/4 tbls finely chopped parsley
1.1kg/2½lb chicken, cut in pieces
225g/½lb lean pork, diced

100g/¼lb chorizo, or pork, sausage, sliced
150ml/¼pt olive oil
1 small lobster, cut in pieces
8 large prawns, shelled
1 Spanish onion, finely shopped
4 small garlic cloves, finely chopped
4 large tomatoes, peeled, seeded and chopped
2 canned pimentos, cut in strips
salt
freshly ground black pepper

1.5ml/¼ tsp cayenne pepper
2.5ml/½ tsp ground saffron
*1L/2pt **Basic chicken stock** (see page 66)*
* (optional)*
450g/1lb risotto rice

1. Steam mussels in dry white wine together with 30ml/2 tbls each finely chopped onion and parsley until shells open. Remove mussels from pan. Reserve. Strain liquor and reserve.
2. Sauté chicken pieces, diced pork and sliced sausage in olive oil in a *paella* or thick-bottomed frying pan until golden on all sides. Remove meats from pan. Reserve.
3. Sauté lobster pieces and prawns in the same pan. Remove shellfish from pan. Reserve.
4. Sauté finely chopped onion and 2 finely chopped garlic cloves in the same pan until onion is transparent. Add peeled and chopped tomatoes and pimento strips and simmer mixture for about 5 minutes, stirring constantly.
5. Return sautéed chicken, pork, sausage and half the lobster, prawns and mussels to pan; add reserved mussel liquor; season with salt and freshly ground black pepper, to taste, and cayenne pepper, and heat through.
6. Mix remaining finely chopped garlic and parsley together with ground saffron in 150ml/¼pt hot CHICKEN STOCK, or water; add to remaining CHICKEN STOCK, or water, and pour over meat and seafood mixture; stir well and slowly bring to the boil again. Add risotto rice and cook for 20 minutes, stirring occasionally.
7. Stir well with a wooden spoon, garnish with remaining lobster, prawns and mussels and continue to cook for a few minutes more, or until rice is tender but still moist. Serve from *paella* pan, or transfer to a heated serving dish.

QUICK PAELLA

SERVES 4-6

30ml/2 tbls butter
30ml/2 tbls olive oil
1 Spanish onion, finely chopped
350g/¾lb risotto rice
*900ml/1½pt hot **Basic chicken stock** (see page 66)*
2.5ml/½ tsp ground saffron
1 small can prawns, drained
1 can small minced clams, with liquid
1 small can mushrooms, quartered
1 small can peas, drained
1 small can pimentos, diced
salt and freshly ground black pepper

1. Heat butter and olive oil in a *paella* or thick-bottomed frying pan; place finely chopped onion in pan and cook slowly, stirring constantly, until onion is transparent.
2. Add risotto rice to pan and cook over medium heat, stirring constantly with a wooden spoon. After a minute or two, stir in 150ml/¼pt hot CHICKEN STOCK and ground saffron. Stir in canned prawns, clams with liquid and quartered mushrooms, and continue cooking for 20 minutes, adding CHICKEN STOCK as needed and stirring from time to time.
3. Add canned peas and diced pimentos; season with salt and freshly ground black pepper, to taste, and cook for a few minutes more until all the stock in the pan is absorbed by the rice and the rice is tender but still moist. Serve from *paella* pan, or transfer to a heated serving dish.

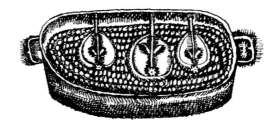

ITALIAN RICE

Italians love rice and are wonderfully creative in their methods of cooking it. Not for them the pallid plain-boiled variety so often served here as a sop for undistinguished gravies of curry and casserole. Instead they combine rice with butter, finely chopped onion and rich chicken stock, and simmer it gently until it is magically tender – neither mushily soft nor unpleasantly hard – but *al dente,* just like their spaghetti. And then they flavour it with saffron, wild mushrooms or, for more special occasions, chicken, shrimps, prawns or thinly sliced white truffles.

Italian cooks respect rice: rarely do they wash it under the tap. Instead they clean it by placing it in cold water for a few minutes, carefully picking out the bits of grit and then they rub it dry, after draining it, between the folds of a tea towel.

For the best results rice should be cooked in only as much liquid as it can absorb, and special care is required in handling it once it is cooked. The grains mash very easily and so, once cooked, they should never be stirred with a spoon, but tossed lightly with a fork. Serve your rice as soon as possible after cooking.

THE RISOTTO

One of the easiest and most delicious methods of cooking rice I know is the risotto. Wash risotto or Italian rice in cold water. Drain and dry thoroughly. Add 45–60ml/3-4 tbls butter; season to taste and add enough chicken stock and dry white wine, beef stock, or a combination of the three, to cover. Bring to the boil, stirring; reduce heat; cover tightly and simmer for 15–18 minutes, adding more liquid if necessary. Uncover, toss lightly with a fork, add a little extra butter and some grated Parmesan cheese and serve. The rice should have absorbed all the liquid and should be separate and moist.

If a rich chicken stock is used in cooking the rice, and you have sautéed the rice with a little finely chopped onion before adding the liquid, it will take on extra strength and flavour. Try adding to it 225g/½lb diced cooked chicken or lamb that has been heated in a little stock with ½ Spanish onion, finely chopped and cooked until golden in 30ml/2 tbls butter. Substitute cooked shrimps, lobster or diced white fish. Then add to any of these 5–10ml/1-2 tsp curry powder, or 2.5ml/½ tsp ground saffron.

RISOTTO ALLA MILANESE

SERVES 4-6

350g/³/4lb risotto rice
butter
60ml/4 tbls raw beef marrow, diced
¹/2 Spanish onion, finely chopped
900ml-1L/1¹/2-2pt hot **Basic beef stock**
  (see page 65)
2.5ml/¹/2 tsp ground saffron
salt and freshly ground black pepper
freshly grated Parmesan cheese

1. Heat 60ml/4 tbls butter and diced raw beef marrow in a thick-bottomed saucepan; place finely chopped onion in pan and cook slowly for 2 to 4 minutes, taking care that the onion does not become brown.
2. Add risotto rice to pan and cook, stirring constantly, until rice is golden. After a minute or so stir in 150ml/¹/4pt hot BEEF STOCK and ground saffron. Continue cooking, adding stock as needed and stirring from time to time, until rice is cooked, 20 to 25 minutes. Season with salt and freshly ground black pepper, to taste. By this time all the stock in the pan should have been absorbed by the rice. Transfer to a heated serving dish and serve with extra butter and Parmesan cheese.

EASY SAFFRON RICE

SERVES 4

350g/³/4lb long-grain rice
2.5ml/¹/2 tsp ground saffron
90ml/6 tbls dry white wine
900ml/1 ¹/2pt hot **Basic chicken stock** *(see*
  page 66)
salt and freshly ground black pepper

1. Stir ground saffron into dry white wine; add to hot CHICKEN STOCK and combine in a thick-bottomed saucepan with rice. Season

with salt and black pepper, to taste.
2. Cover pan and simmer until all the liquid is absorbed and the rice is tender, but still moist.

SAFFRON RICE SALAD

SERVES 4

350g/³/4lb **Saffron rice** *(see recipe above)*
90-120ml/6-8 tbls olive oil
30ml/2 tbls red wine vinegar
60ml/4 tbls finely chopped parsley
1-2 garlic cloves, finely chopped
dry mustard
350g/³/4lb haddock, cooked and flaked
salt and freshly ground black pepper
4 tomatoes, sliced
ripe olives

1. Make a high-flavoured dressing with olive oil and wine vinegar (3 to 4 parts olive oil to 1 part wine vinegar) with parsley, garlic and dry mustard, to taste.
2. Toss cooked SAFFRON RICE and flaked fish in dressing and season generously with salt and freshly ground black pepper, adding more olive oil and wine vinegar if necessary.
3. Transfer salad to a serving platter; garnish with sliced tomatoes and ripe olives and serve.

RISI E BISI

SERVES 4

350g/³/4lb long-grain rice
butter
1 Spanish onion, chopped
2 slices bacon, chopped
225g/¹/2lb fresh peas, shelled, or frozen peas
30ml/2 tbls chopped parsley
900ml-1L/1 ¹/2-2pt **Basic beef stock** *(see page*
  65), or **Basic chicken stock** *(see page 66)*
salt and freshly ground black pepper
freshly grated Parmesan cheese

1. Melt 60ml/4 tbls butter in a thick-bottomed saucepan and sauté chopped onion and bacon until onion is soft and lightly golden.

2. Stir in peas and parsley; pour over half the hot stock; cover and simmer for 15 to 20 minutes (5 minutes only if frozen peas are used).

3. Add rice, cover and cook for 20 minutes, stirring occasionally. Add stock from time to time when needed. Season with salt and freshly ground black pepper, to taste. When rice is done, all the stock in the pan should have been absorbed by the rice, which should be quite moist. Transfer to a heated serving dish and serve sprinkled with freshly grated Parmesan cheese and dotted with butter.

ITALIAN GREEN RICE

SERVES 4

350g/³⁄4lb risotto rice
salt
1 garlic clove
2.5ml/¹⁄2 tsp dried sage
100g/¹⁄4lb butter
30ml/2 tbls cooked strained spinach, or
*   watercress, finely chopped*
50g/2oz Parmesan cheese, freshly grated

1. Cook risotto rice in boiling salted water for 20 to 25 minutes, until rice is tender but still moist.

2. A few minutes before rice is done, gently sauté garlic and sage in butter, being careful not to let butter become brown. Discard garlic as soon as it becomes lightly golden. Set butter aside.

3. Drain rice and place in a heated serving dish. Stir in finely chopped spinach or watercress, and pour over hot garlic-flavoured butter. Mix well; Sprinkle with freshly grated Parmesan cheese and serve immediately.

RISOTTO PROVENCAL

SERVES 4

225g/¹⁄2lb risotto rice
60ml/4 tbls olive oil
1 Spanish onion, finely chopped
salt and freshly ground black pepper

RISOTTO SAUCE

60ml/4 tbls olive oil
30ml/2 tbls finely chopped onion
150ml/¹⁄4 pt dry white wine
4-6 tomatoes, peeled, seeded and coarsely chopped
salt and freshly ground black pepper
2 garlic cloves
60ml/4 tbls finely chopped parsley
1.5ml/¹⁄4 tsp ground saffron
¹⁄2 green pepper, seeded and finely chopped

1. Heat olive oil in a thick-bottomed saucepan and sauté onion until golden.

2. Stir in risotto rice and cook, stirring continuously, until rice is golden. Moisten with 300ml/¹⁄2pt hot water and simmer, stirring from time to time and adding more hot water as liquid is absorbed by the rice. Continue cooking in this way until rice is tender, but still moist, 20 to 25 minutes. Season with salt and freshly ground black pepper. Transfer to a heated serving dish and serve with risotto sauce.

3. To make risotto sauce: heat olive oil in a thick-bottomed saucepan and sauté onion until transparent. Stir in dry white wine and peeled, seeded and coarsely chopped tomatoes. Season with salt and freshly ground black pepper, to taste, and add garlic, finely chopped parsley and saffron. Simmer sauce gently for 20 minutes, then add finely chopped pepper and simmer for a further 10 minutes.

Versatile rice comes in many different forms.

CHINESE FRIED RICE

SERVES 4

450g/1lb cold cooked rice
2 eggs
15ml/1 tbls butter
60ml/4 tbls olive oil
½ Spanish onion, finely chopped
60ml/4 tbls diced cooked pork
60ml/4 tbls diced cooked chicken
60ml/4 tbls diced Italian sausage
4 button mushrooms, diced
10ml/2 tsp soy sauce
salt and freshly ground black pepper

1. Make a thin omelette with the eggs and butter; cut into strips and set aside.
2. Heat olive oil in a thick-bottomed frying pan and, when it is very hot add finely chopped onion and sauté until golden. Add cooked rice, diced meats and mushrooms and sauté gently for 3 to 5 minutes.
3. Just before serving, add egg strips, soy sauce and salt and freshly ground black pepper, to taste. Transfer to a heated dish and serve immediately.

ORANGE RICE WITH BANANAS

SERVES 4

350g/¾lb risotto rice
90ml/6 tbls butter
2 celery stalks, finely chopped
1 Spanish onion, finely chopped
2 garlic cloves, finely chopped
30ml/2 tbls finely chopped parsley
salt and freshly ground black pepper
juice of 2 oranges
*1L/2pt **Basic chicken stock** (see page 66)*
2 bananas, sliced
10ml/2 tsp grated orange rind

1. Melt 60ml/4 tbls butter in a thick-bottomed

saucepan and sauté finely chopped vegetables until soft but not brown.
2. Stir in risotto rice and cook, stirring continuously, until golden. Add finely chopped parsley and season with salt and freshly ground black pepper, to taste. Add orange juice and hot CHICKEN STOCK; cover and simmer, stirring occasionally, for 20 to 25 minutes, or until rice is tender, but still moist.
3. Meanwhile, sauté sliced bananas in remaining butter until golden. Sprinkle with grated orange rind and stir gently into rice mixture. Transfer to a heated serving dish and serve.

RISOTTO AL TONNO

SERVES 4

350g/¾lb risotto rice
60ml/4 tbls olive oil
butter
1 Spanish onion, finely chopped
30ml/2 tbls tomato purée
175ml/6fl oz dry white wine
212g/7½oz tuna fish, drained and pounded
*900ml-1L/1½-2pt **Basic chicken stock** (see page 66)*
salt and freshly ground black pepper
freshly grated Parmesan cheese

1. To make sauce: heat olive oil and 30ml/2 tbls butter in a thick-bottomed saucepan and sauté half the finely chopped onion until golden. Combine tomato purée and 90ml/6 tbls dry white wine and stir into onion mixture together with pounded tuna fish. Heat through, stirring constantly. Keep warm.
2. To make risotto: sauté remaining onion in 60ml/4 tbls butter until transparent. Add risotto rice and cook, stirring continuously, until rice is golden. Add 90ml/6 tbls dry white wine and hot CHICKEN STOCK and simmer, stirring occasionally, for 20 to 25 minutes, or until rice is tender, but still moist.

3. 5 minutes before serving, stir in tuna sauce. Season with salt and freshly ground black pepper, to taste. Transfer to a heated serving dish and serve with additional butter and freshly grated Parmesan cheese.

RICE PILAFF

SERVES 4

350g/³⁄₄lb long-grain rice
90ml/6 tbls butter
½ Spanish onion, finely chopped
*600-900ml/1-1¹⁄₂pt **Basic chicken stock**
  (see page 66)*
salt and freshly ground black pepper
100g/4oz mushrooms, sliced and sautéed in butter

1. If using, preheat oven to moderate (190°C/375°F/gas 5).
2. Melt 60ml/4 tbls butter in a thick-bottomed ovenproof casserole and brown finely chopped onion.
3. Add rice to casserole and stir for a minute or two, until the grains of rice are coated with butter. Add 600ml/1pt hot CHICKEN STOCK and season with salt and freshly ground black pepper, to taste. Cover casserole and bake in preheated oven for about 15 to 20 minutes, or until rice is tender but still moist, stirring occasionally and adding a little more CHICKEN STOCK, if necessary. Or cook over direct heat for about 20 minutes stirring occasionally.
4. Transfer rice to a heated serving dish; add 30ml/2 tbls butter and sautéed sliced mushrooms; toss with a fork and serve immediately.

RISOTTO ALLA PAESANA

SERVES 6

350g/³⁄₄lb risotto rice
100g/4oz red kidney beans, soaked overnight and drained
salt
60ml/4 tbls butter
30ml/2 tbls olive oil
3 slices bacon, diced
1 small onion, finely chopped
50g/2oz carrots, diced
2 courgettes, diced
2 celery stalks, diced
*300ml/¹⁄₂pt **Basic beef stock** (see page 65)*
freshly ground black pepper
freshly grated Parmesan cheese

1. Place beans in a thick-bottomed saucepan with lightly salted water. Bring to the boil; boil for at least 10 minutes, lower the heat, cover and cook for 1 hour, or until tender. Reserve.
2. Combine butter and olive oil in another saucepan and sauté diced bacon and onion until onion is transparent.
3. Add carrots, courgettes and celery and continue to cook, uncovered, for 3 or 4 minutes, stirring occasionally. Pour over hot BEEF STOCK and simmer, until almost all the liquid has evaporated. Add risotto rice to this mixture and cook for 2 minutes over low heat, stirring occasionally.
4. Drain beans, reserving bean stock.
5. Add beans to rice, together with 700ml/1¹⁄₄pt bean stock and cook over medium heat for 20 to 25 minutes, stirring occasionally. Continue adding bean stock as needed until rice is done. When rice is tender, but still moist, season with salt and freshly ground black pepper, to taste, and add freshly grated Parmesan cheese. Transfer to a heated serving dish and serve immediately.

CHAPTER 14

SALADS

— TOSSED GREEN SALAD —

WHAT IS SIMPLER or more summery than a fresh green salad? The very sound of the word evokes visions of crisp green lettuce leaves, carefully washed and dried leaf by leaf, liberally bathed with fruity olive oil and flavoured with a touch of red wine vinegar, a hint of garlic and a dusting of salt and freshly ground black pepper.

There are two secrets to perfect salad dressing: the preparation of the salad itself and the preparation of the dressing. Salad greens must be thoroughly washed and dried and preferably chilled before being mixed with the dressing. No water should be allowed to drip from the greens into the dressing. If you do not own a salad basket, an easy way to dry well-washed salad greens is to pile them loosely in the centre of a clean tea towel and pat the leaves dry. Then gather up the edges and corners of the towel; shake out any remaining moisture over the sink and chill in the refrigerator until crisp.

There seems to be a mystery about a simple so-called French dressing; so many people put sugar, water, paprika or mustard into it; some use Worcestershire sauce or Tabasco. Others depend on bottled preparations rather than use their own initiative and skill to achieve what should be one of the most individual dishes of the entire meal.

I usually prefer to mix my salad dressing directly in the salad bowl – a wooden one, of course, and washed as seldom as possible – blending the olive oil and vinegar with pepper, salt, garlic and herbs, before I add the lettuce and salad greens. Then all one has to do at table is to give a final toss to the ingredients to ensure that every leaf is glistening with the dressing. A final check for flavour, and the salad is ready to serve.

Vary a tossed green salad with an assortment of colourful vegetables such as tomatoes and red peppers.

SALAD DRESSINGS

Here is my recipe for salad dressing to make a tossed salad for 4 to 6.

FRENCH DRESSING: To 30ml/2 tbls of red wine vinegar add salt and freshly ground black pepper, to taste; stir the mixture well; add 90-120ml/6-8 tbls olive oil and beat with a fork until the mixture thickens. For a creamier dressing, put an ice cube in the mixing bowl and stir the dressing for a minute or two longer. Remove the cube and serve.

TARRAGON DRESSING: Add 5ml/1 tsp finely chopped tarragon leaves to French dressing.

CURRY DRESSING: Add 2.5ml/½ tsp curry powder and 5ml/1 tsp finely chopped shallots to French dressing.

CAPER DRESSING: Add 5ml/1 tsp chopped capers, ½ clove garlic, crushed, and anchovy paste, to taste, to French dressing.

ROQUEFORT DRESSING: Add 30-60ml/2-4 tbls crumbled Roquefort cheese to French dressing and blend well. Chill thoroughly before using.

TO MAKE SALAD

Wash lettuce well in a large quantity of water. Drain well and dry thoroughly in a cloth or a salad basket so that there is no water on them to dilute the dressing. Break lettuce leaves into a salad bowl. Leaves should be left whole, or torn, never cut.

For variety's sake, the lettuce can be augmented with other salad greens in season – cos lettuce, endive, chicory, spinach leaves if they are very young and tender, watercress and French *mâche*. Fresh green herbs – chervil, basil and tarragon – are often used to add flavour and freshness to green salads. I also like *eau-de-Cologne* mint, which lends a certain purple spiciness to a summer salad, or even a chopped nasturtium leaf or two from the garden.

Shallots, so finely chopped they are almost minced, are excellent in a tossed green salad, as are chives, especially when combined with diced or finely sliced avocado pear as a garnish. Sometimes a little 'crunch appeal' seems warranted in a summer salad; in these cases I use a little chopped celery, green pepper, or *finocchio,* the green-white root of fennel with its delicate aniseed flavour.

SALADE NICOISE

SERVES 4-6

4 tomatoes, seeded and quartered
½ Spanish onion, sliced
1 green pepper, seeded and sliced
8 radishes, trimmed

2 lettuce hearts
4 celery stalks, sliced
200g/7oz can tuna fish, drained and coarsely
　chopped
8 anchovy fillets
2 hard-boiled eggs, quartered
8 ripe olives

SALAD DRESSING

30ml/2 tbls red wine vinegar, or lemon juice
90ml/6 tbls olive oil
salt and freshly ground black pepper
12 fresh basil leaves, coarsely chopped

1. Arrange prepared vegetables in a salad bowl, placing neatly on top the tuna fish, anchovy fillets and quartered hard-boiled eggs. Dot with ripe olives.
2. Make salad dressing by combining red wine vinegar, or lemon juice, olive oil and basil, and seasoning with salt and freshly ground black pepper, to taste. Sprinkle over salad and serve.

CHILLED WATERCRESS SALAD

SERVES 4-6

4 bunches watercress
2 oranges

CURRY DRESSING
90-120ml/6-8 tbls olive oil
30ml/2 tbls red wine vinegar
15ml/1 tbls lemon juice
15ml/1 tbls curry powder
salt and freshly ground black pepper
5ml/1 tsp finely chopped shallots

1. Wash watercress and remove stalks and any damaged leaves. Dry carefully and chill wrapped in a damp tea towel until ready to use.
2. Peel oranges and cut into thin slices. Chill.
3. To prepare curry dressing: combine olive oil, red wine vinegar, lemon juice and curry powder. Season with salt and freshly ground black pepper, to taste. Chill.
4. Just before serving, place watercress in a salad bowl; arrange orange slices on top; add finely chopped shallots to curry dressing and pour over salad. Toss at the table so that each leaf is glistening.

TOSSED GREEN SALAD WITH AVOCADO

SERVES 4-6

2 heads lettuce
1 bunch watercress
1 avocado pear
lemon juice
1 garlic clove, cut
10ml/2 tsp chives, finely chopped
90-120ml/6-8 tbls olive oil
30ml/2 tbls red wine vinegar
salt and freshly ground black pepper

1. Wash and prepare lettuce and watercress. Shake dry in a salad basket, or dry each lettuce leaf in a tea towel. Wrap in a dry tea towel and allow to crisp in the refrigerator.
2. Cut avocado pear in half; remove stone and peel. Slice and marinate in lemon juice to prevent flesh turning brown.
3. Rub a salad bowl with cut garlic clove. Arrange lettuce and watercress in bowl.
4. Chop garlic finely and sprinkle over salad together with finely chopped chives. Dress with an olive oil and red wine vinegar dressing (3 to 4 parts olive oil to 1 part red wine vinegar) and season with salt and black pepper, to taste. Garnish with avocado slices.

TOSSED GREEN SALAD WITH HERBS

SERVES 4-6

2 heads lettuce
choice of salad greens: endive, young spinach,
*   watercress, chicory, dandelion, mâche, etc.*
1 garlic clove, cut
5ml/1 tsp each finely chopped fresh basil, marjoram,
*   chervil and chives*
90-120ml/6-8 tbls olive oil
30ml/2 tbls red wine vinegar
salt and freshly ground black pepper

1. Wash and prepare lettuce and salad greens of your choice. Shake dry in a salad basket, or dry carefully in a tea towel. Wrap in dry tea towel and allow to crisp in the refrigerator until ready to use.
2. Rub a salad bowl with cut garlic clove. Arrange lettuce and salad greens in bowl.
3. Chop garlic finely and sprinkle over the salad together with finely chopped herbs. Dress with an olive oil and red wine vinegar dressing (3 to 4 parts olive oil to 1 part red wine vinegar) and season with salt and freshly ground black pepper, to taste. Just before serving, toss salad until each leaf is glistening.

DELMONICO SALAD

SERVES 4-6

2 heads lettuce
90-120ml/6-8 tbls olive oil
30ml/2 tbls red wine vinegar
30ml/2 tbls double cream
30ml/2 tbls Roquefort cheese, crumbled
freshly ground black pepper
Tabasco
1 hard-boiled egg, finely chopped
1 rasher cooked bacon, finely chopped

1. Wash and prepare lettuce. Shake dry in a salad basket, or dry each leaf carefully in a tea towel. Wrap in dry tea towel and allow to crisp in the refrigerator until ready to use.
2. To make dressing: combine olive oil and red wine vinegar (3 to 4 parts olive oil to 1 part red wine vinegar), cream and crumbled Roquefort cheese and whisk until smooth. Add freshly ground black pepper and Tabasco, to taste, and stir in finely chopped hard-boiled egg and bacon.
3. Arrange lettuce in a salad bowl. Pour over dressing; toss salad until each leaf is glistening and serve.

CHASEN'S CAESAR SALAD

SERVES 4-6

2 heads Cos lettuce
juice of 1¹/₂ lemons
30ml/2 tbls garlic oil (made by slicing 1 garlic clove into a little olive oil. Leave for 2 hours, then remove garlic)
7.5ml/1¹/₂ tsp Worcestershire sauce
90ml/6 tbls **French dressing** *(see page 304)*
1 one-minute coddled egg
4 slices toast, cut into 1.2cm/¹/₂in squares
freshly ground black pepper
60ml/4 tbls grated Parmesan cheese

1. Wash Cos lettuce and shake dry in a salad basket, or dry each leaf carefully in a tea towel. Break lettuce into fairly big pieces, wrap in a dry tea towel and allow to crisp in the refrigerator until ready to use.
2. Combine lemon juice, garlic oil, Worcestershire sauce, FRENCH DRESSING and coddled egg and whisk lightly until well blended.
3. Just before serving, place lettuce in a salad bowl; add toast *croûtons*, freshly ground black pepper, to taste, and freshly grated Parmesan cheese. Pour over salad dressing and toss until each leaf is coated and there is no excess dressing left in the bottom of the bowl. Serve immediately.

CAESAR SALAD WITH HAM

SERVES 4-6

1 head Cos lettuce
90-120ml/6-8 tbls olive oil
30ml/2 tbls red wine vinegar
90ml/6 tbls freshly grated Parmesan cheese
1-2 fat garlic cloves, mashed
salt and freshly ground black pepper
lemon juice
2 slices bread, rubbed with cut garlic clove and diced
30ml/2 tbls butter

225g/¹/2lb cooked ham, diced
2 egg yolks
6 anchovy fillets

1. Wash and prepare Cos lettuce. Shake dry in a salad basket, or dry each leaf carefully in a tea towel. Break lettuce into fairly big pieces, wrap in a dry tea towel and allow to crisp in the refrigerator until ready to use.
2. Combine olive oil, red wine vinegar, cheese and garlic in a salad bowl and season with salt and freshly ground black pepper and lemon juice, to taste.
3. Sauté diced bread in butter and drain on absorbent paper. Add diced ham and lettuce and toss lightly. Then add egg yolks and toss salad until every leaf glistens. Top with garlic *croûtons* and anchovy fillets and serve.

SALADE PAYSANNE

SERVES 4-6

2 heads lettuce
100g/4oz fat salt pork, finely diced
30ml/2 tbls olive oil
2 hard-boiled eggs, chopped
15ml/1 tbls finely chopped chervil, tarragon, or basil
salt and freshly ground black pepper
red wine vinegar

1. Wash and prepare lettuce. Shake dry in a salad basket, or dry each leaf carefully in a tea towel. Wrap in a dry tea towel and allow to crisp in the refrigerator until ready to use.
2. Sauté finely diced fat salt pork in olive oil until it is golden brown.
3. Place lettuce in a salad bowl; sprinkle with diced pork and hot fat. Add chopped hard-boiled eggs, and herbs. Season with salt, freshly ground black pepper and red wine vinegar, to taste. Mix well and serve immediately.

RUSSIAN SALAD

SERVES 4-6

100g/4oz dried beans, soaked overnight and drained
salt
450g/1lb new potatoes, scraped, cooked and diced
225g/¹/2lb string beans, cooked and sliced
4-6 carrots, cooked and sliced
100g/4oz fresh peas, cooked
30ml/2 tbls red wine vinegar
30ml/2 tbls olive oil
freshly ground black pepper
2-3 hard-boiled eggs
15ml/1 tbls capers
15ml/1 tbls chopped pickles
30ml/2 tbls finely chopped parsley
300-425ml/¹/2-³/4pt well-flavoured **Mayonnaise** *(see page 85)*

1. Place dried beans in a thick-bottomed saucepan with lightly salted water. Bring to the boil, cover and cook for 1 hour, or until tender. Drain.
2. Combine diced potatoes with sliced string beans and carrots, peas and beans, reserving a few of each vegetable for garnish. Moisten with red wine vinegar and olive oil and season with salt and freshly ground black pepper, to taste. Toss and chill.
3. Separate whites and yolks of hard-boiled eggs. Chop egg whites. Sieve egg yolks.
4. Add capers, chopped pickles and finely chopped parsley, chopped egg whites and enough MAYONNAISE to bind mixture loosely. Toss ingredients and mound in a salad bowl. Decorate top and sides with remaining MAYONNAISE and reserved assorted vegetables. Sprinkle sieved egg yolks over top and serve.

CHEF'S SALAD

SERVES 4-6

1 head lettuce
1 bunch watercress
100g/4oz cooked chicken
100g/4oz smoked ox tongue
100g/4oz cooked ham
100g/4oz Swiss cheese
2 hard-boiled eggs, quartered
4 tomatoes, cut in wedges
150ml/¹/4pt **French dressing** *(see page 304)*

1. Wash lettuce. Shake dry in a salad basket, or dry each leaf carefully in a tea towel. Chop lettuce coarsely, wrap in a dry tea towel and allow to crisp in the refrigerator until ready to use.
2. Wash watercress and remove stalks and any damaged leaves. Dry carefully and chill in a damp tea towel until ready to use.
3. Cut chicken, smoked ox tongue, ham and Swiss cheese into thin strips.
4. Arrange coarsely chopped lettuce in the bottom of a salad bowl and arrange meat and cheese strips, according to colour, on bed of lettuce. Garnish with quartered hard-boiled eggs and tomato wedges. Place a cluster of watercress in centre of bowl and serve with well-flavoured FRENCH DRESSING.

SALADE CAROLINE COCHONNE

SERVES 4-6

350g/³/4lb Gruyère cheese, diced
350g/³/4lb ham, diced
175-225ml/6-8fl oz olive oil
60-90ml/4 tbls red wine vinegar
salt and freshly ground black pepper
1 head lettuce
finely chopped parsley

1. Combine diced Gruyère cheese and ham in

a porcelain or earthenware bowl (not metal).
2. Prepare salad dressing by combining olive oil and red wine vinegar and seasoning with salt and freshly ground black pepper, to taste.
3. Pour half the dressing over cheese and ham, toss well and allow to marinate in the refrigerator for 1 hour.
4. Meanwhile wash and prepare lettuce, shake dry in a salad basket, or dry each leaf carefully in a tea towel. Wrap in a dry tea towel and allow to crisp in the refrigerator until ready to use.
5. Just before serving, arrange lettuce in the bottom of a salad bowl. Drain diced cheese and ham and place in the centre. Sprinkle with finely chopped parsley and serve with remaining salad dressing.

ITALIAN VEGETABLE SALAD

SERVES 4-6

1 head lettuce
4 tomatoes
red wine vinegar
olive oil
salt and freshly ground black pepper
1 small cucumber
2 small green peppers
100g/4oz button mushrooms
15ml/1 tbls finely chopped parsley
2 hard-boiled eggs, quartered

ITALIAN DRESSING
150ml/¹/4pt olive oil
4 anchovy fillets, finely chopped
juice of 1 large lemon
5ml/1 tsp capers
salt and freshly ground black pepper

1. Wash and prepare lettuce. Shake dry in a salad basket, or dry each leaf carefully in a tea towel. Wrap in a dry tea towel and allow to crisp in the refrigerator until ready to use.

2. Quarter tomatoes and toss lightly in a little red wine vinegar and olive oil seasoned with salt and freshly ground black pepper, to taste.

3. Peel cucumber and slice thinly; toss lightly in a little red wine vinegar and olive oil seasoned with salt and freshly ground black pepper, to taste.

4. Remove seeds and pith from green peppers, slice in thin strips and toss lightly in a little olive oil and red wine vinegar seasoned with salt and freshly ground black pepper, to taste.

5. Slice button mushrooms thinly. Toss lightly in a little wine vinegar and olive oil to which you have added the chopped parsley.

6. Arrange lettuce in the bottom of a salad bowl. Assemble salads on the bed of lettuce; garnish with quartered hard-boiled eggs; sprinkle liberally with Italian dressing and serve.

7. To make Italian dressing: warm the olive oil slightly and add finely chopped anchovy fillets, mashing them with a fork until they are well blended with the warmed oil. Add lemon juice, capers, salt and freshly ground black pepper, to taste.

BEAN AND RAW SPINACH SALAD

SERVES 4-6

350g/³/4lb dried kidney or broad beans, soaked overnight and drained
90-120ml/6-8 tbls olive oil
30ml/2 tbls red wine vinegar, or lemon juice
5ml/1 tsp finely chopped fresh marjoram
5ml/1 tsp finely chopped basil
10ml/2 tsp finely chopped parsley
1 garlic clove, finely chopped
salt and freshly ground black pepper
450g/1lb young spinach leaves, trimmed
1 small onion, thinly sliced into rings

1. Cook kidney or broad beans until tender; cool and drain.

2. Mix beans with a dressing made of olive oil, wine vinegar, or lemon juice, finely chopped herbs and garlic, and season with salt and freshly ground black pepper, to taste.

3. Serve salad on a bed of tender young spinach leaves and garnish with thinly sliced onion rings.

ROASTED OR GRILLED PEPPERS FOR SALADS

Perfectionists prefer to peel the sweet pepper. The easiest way I know of preparing peppers for use in appetiser salads and other dishes, is to grill the peppers as close to the heat as possible, turning them until the skin is charred on all sides. The skins can then be easily rubbed off under cold running water. The peppers are then cored, seeded, sliced into thick strips and marinated in a well-flavoured ***French dressing*** (see page 304). Peppers prepared in this way will keep a long time under refrigeration if packed in oil in tightly lidded sterilised jars. Serve as a salad on a bed of lettuce with a lattice of anchovy fillets for garnish.

PROVENCAL PEPPER SALAD

SERVES 6

2 large green peppers
2 large sweet red peppers
6 firm tomatoes
6 hard-boiled eggs
24 anchovy fillets
24 ripe olives

HERB DRESSING
2 garlic cloves, finely chopped
15ml/1 tbls each finely chopped parsley, tarragon, chervil and chives
90-120ml/6-8 tbls olive oil
30ml/2 tbls red wine vinegar
salt and freshly ground black pepper

1. Preheat grill to high.

2. Prepare herb dressing by combining finely chopped garlic and herbs with olive oil, wine vinegar, salt and black pepper, to taste.

3. To prepare peppers: place peppers under preheated grill, as close to the heat as possible. Cook, turning peppers continually, until skin on all sides has charred. Rub skin off under cold water. Cut peppers in lengths, 4 or 6 to each pepper, keeping colours separate. Wash off seeds and excess fibre; drain on absorbent paper.

4. Slice tomatoes thickly and cover bottom of a flat serving dish with slices. Sprinkle with a quarter of the herb dressing; add a layer of prepared green pepper slices; sprinkle with herb dressing; add a layer of red pepper slices and sprinkle with herb dressing.

5. Slice hard-boiled eggs into rings; cover red pepper with a layer of sliced eggs and pour over remaining herb dressing.

6. Arrange anchovy fillets in a lattice on top of sliced eggs and place a ripe olive in the centre of each lattice square. Chill salad in refrigerator for at least 30 minutes before serving.

GERMAN POTATO SALAD

SERVES 4-6

1kg/2lb new potatoes
1 head lettuce
salt
15ml/1 tbls sugar
30ml/2 tbls red wine vinegar
150ml/¼pt soured cream
5ml/1 tsp prepared mustard
½ Spanish onion, finely chopped
5ml/1 tsp celery seeds
lemon juice
freshly ground black pepper
30ml/2 tbls finely chopped parsley
tomato wedges
2 hard-boiled eggs, sliced

1. Wash and prepare lettuce. Shake dry in a salad basket, or dry each leaf carefully in a tea towel. Wrap in a dry tea towel and allow to crisp in the refrigerator until ready to use.

2. Scrub new potatoes; cook in boiling salted water until just tender, 15 to 20 minutes. Drain. Peel and slice.

3. Place potatoes in a bowl and sprinkle with sugar and red wine vinegar. Add soured cream, blended with mustard, finely chopped onion, celery seeds, lemon juice and salt and black pepper, to taste. Toss well.

4. Line a salad bowl with lettuce. Arrange potato salad in lettuce-lined bowl, garnish with finely chopped parsley, tomato wedges and sliced hard-boiled eggs and serve.

WATERCRESS AND RADISH SALAD

SERVES 4-6

1 head lettuce
1 bunch watercress
1 bunch radishes

FRENCH DRESSING

90-120ml/6-8 tbls olive oil
30ml/2 tbls red wine vinegar
dry mustard
salt and freshly ground black pepper
1 garlic clove, finely chopped (optional)

1. Wash and prepare lettuce. Shake dry in a salad basket, or dry each leaf carefully in a tea towel. Wrap in a dry tea towel and allow to crisp in the refrigerator until ready to use.

2. Wash watercress and remove stalks and any damaged leaves. Dry carefully and chill in a damp tea towel until ready to use.

3. Trim radishes and slice paper thin. Chill.

4. To make French dressing: combine olive oil and red wine vinegar and season with dry mustard, salt and freshly ground black pepper, to taste. Finely chopped garlic may be added.

5. To assemble salad: arrange lettuce in a salad bowl and spread watercress on top. Scatter radishes over this, pour over French dressing and toss until every ingredient glistens.

ITALIAN TUNA SALAD

SERVES 4-6

1 head lettuce
4 boiled new potatoes, sliced
4 ripe tomatoes, sliced
4 black and 4 green olives, quartered
2 celery stalks, sliced
200g/7oz can tuna fish, drained and flaked
60-90ml/4-6 tbls olive oil
30ml/2 tbls lemon juice
15ml/1 tbls chopped anchovy fillets
30ml/2 tbls finely chopped parsley
salt and freshly ground black pepper

1. Wash and prepare lettuce. Shake dry in a salad basket, or dry each leaf carefully in a tea towel. Wrap in a dry tea towel and allow to crisp in the refrigerator until ready to use.
2. Line a salad bowl with lettuce. Arrange a layer of sliced potatoes in lettuce-lined bowl; top with a layer of sliced tomatoes and sprinkle with quartered olives, sliced celery stalks and flaked tuna fish.
3. Make a dressing by combining lemon juice, olive oil, chopped anchovy fillets and parsley. Season with salt and freshly ground black pepper, to taste, and pour over salad. Just before serving, toss salad until ingredients glisten.

LEEK AND TOMATO SALAD

SERVES 4-6

1 head Cos lettuce
2 leeks
4 ripe tomatoes
5ml/1 tsp each parsley and basil, finely chopped

FRENCH DRESSING
90-120ml/6-8 tbls olive oil
30ml/2 tbls red wine vinegar
dry mustard
salt and freshly ground black pepper
1 garlic clove, finely chopped (optional)

1. Wash and prepare Cos lettuce. Shake dry in a salad basket, or dry each leaf carefully in a tea towel. Wrap in a dry tea towel and allow to crisp in the refrigerator until ready to use.
2. Wash leeks carefully and cut off roots and green tops. Chop white parts coarsely.
3. Cut tomatoes in wedges.
4. To make French dressing: combine olive oil and red wine vinegar and season with dry mustard, salt and black pepper, to taste and finely chopped garlic, if desired.
5. Place lettuce in a salad bowl. Arrange coarsely chopped leeks and tomato wedges in bowl; sprinkle with finely chopped parsley and basil and pour over French dressing. Just before serving, toss salad until every ingredient glistens.

WALDORF SALAD

SERVES 4-6

1 head lettuce
6 red-skinned eating apples
juice of 2 lemons
6 celery stalks, sliced
50g/2oz halved walnuts
Mayonnaise *(see page 85), or* **French dressing**
  (see above)

1. Wash and prepare lettuce. Shake dry in a salad basket, or dry each leaf carefully in a tea towel. Wrap in a dry tea towel and allow to crisp in the refrigerator until ready to use.
2. Core and dice apples and sprinkle with lemon juice.
3. Add sliced celery stalks to diced apples, to-

gether with walnut halves and toss in MAYON-NAISE, or FRENCH DRESSING, according to taste.
4. Line a salad bowl with lettuce. Pile Waldorf salad into lettuce-lined bowl and then serve.

CHICKEN WALDORF

SERVES 4-6

350g/³/4lb cooked chicken, diced
1 head lettuce
6 red-skinned eating apples
juice of 2 lemons
6 celery stalks, sliced
50g/2oz halved walnuts
Mayonnaise *(see page 85), or* **French dressing**
*   (see page 304)*

1. Wash and prepare lettuce. Shake dry in a salad basket, or dry each leaf carefully in a tea towel. Wrap in a dry tea towel and allow to crisp in the refrigerator until ready to use.
2. Core and dice apples and sprinkle with lemon juice.
3. Add diced chicken to diced apples together with sliced celery and walnut halves and toss in MAYONNAISE, or FRENCH DRESSING, according to taste.
4. Line a salad bowl with lettuce. Pile salad into lettuce-lined bowl and serve.

APPLE HERRING SALAD

SERVES 4-6

2 filleted salt herrings
olive oil
red wine vinegar
4 boiled potatoes, sliced
4 tart apples, diced
2 hard-boiled eggs, chopped
1 dill pickle, chopped
60ml/4 tbls stuffed olives, sliced

1 small onion, finely chopped
salt and freshly ground black pepper

1. Cut filleted herrings in small pieces and place in a porcelain or earthenware bowl (not metal). Pour over enough olive oil and red wine vinegar to cover; cover bowl and marinate in the refrigerator for 2-3 hours. Drain.
2. Combine potatoes, apples, eggs, pickle, olives and onion in a salad bowl. Add herring pieces.
3. Make a dressing of olive oil and red wine vinegar (3 to 4 parts olive oil to 1 part red wine vinegar) and season with salt and freshly ground black pepper, to taste. Pour over salad.

SPANISH SEAFOOD SALAD

SERVES 6-8

1 head lettuce
1 head Cos lettuce
225g/¹/2lb prawns, shelled
225g/¹/2lb cooked lobster meat, cut into 1.2cm/
*   ¹/2in cubes*
225g/¹/2lb cooked white fish, cut into 1.2cm/
*   ¹/2in cubes*
225g/¹/2lb cooked crabmeat, flaked
4 tomatoes, cut into wedges
8 large ripe olives
French dressing *(see page 304) (optional)*

SAFFRON DRESSING (optional)
150ml/¹/4pt **Mayonnaise** *(see page 85)*
60ml/4 tbls lemon juice
30ml/2 tbls grated onion
5ml/1 tsp prepared mustard
salt and white pepper
generous pinch of ground saffron

1. Wash and prepare lettuce and Cos lettuce. Shake dry in a salad basket, or dry each leaf carefully in a tea towel. Wrap in a dry tea towel and allow to crisp in the refrigerator.

An attractive salad for a dinner party, cauliflower salad is garnished with a lattice of anchovies.

2. Line a salad bowl with lettuce. Arrange prawns, lobster, white fish, and crabmeat, cut in cubes, in lettuce-lined bowl and garnish with tomato wedges and ripe olives. Serve salad with a well-flavoured FRENCH DRESSING or saffron dressing.

3. To make saffron dressing: combine MAYONNAISE with lemon juice, grated onion and prepared mustard and season with salt and white pepper, to taste. Dissolve ground saffron in a little hot water and stir into dressing. Chill before use.

CAULIFLOWER SALAD

SERVES 4-6

1 head cauliflower
salt
6 anchovy fillets, finely chopped
12 black olives, pitted and chopped
45ml/3 tbls finely chopped parsley
1 garlic clove, finely chopped
15ml/1 tbls finely chopped capers
90ml/6 tbls olive oil

30ml/2 tbls red wine vinegar
freshly ground black pepper

1. Remove green leaves from cauliflower, trim stem and cut off any bruised spots. Break or cut cauliflower into flowerets and poach in lightly-salted water for about 5 minutes. Drain and place in a bowl of cold salted water until ready to use. Drain again. Dry thoroughly.

2. Mix finely chopped anchovies, olives, parsley, garlic and capers with olive oil and red wine vinegar; add cauliflowerets and season with salt and freshly ground black pepper, to taste. Arrange in a salad bowl and serve.

RAW MUSHROOM SALAD

SERVES 6

450g/1lb button mushrooms
120ml/8 tbls olive oil
juice of 1 lemon
salt and freshly ground black pepper
5ml/1 tsp finely chopped chives
5ml/1 tsp finely chopped parsley

1. Remove stems from mushrooms; wipe caps clean with a damp cloth.
2. Slice caps thinly, and arrange them in a salad bowl.
3. Make a dressing by combining olive oil and lemon juice with salt and freshly ground black pepper, to taste. Pour over mushrooms; toss carefully and chill in the refrigerator for 2 hours.
4. Sprinkle salad with finely chopped chives and parsley to serve.

COURGETTES EN SALADE

SERVES 4

1 head lettuce
8 courgettes, 10cm/4in long
salt
½ Spanish onion, finely chopped
1 garlic clove, finely chopped
*well-flavoured **French dressing** (see page 304)*
4 tomatoes, peeled, seeded and finely chopped
½ small green pepper, seeded and finely chopped
¼ Spanish onion, finely chopped
15ml/1 tbls capers, finely chopped
5ml/1 tsp each finely chopped parsley and basil

1. Wash and prepare lettuce. Shake dry in a salad basket, or dry each leaf carefully in a tea towel. Wrap in a dry tea towel and allow to crisp in the refrigerator until ready to use.
2. Simmer courgettes in salted water for about 8 minutes. Cut them in half lengthwise, and carefully scoop out seeds. Lay courgettes, cut sides up, in a flat dish.
3. Combine finely chopped onion and garlic clove and cover courgettes with this mixture. Sprinkle half the FRENCH DRESSING over them; cover with aluminium foil and allow to marinate in the refrigerator for at least 4 hours.
4. When ready to serve, remove onion and garlic mixture from courgettes and drain off the marinade. Arrange lettuce on a flat serving platter; place courgette halves on lettuce and fill the hollows with remaining FRENCH DRESSING to which you have added finely chopped tomatoes, pepper, onion, capers, parsley and basil. Serve immediately.

TRUFFLED CHICKEN SALAD

SERVES 4

1 head lettuce
*60ml/4 tbls **Mayonnaise** (see page 85)*
salt and freshly ground black pepper
celery salt
1 small can black truffles, drained (reserving juice) and finely sliced
3 hard-boiled eggs, finely chopped
350g/¾lb cooked chicken, diced
4 celery stalks, diced
100g/3½oz can tuna fish, drained and flaked

1. Wash lettuce. Shake dry in a salad basket, or dry each leaf carefully in a tea towel. Finely shred lettuce. Wrap in a dry tea towel and allow to crisp in the refrigerator until ready to use.
2. Thin MAYONNAISE with reserved truffle juice and season with salt, freshly ground black pepper and celery salt, to taste.
3. Add finely sliced truffles to sauce and combine with shredded lettuce, finely chopped eggs, diced chicken, celery stalks and tuna fish. Mix well. Add more MAYONNAISE and seasoning, if desired. Arrange in a salad bowl and serve.

SARDINE SALAD

SERVES 4

2 100g/3½oz cans sardines in oil, drained
1 head lettuce
90ml/6 tbls olive oil
30ml/2 tbls lemon juice

salt and freshly ground black pepper
1 small onion, cut into rings
4 hard-boiled eggs, quartered
1 small cooked beetroot, diced
30ml/2 tbls finely chopped parsley

1. Wash and prepare lettuce. Shake dry in a salad basket, or dry each leaf carefully in a tea towel. Wrap in a dry tea towel and allow to crisp in the refrigerator until ready to use.
2. Arrange lettuce in a salad bowl.
3. Combine olive oil and lemon juice and season with salt and freshly ground black pepper, to taste.
4. Toss onion rings, quartered hard-boiled eggs and diced beetroot in dressing and pile into salad bowl. Arrange sardines in centre of bowl; sprinkle with chopped parsley and serve.

COLE SLAW

SERVES 4-6

1 head cabbage, about 1kg/2lb
60ml/4 tbls tarragon vinegar
30ml/2 tbls sugar
salt and freshly ground black pepper
paprika
1 small green pepper, seeded and chopped
15ml/1 tbls spring onions, finely chopped
1.5ml/¼ tsp celery seeds
1.5ml/¼ tsp caraway seeds
*90ml/6 tbls **Mayonnaise** (see page 85)*
150ml/¼pt soured cream

1. Shred the cabbage and then crisp in cold water for ½ hour. Drain and dry thoroughly.
2. Combine tarragon vinegar, sugar, salt, freshly ground black pepper and a sprinkling of paprika to taste, in a porcelain or earthenware bowl (not metal). Add shredded cabbage, toss well and marinate for 1 hour. Drain.
3. Combine cabbage with chopped pepper, finely chopped spring onions, celery seeds and caraway seeds in a salad bowl and toss lightly.
4. Combine MAYONNAISE and soured cream and pour over the cabbage mixture. Toss lightly, correct seasoning and serve.

RED CABBAGE SALAD

SERVES 4-6

1 red cabbage, about 1kg/2 lb
salt
tarragon vinegar
freshly ground black pepper
4 hard-boiled egg yolks
300ml/½pt double cream
juice of 1 large lemon
15ml/1 tbls each finely chopped chervil, chives and
*   fennel*
½ cucumber, thinly sliced
radishes, thinly sliced

1. Shred cabbage and blanch in boiling salted water. Drain; place in cold water, then drain again.
2. Combine tarragon vinegar with salt and freshly ground black pepper, to taste, in a porcelain or earthenware bowl (not metal). Add shredded cabbage, toss well and marinate for at least 1 hour, turning from to time. Drain.
3. Pass hard-boiled egg yolks through a fine sieve; combine with cream and lemon juice and add salt and freshly ground black pepper, to taste. Add finely chopped herbs and mix well with red cabbage.
4. Pile salad into a salad bowl and serve decorated with thinly sliced cucumber and radishes.

RED BEAN SALAD

SERVES 4-6

*350g/¾lb dried kidney beans, soaked overnight
  and drained*
salt
1 head lettuce
1 Spanish onion, finely chopped
30ml/2 tbls parsley, finely chopped
90ml/6 tbls olive oil
60ml/4 tbls red wine vinegar
freshly ground black pepper
generous pinch of dry mustard

1. Place beans in a thick-bottomed saucepan with lightly salted water. Bring to the boil; boil for 10 minutes, reduce the heat, cover and cook for about 1 hour, or until tender. Drain and reserve.
2. Wash and prepare lettuce. Shake dry in a salad basket, or dry each leaf carefully in a tea towel. Wrap in a dry tea towel and allow to crisp in the refrigerator until ready to use.
3. Add finely chopped onion and parsley to beans; moisten with olive oil and red wine vinegar and season with salt and freshly ground black pepper, to taste, and a generous pinch of dry mustard. Mix the salad lightly and chill.
4. Arrange lettuce in a salad bowl. Place bean salad on lettuce; sprinkle generously with finely chopped parsley and serve.

MOROCCAN ORANGE SALAD

SERVES 6-8

6 ripe oranges
6-8 dates, chopped
6-8 blanched almonds, slivered
*orange flower water, or lemon juice and ground
  sugar*
ground cinnamon

1. Peel oranges, removing all pith, and slice crosswise.

2. Place sliced oranges in a salad bowl with chopped dates and slivered almonds and flavour with orange flower water, or lemon juice and sugar, to taste. Chill.
3. Just before serving, sprinkle lightly with ground cinnamon.

SUMMER FRUIT SALAD

SERVES 6-8

1 ripe cantaloupe melon
juice of 2 lemons
50g/2oz cherries, pitted
50g/2oz strawberries, hulled
2 peaches, peeled and sliced
2 oranges, peeled and sliced
2 pears, unpeeled and diced
2 red apples, unpeeled, diced
sprigs of mint

PAPRIKA DRESSING
90ml/6 tbls pineapple juice
90ml/6 tbls lemon juice
3 eggs, beaten until light
75g/3oz sugar
pinch salt
5ml/1 tsp paprika

1. Cut a ripe cantaloupe melon partway down into 6 or 8 sections so that it opens out slightly. Remove the seeds carefully; brush segments with lemon juice; cover with aluminium foil and chill in refrigerator until ready to use. Reserve remaining lemon juice for diced apples and pears.
2. Just before serving, place cut melon on a serving platter. Pile assorted fruits – pitted cherries, hulled strawberries, sliced peaches and oranges, and unpeeled diced apples and pears which you have brushed with reserved lemon juice to prevent discolouration – into cut melon; garnish with sprigs of mint and serve with paprika dressing.

3. To make paprika dressing: combine all ingredients in the top of a double saucepan and cook over boiling water until thick, stirring constantly. Chill before use.

PEARS VINAIGRETTE

SERVES 4

4 ripe dessert pears
1 head lettuce

MINT VINAIGRETTE SAUCE
90ml/6 tbls olive oil
45ml/3 tbls red wine vinegar
30ml/2 tbls mint, finely chopped
30ml/2 tbls parsley, finely chopped
salt and freshly ground black pepper
dry mustard

1. Wash and prepare lettuce. Shake dry in a salad basket, or dry each leaf carefully in a tea towel. Wrap in a dry tea towel and allow to crisp in the refrigerator until ready to use.
2. Peel, core and slice pears.
3. To make mint vinaigrette sauce: combine olive oil, red wine vinegar, finely chopped mint and parsley and season with salt and freshly ground black pepper and a little dry mustard to taste.
4. Toss ripe dessert sliced pears in mint vinaigrette sauce.
5. Place lettuce in a salad bowl. Arrange pears vinaigrette in bowl and serve.

ORANGES VINAIGRETTE

SERVES 6-8

6 ripe oranges

OLIVE AND HERB VINAIGRETTE SAUCE
90ml/6 tbls olive oil
30ml/2 tbls red wine vinegar
12-18 black olives, pitted and finely chopped

½ Spanish onion, finely chopped
15ml/1 tbls finely chopped mint
15ml/1 tbls finely chopped parsley
15ml/1 tbls finely chopped basil
salt and freshly ground black pepper
cayenne pepper

1. Peel oranges, removing all pith, and slice crosswise.
2. To make olive and herb vinaigrette sauce: combine olive oil, red wine vinegar, finely chopped olives, onion and herbs and season with salt and freshly ground black pepper and cayenne pepper, to taste.
3. Toss orange slices in olive and herb vinaigrette sauce. Arrange in a salad bowl and serve.

APPLE AVOCADO SALAD

SERVES 6-8

4 eating apples
1 avocado pear
1 bunch watercress
juice of 2 lemons
25-50g/1-2oz salted mixed nuts
French dressing *(see page 304)*

1. Wash watercress and remove stalks and any damaged leaves. Dry carefully and chill in a damp tea towel until ready to use.
2. Core apples but do not peel. Slice 3mm/⅛in thick.
3. Cut avocado pear in half; remove stone and peel. Slice into wedges 3mm/⅛in thick.
4. Cover apple and avocado slices with lemon juice to prevent discolouration.
5. Just before serving, drain apple and avocado slices. Arrange in a salad bowl with salted mixed nuts and watercress and pour over FRENCH DRESSING to which you have added some of the drained lemon juice. Toss lightly until every ingredient glistens.

CHAPTER 15

DESSERTS

— RUM BABA —

KING STANISLAS of Poland, father-in-law of Louis XV of France, Duke of Lorraine and Bar, was an ardent cook. Among the many creations credited to this noble *cuisinier* is the *baba-au-rhum,* one of the world's most delicious sweets. History tells us that Stanislas dunked his favourite *kugelhupf* in a rum-flavoured syrup and declared the result a triumph! Later generations of cooks added a scattering of raisins to the dough, and the baba as we know it was born. Based on a *savarin* recipe, the rum baba is a featherlight concoction of flour, sugar and eggs, made airy with fresh or dried yeast and moistened with syrup and rum. I like it best baked in a ring mould and filled with a *macédoine* of fresh fruits or *marrons glacés* in a rum-flavoured syrup.

The *savarin* cake mixture, which is the basis of rum baba as well as many other famous sweets, is quite easy to make if you follow these rules: dissolve yeast in liquid (water, milk or a mixture of the two) just a littler warmer than body temperature. The liquid should feel warm, not hot.

Warm a mixing bowl with boiling water. Dry it thoroughly. Sift flour into warm bowl; gradually add yeast mixture and beaten eggs and blend batter ingredients by hand. (The warmth of your hand is important to the handling of the yeast).

Beat by hand until batter is smooth and well blended, cover it with a warm towel and leave to rise in a warm place protected from draughts.

Do not allow batter to stand too long, at most 45 minutes to an hour, or until it doubles in bulk. Yeast will rise even in a refrigerator if left long enough, so it is quite unnecessary to put yeast dough on a radiator or near a stove or heater to make it rise. Just keep it out of draughts.

One of the world's classic desserts—light, airy Savarin aux Marrons is topped with delicious chestnuts in rum-flavoured syrup. I also like to serve a savarin filled with fresh fruits.

Punch the batter down and beat it again, using the bread hook of your electric mixer, if you have one, to facilitate this task, until the dough leaves the sides of bowl, about 5 minutes with mixer.

Butter moulds: fill one-third full with yeast batter; cover with a warm towel and leave for final rising, about 45 minutes. When batter rises to top of the moulds, the cakes are ready for baking and should be put into the oven immediately.

Bake small shapes in a preheated moderate oven (190°C/375°F/gas 5) for 30 to 40 minutes until they acquire a rich brown colour.

To turn out: invert moulds on a wire cake rack for 5 to 10 minutes; then loosen with a knife and turn out of moulds. Saturate with hot syrup while the cake is still warm, spooning the syrup over the cake until most of it is absorbed.

BASIC SAVARIN RECIPE

SERVES 8

225g/¹/₂lb flour
15g/¹/₂oz fresh yeast, or 7g/¹/₄oz dried yeast
25g/1oz castor sugar
about 150ml/¹/₄pt lukewarm milk
4 egg yolks
grated rind of ¹/₂ lemon
melted butter, for mould

1. Sift flour into a warm bowl and leave in a warm place while you make a sponge yeast: mix fresh yeast with 5ml/1 tsp sugar; add 10ml/2 tsp flour and enough of the milk to give a batter-like consistency. Leave in a warm place until bubbly. (If using dried yeast, sprinkle yeast over 60ml/4 tbls lukewarm milk; beat well with a fork and leave for 30 minutes until liquid is frothy and yeast granules have completely dissolved. Then make batter as above with flour and sugar.)
2. Beat egg yolks with remaining sugar and grated lemon rind until fluffy.

3. In a small thick-bottomed saucepan melt butter over a very low heat, taking care not to let it sizzle. Remove from heat and allow sediment to fall to the bottom. Then carefully strain butter through fine muslin, discarding sediment.
4. When yeast mixture is spongy, make a well in the flour. Pour in yeast mixture and beaten eggs, and mix thoroughly by hand, adding milk gradually to make a very soft dough (precise amount of milk will depend on the quality of your flour). Continue to work dough until very smooth; then gradually add clarified butter, kneading and punching dough, which will be very soft indeed by this stage – a very thick batter, in fact – until it no longer sticks to the palm of your hand. Cover bowl with a warm towel and leave dough to rise in a warm place until doubled in bulk.
5. Preheat oven to moderate (190°C/375°F/gas 5).
6. Brush a 1.7L/3pt *savarin* mould generously with melted butter.
7. When dough is well risen, punch it down

320

and beat again, using bread hook of electric mixer, if you have one, until dough leaves sides of bowl.

8. Fill mould one-third full; cover and allow to rise again until dough comes almost to top of mould.

9. Bake *savarin* in preheated oven for 30 to 40 minutes until a rich brown colour. A thin metal skewer pushed through the thickest part should feel quite dry to the touch. Allow to cool slightly before turning out.

SAVARIN AUX MARRONS

SERVES 8

1 Basic savarin recipe (see page 320)
melted butter, for mould
1 can chestnuts, in syrup
30ml/2 tbls Jamaica rum or kirsch
whipped cream or Crème pâtissière (see page 322)

SYRUP
225g/¹/₂lb sugar
strip of orange peel
vanilla pod
90ml/6 tbls Jamaica rum or kirsch

APRICOT GLAZE
300ml/¹/₂pt apricot jam
kirsch

1. Preheat oven to moderate (190°F/375°C/ gas 5).

2. To make *savarin*: follow BASIC SAVARIN RECIPE, baking mixture in a 1.7L/3 pt well-buttered *savarin* mould in preheated oven.

3. When *savarin* is lukewarm prick rounded sides with a skewer and place, rounded side up, in a dish just large enough to hold it. Pour lukewarm syrup over *savarin* and allow to stand for at least ¹/₂ hour.

4. When ready to serve: pour off excess syrup from *savarin* into chestnuts in syrup. Transfer

savarin to a clean serving dish. Sprinkle with dark rum or *kirsch;* paint with apricot glaze and fill centre with whipped cream, or CREME PATISSIERE. Top cream with chestnuts in rum-flavoured syrup and serve.

5. to make syrup: combine sugar, 425ml/ ³/₄pt water, strip of orange peel and vanilla pod in a thick-bottomed saucepan. Cook to syrup stage and then add Jamaica rum or *kirsch*.

6. To make apricot glaze: add 60-90ml/4-6 tbls water to apricot jam in a thick-bottomed saucepan and heat, stirring constantly, until liquid. Flavour with *kirsch,* to taste.

BABA-AU-RHUM

SERVES 8

1 Basic savarin recipe (see page 320)
30ml/2 tbls currants
15ml/1 tbls sultanas
melted butter, for mould
Jamaica rum (optional)

SYRUP FOR BABA
225g/¹/₂lb sugar
90ml/6 tbls Jamaica rum

1. Follow first 7 steps of basic recipe.

2. Add currants and sultanas to dough and mix well. Then put dough into a 1.7L/3pt well-buttered *savarin* mould, or into small individual moulds, filling moulds only up to one-third of their height. Put moulds in a warm place, covered with a warm towel, until dough rises almost to the top of mould.

3. Preheat oven to moderate (190°C/375°F/ gas 5).

4. Bake *baba* for 30 to 40 minutes until a rich brown colour. A thin metal skewer through the thickest part should feel quite dry to the touch. Allow to cool slightly before turning out.

5. To make syrup: combine sugar and 300ml/

½pt water in a saucepan. Simmer gently until it thickens. Stir in rum.

6. Prick *baba* all over with a fork and spoon over syrup. If desired, pour a little more rum over *baba* just before serving.

SAVARIN AUX POMMES

SERVES 8

*1 **Basic savarin recipe** (see page 320)*
melted butter, for mould
60-90ml/4-6 tbls warmed apricot jam
300ml/½pt whipped cream

CREME PATISSIERE

4 egg yolks
50g/2oz sugar
10ml/2 tsp flour
300ml/½pt warm milk
1.5ml/¼tsp vanilla essence

POACHED APPLE HALVES

3-4 eating apples
juice of 1 lemon
60ml/4 tbls sugar
vanilla essence

RUM-FLAVOURED APPLE SAUCE

700g/1½lb cooking apples
2 lemon slices
20ml/1½ tbls sugar
30-60ml/2-4 tbls Jamaica rum

1. Preheat oven to moderate (190°C/375°F/gas 5).

2. To make *savarin:* follow BASIC SAVARIN RECIPE, baking mixture in a 1.7L/3pt buttered *savarin* mould in preheated oven. Allow to cool slightly before turning out.

3. To make *crème pâtissière:* beat egg yolks and sugar together until mixture is lemon-coloured. Mix in flour, then add warm milk and vanilla essence and mix thoroughly. Place mixture in thick-bottomed saucepan over a low heat and cook, stirring constantly, until cream reaches boiling point. Cook until thick; remove from heat; put through sieve and allow to cool.

4. To poach apples: peel and core eating apples; slice in half and poach gently in water with lemon juice, sugar and vanilla essence, to taste, until they have softened slightly. Drain apples and reserve.

5. To make rum-flavoured apple sauce: peel and core cooking apples; cut into thick slices and put into a thick-bottomed saucepan together with 30-60ml/2-4 tbls water, lemon slices and sugar. Bring to the boil; cover tightly and simmer gently for 10 minutes, or until apples are fluffy. Remove lemon slices and purée sauce through a fine sieve. Stir in Jamaica rum.

6. To assemble: fill centre of *savarin* with equal quantities of *crème pâtissière* and rum-flavoured apple sauce. Place a ring of poached apple halves around *savarin*. Brush apple halves with warmed apricot jam and serve with whipped cream.

KUGELHUPF

SERVES 8

15g/½oz fresh yeast or 7g/¼oz dried yeast
30ml/2 tbls sugar
flour
icing sugar
2.5ml/½ tsp salt
2.5ml/½ tsp vanilla essence
grated rind of 1 lemon
2 eggs, beaten
50g/2oz melted butter
warm milk
50g/2oz raisins
melted butter, for mould

1. See BASIC SAVARIN RECIPE (see page 320) if

using fresh yeast. Dissolve dried yeast in 60ml/ 4 tbls warm water; add sugar. Cover mixture with a warm towel and put in a warm place for ½ hour.

2. Sift 450g/1lb flour, 90ml/6 tbls icing sugar and the salt into a warm mixing bowl. Add vanilla essence and grated lemon rind and mix well. Make a well in the centre of the flour and pour in the yeast mixture. Stir well, incorporating as much flour into the mixture as possible. Stir in beaten eggs and melted butter gradually, and continue to mix flour in with hands. Work in enough warm milk (about 300ml/½pt) to form a smooth dough. Dust with flour, cover with a warm towel and let dough rise in a warm place until doubled in bulk.

3. Preheat oven to moderate (190°C/375°F/ gas 5).

4. Add raisins and beat until they are well distributed. Fill a 1.7L/3pt well-buttered *kugelhupf* mould, or a tube pan, one-third full with the dough. Cover with a warm towel and allow to rise in a warm place until doubled in bulk and the pan is almost full. Cover with a piece of aluminium foil and bake in preheated oven for about 1 hour.

5. Allow to cool slightly before turning out. Dust with icing sugar. Leave *kugelhupf* cake to stand overnight before slicing.

GENOESE SPONGE

melted butter and flour, for cake tin
4 eggs
125g/4oz castor sugar
2.5ml/½ tsp vanilla essence, or grated rind of
*   ½ lemon*
75g/3oz flour
25g/1oz cornflour
unsalted butter

1. Preheat oven to moderate (180°C/350°F/ gas 4).

2. Brush base and sides of a 20cm/8in cake tin with melted butter. Line base of tin with a circle of greaseproof paper and brush paper with melted butter. Lightly dust base and sides of tin with flour and shake off excess.

3. Combine eggs, sugar and vanilla or grated lemon rind, and whisk in the top of a double saucepan until mixture is very light and thick and lukewarm. Transfer to electric mixer and whisk at high speed for 5 minutes, or until mixture holds its shape.

4. Sift together flour and cornflour and fold carefully into egg mixture, a little at a time.

5. Melt 120ml/8 tbls unsalted butter in the top of a double saucepan, taking care that it does not bubble or separate; add immediately to sponge mixture and pour into prepared cake tin. Bake in preheated oven for 40 to 45 minutes, or until golden brown. The sponge is cooked when it shrinks away slightly from the sides of the tin and springs back into shape when pressed. If desired, the mixture may be put in 2 shallow 8in tins and baked for 15 to 20 minutes. Invert sponge onto a wire rack to cool. When cool, loosen edges and remove from tin. Slice into two layers; sandwich and ice to choice. Excellent for all layer cakes, iced cakes and *petits fours*.

SPONGE CAKE

melted butter and flour, for sandwich tins
4 eggs, separated
175g/6oz castor sugar
20ml/1½ tbls lemon juice
generous pinch of salt
50g/2oz flour
25g/1oz cornflour

1. Preheat oven to moderate (180°C/350°F/ gas 4).

2. Brush base and sides of two 19cm/7½in sandwich tins with melted butter; line base of tins with a neat circle of greaseproof paper and brush paper with melted butter. Lightly dust base and sides of tins with flour shaking off excess.

3. Whisk egg yolks, castor sugar, lemon juice, or water, and a generous pinch of salt (5 minutes in mixer at high speed).
4. Sift flour and cornflour together.
5. Whisk egg whites until soft peaks form.
6. Gradually resift flour and cornflour over surface of egg yolk mixture, at the same time folding lightly but thoroughly. Fold in beaten egg whites. Divide batter evenly between prepared sandwich tins and bake in preheated oven for 20 to 25 minutes, or until golden brown. The sponges are cooked when they shrink away slightly from the sides of the tins and spring back into shape when pressed lightly with a finger. Invert sponges onto wire racks to cool. When cool, loosen edges and remove from tins. Peel off greaseproof paper. Sandwich and ice layers to choice.

SUMMER LEMON CAKE

CAKE MIXTURE
6 eggs, separated
175g/6oz castor sugar
grated rind of 1 lemon
generous pinch of salt
75g/3oz flour
25g/1 oz cornflour
butter and flour, for cake tin
100g/4oz chopped toasted almonds

LEMON TOPPING
1 egg
150g/5oz sugar
grated rind and juice of 1 lemon made up to
*   150ml/¼pt with water*
25g/½oz sifted flour
300ml/½pt double cream, whipped
100g/4oz chopped toasted almonds

1. Preheat oven to slow (170°C/325°F/gas 3).
2. To make cake: whisk egg yolks, sugar, 30ml/2 tbls water, lemon rind and a generous pinch of salt until light and fluffy (5 minutes in mixer at high speed). Sift flour and cornflour and fold carefully into egg yolk mixture a little at a time. Whisk egg whites until stiff but not dry and fold gently into egg yolk mixture. Pour equal quantities of batter into three 20cm/8in sandwich tins which have been buttered and lightly dusted with flour. Bake in preheated oven for 45 minutes, or until golden brown. The layers are cooked when they shrink away slightly from the sides of the tins and spring back into shape when pressed lightly with a finger. Invert layers onto wire racks. When cool, loosen edges and remove from tins.
3. To make lemon topping: whisk egg, sugar and lemon rind together until foamy; add sifted flour and lemon juice, which you have made up to 150ml/¼pt with water, and cook in the top of a double saucepan, stirring all the time, until smooth and thick. Cool. Fold in whipped cream.
4. Spread 2 cake layers with lemon topping and sandwich together. Cover top and sides of cake with remaining topping and pat chopped toasted almonds firmly around the sides and serve.

CHOCOLATE DATE NUT TORTE

175g/6oz castor sugar
30ml/2 tbls flour
5ml/1 tsp baking powder
2 eggs
100g/4oz coarsely chopped walnuts
225g/8oz coarsely chopped dates
50g/2oz finely grated bitter chocolate
butter and flour, for cake tin
1.5ml/¼ tsp ground cinnamon
Crème chantilly *(see page 325)*

1. Preheat oven to very slow (150°C/300°F/gas 2).
2. Sift 150g/5oz castor sugar together with flour and baking powder.
3. Beat eggs until light and fluffy. Add dry ingredients and mix well.
4. Fold coarsely chopped nuts and dates and finely grated chocolate into the mixture. Pour into a 23cm/9in well-buttered and floured cake tin. Sprinkle with a mixture of the remaining sugar and ground cinnamon and bake in preheated oven for 1 hour, or until golden brown. Allow *torte* to cool. When cool, loosen edges and remove from tin. Invert onto a serving plate; spread cake with CREME CHANTILLY and serve.

TROPICAL BANANA CAKE

2 ripe bananas
100g/4oz butter
5ml/1 tsp grated lemon rind
225g/8oz castor sugar
2.5ml/¹/2tsp vanilla essence
2 eggs
225g/8oz sifted flour
12ml/2¹/2 tsp baking powder
4ml/³/4 tsp salt
60ml/4 tbls milk
butter and flour, for layer tins

BANANA ICING
450g/1lb icing sugar
2.5ml/¹/2 tsp salt
100g/4oz butter
1 ripe banana, mashed
5-10ml/1-2 tsp Jamaica rum

1. Preheat oven to moderate (190°C/375°F/gas 5).
2. Combine butter, lemon rind, sugar and vanilla and beat until light and fluffy. Beat in eggs, one at a time, until thoroughly mixed.

3. Peel bananas and mash to a pulp.
4. Sift flour, baking powder and salt and fold carefully into egg mixture in 3 portions, alternating with banana pulp and milk. Beat after each addition until smooth. Pour batter into two 23cm/9in buttered and floured layer tins and bake in preheated oven for 25 minutes, or until golden brown. The layers are cooked when they shrink away slightly from the sides of tins and spring back into shape when pressed lightly with a finger. Invert layers onto wire racks. When cool, loosen edges and remove from tins.
5. To make banana icing: beat sugar, salt and butter until mixture is glossy and smooth. Add the remaining ingredients and beat until well mixed.
6. Spread banana icing between layers and sandwich together. Frost with remaining icing.

CAPRICE SAINT SYLVESTRE

CAKE MIXTURE
100g/4oz castor sugar
4 eggs
100g/4oz flour
25g/1oz unsweetened cocoa powder
100g/4oz melted butter, cooled
butter, for cake tin, or ring mould
finely chopped almonds
30-60ml/2-4 tbls Jamaica rum
30-60ml/2-4 tbls vanilla syrup
8 marrons glacés
100g/4oz slightly sweetened melted
  chocolate

CREME CHANTILLY
300ml/¹/2pt double cream
30ml/2 tbls castor sugar
30ml/2 tbls iced water
few drops of vanilla essence
4 marrons glacés, coarsely chopped

1. Preheat oven to moderately hot (200°C/400°F/gas 6).
2. Combine castor sugar and eggs and whisk for 5 minutes.
3. Sift flour and cocoa together and fold into egg mixture, followed by cooled melted butter. Pour mixture into a 20cm/8in buttered, round cake tin, or ring mould, which you have sprinkled with finely chopped almonds and bake in preheated oven for 25 to 30 minutes. The cake is cooked when it shrinks away slightly from the sides of the tin, or mould, and springs back when pressed lightly with a finger. Invert cake onto a wire rack to cool. When cool, loosen edges and remove from tin, or mould.
4. Split cake in 2, moisten the cut sides with equal quantities of Jamaica rum and vanilla syrup, and spread with *crème chantilly* to which you have added 4 coarsely chopped *marrons glacés*.
5. Ice cake with slightly sweetened melted chocolate and decorate with remaining *marrons glacés*.
6. To make *crème chantilly:* whip double cream with castor sugar until stiff; add iced water and vanilla essence, to taste, and whip again until cream is soft and fluffy. Chill.

AMERICAN STRAWBERRY SHORTCAKE

SERVES 4

SHORTCAKE MIXTURE
flour
10ml/2 tsp baking powder
1.5ml/¼ tsp salt
45ml/3 tbls castor sugar
softened butter
150ml/¼pt milk
2 egg yolks, lightly beaten
butter, for baking sheet
300ml/½pt double cream

STRAWBERRY MIXTURE
fresh strawberries, hulled and halved
sugar
juice of ½ lemon

1. Preheat oven to fairly hot (220°C/425°F/gas 7).
2. To make shortcake mixture: sift 225g/8oz flour with baking powder, salt and sugar. Work in softened butter with a fork. Add milk and egg little by little, stirring continuously, until mixture holds together but is still soft. Drop 4 rounds of the mixture into a buttered baking sheet and bake in preheated oven for 10 to 15 minutes, or until shortcake turns golden brown.
3. Combine halved strawberries with sugar, to taste, and lemon juice.
4. To serve: split shortcake carefully with a fork, spread with softened butter and spoon the fresh halved strawberries between layers and over the top. Serve warm with double cream.

AMERICAN BAKING POWDER BISCUITS

MAKES 10

plain flour
20ml/4 tsp baking powder
2.5ml/½ tsp salt
60-90ml/4-6 tbls softened butter
150ml/¼pt milk
butter, for baking sheet

1. Preheat oven to hot (230°C/450°F/gas 8).
2. Sift together 225g/½lb flour, baking powder and salt. Rub softened butter into mixture with pastry blender, or your fingers; then add milk, stirring mixture quickly, until you have soft but not sticky dough.
3. Knead dough with floured fingertips on a lightly floured board just enough to shape

dough into a smooth ball; roll or pat out lightly to 1.2cm/½in thickness and cut in rounds with floured glass, or biscuit cutter. Bake on buttered baking sheet in preheated oven for about 15 minutes, or until biscuits are golden brown.

THE BOMBE

I ce cream first reached these shores eight centuries ago in the form of a recipe for orange ice, brought back from the Crusades by Richard Coeur de Lion. It was given to him by Saladin, the great warrior Sultan of Egypt and Syria. Ever since, ices have been firm favourites of the English; the ice-houses buried in hillsides on great estates all over the country bear solid witness to that. Unprotected by our blanket of smog, winters were colder in the past, summers hotter, and only by burying the thick blocks of ice sawn from rivers and ponds after Christmas could they be preserved throughout the summer to provide the delights of iced sweets.

'Take two Pewter Basons, one larger than the other,' wrote Mrs. Glasse in 1747. 'The inward one must have a close Cover, into which you are to put your Cream, and mix it with Raspberries or whatever you like best, to give it a Flavour and a Colour. Sweeten it to your Palate; then cover it close, and set it into the larger Bason. Fill it with Ice, and a Handful of Salt; then let it stand in this Ice three Quarters of an Hour, then uncover it, and stir the Cream well together; cover it close again, and let it stand Half an Hour longer, after that turn it into your Plate.'

The method was cumbersome but the principle was sound. Fresh fruit and fresh cream are the only possible foundation for ice cream, even if you do only have to pop it into the refrigerator to freeze. The juice of peaches, of white grapes, of plums and strawberries and currants, of apples and pears even, will provide the climax to any summer meal.

But to get this perfection, you will have to make the ice cream yourself. Gunter's used to make fresh fruit ice cream in London before the war; many shops in Paris still do. But it is in the tiny village of St. Tropez that the best ices in the world exist. In a side turning at the end of the port, Mme. Lamponi makes ice cream of such perfection that her customers have been down on bended knees, begging her to open in Paris. They have promised her backing, they have found her a shop, they have guaranteed her a clientele, but nothing will budge her. As the last yacht leaves the harbour in the autumn, she puts up her shutters and firmly remains closed until

327

spring brings the first boats nosing once more into the little port. Then she opens again and all summer long a procession of people can be seen leaving her shop, bearing the round cylinders in which the best ice cream in the world is packed. Mme. Lamponi is wise. By opening during the summer months only, she need use nothing but fresh fruit purées in her confections . . . and fresh is the operative word, for no finer tastes have been devised than the blends of fresh fruits, butterscotch and praline that she makes in her little shop.

Experiment yourself with different flavours. Quince and tangerine, fresh lime or bananas will amaze you with their flavour in this new setting. Almost anything will work, as I found myself from Mme. Lamponi. I had heard of a legendary ice served by Gunter's at garden parties before the war – a grape ice cream. When I asked Mme. Lamponi to make some for me, she told me indignantly that it could not be done – the flavour was too subtle to be captured. Disappointed, I gave up; but she did not. Behind her closed shutters she worked away all winter, experimenting, until she had perfected the new flavour. And when I visited St. Tropez the next year, grape ice cream was her top seller!

Home-made fresh fruit ices, iced soufflés and glamorous iced *bombes* can add enormously to the excitements of summer entertaining. A *bombe,* so named because it is usually made in a round or conical-shaped mould, is always a combination of two or more creams or ices frozen together. In most cases an ice or ice cream is used to line the mould and a creamy *bombe* mousse is used to fill the centre.

Bombes make a wonderfully elegant ending to a meal. And as they can be prepared the day before the event, they provide a perfect iced pudding for a small dinner party. Well-flavoured fruit ices or ice creams can be bought in most areas for the outside casing and all that is required is a home-made centre for a personal touch.

A delicious basic *bombe* mixture for the filling can be made of egg yolks, sugar and water. It will keep in a well-sealed jar in the refrigerator for a week and is added to whipped cream with the desired flavourings and garnishes when ready to use. Fruits, nuts, crushed macaroons, cake crumbs, raisins or coarsely grated chocolate are wonderful additions to *bombe* mixtures.

Glamorous ice bombes and home-made ices and ice creams make an elegant end to any meal.

BASIC BOMBE MIXTURE

1. Bring 150g/5oz granulated sugar and 150ml/¼pt water to the boil, stirring continuously, and cook over medium heat until thermometer reads 105°C/217°F. Set aside to cool.
2. Beat 5 egg yolks until light and creamy. Place beaten yolks over boiling water in the top of a double saucepan and add cooled sugar syrup gradually, beating constantly, until well mixed. Cook the mixture, still beating, until it is thick and doubled in volume, about 15 minutes.
3. Remove from heat; set in a pan of iced water and whisk again until mixture is smooth and cold. Use immediately or store in a sealed container in the refrigerator for up to 7 days.
4. Add 300ml/½pt whipped cream flavoured with vanilla essence, rum, cognac or the liqueur of your choice. Stir in any one of the following garnishes and pour into the centre of a well-chilled mould lined with ice or ice cream of a contrasting colour. Chill until ready to serve (2 to 4 hours).

BOMBE GARNISHES

Coarsely grated chocolate, crumbled macaroons, finely chopped glacé cherries, chopped toasted almonds, halved strawberries, crushed raspberries, chopped peaches, bananas or pears and chopped nuts make delicious additions to a *bombe.*

RASPBERRY BOMBE

SERVES 4-6

½ recipe **basic bombe mixture** *(see above)*
1L/2pt **Raspberry ice** *(see this page)*
300ml/½pt double cream
15ml/1 tbls grated orange rind
15-30ml/1-2 tbls Grand Marnier
1 egg white, stiffly beaten
15-30ml/1-2 tbls coarsely chopped nuts

1. Line a 1.4L/2½pt chilled mould with RASPBERRY ICE and smooth into a coating about 2cm/¾in thick. Chill lined mould.
2. In the meantime, whip double cream until stiff and flavour with grated orange rind and Grand Marnier to taste. Whisk into BASIC BOMBE MIXTURE. Fold in stiffly beaten egg white and coarsely chopped nuts and pour into lined mould. Freeze overnight. Unmould before serving.

RASPBERRY ICE

SERVES 4-6

1kg/2lb raspberries
350g/12oz sugar
30ml/2 tbls lemon juice

1. Purée raspberries in an electric blender, or food processor, until smooth. Rub pulp through a sieve.
2. Place sugar in a saucepan with 600ml/1pt water. Bring to the boil and let the mixture boil for 10 minutes. Cool slightly and stir in puréed raspberries and lemon juice. Cool completely.
3. Strain raspberry purée; pour into a freezing tray and freeze until mixture freezes firm 2.5cm/1in around sides of tray. Whisk to break up ice particles and return to freezer until firm. Transfer raspberry ice to main cabinet of refrigerator about 1 hour before serving.

BOMBE AU CHOCOLAT

SERVES 4-6

½ recipe **Basic bombe mixture** *(see this page)*
1L/2pt **Chocolate ice cream** *(see page 331)*
5-7.5ml/1-1½ tsp instant coffee
30ml/2 tbls kirsch
300ml/½pt double cream, whipped stiffly
1 egg white, stiffly beaten

1. Line a 1.4L/2½pt chilled mould with CHOCOLATE ICE CREAM and smooth into a coating about 2cm/¾in thick. Chill lined mould.
2. In the meantime, dissolve instant coffee in *kirsch* and whisk into BASIC BOMBE MIXTURE. Fold mixture gently into whipped cream. Fold in stiffly beaten egg white and pour into lined mould. Freeze overnight. Unmould before serving.

ICED SOUFFLES

SERVES 6

60ml/4 tbls diced sponge cake
60ml/4 tbls Grand Marnier
4 eggs
100g/4oz sugar
30ml/2 tbls orange juice
grated rind of 1 orange
275ml/½pt double cream
powdered chocolate, or cocoa powder

1. Soak diced sponge cake in 30ml/2 tbls Grand Marnier.
2. Separate eggs and beat yolks with sugar until the mixture is lemon-coloured and thick. Stir in remaining Grand Marnier, orange juice and grated orange rind.
3. Whisk cream and egg whites separately and fold into egg yolk mixture.
4. Half-fill 6 individual soufflé dishes, or custard cups, with soufflé mixture; divide diced sponge cake among the dishes, or cups; add remaining soufflé mixture and freeze soufflés for 4 hours. Dust with powdered chocolate, or cocoa powder before serving.

CHOCOLATE ICE CREAM

MAKES 1.1L/2pts

4 egg yolks
100/4oz sugar

1 pinch of salt
425ml/¾pt single cream
50g/2oz chocolate, melted
5ml/1 tsp vanilla essence
300ml/½pt double cream, whipped

1. Beat egg yolks, sugar and salt until light and lemon-coloured.
2. Scald single cream and add to egg and sugar mixture, whisking until mixture is well blended. Pour mixture into the top of a double saucepan and cook over water, stirring continuously, until custard coats the spoon.
3. Pour custard into melted chocolate, whisking continuously until blended. Strain through a fine sieve, add vanilla and chill.
4. Mix whipped cream with chocolate custard mixture; pour into a freezing tray and freeze, stirring mixture vigorously with a fork every ½ hour until half frozen, then leaving for a further 2 to 3 hours until frozen hard. Transfer ice cream to main cabinet of refrigerator about 1 hour before serving.

ORANGE ICE

SERVES 6

350g/¾lb sugar
425ml/¾pt orange juice
150ml/¼pt lemon juice
finely grated rind of 1 orange and 1 lemon

1. Bring sugar and 900ml/1½pt water to the boil; boil for 10 minutes.
2. Cool slightly and add orange juice, lemon juice and finely grated orange and lemon rind. Cool completely.
3. Strain orange mixture; pour into a freezing tray and freeze until mixture freezes firm 2.5cm/1in around sides of tray. Whisk to break up ice particles and return to freeze until firm. Transfer orange ice to main cabinet of refrigerator about 1 hour before serving.

COUPE CREOLE

SERVES 6

150ml/¼pt milk
300ml/½pt double cream
4 egg yolks
100g/4oz castor sugar
4ml/¾ tsp vanilla essence
90ml/6 tbls crème de marrons
300ml/½pt double cream, whipped
100g/4oz chocolate, melted
6 marrons glacés
toasted slivered almonds

1. To make vanilla ice cream: scald milk and cream in a thick-bottomed saucepan and bring to the boil. Whisk egg yolks, adding castor sugar slowly, until mixture is light-coloured and creamy. Pour hot cream mixture over egg and sugar mixture, stirring well. Cook over very low heat until thickened sufficiently to coat back of wooden spoon. Do not let mixture come to the boil, or it will curdle. Strain. Pour into freezer tray and allow to cool. Stir in vanilla essence and freeze, stirring vigorously with a fork every ½ hour until half frozen, then leaving a further 2 to 3 hours until frozen hard. Transfer to main cabinet of refrigerator about 1 hour before serving.

2. Just before serving, place 15ml/1 tbls *crème de marrons* in the bottom of 6 individual *coupes* or champagne glasses, together with a little whipped cream. Place a large ball of ice cream on top and cover with melted chocolate. Top with a *marron glacé* and garnish with remaining whipped cream and toasted slivered almonds.

TULIPE GLACEE

SERVES 8

150g/5oz flour
150g/5oz icing sugar
2 egg yolks

3 egg whites
butter
2 large oranges, greased, to form pastry shapes
1 fresh pineapple, peeled, cored and diced
60ml/4 tbls kirsch
*600ml/1pt **Vanilla ice cream** (see this page)*
300ml/½pt double cream, whipped

1. Preheat oven to moderate (180°C/350°F/gas 4).

2. Sift flour and icing sugar together; add egg yolks and whites and mix well.

3. Butter a cold baking sheet and mark 2 circles on it with a saucer. Spread 12ml/1 dessertspoon of mixture over each circle, using back of teaspoon. Bake in preheated oven for 5 to 6 minutes, or until just turning brown at edges.

4. Remove each round from baking sheet; turn over and, working quickly, place each circle over top of a greased orange. Place tea towel over pastry to prevent burning your hands and mould pastry to fit orange. Remove and continue as above, baking 2 each time and shaping them over oranges as you go. Cases will keep for days in a biscuit tin. This recipe makes 12 to 16 *tulipes*.

5. Marinate diced pineapple in *kirsch* for 10 minutes. Drain.

6. To serve: fill 8 cases with marinated pineapple; add a scoop of VANILLA ICE CREAM and finally decorate *tulipes* with whipped cream.

ANANAS GLACE 'LAURENT'

SERVES 4

4 slices fresh pineapple
3 oranges, peeled and segmented into quarters
*4 scoops **Vanilla ice cream** (see this page)*
150ml/¼pt double cream, whipped
chocolate vermicelli
toasted slivered almonds

1. Remove hard central core from slices of pineapple. Arrange on 4 individual serving plates; add orange segments in a flower shape and keep cool.

2. Just before serving, place a scoop of VANILLA ICE CREAM in the hollow of the pineapple; top with whipped cream and sprinkle with chocolate *vermicelli* and toasted slivered almonds.

BAKED APPLE COMPOTE

SERVES 4

1kg/2lb cooking apples, peeled and cored
butter
juice and grated rind of 1 lemon
100g/4oz brown sugar
double cream

1. Preheat oven to moderate (190°C/375°F/gas 5).

2. Slice peeled and cored cooking apples into a buttered baking dish.

3. Sprinkle apple slices with lemon juice, grated lemon rind and brown sugar. Dot with butter and bake, uncovered, in preheated oven for 30 minutes, or until tender. Serve with double cream.

POIRES A LA BOURGUIGNONNE

SERVES 4

8 small pears
225g/8oz sugar
1/2 cinnamon stick
300ml/1/2pt red Burgundy
whipped cream

1. Peel pears but do not core them.

2. Put pears in a thick-bottomed saucepan with sugar, 150ml/1/4pt water and 1/2 cinnamon stick. Simmer, covered, for about 15 minutes. Add wine and continue to cook over a low heat, uncovered, for 15 minutes.

3. Transfer pears to a deep serving dish. Reduce liquid over a medium heat to the consistency of a light syrup. Pour syrup over the pears and chill. Serve with whipped cream.

PEACHES IN WHITE WINE

SERVES 4-6

4-6 large peaches, or 8-12 small peaches
450g/1lb sugar
2 cloves
3 cinnamon sticks
2-3 strips of orange and lemon peel
400ml/1/2pt dry white wine

1. In a saucepan dissolve sugar in 300ml/1/2pt water over low heat; add cloves, cinnamon and orange and lemon peel.

2. Carefully drop peaches into syrup and simmer, uncovered, for 10 minutes. Add dry white wine and continue to simmer for a further 10 minutes, taking care not to let peaches become mushy. Remove from heat.

3. Take peaches, one by one, from syrup with a slotted spoon and holding gently with a towel so as not to burn your hand, carefully peel off skin with your fingers. Arrange skinned peaches in a serving dish.

4. Simmer cooking juices until reduced to a light syrup. Cool syrup and spoon over peaches. Chill until ready to serve.

MARQUISE A L'ANANAS

SERVES 4

2 small fresh pineapples
sugar
300ml/1/2pt pineapple juice
grated rind and juice of 1 lemon
300ml/1/2pt double cream, whipped
45ml/3 tbls kirsch

1. Cut pineapples in half lengthwise leaving on the green tops. With a fork, scrape the flesh and juice into a bowl, discarding the hard core and being careful not to break through the shell. Sprinkle the insides of the shells with a little sugar and chill until ready to use.

2. Mash flesh of the two pineapples. Add pineapple juice, 150ml/¼pt water, 225g/8oz sugar and grated lemon rind. Bring to the boil and boil for 5 minutes.

3. Strain pineapple mixture into a freezing tray; stir in lemon juice and freeze until mixture freezes firm 2.5cm/1in around sides of tray. Whisk to break up ice particles and return to freezer for 30 minutes.

4. Whisk mixture until smooth; fold in whipped cream and *kirsch* and return to freezer until mixture is firm.

5. Just before serving, spoon mixture into chilled pineapple shells.

FRESH FRUIT COMPOTE

SERVES 4–6

1 medium-sized pineapple
4 pears, peeled, cored and sliced
4 Cox's orange pippins, peeled, cored and sliced
4 plums, sliced
1 bunch grapes, halved and seeded
icing sugar
30ml/2 tbls brandy
30ml/2 tbls lemon juice
¼ bottle champagne

1. Peel, core and slice pineapple into rings. Reserve top. Slice each ring in half and combine with peeled, cored and sliced pears and apples, sliced plums and halved and seeded grapes. Dust with icing sugar; add brandy and lemon juice; toss well and chill.

2. Just before serving, transfer fruits to a serving bowl; pour over champagne and decorate with pineapple top.

BAKED PEARS IN WHITE WINE

SERVES 6

6 large pears
425ml/¾pt dry white wine
90ml/6 tbls sugar
whipped cream, to serve

1. Preheat oven to moderate (190°C/375°F/gas 5).

2. Peel pears and place upright in an oven-proof baking dish. Combine dry white wine and sugar in a thick-bottomed saucepan and bring to the boil.

3. Pour syrup over pears; cover with foil and bake in preheated oven for 45 minutes, or until tender. Serve cool, or chilled, with whipped cream.

FIGS IN WINE AND HONEY

SERVES 4

450g/1lb fresh figs, trimmed
dry white wine
125ml/4 fl oz clear honey
double cream

1. Place figs in a saucepan with enough white wine to cover. Bring to the boil; add honey and simmer until figs are tender.

2. Transfer figs to a serving dish and chill. Serve with double cream.

Peaches in White Wine are marvellously refreshing on a warm summer evening. Serve them with sticks of cinnamon to give this dessert an extra tang.

ELIZABETH MOXON'S LEMON POSSET

SERVES 6

grated rind and juice of 2 lemons
600ml/1pt double cream
150ml/¼pt dry white wine
sugar
whites of 3 eggs

1. Add grated lemon rind to double cream and whisk until stiff. Stir in lemon juice and dry white wine. Add sugar, to taste.
2. Whisk egg whites until they form peaks and fold into whipped cream mixture. Transfer to a glass serving dish, or 6 individual glasses, and serve.

ENGLISH TRIFLE

SERVES 8-10

1 can whole peeled apricots
19cm/7½in **Sponge cake** *(see page 323)*
150ml/¼pt sweet Marsala
30ml/2 tbls cornflour
sugar
300ml/½pt hot milk
3 eggs
50g/2oz macaroons, crumbled
600ml/1pt double cream
2.5ml/½ tsp vanilla essence
fresh or crystallised fruits

1. Drain syrup from a can of whole peeled apricots. Remove pits and purée apricots in an electric blender, or food processor.
2. Cut SPONGE CAKE into 2 layers and spread half the apricot purée between layers. Assemble cake again and cut into pieces 5 x 2.5cm/2 x 1in. Arrange cake strips in the bottom of a glass serving bowl. Pour sweet Marsala over cake and spread remaining apricot purée on top.

3. To prepare custard: mix cornflour and 30ml/2 tbls sugar with a little hot milk to form a smooth paste; combine with remaining hot milk in the top of a double saucepan and bring to the boil. Cook over water, stirring continuously, until the mixture thickens. Remove from heat and beat in eggs, one by one. When well blended, simmer gently over water, stirring continuously, for 10 minutes. Stir in crumbled macaroons and leave to soak until soft. Beat well to dissolve macaroons. Allow custard to cool, then pour over apricot purée. Chill for 2 hours.
4. Just before serving, whisk double cream with vanilla essence and 60ml/4lbs sugar until thick. Cover custard with whipped cream mixture; decorate TRIFLE with fresh or crystallised fruits and serve.

RUM CHARLOTTES

SERVES 6

100g/4oz castor sugar
90ml/6 tbls Jamaica rum
100g/4oz unsweetened chocolate
150ml/¼pt coffee
30ml/2 tbls brown sugar
50g/2oz butter
4 eggs, separated
10ml/2 tsp gelatine
30 sponge fingers
unsweetened whipped cream, to serve

1. Make a rum syrup by boiling 150ml/¼pt water, sugar and rum together for 3 to 5 minutes.
2. Make a chocolate sauce by combining unsweetened chocolate and coffee in a thick-bottomed saucepan, cook over a very low heat, stirring, until chocolate has melted. Cook for a further 5 minutes. Remove pan from heat; add brown sugar, butter and egg yolks and mix well. Allow to cool.

3. Soften gelatine in cold water and dissolve over hot water. Stir into the chocolate sauce mixture.

4. Place chocolate mixture over a bowl of ice and stir until it is on the point of setting.

5. Stiffly beat egg whites and fold into chocolate mixture.

6. Line 6 small moulds with sponge fingers which have been sprinkled with some of the rum syrup. Pour in chocolate mixture. Arrange more sponge fingers over top of moulds to cover, filling moulds completely. Chill for 12 hours.

7. Unmould; sprinkle with remaining rum syrup and serve with unsweetened whipped cream.

FRENCH RICE PUDDING

SERVES 4-6

50-75g/2-3oz patna rice
600ml/1pt milk
100g/4oz sugar
1.5ml/¼ tsp salt
2 egg yolks
2 egg whites, stiffly beaten
2.5ml/½ tsp vanilla essence
butter

1. Preheat oven to fairly hot (220°C/425°F/ gas 7).

2. Cook rice in milk and a little water with sugar and salt until tender, but not mushy.

3. Beat egg yolks and add hot rice mixture slowly. Cook in the top of a double saucepan over hot water until thick.

4. Cool rice mixture slightly and fold in stiffly-beaten egg whites. Flavour with vanilla essence, and if necessary, more sugar. Pour rice mixture into a buttered ovenproof serving dish and bake pudding in preheated oven for 5 to 10 minutes, or until golden brown. Serve immediately.

ZABAGLIONE PUDDING

SERVES 6

6 egg yolks
50g/2oz sugar
90-120ml/6-8 tbls Marsala, or medium dry sherry
7g/¼oz gelatine
45ml/3 tbls brandy
300ml/½pt double cream, whipped

ZABAGLIONE SAUCE

3 egg yolks
25g/1oz sugar
45-60ml/3-4 tbls Marsala, or medium dry sherry
22ml/1½ tbls brandy

1. To make pudding: in the top of a double saucepan, combine the egg yolks with sugar and Marsala, or medium sherry, and whip mixture over hot but not boiling water until it thickens. Stir in gelatine, which you have softened in cold water and dissolved over hot water. Put pan in a bowl of ice and stir the *zabaglione* well until it is thick and free of bubbles. When it is almost cold, fold in brandy and whipped cream and pour into 6 individual moulds. Chill *zabaglione* until ready to serve. Unmould and serve with *zabaglione* sauce.

2. To make zabaglione sauce: repeat the process as above, stirring egg yolks and sugar over hot water until the sauce is of the desired consistency. Stir in Marsala, or medium sherry, and brandy.

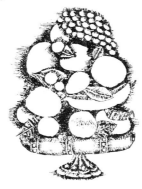

CREME RENVERSEE AU GRAND MARNIER

SERVES 6

425ml/³/4pt single cream
45ml/3 tbls Grand Marnier
4 eggs
4 egg yolks
100g/4oz sugar
butter

1. Preheat oven to moderate (180°C/350°F/ gas 4).
2. Scald single cream with Grand Marnier and let it cool slightly.
3. Beat whole eggs and egg yolks with sugar until light and lemon-coloured. Add flavoured cream, stirring constantly, until mixture is well blended together. Strain through a fine sieve into a buttered 1.4L/2½pt baking dish. Set dish in a pan of hot water; cover and bake in preheated oven for 35 to 45 minutes, or until the custard has set.
4. To serve: cool custard, loosen it from the sides of the dish with a knife and invert onto a serving platter.

BREAD AND BUTTER PUDDING

SERVES 4

25g/1oz currants
butter
4 slices bread
4 egg yolks
3 egg whites
100g/4oz sugar
freshly grated nutmeg
600ml/1pt warm milk
1.5-2.5 ml/¼-½ tsp vanilla essence

1. Preheat oven to moderate (190°C/375°F/ gas 5).
2. Wash and pick currants and scatter a few in the bottom of a 1.4L/2½pt well-buttered ovenproof serving dish.
3. Trim crusts from bread; cut each slice in half; butter each piece generously and place in layers in dish, scattering currants between each layer.
4. Twenty minutes before you are ready to bake the pudding: beat egg yolks and egg whites together with sugar and a little freshly grated nutmeg. Stir in warm milk and vanilla essence, to taste, and pour over sliced bread and currants. Bake in preheated oven for about ¾ hour, or until pudding is set and lightly browned. Serve immediately.

CREPES SUZETTE

Pancakes, in one form or another, have been a universal delight since man first discovered that if he mixed crushed grain with water and baked it, he would have a new kind of food.

Under more elaborate conditions – and a host of different names and fillings – they have been enjoyed around the world for centuries. In Mexico, it is the peasant *tortilla;* in China, the crisp egg roll; while America prefers hers for breakfast, swimming in melted butter and maple syrup; and the Russians like theirs as *blinis,* a delicious appetiser topped with caviare and sour cream.

But of all the pancake recipes in the world, the greatest – *crêpes suzette* – originated in France. The legends of the origin of this famous dish are as varied as the recipes for making it. The one I like best is the version recounted by Morrison Wood in his excellent cookery book, *With a Jug of Wine.* According to Mr. Wood, a well-known French chef, Henri Carpentier, was preparing *crêpes* in liqueur for Edward VII when the dish accidentally burst into flames. Chef Henri, not at all abashed at this misadventure, carried the flaming pan in which the *crêpes* were immersed to the table, and when the fire had died out, he served the little pancakes to the king and his party.

Edward pronounced them delicious and asked what they were called. 'They have just been invented, sir,' Henri replied, 'and they shall be called *crêpes Princesse.'* The king smiled, but shook his head. 'Where is your gallantry, Henri?' he asked. Then, indicating the young daughter of his host, he announced: 'They shall be called *crêpes Suzette,* in Mademoiselle's honour.' Whatever you call them, these paper-thin pancakes are wonderfully easy to make. They can be prepared hours or even the day before you plan to serve them, as their flaming sauce calls more for showmanship than for skill.

You will need a good *crêpe* pan made of cast iron or lined copper, for the delicate pancakes may scorch in lighter materials. It should be the size of the ultimate pancake (about 15cm/6in across), for the batter should be so creamy and thin that it will run ragged over a larger pan. And your pan should have rounded or sloping sides so that you will be able to turn the pancakes over with your spatula without tearing them.

Season your *crêpe* pan before using: fill it with vegetable oil; bring the oil slowly to a simmer; remove from heat and let the oil-filled pan stand until oil is cold. Then pour out the oil and wipe the pan clean with cloth or absorbent paper. To keep your pan in prime condition: wipe it out with oil, never with water, after every use, and your *crêpes* will never stick.

BASIC CREPES MIXTURE

MAKES 24 CREPES

225g/8oz flour
15ml/1 tbls sugar
2.5ml/½ tsp salt
3 eggs

425ml/¾pt milk
butter
olive oil
30ml/2 tbls cognac, or Jamaica rum

1. Sift together flour, sugar and salt.
2. Beat eggs and add them to the dry ingre-

dients. Mix in milk 30ml/2 tbls melted butter, or olive oil, and cognac, or rum, doing it gradually to avoid lumps. Strain through a fine sieve and leave batter to stand for at least 2 hours before cooking *crêpes*. Batter should be as thin as cream.

3. Heat a 15cm/6in thick-bottomed frying pan. Rub all over with a thick wad of absorbent paper smeared with olive oil. For each *crêpe,* spoon about 30ml/2 tbls batter into pan, swirling pan to allow batter to cover entire surface thinly; rub a piece of butter around edge of pan with the point of a knife and cook over a medium heat until just golden, about 1 minute each side. Repeat until all the *crêpes* are cooked, stacking them on a warm plate as they are ready. Keep warm if *crêpes* are to be filled immediately, and cover with waxed paper, or aluminium foil, to prevent drying.

LEMON CREPES MIXTURE

MAKES 24 THIN LEMON PANCAKES

100g/4oz flour
15ml/1 tbls sugar
pinch of salt
2 eggs
2 egg yolks
425ml/³/4pt milk
butter
5ml/1 tsp grated lemon rind
30ml/2 tbls lemon juice
olive oil

1. Sift together flour, sugar and pinch of salt.
2. Beat together whole eggs and egg yolks and add them to the dry ingredients. Mix in milk, 30ml/2 tbls melted butter, grated lemon rind and lemon juice, stirring until smooth. Strain through a fine sieve and leave batter to stand for at least 2 hours before cooking the *crêpes*. Batter should be as thin as cream.
3. Heat a 15cm/6in thick-bottomed frying

pan. Rub all over with a thick wad of absorbent paper smeared with olive oil. For each *crêpe,* spoon about 30ml/2 tbls batter into pan, swirling pan to allow batter to cover entire surface thinly; rub a piece of butter around edge of pan with the point of a knife and cook over a medium heat until just golden, about 1 minute each side. Repeat until all the *crêpes* are cooked, stacking them on a warm plate as they are ready. Keep warm by covering with waxed paper or foil to prevent the *crêpes* from drying out.

VARIATIONS ON THE BASIC CREPES THEME

1. APPLE CREPES
Simmer 3 to 4 apples, peeled and sliced, with 2.5ml/½ tsp ground cinnamon, 60ml/4 tbls brown sugar and 60ml/4 tbls butter for 15 minutes, or until apples are soft. Cook *crêpes* as above; place 15-30ml/1-2 tbls of apple filling on each; roll up and brown in butter. Sprinkle with ground cinnamon and sugar before serving.

2. FRESH BERRY CREPES
Cook *crêpes* as above and fill with crushed raspberries or strawberries which have been mixed with whipped cream. Garnish with whole berries.

3. APRICOT CREPES
Cook *crêpes* as above and fill with a combination of chopped fresh pineapple and apricot jam flavoured with *kirsch*.

4. MARRON CREPES
Cook *crêpes* as above and butter them generously with *crème de marrons* (tinned puréed chestnuts); roll them up and cover with a sauce made of heated apricot jam. Top with toasted slivered almonds.

CREPES SUZETTE

SERVES 6

*¹/₂ **Basic crêpes mixture** (see page 339)*
100g/4oz butter
50g/2oz icing sugar
grated rind of 2 lemons
grated rind and juice of 1 orange
90ml/6 tbls Cointreau, Curaçao, or
 Grand Marnier
sugar
60ml/4 tbls cognac, warmed

1. Cream butter and icing sugar together; add grated lemon and orange rind, orange juice and 60ml/4 tbls Cointreau. (You can substitute either Curaçao or Grand Marnier.)
2. Make 12 *crêpes*, stacking them on a warm plate as they are ready. Keep warm, covered with waxed paper or foil to prevent drying.
3. When ready to serve: heat orange-flavoured butter in a hot chafing dish, or thick-bottomed frying pan, for a few minutes until butter bubbles and reduces a little. Dip each cooked *crêpe* into this hot mixture; then fold in quarters, using a fork and spoon, and push to one side of dish, or pan. When all *crêpes* are used, sprinkle with a little sugar and add remaining Cointreau to the pan together with warmed cognac. Stand well away from the pan and light the liquid with a match. Spoon flaming liquid over *crêpes* and serve when flames die down.

DESSERT CREPES

SERVES 6

*¹/₂ **Lemon crêpes recipe** (see page 340)*
100g/4oz strawberry jam
450g/1lb can pineapple chunks, drained
60ml/4 tbls kirsch
15ml/1 tbls Curaçao
60ml/4 tbls slivered almonds
***Zabaglione sauce** (see page 337)*

1. Make 12 lemon *crêpes*, stacking them on a warm plate as they are ready. Keep warm, covered with waxed paper or foil to prevent them drying.
2. Mix strawberry jam and pineapple chunks. Flavour with *kirsch* and Curaçao. Add slivered almonds.
3. Fill *crêpes* with pineapple mixture; roll and arrange them on a heated serving platter. Garnish with ZABAGLIONE SAUCE and serve.

STRAWBERRY DESSERT PANCAKES

SERVES 6

*¹/₂ **Lemon crêpes recipe** (see page 340)*
1 punnet strawberries, hulled
sugar
kirsch, or Grand Marnier
butter
blanched, shredded and lightly-toasted almonds
whipped cream, flavoured with kirsch, or
 Grand Marnier

1. Make 12 *crêpes,* stacking them on a warm plate as they are ready. Keep warm, covered with waxed paper or foil to prevent them drying.
2. Preheat grill to high.
3. Slice strawberries; add sugar and a little *kirsch* or Grand Marnier, to taste, and spoon 30ml/2 tbls sliced and sugared strawberries onto each pancake. Roll *crêpes* to enclose the filling and arrange them side by side in a buttered baking dish. Sprinkle with lightly-toasted almonds and put dish under preheated grill for a few minutes. Serve hot with whipped cream which you have flavoured with a little *kirsch,* or Grand Marnier.

ENGLISH APPLE PIE

It is quite amazing the subtleties of flavour that our ancestors managed to create when you realise how few ingredients they had to play with.

Sated as we are with the riches of the world (asparagus from Kenya, strawberries from California and courgettes from Morocco as early as January), we can hardly imagine that the cabbage and the carrot were once exotic imported vegetables, that Henry VIII himself brought back from the Field of the Cloth of Gold the first cherries ever to be seen here, and that the pineapple was considered so extraordinary when it first arrived on these shores that the reigning monarch, Charles II, was painted receiving the first specimen as if it were a rare treasure.

But for nearly two thousand years, ever since the Romans first planted apple trees in Somerset and found that the flavour of the fruit surpassed that of any in all their Empire, the apple has been our dominant fruit, and by far and away our favourite.

Along with roast beef, game and salmon, the apple pie is one of the great dishes of this island, and one that has spread right round the world, recognisably British still, perfected over the centuries, impossible to improve.

I find a special satisfaction, in these days of quick and easy cooking, in making this traditional dish just for the sheer pleasure of it. The warm and spicy smell of apple pie baking in the oven – its filling rich with cinnamon and nutmeg and the tart rind of lemon, its crust part butter, part flour and part poetry – is one of the most tantalising and appetising aromas I know. For British cooks have been making superb apple pies ever since 1296 when the first British cooking apple of real importance, the Costard, came on the scene.

Costards are no longer to be had today, for time has marched over them. But from those far-off origins stem their descendants, the Lord Derby, the Grenadier, The Newton Wonder, and my own personal favourite, Bramley's Seedling.

The Bramley keeps firm and well, and cooks to perfection. Tart, but not too tart, juicy, but not too juicy, its highly-flavoured flesh breaks down when cooked to a fluffy mass that is as delicious hot as it is cold. It is the perfect apple for making apple sauce and baked apples and, of course, apple pie.

ENGLISH APPLE PIE

700g/1¹/₂lb cooking apples
juice of ¹/₂ lemon
Fingertip pastry *for shell and top*
  (see page 347)
100g/4oz sugar
50g/2oz dark brown sugar
15ml/1 tbls flour
large pinch of ground nutmeg
1.5ml/¹/₄ tsp ground cinnamon
grated rind of ¹/₂ orange
grated rind of ¹/₂ lemon
50g/2oz raisins and sultanas, chopped
30ml/2 tbls orange juice
15ml/1 tbls butter
double cream (optional)
cheddar cheese (optional)

1. Preheat oven to moderately hot (200°C/ 400°F/gas 6).
2. Pare and core apples and slice thickly. Soak slices in water to which you have added lemon juice to keep their colour and prevent them going brown.
3. Line a deep 23cm/9in pie dish with FINGER-TIP PASTRY.
4. Combine sugar, dark brown sugar, flour, a large pinch of ground nutmeg and ground cinnamon and rub a little of this mixture into pastry lining.
5. Add grated orange and lemon rind to remaining sugar mixture.
6. Drain apple slices and cover bottom of pastry shell; sprinkle over with a few chopped raisins and sultanas and some of the sugar mixture. Repeat layers until pastry shell is richly filled. Sprinkle with orange juice; dot with butter and fit over top crust, pressing the edges together, or fluting them (see page 30). Decorate pastry; cut slits in top crust to release steam and bake in preheated oven for 35 to 40 minutes, or until tender. Serve warm, with double cream, or cheddar cheese.

FRENCH APPLE FLAN

25cm/10in **Fingertip pastry** *shell (see page 347)*
  fully baked blind (see page 26)
700g/1¹/₂lb cooking apples
30ml/2 tbls butter

FRENCH PASTRY CREAM
100g/4oz sugar
15ml/1 tbls cornflour
425ml/³/₄pt milk
5 egg yolks
2.5-5ml/¹/₂-1 tsp vanilla essence
10ml/2 tsp kirsch

APRICOT GLAZE
90ml/6 tbls apricot jam
15ml/1 tbls Jamaica rum, brandy, or kirsch
  (optional)

1. To make French pastry cream: combine sugar and cornflour in the top of a double saucepan. Stir in milk and cook over direct heat, stirring continuously, until mixture comes to the boil. Boil for 1 minute. Beat egg yolks slightly, add a little hot milk mixture and pour into milk and sugar mixture, stirring. Cook, stirring, over hot but not boiling water for 5 to 10 minutes. Strain and allow to cool. Add vanilla essence and *kirsch* to cream; cover with waxed paper and chill before use.
2. Preheat grill to high.
3. Half-fill baked pastry shell with French pastry cream.
4. Peel, core and slice cooking apples as thinly as possible. Arrange in overlapping concentric circles on top of pastry cream. Dot with knobs of butter and grill under preheated grill for 3 to 5 minutes. Coat with apricot glaze and serve.
5. To prepare apricot glaze: heat apricot jam and 45ml/3 tbls water in thick-bottomed saucepan, stirring constantly, until mixture melts. Strain and, if desired, stir in rum, brandy, or *kirsch*.

CREAMY APPLE PIE

23cm/9in **Fingertip pastry** *shell (see page 347)*
1kg/2lb cooking apples
175g/6oz sugar
25g/1oz flour
1.5ml/¼ tsp salt
1.5ml/¼ tsp ground cinnamon
300ml/½pt double cream

1. Preheat oven to moderately hot (200°C/ 400°F/gas 6).
2. Bake pastry shell blind in preheated oven (see page 26). Remove from oven. Adjust oven temperature to moderately hot (200°C/400°F/ gas 6).
3. Peel, core and slice cooking apples thickly.
4. Combine sugar, flour, salt and ground cinnamon and add to apples. Toss lightly and turn into pastry shell. Bake in preheated oven for 20 minutes.
5. Pour 150ml/¼pt double cream over pie and bake for a further 10 minutes, or until apples are tender and cream slightly caramelised. Serve warm with remaining double cream.

LEMON MERINGUE PIE

20cm/8in **Fingertip pastry** *shell (see page 347)*
  fully baked blind (see page 26)
60ml/4 tbls cornflour
salt
450g/1lb castor sugar
15ml/1 tbls butter
90ml/6 tbls lemon juice
grated rind of ½ lemon
4 eggs yolks, slightly beaten
3 egg whites

1. Preheat oven to fairly hot (220°C/425°F/ gas 7).
2. Combine cornflour, 2.5ml/½ tsp salt, 275g/10oz sugar and 425ml/¾pt boiling water in the top of a double saucepan and cook over direct heat, stirring continuously, until mixture comes to the boil. Turn down heat and cook over simmering water for 15 minutes, stirring from time to time.
3. Beat in butter and lemon juice and rind. Stir in slightly-beaten egg yolks and cook over water until thick. Allow to cool.
4. Fill baked pastry shell with this mixture.
5. Make a meringue with egg whites, beaten until stiff with a pinch of salt, and 175g/6oz sugar added in 4 batches. Spoon meringue onto pie and bake in preheated oven for 15 minutes, or until golden grown. Serve.

FRENCH LEMON TARTS

MAKES 16 TARTS

PASTRY
100g/4oz butter
50g/2oz icing sugar
juice of 1 lemon
175g/6oz flour
2.5ml/½ tsp salt

FILLING
2 eggs
275g/10oz sugar
juice and grated rind of 2 lemons
100g/4oz softened butter

1. Preheat oven to moderately hot (200°C/ 400°F/gas 6).
2. To make pastry: cream butter and icing sugar. Add lemon juice. Sift flour and salt and add to butter mixture. Mix quickly to a firm paste using a little water. Chill for 15 minutes.
3. Roll out pastry and fit into 16 6.5cm/2½in tart cases. Prick bases lightly and bake blind in preheated oven (see page 26). Lower oven temperature to slow (170°C/325°F/gas 3).
4. To make filling: beat eggs with sugar until

25

light and creamy; add juice and grated rind of lemons and softened butter, and continue to beat to a smooth paste.

5. Fill tart shells with this mixture and bake in preheated oven for 10 to 15 minutes, or until surface forms a crust. Cool before serving.

STRAWBERRY FLAN CHANTILLY

20cm/8in **Fingertip pastry** *shell (see page 347)*
  fully baked blind (see page 26)
450g/1lb strawberries
90ml/6 tbls Grand Marnier
sugar
1 egg white
300ml/¹/2pt double cream, whipped

1. Wash, hull and slice strawberries into a porcelain or earthenware bowl (not metal). Pour Grand Marnier over them; add sugar to taste; stir and marinate in the refrigerator for at least 30 minutes.
2. Beat egg white until stiff and fold into whipped cream.
3. Just before serving, fold sliced strawberries and marinade into *chantilly* mixture; correct flavouring with sugar, to taste and pile into baked flan case. Serve immediately.

BRIOCHES

Start the dough the day before you wish to serve *brioches*.

MAKES 12 BRIOCHES

25g/1oz fresh yeast, or 15g/¹/2oz dried yeast
550g/1¹/4lb flour
60ml/4 tbls castor sugar
2.5ml/¹/2 tsp salt
4 eggs
120ml/8 tbls lukewarm milk
5ml/1 tsp vanilla essence

100g/4oz softened butter
melted butter, for moulds
1 egg yolk, beaten with a little water
flour

1. If using fresh yeast, cream with 120ml/8 tbls lukewarm water. If using dried yeast, sprinkle over 120ml/8 tbls lukewarm water; beat well and leave for about 10 minutes until liquid is frothy and yeast granules have completely dissolved.
2. Sift flour, sugar and salt together into a warmed bowl and make a well in the centre.
3. Beat eggs with lukewarm milk; stir in vanilla essence and add to flour mixture together with dissolved yeast. Mix well.
4. Add half the softened butter, diced, and beat until dough is smooth. The dough will be very soft at this stage. Dot surface with remaining butter; cover bowl with a clean cloth and leave in a warm place to rise until doubled in bulk.
5. Punch dough down and beat vigorously by hand for 5 minutes, or until dough no longer sticks to the sides of the bowl (flour your hands from time to time while beating).
6. Cover bowl tightly and refrigerate overnight. *Brioche* dough is very sticky and chilling overnight helps to make it easier to handle.
7. The following day, brush 12 individual *brioche* moulds with melted butter.
8. Turn dough out onto a lightly floured surface and knead a few times until smooth again. Weigh dough and cut off a quarter, making 2 balls. Divide each ball into 12 pieces of equal size. Roll 12 larger pieces into balls and place them in prepared moulds. Roll each of the smaller pieces into a ball; snip top of each larger ball twice with scissors to form a cross and set 1 of the smaller balls on top. Place moulds on a baking sheet and leave to rise again until doubled in bulk, about 30 minutes.
9. Preheat oven to moderately hot (200°C/ 400°F/gas 6).

10. When *brioches* have risen brush tops with egg yolk which you have beaten with a little water and bake in preheated oven for 15 to 20 minutes, or until firm and well risen and a rich golden colour. Turn out onto a wire rack and allow to cool. Store in an airtight container.

BRIOCHES AUX PECHES

SERVES 6

*6 **Brioches** (see page 345)*
6 small peaches
225g/8oz sugar
ground cinnamon
150ml/¹/₄pt red Burgundy
100g/4oz softened butter

1. Pour boiling water over peaches and peel. Slice in half and remove stones.
2. Poach peaches, uncovered, in syrup made of sugar and 150ml/¹/₄pt water with ground cinnamon, to taste, for about 15 minutes. Add wine and continue to cook, uncovered, over a low heat until fruit is tender, about 15 minutes.
3. Preheat oven to moderately hot (200°C/400°F/gas 6).
4. Transfer peaches to a deep bowl. Reduce poaching liquid to the consistency of a light syrup; pour syrup over the peaches and chill.
5. Slice off tops of BRIOCHES and remove the interiors, leaving a thin shell. Coat insides of BRIOCHES with softened butter and bake in preheated oven for a few minutes until crisp and golden. Re-form peach and set inside each case; glaze with reduced syrup and serve.

FLAKY PASTRY

MAKES 450g/1lb

450g/1lb flour
5ml/1 tsp salt
50g/2oz vegetable shortening
50g/2oz lard
225g/8oz butter
iced water
15ml/1 tbls lemon juice
flour

1. Sift 450g/1lb flour and salt together into a mixing bowl. If convenient, place bowl in the refrigerator until needed.
2. Work vegetable shortening and lard together with a knife until thoroughly blended. Shape into a brick; divide in half and refrigerate until firm again.
3. Remove flour from the refrigerator. Dice half the butter into bowl and rub into flour with your fingertips until mixture resembles fine breadcrumbs. Make a well in the centre.
4. Carefully measure 150ml/10 tbls iced water into well, together with lemon juice. Stir vigorously with a knife, gradually incorporating flour from sides of well; then start mixing in remaining flour, adding more iced water, if necessary, 5ml/1 tsp at a time, until you have a ball of dough that is neither too sticky, nor too dry, ie of such a consistency that you can use it to wipe the sides of the bowl clean. It will be easier to judge this if, in the final stages, you use your hands to push the dough gently together. In all you will probably need 45-60ml/3-4 tbls iced water, depending on the quality of your flour.
5. Turn dough out onto a lightly floured surface. Work dough lightly with just a few turns (kneading would be too strong a word) to smooth out the texture without developing any elasticity.
6. Roll dough out into a rectangle 40 x 20cm/16 x 8in, pushing sides straight and corners as square as you can with the side of a ruler. If dough was kneaded too vigorously, it will probably start resisting before it has reached the right dimensions, but you will get it there if you keep on rolling with gentle perseverance.
7. With the back of a knife make a light inden-

tation across the width of the rectangle one-third from the bottom.

8. Use the tip of the knife to dot the upper two-thirds of the rectangle with half the white fat mixture, covering the area down to the indentation with nut-sized flicks and leaving 1.2cm/½in border clear on the 3 outer sides – if fat is put too near edge it may ooze out during rolling.

9. Fold rectangle in 3 as follows: fold the clear (ie free of fat) third of dough up towards the centre; then fold the remaining third down over the top. Seal all edges.

10. Wrap pastry in greaseproof paper, then in a tea towel and chill for 15 minutes. (Make a note for yourself to indicate that pastry has had its first rolling, or 'turn').

11. Unwrap pastry and lay on a lightly floured surface so that the fold is on your left-hand side and the longest sealed edge on your right (think of a closed book lying with its cover upwards). Roll out again into a rectangle 40 x 20cm/16 x 8in using firm even strokes down towards you from the centre and upwards away from you – *never* roll pastry sideways, or in different directions.

12. Repeat steps 7 to 10, this time using half of the remaining butter and return to the refrigerator for 25 minutes. Make a note of the second 'turn'.

13. Give pastry its third and fourth 'turns', using remaining fat for the third and remaining butter for the fourth and final 'turn' and chilling pastry for 15 minutes in between.

14. After the final folding, seal edges of pastry; wrap in greaseproof paper, followed by the tea towel, and leave to rest in the refrigerator overnight, or for several hours at least.

NOTE: Once you have mastered the technique of making flaky pastry you will probably find that you can work much more quickly and that, consequently, the fat stays firm enough to allow you to complete 2 turns at a time.

Nevertheless, in very hot weather, or at the slightest suspicion of oozing, you would be well advised to follow the recipe step-by-step as described.

CRESCENTS OF FLAKY PASTRY

MAKES 20 CRESCENTS

*100g/4oz **Flaky pastry** (see page 346)*
flour

1. Preheat oven to fairly hot (220°C/425°F/ gas 7).

2. Roll pastry out 6mm/¼in thick on a lightly floured board and with a 6.5cm/2½in floured round pastry cutter cut a small crescent and discard (as this is not crescent shaped).

3. Place cutter on pastry, above cut out piece, to form a crescent. Repeat to make 20.

4. Transfer pastry crescents to a baking sheet and bake in preheated oven for 10 minutes, or until golden and risen.

FINGERTIP PASTRY

MAKES 225g/8oz PASTRY

225g/½lb flour
15ml/1 tbls icing sugar
generous pinch of salt
150g/5oz butter, slightly softened and diced
1 egg yolk
60ml/4 tbls iced water

1. Sieve together flour and icing sugar into a mixing bowl. Add a generous pinch of salt and slightly softened butter. Lift flour gently over the butter cubes with your hands and then rub in the butter gradually with the tips of your fingers – lifting flour and butter out of the bowl each time – until the mixture resembles fine breadcrumbs. Do this very gently and lightly, or the mixture will become greasy and heavy.

More pastry has been ruined by over-handling than by under-handling.

2. Mix egg yolk with 60ml/4 tbls iced water; sprinkle over pastry mixture and work in lightly with your fingers.

3. Shape moist dough lightly into a slightly flattened smooth round; wrap in greaseproof paper, then in a tea towel and put in the refrigerator for at least 1 hour to 'ripen' and become firm. If chilled dough becomes too firm for easy handling, let it stand at room temperature until it softens slightly. Turn dough out onto a floured board and roll as required.

PROFESSIONAL CHEF PUFF PASTRY

MAKES APPROXIMATELY 1.2kg/2¾lb

450g/1lb strong flour
450g/1lb unsalted butter
2.5ml/½ tsp salt
30ml/2 tbls lemon juice, or white wine vinegar

1. Chill flour, butter, salt, 250ml/9fl oz water, lemon juice, or vinegar and the mixing bowl in the refrigerator several hours before use.

2. Finely dice 40g/½oz of the cold butter. Place remaining butter on a lightly floured board and knock it with your fist into a rectangle approximately 12.5 x 1.5cm/5 x 6in. Chill.

3. Sift flour and salt into chilled mixing bowl; add finely diced butter and work with your fingers until butter is thoroughly coated with flour.

4. Add chilled water and lemon juice, or vinegar, and work to a moist, but not sticky, dough. Add more water if necessary.

5. Turn dough out onto a floured board and knead into a ball, adding flour to board and dough, until dough is no longer moist. Flatten dough ball to 2.5cm/1in thick, wrap in greaseproof paper, then in a tea towel, and refrigerate for 15 minutes.

6. Remove dough ball from the refrigerator, then, with plenty of flour on the board, pat pastry down a little with your hands and roll dough into a rectangle, being careful to always roll dough from the centre so it doesn't stretch. NOTE: Use plenty of flour to prevent pastry from sticking to the board, but brush all excess flour off pastry before doing the turns.

7. Brush excess flour off pastry, place 'brick' of butter in centre of rectangle and fold over the 4 edges to make a package. Seal by pressing gently with your fingertips.

8. To make 1 x 3 and 1 x 4 turns: FIRST TURN. Roll the pastry out to a rectangle measuring 30 x 38cm/12 x 15in. With the long side towards you, mark out pastry into 3 equal segments with your fingers. Then fold the left-hand third across the centre to meet the second mark; fold remaining right-hand third on top of it, making sure that edges fit exactly. Seal pastry joins pressing gently with your fingertips. Turn the pastry through 90°. (Make a note to remind you that pastry joins have had a 1 x 3 turn.) SECOND TURN. Roll out the pastry to a rectangle measuring 30 x 38cm/12 x 15in. With the long side towards you mark centre of pastry with your fingertips. Fold the short outer edges of the dough to meet in the centre at the mark. Then fold one half on top of the other as if you were closing a book. Seal pastry joins by pressing gently with your fingertips. Turn pastry round 90°. (The pastry has now had a 1 x 4 turn).

9. To mature pastry: wrap pastry in greaseproof paper and a tea towel and place in the refrigerator for at least 15 minutes.

10. Repeat '1 x 3 turns' and '1 x 4 turns' as described in Step 8 above.

11. To mature pastry: wrap pastry in greaseproof paper and a tea towel and place in the refrigerator for at least 15 minutes.

12. The pastry is now ready for use. Roll to the desired shape and leave to relax in the refrigerator for 1 hour before baking.

· INDEX ·

Picture Credits

ILLUSTRATION FOR ENDPAPERS
JILL MOORE

ANTHONY BLAKE: 2, 6
MICHAEL BOYS: 15, 74, 109, 133, 177, 203, 227, 247, 283, 303, 329
JOHN MILLER: 79, 155, 251, 254
JAMES MORTIMER: 193
JACK NISBERG: 27, 33, 40, 121, 127, 319
BRUCE PINKARD: 46/7, 335
JOHN STEWART: 19, 39, 55, 59, 91, 145, 165, 195, 210/1, 238/9, 263, 271, 299, 313

Robert Carrier's Kitchen Garden

Lavender border

Tarragon 3b

Lavender border

3a Tomatoes

Beans on Bamboo Wigwam

with Nasturtium border (2b)

2a&b

with Wild Strawberry border (2a)

1 Beech Hedge

4 Basil with Marjoram border

5 Green Pepper with Rosemary border

6 Salad Bowl Lettuce with Chive border

7 Tomato with Flat Leaved Parsley border

8 Celery

with Sweet Allysum border

Batavia

Chicory

9

Escarole

Curly Endive

10 Romaine Lettuce

with Marigold border

11 with Clipped Santolina border

Wild Strawberry and Bay Tree

Roquette

Purslane

12a Purple Basil